BARC

Work Assistant Exam

Latest Edition
Practice Kit

20 Tests
20 Mock Test

Based On Real Exam Pattern

✓ Thoroughly Revised and Updated

✓ Detailed Analysis of all MCQs

<table>
<tr><td>Title</td><td>: BARC Work Assistant Exam</td></tr>
<tr><td>Author Name</td><td>: Mr. Rohit Manglik</td></tr>
<tr><td>Published By</td><td>: EduGorilla Community Pvt. Ltd.</td></tr>
<tr><td>Publishers Address</td><td>: 12/651, First Floor Opp. Arvindo Park, Near Jama Masjid,
Indira Nagar, Lucknow, Uttar Pradesh-226016, India</td></tr>
</table>

Copyright EduGorilla

Disclaimer EduGorilla

ROHIT MANGLIK
CEO, EduGorilla

Dear Applicants,

People say *"Success comes to those who work hard."* But I've seen people working hard for their exams day in and day out for marginal success. While others succeed in their examinations by putting in just half the work. So are they God Gifted? No! I believe that it's because they work *smart* and not just *hard*. Similarly, for your exams, you should strategize your preparation so as to increase the likelihood of success. Well with EduGorilla get ready to increase your *chances of selection* in your exam by *16x*.

EduGorilla helps you in not only working *hard* but also working in a *smart and strategic* manner. With EduGorilla's preparation package, you get a chance to make your exam preparation easy, and a fun learning path towards selection. Finding the right path to your preparations can be difficult if you don't know in which direction to head. Don't worry, we have you covered! EduGorilla will be your guide to success in your journey. With our Preparation Package, you can prepare strategically and beat the exam in just one attempt.

EduGorilla's Preparation Package includes-

• **Test Series** • **Books**

Our preparation package is handcrafted as per the latest changes, expert opinions, and students' discretion. Thus, enabling you to get through each stage of the selection process for your exam.

Our Books are designed by the teachers and experts of the respective exam with a combined 150+ years of experience; to provide you with easy, efficient, and effective learning. Our books are smart, in the sense that not only do they give you the answers to the questions but also provide similar questions for practice.

EduGorilla's competent Test Series gives you real-time experience and confidence through which you can clear your offline or online exam in just one attempt. We currently host 83,000+ mock tests for 1,440+ competitive and academic exams.

Thus, EduGorilla misses no chance to assist you in your preparation and covers all stages of the exam, so that you don't have to look anywhere else.

We provide complete preparation packages for defense, banking, teaching, and other National & State-Level exams. Hence, it doesn't matter which exam you aspire to because you will reach your success.

ALL THE BEST !
Let EduGorilla be your Guide to Success.

Rohit Manglik,
Founder and CEO, EduGorilla

INTRODUCTION

EduGorilla focuses on guiding students to succeed in their examinations. With that in mind, our book, titled "BARC : Work Assistant Exam", has been drafted through the collective efforts of our distinguished experts with 150+ years of combined experience. This book consists of questions that are created following the latest changes in the syllabus and exam pattern. We compiled the book on the basis of questions that are most likely to appear in the BARC Work Assistant Exam. Through EduGorilla's "BARC : Work Assistant Exam" your chances of success will increase 16x.

EduGorilla does this through our Complete Preparation Package. This package consists of well-conceptualized and structured content in the form of questions that are tailor-made according to your needs and will help you practice for exams in a smart way by pinpointing all the necessary information. It also provides hints and solutions, along with a smart answer sheet for your self-evaluation. You can assess your shortcomings and work accordingly on areas that may require more of your attention.

EduGorilla promises to help you succeed in your examination and accomplish your dream goals. We believe in our aspirants and see them at the top of the merit list. And the first step towards the top is to start preparing with us. EduGorilla's "BARC : Work Assistant Exam" includes the following attributes.

➤ Well-Researched Content

➤ Top-Notch Quality

➤ Detailed Answers and Analysis

➤ Smart Answer Sheet

➤ Exam Relevant Questions

Therefore, EduGorilla fortifies your preparation and makes it durable enough to help you stand tall and beat the examination.

BARC Work Assistant Exam
Scan QR code for Eligibility, Exam Pattern, Syllabus and more.

Book ID: 0178

TABLE OF CONTENTS

Mathematics

Q.1 Speed of a boat in standing water is 9kmph and the speed of the stream is 1.5kmph. A man rows to a place at a distance of 10.5 km and comes back to the starting point. Find the total time taken by him.

A. 24 hours   **B.** 16 hours   **C.** 20 hours   **D.** 15 hours

Q.2 A man rows to a place 48km distant and back in 14 hours. He finds that he can row 4km with the stream in the same time as 3km against the stream. Find the rate of the stream.

A. 2 km/hr   **B.** 1 km/hr   **C.** 3 km/hr   **D.** 3.5km/hr

Q.3 If $a - b = 7$ and $a^2 + b^2 = 53$, find the value of ab.

A. 5   **B.** 3   **C.** 1   **D.** 2

Q.4 45% of 870 + 67% of 1250 − 21% of 540 = ?

A. 1087   **B.** 1115   **C.** 1439   **D.** 1560

Q.5 Ravi found that he had made a loss of 10% while selling his smartphone. He also found that had he sold it for Rs.100 more, he would have made a profit of 10%. The initial loss was what percentage of the profit earned, had he sold the smartphone for a 10% profit ?

A. 100%   **B.** 118%   **C.** 75%   **D.** 85%

Q.6 A, B and C invests rupees 8000, 12000 and 10000 respectively in a business. At the end of the year the balance sheet shows a loss of 40% of the initial investment. Find the share of loss of B.

A. 4000   **B.** 4500   **C.** 4800   **D.** 5000

Q.7 Rakesh travelled 2000 kilometre by air which formed 3/5 of the total journey. He travels 1/4 of the trip by car and the remaining trip by train. Find the distance travelled by train.

A. 2800   **B.** 4500   **C.** 2500   **D.** 3800

Q.8 Rahul has to travel from one point to another point in a certain time. Travelling at a speed of 6kmph he reaches 40m late and travelling at a speed of 8kmph he reaches 12 m earlier.What is the distance between this two points ?

A. 27km   **B.** 18km   **C.** 15km   **D.** 21km

Q.9 One year back, Ria was six times as old as her daughter. Six years hence, Ria's age will exceed her daughter's age by 15 years. The ratio of the present ages of Ria and her daughter is?

A. 15 : 4   **B.** 19 : 4   **C.** 15 : 2   **D.** 17 : 2

Q.10 Suresh age is 125% of what it was ten years ago, but 250/3% of what it will be after ten years. What is the present age of Suresh?

A. 60 years
B. 50 years
C. 40 years
D. Cannot be determined

Q.11 The difference between the compound and simple interest on a certain sum at 12% per annum for two years is Rs. 90. What will be the value of the amount at the end of 3 years if compounded annually?

A. Rs 8780.80   **B.** Rs 2808.80
C. Rs 315.80   **D.** Rs 3250.80

Q.12 A man with a sum of Rs3903 wants to deposit in the bank account of his two sons so that both will get equal money after 5yrs and 7yrs respectively at the rate of 4% compounded annually. Find the part of amount deposited into the account of first son?

A. 2020   **B.** 2025   **C.** 2028   **D.** 2220

Q.13 A got 30% of the maximum marks in an examination and failed by 10 marks. However, B who took the same examination got 40% of the total marks and got 15 marks more than the passing marks. What were the passing marks in the examination?

A. 65   **B.** 75
C. 80   **D.** None of these

Q.14 The population of a town is 15000. It increases by 10 percent in the first year and 20 percent in the second year. But in the third year it decreases by 10 percent. What will be the population after 3 years.

A. 16820   **B.** 15820   **C.** 17820   **D.** 19820

Q.15
A train can travel 50% faster than a car. Both start from point A at the same time and reach point B 75 kms away from A at the same time. On the way, however, the train lost about 12.5 minutes while stopping at the stations. The speed of the car is:

A. 100 kmph   **B.** 120 kmph
C. 130 kmph   **D.** None of above

Q.16 There are 3 bags : first containing 1 white, 2 red, 3 green balls; second 2 white, 3 red, 1 green balls and third contains 3 white, 1 red and 2 green balls. two balls are drawn from a bag chosen at random. these are found to be 1 white and 1 red. find the probability that the ball so drawn came from the second bag

A. 1/2   **B.** 11/12   **C.** 11/49   **D.** 12/49

Q.17 Two pipes P and Q can fill a tank in 10 min and 12 min respectively and a waste pipe can carry off 12 litres of water per minute. If all the pipes are opened when the tank is full and it takes one hour to empty the tank. Find the capacity of the tank.

A. 30   **B.** 45   **C.** 60   **D.** 75

Q.18 One pipe fill 1/4 of the tank in 4 minutes and another pipe fills 1/5 of the tank in 4 minutes. Find the time taken by both pipe together to fill half the tank?

A. 40/9 minutes   **B.** 50/9 minutes
C. 44/9 minutes   **D.** 53/9 minutes

Q.19 The ratio of students of three classes is 2:3:4. If 12 students are increased in each classes then their ratio turns into 13:18:23. What was the total number of students in all the three classes originally ?

A. 250   **B.** 215   **C.** 225   **D.** 190

Q.20 Ravi and Govind have money in the ratio 5 : 12 and Govind and Kiran also have money in the same ratio 5 : 12. If Ravi has Rs. 500, Kiran has

A. Rs.2500   **B.** Rs.2880   **C.** Rs.1850   **D.** Rs.3100

Science

Q.21 A cylindrical rod with one end in a steam chamber and the other end in ice results in melting of 0.1gm of ice per second. If the rod is replaced by another with half the length and double the radius of the first and if the thermal conductivity of material of second rod is 1/4 that of first, the rate at which ice melts in gm/sec will be

A. 3.2   **B.** 1.6   **C.** 0.2   **D.** 0.1

Q.22 One end of a copper rod of length 1.0 m and area of cross-section 10^{-3} is immersed in boiling water and the other end in ice. If the coefficient of thermal conductivity of copper is 92cal/m–s–°C and the latent heat of ice is 8×10^4cal/kg, then the amount of ice which will melt in one minute is

A. 9.2×10^{-3}kg   **B.** 8×10^{-3}kg
C. 6.9×10^{-3}kg   **D.** 5.4×10^{-3}kg

Q.23 If the r.m.s. velocity of a gas at a given temperature (Kelvin scale) is 300 m/s, whathat will be the r.m.s. velocity of a gas having twice the molecular weight and half the temperature on Kelvin scale =

A. 300 m/sec   **B.** 600 m/sec
C. 75 m/sec   **D.** 150 m/sec

Q.24 The ratio of two specific heats $\dfrac{C_p}{C_v}$ of CO is:

A. 1.33   **B.** 1.40   **C.** 1.29   **D.** 1.66

Q.25 The energy of a gas per litre is 300 joules, then its pressure will be

A. 3×10^5Nm^2 **B.** 6×10^5Nm^2
C. 10^5Nm^2 **D.** 2×10^5Nm^2

Q.26 Which of these does not influence the rate of reaction?

A. Nature of the reactants
B. Concentration of the reactants
C. Temperature
D. Molecularity

Q.27 For the reaction A + B → C, it is found that doubling the concentration of A increases the rate by 4 times and doubling the concentration of B doubles the reaction rate. What is the overall order of the reaction?

A. 4   **B.** 3/2   **C.** 3   **D.** 1

Q.28 The rate at which a substance reacts depends upon:

A. Atomic weight   **B.** Atomic number
C. Molecular weight   **D.** Active mass

Q.29 Which one among the following is a thermosetting plastic?

A. PVC   **B.** PVA   **C.** Bakelite   **D.** Perspex

Q.30 Based on the mode of their formation, polymers can be classified as?

A. As addition polymers only
B. As condensation polymers only
C. As copolymers
D. Both as addition and condensation polymers

Q.31 Which of the following is a product when caprolactum is heated with water at a high temperature?

A. Nylon 6,6   **B.** Nylon 6
C. PVC   **D.** Bakelite

Q.32 The IUPAC name of the following compound is?

$$CH_3 - CH_2 - CH_2 - \overset{\displaystyle |}{\underset{\displaystyle CH_3}{CH}} - CH_2 - \overset{\displaystyle CH_3}{\underset{\displaystyle |}{CH}} - CH_3$$

A. 2,4-Dimethylheptane
B. 4,6-Dimethylheptane
C. 2,4-Methylheptane
D. 2,3-Ethylheptane

Q.33 The systematic (IUPAC) name of tertiary butyl chloride is:

A. t-Butyl-chloride
B. tert-Butyl-chloride
C. 1-Chloro-3-methylpropane
D. 2-Chloro-2-methylpropane

Q.34 IUPAC name of the following compound is $CH_3 - CH = CH - C \equiv H$?

A. 5-Pentyn-3-ene   **B.** 3-Penten-1-yne
C. 1-Pentyn-3-ene   **D.** None of these

Q.35 It has been observed that gaseous hydrogen chloride is a very poor conductor of electricity but a solution of hydrogen chloride gas in water is a good conductor of electricity. This is due to the fact that

A. Water is good conductor of electricity
B. Hydrogen chloride gas ionizes in water
C. A gas is an electronic conductor but a liquid is always an electrolytic conductor
D. Gas does not obey Ohm's law whereas a solution does

Q.36 Which colorless gas evolves, when NH_4Cl reacts with zinc in a dry cell battery

A. NH_4 **B.** N_2 **C.** H_2 **D.** Cl_2

Q.37 Which of the following represents the anode half-cell reaction for the following galvanic cell:

$Cu(s)|Cu^{2+}(aq)||Ag+(aq)|Ag(s)$

A. $Cu(s)+2Ag^+(aq) \rightarrow Cu^{2+}(aq)+2Ag(s)$
B. $Cu(s) \rightarrow Cu^{2+}(aq)+2e-$
C. $2Ag^+(aq)+2e^- \rightarrow 2Ag(s)$
D. $Ag^+(aq)+e^- \rightarrow Ag(s)$

Q.38 Deficiency of which vitamin causes rickets?

A. Vitamin-D
B. Vitamin-B
C. Vitamin-A
D. Vitamin-K

Q.39 Assertion : Sucrose is a non-reducing sugar.

Reason : It has a glycosidic linkage.

A. If both assertion and reason are true and the reason is the correct explanation of the assertion.
B. If both assertion and reason are true but reason is not the correct explanation of the assertion.
C. If assertion is true but reason is false.
D. If the assertion and reason both are false.

Q.40 Vitamin B_{12} contains metal

A. Ca (II)
B. Zn (II)
C. Fe (II)
D. Co (III)

General Awareness

Q.41 Among the following states, which one does not have any significant coal resources?

A. Andhra Pradesh
B. Bihar
C. Chhattisgarh
D. Maharashtra

Q.42 The term 'Duck' is associated with :

A. Soccer
B. Volleyball
C. Golf
D. Cricket

Q.43 With which game is Brookland associated?

A. Hockey
B. Golf
C. Football
D. Tennis

Q.44 How may squares are there in a Chess Board??

A. 36
B. 48
C. 64
D. 72

Q.45 Which of the following places is known as the 'Mecca of Indian Football'?

A. Delhi
B. Bombay
C. Kolkata
D. Ambaia

Q.46 Merdeka Cup is associated with

A. Cricket
B. Football
C. Ragbi
D. Hockey

Q.47 What is the length of each stump in cricket?

A. 28 inches
B. 32 inches
C. 2 ft
D. 2 ½ ft

Q.48 The first Asian Games were held in

A. Manila
B. Tokyo
C. Jakarta
D. New Delhi

Q.49 Where did the 1st ODI match was played in India?

A. New Delhi
B. Ahmedabad
C. Kolkata
D. Mumbai

Q.50 Who has the written the book ''Two Lives'?

A. Salman Rushdie
B. Arundhati roy
C. Vikram Seth
D. Shiv Khera

// Smart Answer Sheet //

Correct   Indicates percentage of students who answered questions correctly.

Skipped   Indicates percentage of students who skipped questions.

Q.	Ans.	Correct / Skipped
1	A	84.43 % / 10.94 %
2	B	84.41 % / 10.73 %
3	D	77.7 % / 21.57 %
4	B	84.5 % / 14.2 %
5	A	80.79 % / 14.56 %
6	C	80.24 % / 15.24 %
7	C	89.62 % / 10.3 %
8	D	80.72 % / 18.02 %
9	B	86.94 % / 11.54 %
10	B	80.99 % / 11.0 %

Q.	Ans.	Correct / Skipped
11	A	81.13 % / 17.31 %
12	C	77.53 % / 20.76 %
13	D	88.71 % / 10.14 %
14	C	76.89 % / 10.9 %
15	B	77.38 % / 11.66 %
16	A	87.54 % / 10.68 %
17	C	80.47 % / 18.71 %
18	A	88.49 % / 10.29 %
19	C	88.87 % / 10.09 %
20	B	76.82 % / 21.81 %

Q.	Ans.	Correct / Skipped
21	C	86.95 % / 12.16 %
22	C	84.18 % / 14.7 %
23	D	81.81 % / 16.18 %
24	B	76.6 % / 15.9 %
25	D	78.43 % / 18.29 %
26	D	86.76 % / 11.11 %
27	C	80.35 % / 16.44 %
28	D	85.01 % / 13.5 %
29	C	76.39 % / 10.91 %
30	D	88.97 % / 10.33 %

Q.	Ans.	Correct / Skipped
31	B	81.08 % / 12.97 %
32	A	78.93 % / 19.73 %
33	D	77.34 % / 21.32 %
34	B	83.37 % / 10.45 %
35	B	87.59 % / 10.56 %
36	C	77.06 % / 10.23 %
37	B	83.42 % / 11.88 %
38	A	89.93 % / 10.06 %
39	A	86.05 % / 11.9 %
40	D	79.69 % / 13.02 %

Q.	Ans.	Correct / Skipped
41	B	78.06 % / 19.17 %
42	D	86.09 % / 11.46 %
43	C	77.47 % / 15.29 %
44	C	78.73 % / 19.6 %
45	C	84.28 % / 11.98 %
46	B	83.73 % / 12.38 %
47	A	86.01 % / 10.35 %
48	D	83.04 % / 14.31 %
49	B	80.86 % / 17.22 %
50	C	84.7 % / 10.97 %

Performance Analysis

Avg. Score (%)	55.33%
Toppers Score (%)	70.67%
Your Score	

//Hints and Solutions//

1. Basic Formula:

i. speed = distance traveled / time taken

ii. speed of the stream = ½ (a-b) km/hr

iii. speed in still water = ½ (a+b) km/hr

Explanation:

Speed in still water= ½ (a+b) = 9km ph

= a+b = 18 1

speed of the stream = ½ (a-b) = 1.5 kmph

= a-b = 3 kmph............2

solving 1 and 2 gives a = 10.5km/hr ; b=7.5 kmphr

Total time taken by him = 105/10.5 + 105/7.5 = 24 hours

2. Basic Formula:

Speed of the stream = ½ (a-b) km / hr

Speed = distance traveled / time taken

Explanation:

Suppose he moves 4km downstream in x hours

Then, downstream a= 4 / x km/hr

Speed upstream b = 3/ x km/hr

48 / (4 /x) + 48 / (3/x) = 14

12x + 16x = 14

x = 1/2

a=8 km/hr ,b = 6 km/hr

rate of stream = ½ (8 – 6)

= 1 km/hr

3. $2ab = (a^2 + b^2) – (a – b)^2$

2ab = 53-49 =4

ab =4/2 = 2

4. [(45/100)* 870] + {(67/100)*1250} -{(21/100)*540}

=391+837-113

=1115

5. Profit= 10%

10% of CP = Rs. 100

CP = Rs. 1000

Now, Loss% = 10%

Loss =Rs. 100

Required % = (100/100)*100 = 100%

6. Total loss after one year = 30000*40/100 = 12000

share of B = (40/10)*12000 = 4800

7. 3=2000

5=10000/3

Distance by train=3×10000/3×4=2500

Another method :

Total 20

12=====2000

20=====2000*20/12

5======2000*5/12

3======2000*5*3/12=2500

8. t +40/60 = d/6

t – 12/60 = d/8

By the solving these two equations we get.

d = 20.8 km ~ 21 km

Another method :

6.................4.   (40m late)

.........24............

8.................3.   (12 m ear)

60 = 52

1 = 52/60 = 13/15

So distance = 24 *13/15

= 8*13/5 = 104/5 = 20.8km

9. Ages of Ria and her daughter = 6x, x

[6x + 1 + 6] – [x + 1 + 6] = 15

5x = 15; x = 3

Ratio = 6x + 1 : x + 1 = 19 : 4

10. Suresh's age before 10 years = x

125x/100 = x + 10

125x = 100x + 1000 => x = 40

Present age = x + 10 = 50

11. Here, in this question, the difference is already given to us and we are required to find the principal amount. And using that principal amount we are required to find the amount compounded after three years. The difference is given for two years. So, the formula will be,

Difference $= P(R)^2/100^2$

Now, putting the values into the equation, we will find that,

$$90 = P(12)^2/(100)^2$$
$$90 \times 100^2/12^2 = P$$
$$P = Rs.\,6250$$

Now, calculating the compound interest on Rs. 6250 will be,

$$A = 6250(1 + 12/100)^3$$

$$A = 6250(112/100)^3 => 6250(1.12)^3 => Rs\,.8780.80$$

So, the compounded amount after three years will be Rs. 8780.80

12. Option C
Some Extra:

$$A(1 + 4/100)^5 = B(1 + 4/100)^7$$
$$A/B = (1 + 4/100)^2 = 676/625$$
$$676 + 625 = 3903$$
$$1 = 3$$
$$676 = 2028$$

13. (30/100)*T = P -10

(40/100)*T = P + 15

U will get P = 85

14. [15000*(11/10)*(12/10)*(9/10)]

= 17820

15. Let speed of the car be x kmph.

Then, speed of the train $= \dfrac{150}{100}x = \left(\dfrac{3}{2}x\right) kmph$

$\therefore \dfrac{75}{x} - \dfrac{75}{(3/2)x} = \dfrac{125}{10 \times 60}$

$\Rightarrow \dfrac{75}{x} - \dfrac{50}{x} = \dfrac{5}{24}$

$\Rightarrow x = \left(\dfrac{25 \times 24}{5}\right) = 120 kmph$

16. Total no.of balls are 6

the probability of getting a white ball from second bag is 2/6=1/3

the probability of getting a red ball = 3 / 6

=1/2

17. Let the waste pipe take 'T' time to empty the tank.

(1/10 + 1/12 – 1/T)*60 = -1

We will get T = 5 min

So capacity = 5*12 = 60ltr

18. First pipe will take 16 minutes to fill the tank alone. Similarly second pipe will take 20 minutes to fill the tank alone. Let T is the time in which both the pipes will fill half the tank

(1/16 + 1/20)*T = 1/2, we get T = 40/9 minutes

19. 50:75:100

15 students increased

65:90:115 => 13:18 :23

Total no of students = 50+75+100 = 225

20. Ravi : Kiran = 5/12* 5/12 = 25/144

Kiran = 144*500/25 = 2880

21. $\dfrac{Q}{t} = \dfrac{KA\Delta\theta}{l} \Rightarrow \dfrac{mL}{t} = \dfrac{K(xr^2)\Delta\theta}{l}$

$\Rightarrow$ Rate of melting of ice $\left(\dfrac{m}{t}\right) \propto \dfrac{Kr^2}{l}$

since for second rod K becomes $\dfrac{1}{4}th$ r becomes double and length

becomes half, so rate of melting will be twice i.e. $\left(\dfrac{m}{t}\right)_2 =$

$2\left(\dfrac{m}{t}\right)_1 = 2 \times 0.1 = 0.2gm/\text{sec}$

22. Heat transferred in one minute is utilised in melting the ice so,

$$\dfrac{KA(\theta_1 - \theta_2)t}{l} = m \times L$$

$$\Rightarrow m = \dfrac{10^{-3} \times 92 \times (100-0) \times 60}{1 \times 8 \times 10^4} = 6.9 \times 10^{-3} kg$$

23. $v_{max} = \sqrt{\dfrac{3RT}{M}} \Rightarrow V_{max} \infty \sqrt{\dfrac{T}{M}}$

$\dfrac{\pi_2}{\tau_1} = \sqrt{\dfrac{M_1}{M_2} \times \dfrac{T_2}{T_1}} \sqrt{\dfrac{1}{2} \times \dfrac{1}{2}} \Rightarrow v_2 = \dfrac{v_1}{2} = \dfrac{300}{2} = 150$ m/sec

24. CO is diatomic gas, for diatomic gas

$$C_p = \dfrac{7}{2}R \text{ and } C_v = \dfrac{5}{2}R \Rightarrow \gamma = \dfrac{C_p}{C_v} = \dfrac{\frac{7R}{2}}{\frac{5R}{2}} = 1.4$$

25. Energy $= 300$ J/litre $= 300 \times 10^3 J/m^3$

$P = \dfrac{2}{3}E = \dfrac{2 \times 300 \times 10^3}{3} = 2 \times 10^5 N/m^2$

26. The Molecularity of the reaction does not influence the rate of reaction.

27.

$$\text{rate } = k[A]^x[B]^y$$
$$4 = k[2]^x \qquad 2 = k[2]^y$$
$$x = 2 \qquad\qquad y = 1$$

x+y=3

28. The rate of a reaction depends on the active mass of the reactants

29. Bakelite is thermosetting polymer. It becomes infusible on heating and cannot be remoulded.

30. On the basis of the mode of their formation, the polymers can be classified as addition polymers and condensation polymers.

31. Caprolactum is heated with water at a high temperature to obtain Nylon 6.

32. Our first step should be to choose the longest chain from the given alkane.

Although there are 9 carbon atoms in total, the longest chain contains only 7 carbon atoms.

$$\overset{①}{CH_3} - \overset{②}{CH_2} - \overset{③}{CH_2} - \overset{④}{CH} - \overset{⑤}{CH_2} - \overset{⑥}{CH} - \overset{⑦}{CH_3}$$

with CH_3 groups at positions ④ and ⑥

Our first step should be to choose the longest chain from the given alkane.

Although there are 9 carbon atoms in total, the longest chain contains only 7 carbon atoms.

$$CH_3 - CH_2 - CH_2 - \overset{④}{CH} - CH_2 - CH - CH_3$$

Now we have substituents at C_2 and C_4. In both cases, there are exactly two substituents.

We choose the numbering direction that gives the lowest set of locants.

Hence, secondary prefix = 2,4-dimethyl (since there are two methyl groups-one each at C_2 and C_4

Hence, the IUPAC name is **2,4-Dimethylheptane**

33. The given compound tertiary butyl chloride is

$$\overset{①}{CH_3}$$
$$CH_3 - \overset{②}{C} - Cl$$
$$\overset{③}{CH_3}$$

It is numbered as shown.

The longest chain clearly includes 3 carbon atoms

⇒ root word = prop

primary suffix = ane

Secondary prefix = 2-chloro-2-methyl

Hence the name (systematic IUPAC) of given compound is:

(d) 2-Chloro-2-methylpropane

34.

$$\underset{5}{CH_3} - \underset{4}{CH} = \underset{3}{CH} - \underset{2}{C} \equiv \underset{1}{CH}$$

From lowest sum rule, we will select 1,3 and not 2,4

Five carbons ⇒ word root = pent

3-Penten-1-yne

35. HCl gas ionizes in water solution and the ions so formed act as charge carriers.

36. $2NH_4Cl + Zn \rightarrow 2NH_3 + ZnCl_2$ $H_2\uparrow$

37. Reduction reaction takes place at cathode and oxidation reaction takes place at anode.

Cathode : $2Ag^+(aq) + 2e^- \rightarrow 2Ag(s)$

Anode : $Cu(s) \rightarrow Cu^{2+}(aq) + 2e^-$

Cell reaction : $Cu(s) + 2\,Ag^+(aq) \rightarrow Cu^{2+}(aq) + 2Ag(s)$

38. The most common cause of rickets is a lack of vitamin D or calcium in a child's diet. Both are essential for children to develop strong and healthy bones.

39. Sucrose is a non reducing-sugar as it does not reduce Tollen's or Fehling's reagent, due to absence of free aldehyde or ketone groups. It contains stable acetal or ketal structure which cannot be opened into a free carboxyl group.

Sucrose is composed of alpha-D-glucopyranose unit and ß-D-fructofuranose unit. These units are joined by a-b-glycosidic linkage between C-1 of the glucose unit and C- 2 of the fructose unit.

Glucose

Fructose

40. Vitamin B_{12} also called as CyanoCOBALamine(COBALT)

41. Coal deposits are primarily found in eastern and south-central India. Jharkhand, Odisha, Chhattisgarh, West Bengal, Madhya Pradesh, Telangana and Maharashtra accounted for 98.26% of the total known coal reserves in India.

42. A batsman who is dismissed without facing a ball (most usually run out from the non-striker's end, but alternatively stumped or run out off a wide delivery) is said to be out for a diamond duck, but in some regions that term has an alternative definition.

43. Football game is Brook land associated and it commonly called as the football or also known as the soccer. It is team sport player among two team with the 11 players and also spherical ball.

44. there are 64 squares in a Chess Board.

45. Kolkata, hands down. No city even comes close to the frenzy the game creates here. East Bengal and Mohun Bagan are the biggest football clubs in the city, and during a Derby, Kolkata basically splits into two warring factions, the Ghotis and the Bangals.

46. Pestabola Merdeka or Merdeka Tournament is a football friendly tournament held in Malaysia to honour the Independence Day.

47. Each stump is 28 inches (71.1 cm) tall with maximum and minimum diameters of 1½ inches (3.81 cm) and 1⅜ inches (3.49 cm).

48. The 1951 Asiad were originally scheduled to be held in 1950, but postponed until 1951 due to delays in preparations. On 13 February 1949, the Asian Games Federation was formally established in Delhi, with Delhi unanimously announced as the first host city of the Asian Games.

49. The 1st ODI match was played in India in Ahmedabad.

50. Vikram Seth has written the book ''Two Lives''.

Mathematics

Q.1 A man goes downstream 60 km and upstream 20 km, taking 4 hrs each. What is the velocity of current?
A. 4 km/hr   **B.** 8 km/hr   **C.** 6 km/hr   **D.** 5 km/hr

Q.2 A man can row 30 km upstream and 44 km downstream in 10 hrs. Also, he can row 40 km upstream and 55 km downstream in 13 hrs. Find the speed of the man in still water.
A. 5 km/hr   **B.** 8 km/hr   **C.** 10 km/hr   **D.** 12 km/hr

Q.3 23.56 + 4142.25 + 134.44 = ?
A. 4010.05   **B.** 4000.15   **C.** 4100.25   **D.** 4300.25

Q.4 ($\sqrt{7744} * 66$) ÷ (203 + 149)= ?
A. 12.5   **B.** 14.5   **C.** 13.5   **D.** 16.5

Q.5 David sells his Laptop to Goliath at a loss of 20% who subsequently sells it to Hercules at a Profit of 25%. Hercules, after finding some defect in the laptop, returns it to Goliath but could recover only Rs. 4.50 for every Rs. 5 he had paid. Find the amount at Hercules' loss if David had paid Rs. 1.75 lakh for the laptop.
A. Rs.6000   **B.** Rs.7000
C. Rs.2000   **D.** Rs.17,500

Q.6 A reduction of 20% in the price of sugar enables a housewife to purchase 6 kg more for Rs. 240. What is original price per kg of sugar?
A. Rs.10 per Kg   **B.** Rs.8 per Kg
C. Rs.6 per Kg   **D.** Rs.5 per Kg

Q.7 A boat running upstream takes 8 hours 48 minutes to cover a certain distance, while it takes 4 hours to cover the same distance running downstream. What is the ratio between the speed of the boat and speed of the water current respectively?
A. 5:2   **B.** 7:4   **C.** 6:1   **D.** 8:3

Q.8 A boat can travel 20 km downstream in 24 min. The ratio of the speed of the boat in still water to the speed of the stream is 4 : 1. How much time will the boat take to cover 15 km upstream?
A. 20 min   **B.** 22 min   **C.** 25 min   **D.** 30 min

Q.9 The average expenditure of the hotel when there are 10 guests is Rs. 80 per guests and the average expenditure is Rs.40 when there are 30 Guests. If it is known that there are some fixed expenses irrespective of the number of guests then the average expenditure per guest when there are 50 guests in the hotel.?
A. Rs. 25   **B.** Rs. 35   **C.** Rs. 50   **D.** Rs. 45

Q.10 The average marks of Sumit decreased by one, when he replaced the subject in which he has scored 40 marks by the other two subjects in which he has just scored 23 and 25 marks

respectively. Later he has also included 57 marks of Computer Science, then the average marks increased by two. How many subjects were there initially?
A. 12   **B.** 14   **C.** 10   **D.** 15

Q.11 Find the least number of years in which the sum put at 25% rate of interest will be more than doubled.
A. 2 years   **B.** 3 years   **C.** 4 years   **D.** 5 years

Q.12 A sum of rupees 4420 is to be divided between rakesh and prakash in such a way that after 5 years and 7 years respectively the amount they get is equal. The rate of interest is 10 percent. Find the share of rakesh and prakash
A. 2000, 2420   **B.** 2420, 2000
C. 2480, 2420   **D.** 2210, 2210

Q.13
Albert invested an amount of Rs. 8000 in a fixed deposit scheme for 2 years at compound interest rate 5 p.c.p.a. How much amount will Albert get on maturity of the fixed deposit?
A. 5000   **B.** 7820   **C.** 8820   **D.** 1250

Q.14 Mr. Tyagi walked 6 km to reach the station from his house, then he boarded a train whose average speed was 60km/hr and thus he reached his destination. In this way he took total of 3 hours. If the average speed of the entire journey was 32 km/hr then the average speed of walking is:
A. 14 km/hr   **B.** 15 km/hr   **C.** 4 km/hr   **D.** 5 km/hr

Q.15 A lottery is organised by the college ABC through which they will provide scholarship of rupees one lakhs to only one student. There are 100 fourth year students, 150 third year students, 100 second year students and 250 first year students. What is the probability that a second year student is choosen.
A. 1/7   **B.** 2/7   **C.** 3/7   **D.** 4/7

Q.16 A card is drawn from a pack of 52 cards. The card is drawn at random; find the probability that it is neither club nor queen?
A. 4/13   **B.** 5/13   **C.** 7/13   **D.** 9/13

Q.17 Two pipes A and B can fill a tank in 12 hours and 18 hours respectively. The pipes are opened simultaneously and it is found that due to leakage in the bottom of the tank it took 48 minutes excess time to fill the cistern. When the cistern is full, in what time will the leak empty it?
A. 72 hours   **B.** 62 hours   **C.** 64 hours   **D.** 84 hours

Q.18 A tank is normally filled in 6 hours but takes two hours longer to fill because of a leak in the bottom of the tank. If the tank is full the leak will empty it in how many hours?
A. 16 hours   **B.** 18 hours   **C.** 17 hours   **D.** 24 hours

Q.19 180 sweets are divided among friends A, B, C and D in which B and C are brothers also such that sweets divided between A and B are in the ratio 2 : 3, between B and C in the ratio 2 : 5 and between C and D in ratio 3 : 4. What is the number of sweets received by the brothers together?

A. 78 **B.** 84 **C.** 92 **D.** 102

Q.20 Number of students in 4th and 5th class is in the ratio 6 : 11. 40% in class 4 are girls and 48% in class 5 are girls. What percentage of students in both the classes are boys?

A. 62.5% **B.** 54.8% **C.** 52.6% **D.** 55.8%

Science

Q.21 A body initially at 80^0 C cools to $64°$ C in 5 minutes and to $52°$ C in 10 minutes. The temperature of the body after 15 minutes will be

A. 42.7° C **B.** 35° C **C.** 47° C **D.** 40° C

Q.22 A 5cm thick ice block is there on the surface of water in a lake. The temperature of air is $-10°$ C; how much time it will take to double the thickness of the block

$(L=80$ ca/g,$K_{ice}=0.004$ Erg/s$-$k,$d_{ice}=0.92$gcm$^{-3})$

A. 1 hour **B.** 191 hours
C. 19.1 hours **D.** 1.91 hours

Q.23 Four identical rods of same material are joined end to end to form a square. If the temperature difference between the ends of a diagonal is 100° C , then the temperature difference between the ends of other diagonal will be

A. 0^0C
B. $\frac{10\%}{l} C$; where l is the length of each rod
C. $\frac{100°}{21} C$
D. 100°C

Q.24 A vessel of volume V contains an ideal gas at absolute temperature T and pressure P. The gas is allowed to leak till its pressure falls to P. Assuming that the temperature remains constant during leakage, the number of moles of the gas that have leaked is

A. $\frac{V}{RT}(P + P')$ **B.** $\frac{V}{RT}(P - P')$
C. $\frac{V}{RT}(P - P')$ **D.** $\frac{V}{2RT}(P - P')$

Q.25 An air bubble doubles its radius on raising from the bottom of water reservoir to be the surface of water in it. If the atmospheric pressure is equal to 10 m of water, the height of water in the reservoir is

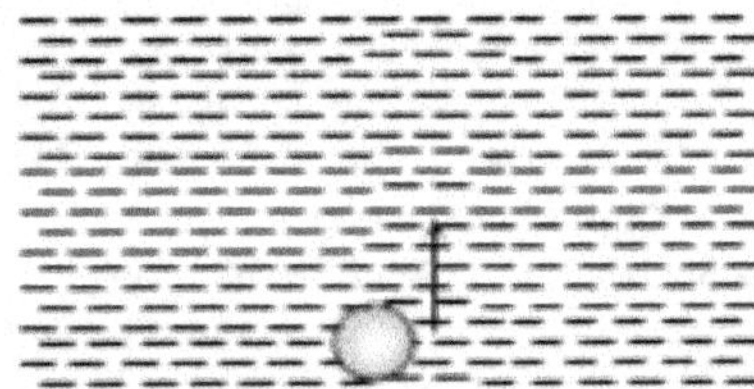

A. 10 m **B.** 20 m **C.** 70 m **D.** 80 m

Q.26 If the r.m.s. velocity of a gas at a given temperature (Kelvin scale) is 300 m/s, whathat will be the r.m.s. velocity of a gas having twice the molecular weight and half the temperature on Kelvin scale =

A. 300 m/sec **B.** 600 m/sec

C. 75 m/sec **D.** 150 m/sec

Q.27 The data for the reaction is A + B → C

S.No.	$[A]_o$	$[B]_o$	Initial Rate
1.	0.012	0.035	0.10
2.	0.024	0.035	0.80
3.	0.012	0.070	0.10
4.	0.024	0.070	0.80

A. $r=k[B]^3$ **B.** $r=k[A]^3$
C. $r=k[A][B]^4$ **D.** $r=k[A]^2[B]^2$

Q.28 The half-life for the reaction, $N_2O_5 \Rightarrow 2NO_2+1/2O_2$ is 12 minutes at 30°C. Starting with 100 g of N_2O_5 how many gram of N_2O_5 will remain after a period of 1 hour 36 minutes.

A. 1.25 g **B.** 0.39 g **C.** 1.77 g **D.** 0.5 g

Q.29 A first order reaction is half completed in 45 minutes. How long does it need for 99.9% of the reaction to be completed?

A. 20 hours **B.** 10 hours
C. 7.5 hours **D.** 5 hours

Q.30 Which of the following is a linear polymer?
A. Nylon
B. Bakelite
C. Low density polythene
D. Melamine-formaldehyde polymer

Q.31 Which of the following is a monomer of natural rubber?
A. Neoprene **B.** Isoprene
C. Chloroprene **D.** Buna-N

Q.32 Which of the following possess the relative strength of intermolecular forces of attraction between that of elastomers and fibres?
A. Terylene **B.** Polythene
C. Bakelite **D.** Nylon

Q.33 The IUPAC name of the following compound is?

$$CH_3-CH_2-CH_2-CH_2-CH_2-C-CH_2-CH_2-CH-CH_3$$

A. 5, 5-(1,1-Dimethylpropyl)-2-methyldecan
B. 5, 5-Bis(1,1-dimethylpropyl)-2-methyldecane
C. 5, 5-Bis(1,1-dipropylmethyl)-2-methyldecane
D. None of these

Q.34 The IUPAC name of this compound is?

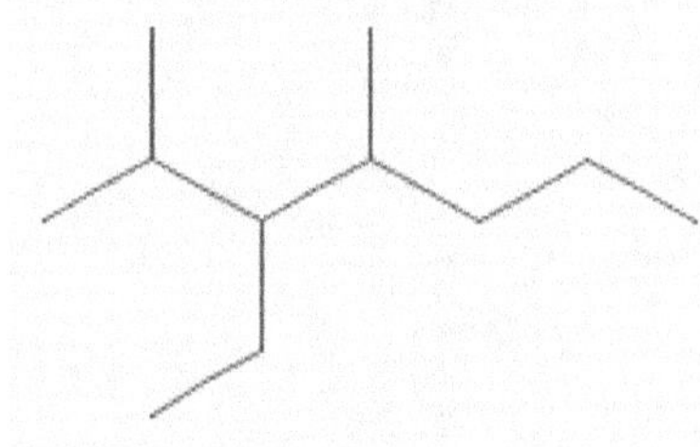

A. 3-Ethyl-4,4-dimethylheptane
B. 1,1-Diethyl-2,2-dimethylpentane
C. 4,4-Dimethyl-5,5-diethylpentane
D. 4,4-Dimethyl-5,5-diethylpentane

Q.35 The IUPAC name of the following compound is?

$$CH_3-CH-\underset{\underset{CH_2-CH_3}{|}}{\overset{\overset{CH_3}{|}}{C}}-CH_2-CH_3$$

with CH_3 below the CH and CH_2-CH_3 below the C

A. 2-Methyl-3,2-methylethylpentane
B. 3-Ethyl-2,3-dimethylpentane
C. 3,2-Methylethyl-2-methylpentane
D. None of these

Q.36 Corrosion of iron is essentially an electrochemical phenomenon where the cell reactions are

A. Fe is oxidised to Fe^{2+} and dissolved oxygen in water is reduced to O^{2-}
B. Fe is oxidised to Fe^{3+} and H_2O is reduced to $O2^{-2}$
C. Fe is oxidised to Fe^{2+} and H_2O is reduced to O^{-2}
D. Fe is oxidised to Fe^{2+} and H_2O is reduced to O^2

Q.37 Which of the following conversion takes place in a galvanic cell?

A. Electrical energy to chemical energy
B. Chemical energy to electrical energy
C. Chemical energy to mechanical energy
D. Mechanical energy to chemical energy

Q.38 The specific conductance of $\frac{N}{10}KCl$ KCl solution at $20°C$ is $0.0212 ohm^{-1}cm^{-1}$ and the resistance of cell containing this solution at $20°C$ is $55 ohm$. The cell constant is

A. 1.166 cm⁻¹
B. 2.173 cm⁻¹
C. 3.324 cm⁻¹
D. 4.616 cm⁻¹

Q.39 An example for a saturated fatty acid, present in nature is

A. Oleic acid
B. linoleic acid
C. Linolenic acid
D. Palmitic acid

Q.40 The chemical name of vitamin C is

A. Ascorbic acid
B. Citric acid
C. Folic acid
D. Nicotinic acid

General Awareness

Q.41 Which of the following sanctuary is well-known for elephants

A. Kanha
B. Gir
C. Kaziranga
D. periyar

Q.42 Which one of the following is not a Baltic state?

A. Belarus
B. Estonia
C. Latvia
D. Lithuania

Q.43 Which one of the following is not an official language of the United Nations?

A. Arabic
B. Chinese
C. Portuguese
D. Spanish

Q.44 In which one of the following State of India is the Pemayangtse Monastery situated?

A. Nagaland
B. Himachal Pradesh
C. Sikkim
D. Arunachal Pradesh

Q.45 Article 370 of the constitution was applicable to the state

A. Nagaland
B. Mizoram
C. Manipur
D. Jammu and Kashmir

Q.46 The Acid in gastric juice is -

A. acetic acid
B. nitric acid
C. hydrochloric acid
D. sulphuric acid

Q.47 On July....., man walked on the Moon for the first time.

A. 20th
B. 21th
C. 19th
D. 18th

Q.48 Who among the following is the author of the book ' The Namesake'?

A. Arundhati Roy
B. Amitav Ghosh
C. Jhumpa Lahiri
D. Kiran Desai.

Q.49 Sabin Awards is given for the conservation of

A. amphibians
B. reptiles
C. birds
D. corals

Q.50 Famous player kevin peterson belong to

A. Kenya
B. England
C. Nigeria
D. Namibia

// Smart Answer Sheet //

Correct Indicates percentage of students who answered questions correctly.

Skipped Indicates percentage of students who skipped questions.

Q.	Ans.	Correct / Skipped
1	D	84.52 % / 10.14 %
2	B	88.13 % / 11.15 %
3	D	88.5 % / 10.13 %
4	D	81.38 % / 13.16 %
5	D	83.1 % / 10.21 %
6	A	80.73 % / 16.06 %
7	D	78.75 % / 14.22 %
8	D	88.12 % / 11.0 %
9	B	76.45 % / 10.52 %
10	D	89.78 % / 10.2 %

Q.	Ans.	Correct / Skipped
11	C	83.91 % / 15.75 %
12	B	79.14 % / 14.54 %
13	C	76.53 % / 15.82 %
14	C	80.42 % / 18.71 %
15	A	78.8 % / 12.97 %
16	D	86.17 % / 10.96 %
17	A	83.7 % / 13.74 %
18	D	80.22 % / 14.63 %
19	B	81.97 % / 17.46 %
20	B	79.07 % / 15.23 %

Q.	Ans.	Correct / Skipped
21	A	78.96 % / 13.73 %
22	C	81.59 % / 14.33 %
23	A	84.58 % / 15.3 %
24	C	77.67 % / 14.59 %
25	C	88.12 % / 10.96 %
26	D	85.05 % / 11.43 %
27	B	76.07 % / 10.76 %
28	B	81.21 % / 16.98 %
29	C	77.76 % / 21.72 %
30	A	77.07 % / 11.0 %

Q.	Ans.	Correct / Skipped
31	B	88.41 % / 10.08 %
32	B	76.61 % / 18.66 %
33	B	88.59 % / 10.51 %
34	A	85.29 % / 14.09 %
35	B	89.13 % / 10.26 %
36	A	80.52 % / 17.78 %
37	B	86.19 % / 11.78 %
38	A	85.6 % / 13.62 %
39	D	89.45 % / 10.12 %
40	A	86.22 % / 10.24 %

Q.	Ans.	Correct / Skipped
41	D	81.2 % / 10.44 %
42	A	76.68 % / 22.04 %
43	C	80.98 % / 10.77 %
44	C	85.46 % / 11.61 %
45	D	77.52 % / 12.28 %
46	C	79.13 % / 16.26 %
47	A	85.18 % / 11.85 %
48	C	85.41 % / 10.82 %
49	A	89.39 % / 10.48 %
50	B	88.98 % / 10.76 %

Performance Analysis	
Avg. Score (%)	36.67%
Toppers Score (%)	74.0%
Your Score	

//Hints and Solutions//

1. Explanation:

Downstream speed = 60/4 = 15 km/hr

Upstream speed = 20/4 = 5 km/hr

Velocity of stream = (15-5)/2 = 5 km/hr

2. Explanation:

Let upstream speed = x, downstream speed = y km/hr

Then, 30/x + 44/y = 10 and 40/x + 55/y = 13

Put 1/x = a, 1/y = b

Solve the equations.

A = 1/5, b = 1/11

So, x = 5, y = 11

Speed in still water = (5+11)/2 = 8 km/hr

3. Explanation :

23.56 + 4142.25 + 134.44 = 4300.25

4. Explanation :

($\sqrt{7744} * 66$)= 5808; 5808/352 = 16.5

5. David (100) == 20% ↓(loss) ⇒ Goliath (80) == 25% ↑(gain) ⇒ Hercules(100) == 10% ↓ (loss) ⇒ Goliath (90)

Hercules's loss corresponds to 10 when David buys the laptop for Rs. 100.

Thus, Hercules's loss would he Rs. 17,500 when David buys the laptop for 1,75,000.

6. Explanation:

Reduction in price = 1/5 = 20%

Increase in Quantity = 25%

25% = 6 Kg.

original amount of Sugar = 6*4 = 24Kg.

Original price of the sugar = 240/24 = Rs. 10 per kg.

7. Let the man's rate upstream be x kmph and that downstream be y kmph. Then, distance covered upstream in 8 hrs 48 min $=$ Distance covered downstream in 4 hrs. $\rightarrow \left(x \times 8\frac{4}{5} \right) = (y \times 4)$

$\rightarrow \frac{44}{4}x = 4y$

$\rightarrow y = \frac{11}{5}x$

$\rightarrow$ Required ratio $= \left(\frac{y+x}{2} \right) : \left(\frac{y-x}{2} \right)$

$= \left(\frac{16x}{5} \times \frac{1}{2} \right) : \left(\frac{6x}{5} \times \frac{1}{2} \right)$

$= \frac{8}{5} : \frac{3}{5}$

$= 8:3$

8. Explanation :

Down speed =20/24*60=50km/hr

4:1 =4x:x

Downstream speed = 4x+x=5x

Upstream speed = 4x-x=3x

5x= 50; x=10

so up speed 3*10=30

Time = 15/30*60= 30min.

9. x + 30y = 1200

x + 10y = 800

y = 20

Total Expenditure = 600 + 40 * 20 = 1400

Average Expenditure = 1400/40 = 35

10. Total subjects = x ; Average Marks = y

(x + 1)(y − 1) = (xy − 40) + (23 + 25)

y − x = 9 −(1)

(x + 2)(y + 1) = (xy − 40) + (23 + 25)+ 57

xy + 2y + x + 2 = xy + 65

2y + x = 63 −(2)

From Equation (1) and (2) => x = 15; y = 24

11. Explanation:

$P\left(1 + \frac{20}{100}\right)^n > 2P \Rightarrow \left(\frac{6}{5}\right)^n > 2$

Now, $\left(\frac{6}{5} \times \frac{6}{5} \times \frac{6}{5} \times \frac{6}{5}\right) > 2$

So, $n = 4$ years.

12. Explanation :

Let the share of rakesh and prakash be R and P

R*(1+10/100)^ 5 = (4420 − R)*(1+10/100)^ 7

We get R = 2420, so P = 2000

13. Explanation:

$$\text{Amount} = \text{Rs.} \left[8000 \times \left(1 + \frac{5}{100}\right)^2 \right]$$
$$= \text{Rs.} \left(8000 \times \frac{21}{20} \times \frac{21}{20} \right)$$
$$= \text{Rs. } 8820$$

14. Correct Option: C

Total distance $= 32 \times 3 = 6 + 60 \times x$

$\Rightarrow x = 1.5$ hours

Thus, the speed of walking $= \frac{6}{1.5} = 4km/hr.$

Hence, option (C) is correct.

15. Second year students = 200

so, P = 100/700 = 1/7

16. 1 – [13/52 + 4/52 – 1/52] = 9/13

17. Work done by the two pipes in 1 hour = (1/12)+(1/18) = (15/108).

Time taken by these pipes to fill the tank = (108/15)hrs = 7 hours 12 min.

Due to leakage, time taken = 7 hours 12 min + 48 min = 8 hours

Work done by two pipes and leak in 1 hour = 1/8.

Work done by the leak in 1 hour =(15/108)-(1/8)=(1/72).

Leak will empty the full cistern in 72 hours.

18. Work done by leak in 1 hr=(1/6-1/8)=1/24

Leak will empty the tank in 24 hours

19. A/B = N1/D1 B/C = N2/D2 C/D = N3/D3

A : B : C : D = N1*N2*N3 : D1*N2*N3 : D1*D2*N3 : D1*D2*D3

A/B = 2/3 B/C = 2/5 C/D = 3/4

A : B : C : D

2*2*3 : 3*2*3 : 3*5*3 : 3*5*4

4 : 6 : 15 : 20

B and C together = [(6+15)/(4+6+15+20)] * 180

7/45 * 180

7 * 12

=84

20. Total students in both = 6x+11x = 17x

Boys in class 4 = (60/100)*6x = 360x/100

Boys in class 5 = (52/100)*11x = 572x/100

So total boys = 360x/100 + 572x/100 = 932x/100 = 9.32x

% of boys = [9.32x/17x] * 100

932/17

54.82%

21. According to Newton law of cooling

$$\frac{\theta_1-\theta_2}{t} = K\left[\frac{\theta_1-\theta_2}{2} - \theta_0\right]$$

For first process: $\dfrac{(80-64)}{5} = K\left[\dfrac{80+64}{2} - \theta_0\right]$ ... ... (i)

For second process: $\dfrac{(80-52)}{10} = K\left[\dfrac{80+52}{2} - \theta_0\right]$ ... (ii)

For third process: $\dfrac{(80-\theta)}{15} = K\left[\dfrac{80+\theta}{2} - \theta_0\right]$ ... ... (iii)

On solving equation (i) and (ii) we get $K = \dfrac{1}{15}$ and $\theta_0 = 24°C$ Putting these values in equation (iii) we get $\theta = 42.7°C$

22. $t = \dfrac{Ql}{KA(\theta_1-\theta_2)} = \dfrac{mLl}{KA(\theta_1-\theta_2)} = \dfrac{V\rho Ll}{KA(\theta_1-\theta_2)}$

$= \dfrac{5\times A\times0.92\times80\times\frac{5+10}{2}}{0.004\times A\times10\times3600} = 19.1$ hours.

23. Suppose temperature difference between A and B is $100°C$ and $\theta_A > \theta_B$

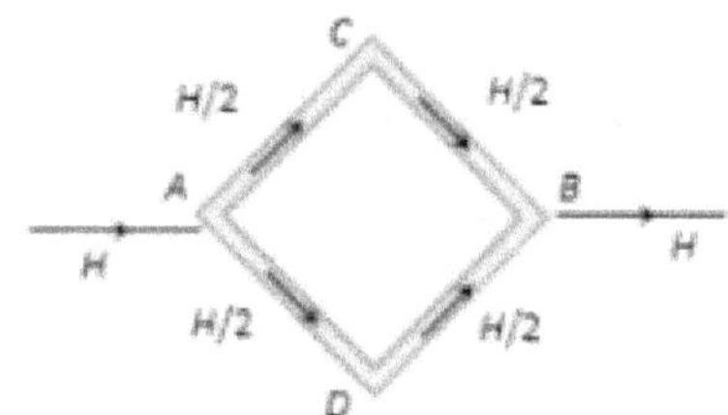

Heat current will flow from A to B via path ACB and ADB. since all the rod are identical so $\Delta\theta)_{AC} = (\Delta\theta)_{AD}$

(Because heat current $H = \dfrac{\Delta\theta}{R}$; here R = same for all.) $\Rightarrow$ $\theta_A - \theta_C = \theta_A - \theta_D \Rightarrow \theta_C = \theta_D$

I.e. temperature difference between C and D will be zero.

24. Number of moles present initially is $n = \dfrac{PV}{RT}$ Let n' be the number of moles of the gas that leaked till

the pressure falls to P'. since volume V of the vessel cannot change

and temperature T remains constant during leakage, we have

$$n' = \frac{P'V}{RT}$$

∴ Number of moles that leaked is

$$\Delta n = n - n' = \frac{PV}{RT} - \frac{P'V}{RT} = \frac{V}{RT}(P - P')$$

25. Accoding to Boyle's law $(P_1V_1)_{\text{bottom}} = (P_2V_2)_{\text{top}}$

$(10 + h) \times \frac{4}{3}\pi r_1^3 = 10 \times \frac{4}{3}\pi r_2^3$ but $r_2 = 2r_1$

∴ $(10 + h)r_1^3 = 10 \times 8r_1^3$ ∴ $10 + h = 80$ ∴ $h = 70m$

26. $v_{\text{max}} = \sqrt{\dfrac{3RT}{M}} \Rightarrow V_{\text{max}} \infty \sqrt{\dfrac{T}{M}}$

$\frac{v_2}{v_1} = \sqrt{\frac{M_1}{M_2} \times \frac{T_2}{T_1}}\sqrt{\frac{1}{2} \times \frac{1}{2}} \Rightarrow v_2 = \frac{v_1}{2} = \frac{300}{2} = 150$ m/sec

27. A quick way to solve this would be to look at rows one and two. Straight away you can tell that rate does not depend on [B]

28. One hour 36 minutes, i.e., 96 minutes is 8 half lives

Hence the amount left over is $\dfrac{100}{2^8} = \dfrac{100}{256} = 0.39g$

29. Each half life would reduce the concentration to half of its original value. So, 99.9% completion takes place in 10 half-lives. Remember 2^{10}=1024 and 1/1024≈0.001

Hence time taken = 45 × 10 minutes = 450 minutes = 7.5 hours.

30. Nylon is a linear polymer.

$$\left(\begin{matrix} H & & O \\ | & & || \\ -N-(CH_2)_5-C- \end{matrix}\right)_n$$

Nylon 6

31.

$$H_3C \quad\quad CH_2$$
$$\backslash \quad\quad /$$
$$C=C$$
$$/ \quad\quad \backslash$$
$$H_2C \quad\quad H$$

32. Thermoplastic polymers possess intermolecular forces of attraction between elastomers and fibres. Polythene is a thermoplastic polymer.

33. Decide the parent chain and give the numbering so that more substituted substituent will get the least number.

$$CH_3$$
$$|$$
$$CH_3-CH_2-C-CH_3$$
$$\overset{⑩}{CH_3}-\overset{⑨}{CH_2}-\overset{⑧}{CH_2}-\overset{⑦}{CH_2}-\overset{⑥}{CH_2}-\overset{⑤}{C}-\overset{④}{CH_2}-\overset{③}{CH_2}-\overset{②}{CH}-\overset{①}{CH_3}$$
$$\quad\quad\quad\quad CH_3-CH_2-C-CH_3 \quad\quad CH_3$$
$$\quad\quad\quad\quad\quad\quad\quad |$$
$$\quad\quad\quad\quad\quad\quad\quad CH_3$$

parent chain

10 carbons ⇒ word root ⇒ dec

single bond ⇒ suffix ⇒ ane

substituents at C_5 and C_2

Now,

$$CH_3$$
$$|$$
$$\overset{③}{CH_3}-\overset{②}{CH_2}-\overset{①}{C}-CH_3$$
$$\quad\quad\quad |$$
$$\quad\quad\quad C$$

⇒ 1, 1-dimethyl propyl
Because it's a substituent

There is one more same substituent on C_5

Therefore,

5,5-Bis-(1,1-dimethyl propyl)

Bis⇒ Because two same substituents are there, and a methyl group at C_2⇒ 2-methyl

Therefore,

5,5-Bis-(1,1-dimethylpropyl)-2-methyldecane

34. 7 carbon ⇒ hept (word root)

Single bonds ⇒ ane (suffix

→ substituent at C_3 and C_4 3-ethyl-4,4-dimethyl(alphabetically)

Therefore, **3-Ethyl-4,4-dimethylheptane**

35. Decide parent chain.

Numbering so that more substituted substituent will get the lowest number.

$$CH_3$$
$$|$$
$$\overset{①}{CH_3}-\overset{②}{CH}-\overset{③}{C}-\overset{④}{CH_2}-\overset{⑤}{CH_3}$$
$$\quad\quad\quad | \quad\quad |$$
$$\quad\quad\quad CH_3 \quad CH_2-CH_3$$

Five carbons ⇒ word root = pent

single bonds = ane(suffix)

→ substituent at C_2 and C_3⇒ 3-ethyl-2, 3-dimethylpentane(alphabetically)

Therefore,

(b) 3-Ethyl-2,3-dimethylpentane

36. Anode:$Fe(s) \rightarrow Fe^{2+}(aq)+2e^-$

Cathode:$4H^+ + O_2 + 4e^- \rightarrow 2H_2O$

37. A galvanic cell is an electrochemical cell that converts the chemical energy of a spontaneous redox reaction to the electrical energy.

38. $K = \dfrac{1}{R} \times$cell constant

Cell constant $= K \times R = 0.0212 \times 55 = 1.166 cm^{-1}$

39. Oleic acid $-C_{17}H_{33}COOH$, linoleic acid $-C_{17}H_{31}COOH$, linolenic acid $-C_{17}H_{29}COOH$,palmitic acid $-C_{15}H_{31}COOH$. Saturated monocarboxylic acids form a homologous series which has a general formula $-C_nH_{2n+1}COOH$ or $-C_nH_{2n}COOH$. Only palmitic acid follows this.

40.

Ascorbic acid (vitamin c)

41. Periyar National Park and Wildlife Sanctuary (PNP) is a protected area near Thekkady in the district of Idukki, Kottayam and Pathanamthitta in Kerala, India. It is notable as an elephant reserve and a tiger reserve.

42. The countries that have shorelines along the Baltic Sea: Denmark, Estonia, Latvia, Finland, Germany, Lithuania, Poland, Russia, and Sweden.

Belarus is not a Baltic state.

43. There are six official languages of the UN. These are Arabic, Chinese, English, French, Russian and Spanish.

44. The Pemayangtse Monastery is a Buddhist monastery in Pemayangtse, near Pelling in the northeastern Indian state of Sikkim, located 110 km west of Gangtok.

45. Article 370 of the constitution was applicable to the state Jammu and Kashmir.
Ayyangar was the chief drafter of Article 370 which granted local autonomy to the state of Jammu and Kashmir.
On 5 August 2019, the Government of India revoked the special status, or limited autonomy, granted under Article 370 of the Indian Constitution to Jammu and Kashmir - a region administered by India as a state which consists of the larger part of Kashmir which has been the subject of dispute among India, Pakistan, and China since 1947.

46. Gastric acid, gastric juice, or stomach acid, is a digestive fluid formed in the stomach and is composed of hydrochloric acid (HCl)

47. Armstrong became the first person to step onto the lunar surface six hours 39 minutes later on July 21 at 02:56 UTC

48. The Namesake (2003) is the first novel by American author Jhumpa Lahiri. It was originally a novel published in The New Yorker and was later expanded to a full-length novel.

49. Sabin award is to the Amphibian conservationists. In 2008 the IUCN recognized Satyabhama Das Biju of Department of Environmental biology, University of Delhi for his dedication for his research and conservation of Frogs and had awarded the Sabin award.

50. Kevin Peter Pietersen MBE (born 27 June 1980) is a former cricketer. He is a right-handed batsman and occasional off spin bowler who played in all three formats for England between 2005 and 2014.

Mathematics

Q.1 8934 – 3257 + 481 = ? + 2578

A. 3250　　**B.** 3580　　**C.** 3560　　**D.** 3480

Q.2 A boat takes 30 hours for travelling downstream from point A to point B and coming back to point C midway between A and B. If the velocity of the stream is 2 kmph and the speed of the boat in still water is 15 kmph, what is the distance between A and B?

A. 342km　　**B.** 356km　　**C.** 316km　　**D.** 308km

Q.3 Arun takes thrice as long to row a distance against the stream as to row the same distance in favour of the stream. The ratio of the speed of the boat in still water and stream is

A. 3:1　　**B.** 1:2　　**C.** 2:1　　**D.** 2:3

Q.4 $(656 \div 164)^2 = \sqrt{?}$

A. 4　　**B.** 16　　**C.** 256　　**D.** 400

Q.5 Rahul purchased an article for Rs. 8400 and sold it for a loss of 5%. From that money he purchased another article and sold it for a gain of 5%. What is the overall gain or loss?

A. Profit of Rs.21　　**B.** Profit of Rs.24
C. Loss of Rs.21　　**D.** Loss of Rs.24

Q.6 A Shop Keeper sells two bags for Rs. 500 each. On one, he gets 14% profit and on the other he gets 14% loss. His profit or loss in the entire transaction was?

A. 64/25 % Gain　　**B.** 49/25 % Gain
C. 64/25 % Loss　　**D.** 49/25 % Loss

Q.7 Two Vans start from a place with a speed of 50 kmph at an interval of 12 minutes. What is the speed of a car coming from the opposite direction towards the place if the car meets the vans at an interval of 10 minutes?

A. 13 kmph　　**B.** 10 kmph　　**C.** 14 kmph　　**D.** 16 kmph

Q.8 A car travels from a place A to B in 7 hour. It covers half the distance at 30 kmph and the remaining distance at 40 kmph, what is the total distance between A and B?

A. 120 Km　　**B.** 250 Km　　**C.** 240 Km　　**D.** 150 Km

Q.9 Eight years ago, Pavi's age was equal to the sum of the present ages of her one son and one daughter. Five years hence, the respective ratio between the ages of her daughter and her son that time will be 7:6. If Pavi's husband is 7 years elder to her and his present age is three times the present age of their son, what is the present age of the daughter?

A. 15 years　　**B.** 23 years　　**C.** 19 years　　**D.** 27 years

Q.10 Ravi's present age is three times his son's present age and 4/5th of his father's present age. The average of the present ages of all of them is 62 years. What is the difference between the Ravi's son's present age and Ravi's father's present age?

A. 62 years　　**B.** 64 years　　**C.** 69 years　　**D.** 66 years

Q.11 A sum of rupees 3200 is compounded annually at the rate of 10 paisa per rupee per annum. Find the compound interest payable after 2 years.

A. 200　　**B.** 842　　**C.** 672　　**D.** 832

Q.12 A certain sum is lent for 3yrs at 10% compound interest p.a. if the C.I for the 3rd year is 242. Then what will be the S.I for 4yrs?

A. 1500　　**B.** 1200　　**C.** 800　　**D.** 1900

Q.13 Deepak was to get a 50% hike in his pay but the computer operator wrongly typed the figure as 80% and printed the new pay slip. He received this revised salary for three months before the organization realized the mistake. What percentage of his correct new salary will get in the fourth month, if the excess paid to him in the previous three months is to be deducted from his fourth month?

A. 30%　　**B.** 40%　　**C.** 45%　　**D.** 25%

Q.14 The prices of two articles are in the ratio 3 : 4. If the price of the first article be increased by 10% and that of the second by Rs. 4, the original ratio remains the same. The original price of the second article is

A. Rs.40　　**B.** Rs.35　　**C.** Rs.10　　**D.** Rs.30

Q.15 10 persons are seated around a round table. What is the probability that 4 particular persons are always seated together?

A. 1/21　　**B.** 4/21　　**C.** 8/21　　**D.** 11/21

Q.16 A box contains 4 red, 5 black and 6 green balls. 3 balls are drawn at random. What is the probability that all the balls are of same colour?

A. 33/455　　**B.** 34/455　　**C.** 44/455　　**D.** 47/455

Q.17 A full tank gets emptied in 8 minutes due to the presence of a leak in it. On opening a tap which can fill the tank at the rate of 9 L/min, the tank get emptied in 12 min. Find the capacity of a tank?

A. 120 L　　**B.** 240 L　　**C.** 216 L　　**D.** 224 L

Q.18 If a pipe A can fill a tank 3 times faster than pipe B. If both the pipes can fill the tank in 42 minutes, then the slower pipe alone will be able to fill the tank in?

A. 148 minutes　　**B.** 124 minutes
C. 154 minutes　　**D.** 168 minutes

Q.19 Two numbers are in the ratio of 5:6 and if 4 is added to the first number and 4 is subtracted from the second number then the ratio becomes 3:2. Find the difference between two numbers.

A. 2.5　　**B.** 3.5　　**C.** 4.5　　**D.** 6.5

Q.20 The income of riya and priya are in the ratio of 4:5 and their expenditure is in the ratio of 2:3. If each of them saves 2000, then find their income.

A. 4000, 6000　　**B.** 4000, 5000

C. 5000, 4000   **D.** 5000, 4000

Science

Q.21 The following figure shows two air-filled bulbs connected by a U-tube partly filled with alcohol. What happens to the levels of alcohol in the limbs X and Y when an electric bulb placed midway between the bulbs is lighted.

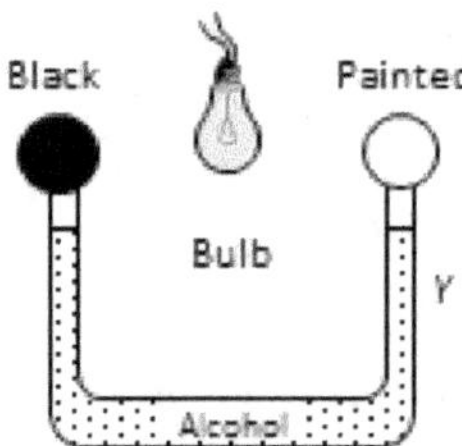

A. The level of alcohol in limb X falls while that in limb Y rises
B. The level of alcohol in limb X rises while that in limb Y falls
C. The level of alcohol falls in both limbs
D. There is no change in the levels of alcohol in the two limbs

Q.22 Two conducting rods A and B of same length and cross-sectional area are connected (i) In series (ii) In parallel as shown. In both combination a temperature difference of $100°$ C is maintained. If thermal conductivity of A is 3K and that of B is K then the ratio of heat current flowing in parallel combination to that flowing in series combination is

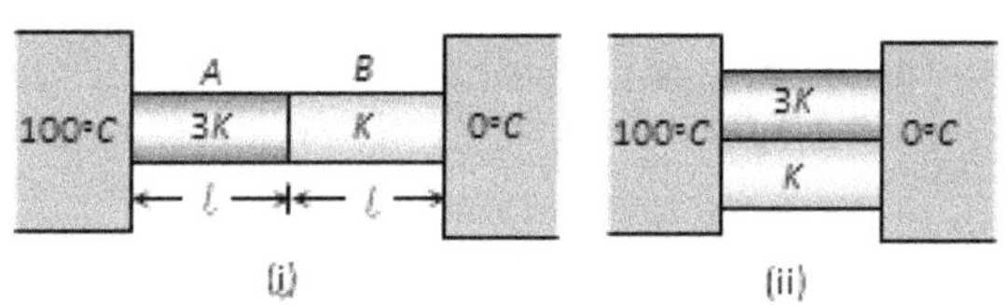

A. 16/3   **B.** 3/16   **C.** 1/1   **D.** 1/3

Q.23 Water and turpentine oil (specific heat less than that of water) are both heated to same temperature. Equal amounts of these placed in identical calorimeters are then left in air

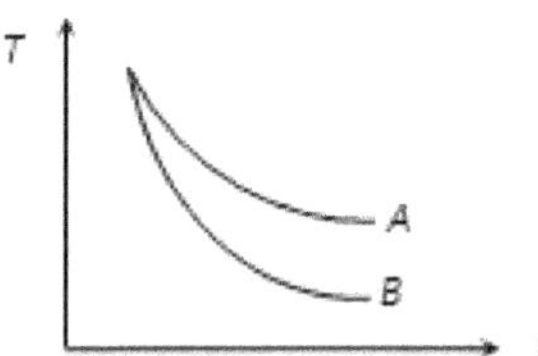

A. Their cooling curves will be identical
B. A and B will represent cooling curves of water and oil respectively
C. B and A will represent cooling curves of water and oil respectively
D. None of the above

Q.24 Two thermally insulated vessels 1 and 2 are filled with air at temperature (T_1, T_2), volume (V_1, V_2) and pressure (P_1, P_2) respectively. If the value joining the two vessels is opened, the temperature inside the vessel at equilibrium will be

A. $T_1 + T_2$ **B.** $\dfrac{T_1 + T_2}{2}$

C. $\dfrac{T_1 T_2 (P_1 V_1 + P_2 V_2)}{P_1 V_1 T_2 + P_2 V_2 T_1)}$ **D.** $\dfrac{T_1 T_2 (P_1 V_1 + P_2 V_2)}{P_1 V_1 T_1 + P_2 V_2 T_2)}$

Q.25 A vessel contains 1 mole of O_2 gas (molar mass 32) at a temperature T. The pressure of the gas is P. An identical vessel containing one mole of He gas (molar mass 4) at a temperature 2T has a pressure of

A. P/8   **B.** P   **C.** 2P   **D.** 8P

Q.26 An enclosure of volume V contains a mixture of 8g of oxygen, 14 g of nitrogen and 22 g of carbon- dioxide at absolute temperature T. The pressure of the mixture of gases is (R is universal gas constant)

A. $\dfrac{RT}{V}$ **B.** $\dfrac{3RT}{2V}$ **C.** $\dfrac{5RT}{4V}$ **D.** $\dfrac{7RT}{5V}$

Q.27 Assertion: Teflon has high thermal stability and chemical inertness.
Reason: Teflon is a thermoplastic.

A. If both assertion and reason are true and the reason is the correct explanation of the assertion.
B. If both assertion and reason are true but reason is not the correct explanation of the assertion.
C. If the assertion and reason both are false.
D. If assertion is false but reason is true.

Q.28 Which of the following statements is correct regarding the drawbacks of raw rubber?
A. It is not elastic in nature
B. It has high durability
C. It doesn't absorb water
D. All of these

Q.29 Which of the following is a monomer of Dacron?
A. Adipic acid   **B.** Terephthalic acid
C. Acetic acid   **D.** Formic acid

Q.30 If in the fermentation of sugar in an enzymatic solution which is initially 0.12 M the concentration of sugar is reduced to 0.06 M in 10 h and to 0.03 M in 20 h, hence order of the reaction is
A. 0   **B.** 1   **C.** 2   **D.** 3

Q.31 The half-life of a first order reaction is 24 hrs. If we start with 10 M initial concentration of the reactant then conc. after 96 hrs will be
A. 6.25 M   **B.** 1.25 M   **C.** 0.125 M   **D.** 0.625 M

Q.32 The half-life for the reaction, $N_2O_5 \Rightarrow 2NO_2 + 1/2O_2$ is 12 minutes at 30°C. Starting with 100 g of N_2O_5 how many gram of N_2O_5 will remain after a period of 1 hour 36 minutes.
A. 1.25 g   **B.** 0.39 g   **C.** 1.77 g   **D.** 0.5 g

Q.33 The IUPAC name of the following compound is

A. 1-Methyl-2-ethylcyclohexane

B. 1-Ethyl-6-Methylcyclohexane
C. 1-Ethyl-2-Methylcyclohexane
D. 1-Methyl-6-ethylcyclohexane

Q.34 C_5H_{12} has a symmetrical structure with one quaternary carbon. Its IUPAC name is:
A. 2-Methylbutane
B. n-Pentane
C. 2,2-Dimethylpropane
D. 1-Methylbutane

Q.35 The systematic IUPAC name of the compound is?

$$CH_2C-C-CH_3$$ with C_2H_5 groups

A. neoheptyl chloride
B. 3-Chloro-2,2-diethylpropane
C. 3-(Chloromethyl)-3-methylpentane
D. None of the above

Q.36 Which of the following statement(s) is(are) true?
A. The conductance of an electrolyte is dependent on the nature of the electrolyte.
B. Conductance of a solution equals the inverse of resistivity of the solution.
C. In an electrolytic cell the flow of electrons is from cathode to anode.
A. A, B   **B.** A,C   **C.** Only A   **D.** Only C

Q.37 During the electrolysis of an electrolyte, the number of ions produced is dependent on
A. Temperature
B. Nature of solvent
C. Nature of the electrolyte
D. All of the above

Q.38 What amount of current is required to be passed during a period of 5 minutes in order to deposit 0.6354gm of copper by electrolysis of aqueous cupric sulphatesolution? (Molar wt. of Copper = 63.5gm/mole)
A. 10.24A   **B.** 6.43A   **C.** 12.68A   **D.** 1930C

Q.39 Identify the correct statement regarding enzymes.
A. Enzymes are specific biological catalysts that cannot be poisoned
B. Enzymes are normally heterogeneous catalysts that are very specific in their action
C. Enzymes are specific biological catalysts that can normally function at very high temperature (T ~ 1000K)
D. Enzymes are specific biological catalysts that possess no well-defined active sites.

Q.40 Hydrolysis reaction of fats, with caustic soda, is known as
A. Acetylation   **B.** Carboxylation
C. Saponification   **D.** Esterification

General Awareness

Q.41 The National Chemical Laboratory is located in
A. Mumbai   **B.** Bengaluru
C. Hyderabad   **D.** Pune

Q.42 The National school of Drama is situated in which of the following cities?
A. Mumbai   **B.** New Delhi
C. Bhopal   **D.** Kolkata

Q.43 The first woman to climb mount Everest was
A. Marie Jose perec
B. Florence Griffith Joyner
C. Junko Tabei
D. Jackie Joyner Kersee

Q.44 The Arjuna Awards were instituted in the year
A. 1965   **B.** 1963   **C.** 1961   **D.** 1975

Q.45 Which one of the following countries is not a member of the OPEC?
A. Algeria   **B.** Indonesia
C. Malaysia   **D.** Nigeria

Q.46 Who is the author of the book ' The Right of Man'?
A. Thomas Hardy   **B.** Thomas Mann
C. Thomas Moore   **D.** Thomas Paine

Q.47 Which one of the following countries is not a member of ASEAN?
A. Brunei Darussalam   **B.** Cambodia
C. Vietnam   **D.** India

Q.48 India first took part in the Olympic Games in the year
A. 1920   **B.** 1928   **C.** 1972   **D.** 1974

Q.49 The first Asian Games were held in
A. China   **B.** India   **C.** Pakistan   **D.** Iran

Q.50 Toda tribes mainly live in
A. Madhya Pradesh   **B.** Tamil Nadu
C. Kerala   **D.** Odisha

// Smart Answer Sheet //

Correct   Indicates percentage of students who answered questions correctly.

Skipped   Indicates percentage of students who skipped questions.

Q.	Ans.	Correct / Skipped	Q.	Ans.	Correct / Skipped	Q.	Ans.	Correct / Skipped	Q.	Ans.	Correct / Skipped	Q.	Ans.	Correct / Skipped
1	B	81.08 % / 11.89 %	11	C	80.78 % / 18.46 %	21	A	80.28 % / 18.44 %	31	D	80.56 % / 17.42 %	41	D	89.33 % / 10.65 %
2	D	81.47 % / 10.93 %	12	C	83.9 % / 10.09 %	22	A	79.64 % / 13.15 %	32	B	78.8 % / 17.75 %	42	B	86.77 % / 11.81 %
3	C	87.1 % / 12.82 %	13	B	78.86 % / 13.75 %	23	B	84.57 % / 14.43 %	33	C	76.37 % / 11.56 %	43	C	79.31 % / 18.13 %
4	C	85.44 % / 14.54 %	14	A	87.99 % / 11.05 %	24	C	86.28 % / 11.01 %	34	C	86.07 % / 13.54 %	44	C	89.51 % / 10.1 %
5	C	76.51 % / 13.63 %	15	A	78.41 % / 16.01 %	25	C	88.6 % / 10.43 %	35	C	87.67 % / 11.39 %	45	C	83.08 % / 10.81 %
6	D	78.67 % / 12.41 %	16	B	84.05 % / 15.09 %	26	C	82.55 % / 13.39 %	36	C	82.36 % / 12.64 %	46	D	81.92 % / 13.18 %
7	B	87.98 % / 10.47 %	17	C	78.05 % / 10.11 %	27	B	80.24 % / 10.92 %	37	D	77.38 % / 10.26 %	47	D	81.56 % / 15.62 %
8	C	88.89 % / 10.96 %	18	D	76.38 % / 23.01 %	28	A	86.34 % / 10.47 %	38	B	81.87 % / 10.48 %	48	A	85.48 % / 11.34 %
9	B	80.53 % / 13.44 %	19	A	87.51 % / 11.29 %	29	B	86.9 % / 11.58 %	39	A	76.95 % / 10.85 %	49	B	87.42 % / 10.3 %
10	D	80.75 % / 14.06 %	20	B	80.44 % / 14.78 %	30	B	84.87 % / 14.56 %	40	C	78.49 % / 12.15 %	50	B	81.97 % / 10.1 %

Performance Analysis

Avg. Score (%)	44.67%
Toppers Score (%)	54.67%
Your Score	

//Hints and Solutions//

1. Explanation :

9415 – 5835 = 3580

2. Explanation :

velocity of the stream = 2 kmph

Speed of the boat in still water is 15 kmph

Speed downstream = (15+2) = 17 kmph

Speed upstream = (15-2) = 13 kmph

Let the distance between A and B be x km

x/17+(x/2)/13=30

x/17+x/26=30

43x/442=30

x=30*442/43 = 308.37 = 308km

distance between A and B = 308 km

3. Explanation :

speed downstream = x kmph

Speed upstream = 3x kmph

(3x+x)/2 : (3x-x)/2

4x/2 : 2x/2 = 2:1

4. Explanation :

656 ÷ 164 = √?

= >42= √?;

√? = 16 ;

? = 256

5. Explanation :

CP = 8400

SP = 8400 * 95/100 = 7980

CP = 7980

SP = 7980 * 105/100 = 8379

Difference = 8400 – 8379 = 21

6. Explanation :

% = x

Loss % = $x^2/100$ = 196/100 = 49/25%

7. Explanation :

50*12/60 = 10/60 * (50+x)

600 = 500 + 10x

x = 10 kmph

8. Explanation :

Total Distance = x

(x/2*30) +(x/2*40) = 7

x = 240

9. Explanation :

P – 8 = S + D —(1)

6D + 30 = 7S + 35 —(2)

H = 7 + P

H = 3S

3S = 7 + P —-(3)

Solving eqn (1),(2) and (3) D = 23

10. Explanation :

Present age of Ravi is = 4/5x

Present age of Ravi's father is = 4/15x

Ratio = 15: 12 : 4

Difference between the Ravi's son's present age and Ravi's father's present age = 62/31 * 3(15 – 4).

= 2*3*11 = 66 year.

11. Explanation :

Rate of interest is 10 paisa per rupee per annum. So for 100 rupees it is 1000 paise i.e. 10 percent

Now, CI = 3200(1+10/100)^ 2 – 3200 = 672

12. $R - 10\% = 1/10m..\,(10)^3 = 1000$, let $P = 1000$

C.I for 3 rd y r $= 121$

$121 = 242$

$1 = 2$

$P = 1000 = 2000$

$S.I = 4{*}10 = 40\%$ of $2000 = Rs800$

13. Explanation:

Assume Deepak's salary =10000

original hike(50%) amount = 5000 ; Revised salary =15000

Wrongly typed(80%) hike amount = 8000

Diff = 3000; For three months = 9000

Fourth Month Salary = 15000-9000=6000

15000*x/100 = 6000 => x=40%

14. Explanation:

Let the price of two articles are 3X and 4X.

After increment the ratio will be:

110% of 3x/(4X+4) = 3/4

x=10

Thus the CP of second article = 4X = 4*10 = Rs. 40.

15. Explanation :

Total outcomes = (10 -1)! = 9!

Favourable outcomes = 6!*4! (4 person seated together and 6 other persons seated randomly, so they will sit in (7-1)! Ways and those 4 persons can be arranged in 4! ways)

So probability = 1/21

16. Total number of combinations of 3 from 15 is 15! / (3! x 12!) = 455

Of those, the number where all the balls are red is 4

... all black is 5! / (2! x 3!) = 10

... all green is 6! / (3! x3!) = 20

so the total number of combinations where all three are the same colour is 34

The probability of all 3 being the same colour is 34/455.

17. Explanation :

a = 8; b = 9; C = 12

Capacity of a tank = a*b*c/c-a

= 8*9*12/4

= 216 Litre.

18. Explanation :

Time is taken by pipe A = x

Time is taken by pipe B = x/3

1/x + 3/x = 1/42

x = 168 minutes

19. Let the rational betweens two numbers be x

Thus the two numbers are smaller 5x and larger 6x.

If four is added to first number and four is subtracted from second number then the ratio become 3 : 2

After addition of 4 in first number it become 5x + 4 and after substraction of 4 from second number it become 6x - 4. Their ratio

(5x + 4)/ (6x - 4) = 3 / 2,

Cross multiplication

2 (5x + 4) = 3 (6x - 4)

10x + 8 = 18x - 12

10x - 18x = - 12 - 8,

--8x = —20

x = 20/8

x = 2.5

Thus two numbers are,

Smaller 5x = 5 × 2.5= 12.5

Larger 6x = 6 × 2.5 = 15

Difference between two numbers

15 - 12.5 = 2.5

Answer :The difference between the two numbers is 2.5.

20. Explanation :

4x – 2y = 2000 ---------1

and 5x – 3y = 2000.-------2

X = 1000 and Y= 1000

X = 1000, so income = 4000 and 5000

21. Black bulb absorbs more heat in comparison with painted bulb. So air in black bulb expands more. Hence the level of alcohol in limb X falls while that in limb Y rises.

22. Heat current $H = \dfrac{\Delta\theta}{R} \Rightarrow \dfrac{H_p}{H_s} = \dfrac{R_\alpha}{R_p}$

In first case $: R, = R_1 + R_2 = \dfrac{l}{(3K)A} + \dfrac{l}{KA} = \dfrac{4}{3KA}$

In second case : $R_p = \dfrac{R_1 R_2}{R_1 + R_2} = \dfrac{\frac{1}{(3K)4} \times \frac{l}{RA}}{\left(\frac{l}{(3K)4} + \frac{l}{KA}\right)} = \dfrac{l}{4KA}$

$\therefore \dfrac{H_p}{H_s} = \dfrac{\frac{d}{3KA}}{\frac{t}{4KA}} = \dfrac{16}{3}$

23.

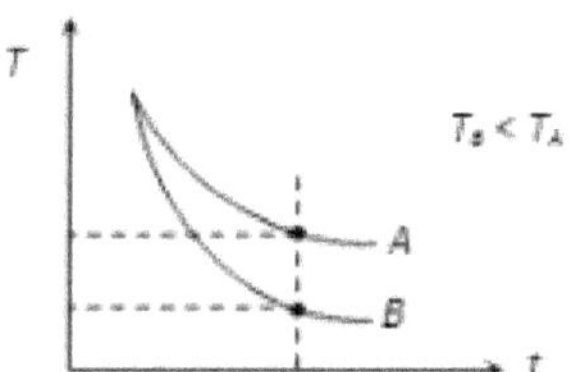

As we know, Rate of cooling $\propto \dfrac{1}{\text{spect fic heat } (c)}$

$\because C_{\text{oil}} < C_{\text{eater}}$

$\Rightarrow (\text{Rate of cooling})_{\text{olt}} > (\text{Rate of cooling})_{\text{vater}}$

It is clear that, at a particular time after start cooling, temperature of oil

will be less than that of water.

So graph B represents the cooling curve of oil and A represents the

cooling curve of water

24. According to the kinetic theory, the average kinetic energy(KE) per molecule of a gas $= \dfrac{3}{2}KT$. Let n_1 and n_2 be the number of moles of air in vessels 1 and 2 respectively. Before mixing, the total KE of molecules in the two vessels is $E_1 =$

$$\frac{3}{2}n_1 kT_1 + \frac{3}{2}n_2 kT_2$$
$$= \frac{3}{2}k(n_1 T_1 + n_2 T_2)$$

After mixing, the total KE of molecules is $E_2 =$
$$\frac{3}{2}(n_1 + n_2)kT$$

Where T is the temperature when equilibrium is established. since there is no loss of energy (Because the vessels are insulated), $E_2 = E_1$ or $\frac{3}{2}(n_1 + n_2)kT = \frac{3}{2}k(n_1 T_1 + n_2 T_2)$

or $T = \frac{n_1 T_1 + n_2 T_2}{n_1 + n_2}$

Now $P_1 V_1 = n_1 R T_1$ and $P_2 V_2 = n_2 R T_2$ which give

$n_1 = \frac{P_1 v_1}{R I_1}$ and $n_2 = \frac{P_2 v_2}{RT_2}$

Using these in Eq. (1) and simplifying, we get $T = \frac{T_1 T_2 (P_1 V_1 + P_2 V_2)}{(P_1 V_1 T_2 + P_2 V_2 T_1)}$

25. For a gas, $PV = nRT$. Hence

$(P)_{O_2} = \frac{(1\,\text{mole})RT}{V}$

and $(P)_{He} = \frac{(1 mole)R(2T)}{V}$

$\therefore \frac{(P)_{He}}{(P)_{O_2}} = 2$ or $(P)_{He} = 2(P)_{O_2}$

26. The pressure exerted by a gas is given by

$P = \frac{nRT}{V}$
$= \frac{mass}{molecular\ vereht} \times \frac{RT}{V}$

Pressure exerted by oxygen $P_1 = \frac{8RT}{32V} = \frac{1RT}{4V}$ Pressure exerted by oxygen $P_2 = \frac{14RT}{28V} = \frac{1RT}{2V}$ Pressure exerted by carbon dioxide $P_3 = \frac{22RT}{4V} = \frac{1RT}{2V}$ From Dalton's law of partial pressures, the total pressure exerted by the mixture is given by

$$P = P_1 + P_2 + P_3$$
$$= \frac{1RT}{4V} + \frac{1RT}{2V} + \frac{1RT}{2V}$$
$$= \frac{5RT}{4V}$$

27. Due to the presence of strong C–F bonds teflon has high thermal stability and chemical inertness.

And it is true that it is a thermoplastic. It changes shape on heating and retains the shape. It cannot be reshaped on further heating.

So, it is true that it is chemically inert but not because it is a thermoplastic.

28. The raw rubber is not elastic when found in nature. It becomes soft at high temperature. It has little durability and it has large water absorption capacity.

29. Dacron is formed by the interaction of ethylene glycol and terephthalic acid.

30. Given, Concentration is reduced from $0.12M$ to $0.06M$ in $10h$.

So, $t_{1/2} = 10h$

Conc reduced from $0.12M$ to $0.03M$ in $20hr$.

So, $t_{3/4} = 20h$

$t_{3/4} = 2 \times t_{1/2}$

This is valid only for 1 st Order Reaction.

So, Order is 1

31. $10 \xrightarrow{24\,\text{hrs}} 5 \xrightarrow{24\,\text{hrs}} 2.5 \xrightarrow{24\,\text{hrs}} 1.25 \xrightarrow{24\,\text{hrs}} 0.625$

32. One hour 36 minutes, i.e., 96 minutes is 8 half lives

Hence the amount left over is $\frac{100}{2^8} = \frac{100}{256} = 0.39g$

33. The numbering is according to the lowest of locants, which gives us two options.

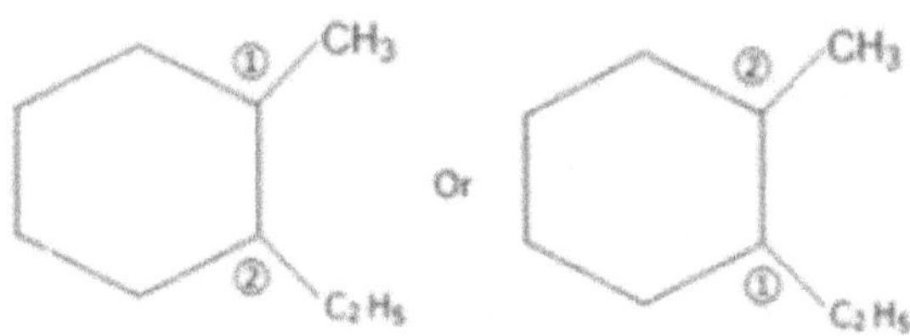

In this case, numbering happens according to alphabetical order. So ethyl group will have the lower number.

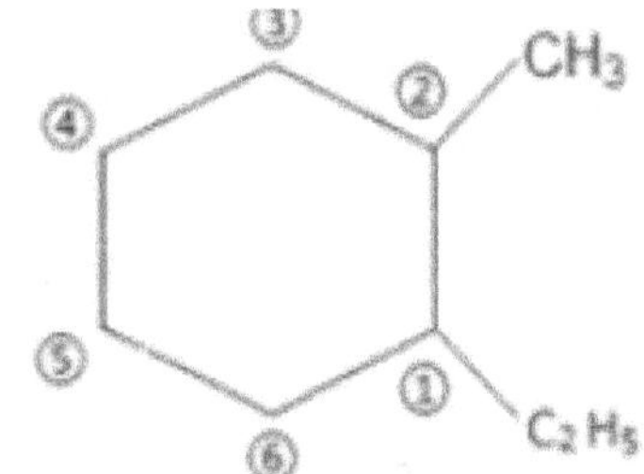

word root = hex

primary prefix = cyclo

secondary prefix = 1-Ethyl-2-methyl

primary suffix = ane

IUPAC name is

(c)1-Ethyl-2-methylcyclohexane

34. $C_5 H_{12}$ is of the form CnH_{2n+2}

Hence it is a saturated alkane. Further, it is given that it has a quaternary carbon. Hence its structure is:

Longest chain $= 3$ carbons $\Rightarrow$ word root $=$ prop

Primary suffix = ane Secondary prefix $= 2,2$ -Dimethyl

IUPAC name is (c) 2,2-Dimethyl propane

35.

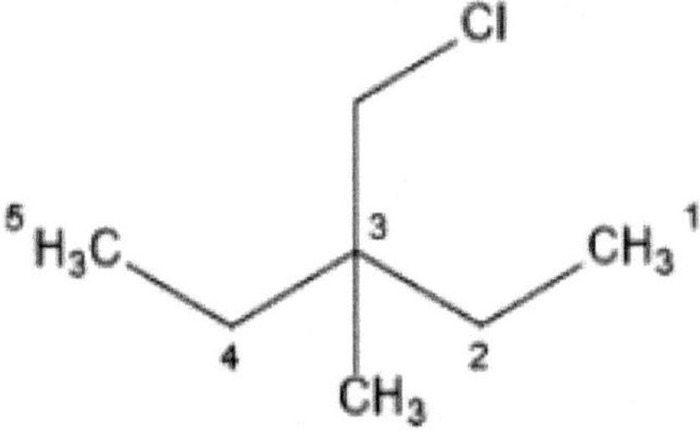

3-chloromethyl-3-methylpentane

Word root = pent

Primary suffix = ane

Lowest locant set = 3,3

Secondary prefixes = 3-(chloromethyl)-3-methyl

IUPAC name is 3-(chloromethyl)-3-methylpentane

36. Conductance of a solution equals the inverse of resistance of the solution, and not the resistivity

In an electrolytic cell the cathode acts as the source of electrons, hence the flow of electrons is from anode to cathode.

37. Number of ions produced depends on degree of dissociation, which depends on factors like nature of electrolyte, nature of solvent, temperature etc.

38. Moles of copper to be obtained $= \dfrac{0.6354}{63.54} = 0.01 moles$

$$Cu^{++} + 2e^- \rightarrow Cu$$

In order to obtain 1 mole of copper , 2 Felectricity is required. so, to obtain 0.01 moles of copper, $0.02F$ of electricity will be needed. $Q = I \times t = 0.02F = 0.02 \times 96500C = 1930C$ of electricity

Or, $I \times (5 \times 60) = 1930$

$\Rightarrow I = \dfrac{193}{30} = 6.43A$

39. Enzymes are specific biological catalysts that cannot be poisoned.

They are not necessarily heterogeneous catalysts: those in solution in the cellular medium are homogeneous, those bound to a membrane are heterogeneous.

We have seen they perform best at the temeperature close to our normal body temperature around 310 K. At very high temperatures, they become denatured.

40. Alkaline hydrolysis of fats is called Saponification.

41. The National Chemical Laboratory (NCL) is an Indian government laboratory based in Pune, in western India.

42. National School of Drama (or NSD) is a theatre training institute situated at New Delhi, India. It is an autonomous organization under Ministry of Culture, Government of India.

43. Junko Tabei (born Ishibashi Junko), 22 September 1939 – 20 October 2016)was a Japanese mountaineer. She was the first woman to reach the summit of Mount Everest, and the first woman to ascend all Seven Summits by climbing the highest peak on every continent.

44. The Arjuna Awards are given by the Ministry of Youth Affairs and Sports, Government of India to recognize outstanding achievement in sports. Started in 1961, the award carries a cash prize of ₹500,000, a bronze statue of Arjuna and a scroll.

45. Malaysia is not a member of the OPEC.
The Organization of the Petroleum Exporting Countries (OPEC) is a group consisting of 14 of the world's major oil-exporting nations. OPEC was founded in 1960 to coordinate the petroleum policies of its members and to provide member states with technical and economic aid. OPEC is a cartel that aims to manage the supply of oil in an effort to set the price of oil on the world market, in order to avoid fluctuations that might affect the economies of both producing and purchasing countries. Countries that belong to OPEC include Iran, Iraq, Kuwait, Saudi Arabia, and Venezuela (the five founders), plus the United Arab Emirates, Libya, Algeria, Nigeria, and five other countries.

46. Rights of Man (1791), a book by Thomas Paine, including 31 articles, posits that popular political revolution is permissible when a government does not safeguard the natural rights of its people.

47. ASEAN is a regional intergovernmental organization comprising ten countries in Southeast Asia, which promotes intergovernmental cooperation and facilitates economic, political, security, military, educational, and sociocultural integration among its members and other countries in Asia.

India is not a member of ASEAN.

48. India sent its first Olympic team to the 1920 Summer Olympics in Antwerp, Belgium, some twenty years after a single athlete (Norman Pritchard) competed for India in 1900

49. The Asian Games, also known as Asiad, is a continental multi-sport event held every four years among athletes from all over Asia. The Games were regulated by the Asian Games Federation (AGF) from the first Games in New Delhi, India.

50. Toda people are a Dravidian ethnic group who live in the Nilgiri Mountains of Tamil Nadu.

Mathematics

Q.1 What value should replace the question mark (?) in the following question?

$456 \div 24 \times 38 - 958 + 364 = ?$

A. 126   **B.** 127   **C.** 128   **D.** 138

Q.2 What value should replace the question mark (?) in the following question?

$5616 \div 18 \div 8 = ?$

A. 34   **B.** 39   **C.** 38   **D.** 37

Q.3 A milkman buys two cows for Rs. 3000. He sells first cow at a profit of 22% and the second cow at a loss of 8%. What is the SP of second cow if in the whole transaction there is no profit no loss?

A. Rs. 2312   **B.** Rs. 2024   **C.** Rs. 2484   **D.** Rs. 2532

Q.4 Sum of CP's of two cows is Rs. 39, 000. Both the cows are sold at a profit of 20% and 40% respectively with their SP's being the same. What is the difference of CP's of both the cows?

A. Rs. 3,000   **B.** Rs. 2, 000
C. Rs. 1, 500   **D.** Rs. 2, 500

Q.5 Two trains 200 m and 160 m long, run at the rate of 60 km/h and 100 km/h respectively on parallel rails. How long will it take a man sitting in the second train to pass the first train if they run in the opposite direction?

A. 4.4 seconds   **B.** 4.5 seconds
C. 3.24 seconds   **D.** 4 seconds

Q.6 A car traveled 80% of the distance from town A to B by traveling at T hours at an average speed of V km/h. The car travels at an average speed of S km/h for the remaining part of the trip. Which of the following expressions represents the average speed for the entire trip?

A. 12VS/(9V+S)   **B.** 5VS/(4S+V)
C. VT/3S   **D.** 9VS/(4S+V)km/h

Q.7 When Rajesh was born, his father age was 29 years older than his Brother and his Mother was 25 years older than his Sister. If his Brother is 2 years elder than his Sister. After 6 years the average age of the family is 20. Then what is the age of Mother when Rajesh was born?

A. 27   **B.** 28   **C.** 29   **D.** 30

Q.8 The ratio of Present age of Madhu and Divya is 6:7. Madhu is 7 years younger than Laxmi. Laxmi's age after 8 years will be 51 years. Then what is the difference between the present ages of Madhu and Divya?

A. 3 Years   **B.** 4 Years   **C.** 5 Years   **D.** 6 Years

Q.9 If a sum of money Rs. 200000 amounts to Rs. 266200 in 3 years at compound interest. Find the rate of interest?

A. 20%   **B.** 30%   **C.** 40%   **D.** 10%

Q.10 Cost of a Mobile Rs.8000. Sudha bought Mobile in EMI. She paid a Down payment of Rs. 2000 and paid rest in 6 equal installments of Rs.1020 for next 6 months. Then what is the SI rate charged?

A. 6.5%   **B.** 6.95%   **C.** 10.5%   **D.** 12.5%

Q.11 Veena bought a watch costing Rs. 1404 including sales tax at 8%. She asked the shopkeeper to reduce the price of the watch so that she can save the amount equal to the tax. The reduction of the price of the watch is?

A. Rs.108   **B.** Rs.104   **C.** Rs.112   **D.** Rs.120

Q.12 A Sales Executive gets a commission on total sales at 8%. If the sale is exceeded Rs.10,000 he gets an additional commission as a bonus of 4% on the excess of sales over Rs.10,000. If he gets the total commission of Rs.950, then the bonus he received is?

A. 40   **B.** 50   **C.** 36   **D.** 48

Q.13 Bag A contains 7 Red Balls, 'X' Green Balls, and 5 Yellow Balls. The probability to pick Green Ball at random is 2/5. Another Bag B contains 'X-3' Red Balls, 'X-4' Yellow Balls and 6 Green Balls. If two balls are picked one after the other from Bag B at random then what is the probability for the Balls to be Red?

A. 1/21   **B.** 2/21   **C.** 3/21   **D.** 4/21

Q.14 Six individual sock are present in a drawer- Two Red, Two Black and Two White. Pradeep picked one sock randomly to wear. Now he draws another sock from the drawer then what is the probability he draws a sock of same color?

A. 1/5   **B.** 1/6   **C.** 1/30   **D.** 11/30

Q.15 How many 3 digit number can be formed with the digits 5, 6, 2, 3, 7 and 9 which are divisible by 5 and none of its digit is repeated?

A. 12   **B.** 16   **C.** 20   **D.** 24

Q.16 In how many different ways can the letter of the word ELEPHANT be arranged so that vowels always occur together?

A. 2060   **B.** 2160   **C.** 2260   **D.** 2360

Q.17 Jeevan went to buy a chocolate worth Rs. x. He gave Rs.10 rupee note to the shopkeeper to buy the chocolate then shopkeeper gave rest of the money in the denominations of 50 paise, 1 rupee, and 2 rupees. If the ratio of the number of coins is 4:2:1 respectively. Then what is the price of the chocolate?

A. 4   **B.** 5   **C.** 6   **D.** 7

Q.18 In a family, there are 'n' persons. The expenditure of rice per month is directly proportional to 4 times the square of the number of persons of the family. If one of them left the family there was a decrease in consumption of 28Kg rice per month. Then initially how many persons were in the family?

A. 3   **B.** 4   **C.** 5   **D.** 6

Q.19 If 60% of $A = 50\%$ of B and $B = x\%$ of A, then the value of x is:

A. 150   **B.** 120   **C.** 200   **D.** 125

Q.20 Two numbers are in the ratio 5 : 6. The product of their H. C. F and L. C. M is 3000. What is the sum of the numbers?

A. 117   **B.** 110   **C.** 84   **D.** 104

Science

Q.21 Given standard electrode potentials

$Fe^{++} + 2e^- \rightarrow Fe; \ E° = -0.440 \ V$

$Fe^{+++} + 3e^- \rightarrow Fe; \ E° = -0.036 \ V$

The standard electrode potential ($E°$) for $Fe^{+++} + e^- \rightarrow Fe^{++}$ is

A. - 0.476 V   **B.** - 0.404 V

C. + 0.404 V   **D.** + 0.772 V

Q.22 In electrical motor ________.

A. Heat is converted into electrical energy

B. Electrical energy is converted into heat

C. Electrical energy is converted into mechanical energy

D. Mechanical energy is converted into electrical energy

Q.23 $E°$ for the cell is Zn $|Zn^{2+}$ (aq)$||Cu^{2+}$ (aq)$|$ Cu at 25°C, the equilibrium constant for the reaction $Zn + Cu^{2+}(aq) \rightleftharpoons Cu + Zn^{2+}$ (aq) is of the order of

A. 10^{-37} **B.** 10^{-28} **C.** 10^{+18} **D.** 10^{+17}

Q.24 To make 2.5 kg of 0.25 molar aqueous solution, determine the mass of urea (NH_2CONH_2) that is required.

A. 32 g   **B.** 37 g   **C.** 35 g   **D.** 40 g

Q.25 Which among the following is a false statement?

A. For a first order reaction $t_{1/2} = 0.693/k$

B. Rate of zero order reaction is independent of initial concentration of reactant

C. Half-life of a third order reaction is inversely proportional to the square of initial concentration of the reactant

D. Molecularity of a reaction may be zero or fraction

Q.26 Certain bimolecular reactions which follow first order kinetics are called

A. Bimolecular reactions

B. Unimolecular reactions

C. First order reaction

D. Pseudo unimolecular reactions

Q.27 The conversion of A to B follows second order kinetics. Doubling the concentration of A increases the rate of formation of B by a factor of

A. 2   **B.** 4   **C.** 1/2   **D.** 1/4

Q.28 Half-life of a reaction is found to be inversely proportional to the cube of initial concentration. The order reaction is

A. 2   **B.** 5   **C.** 3   **D.** 4

Q.29 The mass average molecular weight and number average molecular weight of a polymer are respectively 40000 and 30000. The poly-dispersity index of the polymer will be

A. < 1   **B.** > 1   **C.** 1   **D.** 0

Q.30 Buna-S rubber is which of the following of 1-3-butadiene and styrene

A. Polymers

B. Copolymer

C. Step growth polymer

D. Condensation polymer

Q.31 Which of the following are addition polymers?

I. Nylon

II. Melamine formaldehyde resin

III. Orlon

IV. Polystyrene

A. I, II   **B.** I, III   **C.** II, IV   **D.** III, IV

Q.32 Which among the following is polymer 'A'?

A. Melamine   **B.** Novolac

C. Terylene   **D.** Bakelite

Q.33 The IUPAC name of the following compound is

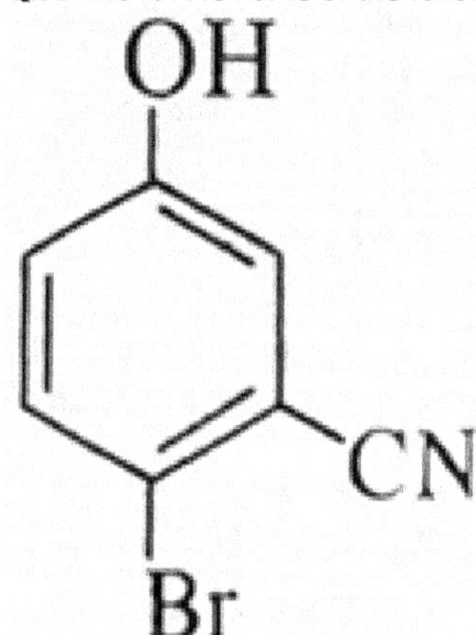

A. 4-Bromo-3-cyamphenol

B. 2-Bromo-5-hydroxybenzonitrile

C. 2-Cyano-4-hydroxybromobenzene

D. 6-Bromo-4-hydroxybenzonitrile

Q.34 C_5H_{12} has a symmetrical structure with one quaternary carbon. Its IUPAC name is:

A. 2-Methylbutane

B. n-Pentane

C. 2,2-Dimethylpropane

D. 1-Methylbutane

Q.35 The systematic IUPAC name of the compound is?

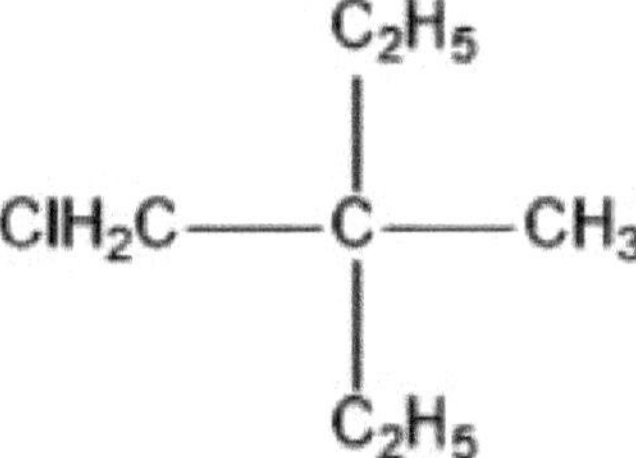

A. neoheptyl chloride
B. 3-Chloro-2,2-diethylpropane
C. 3-(Chloromethyl)-3-methylpentane
D. None of the above

Q.36 The IUPAC name of the following compound is?

$$CH_3-CH_2-CH_2-CH_2-CH_2-\underset{\underset{CH_3-CH_2-\underset{\underset{CH_3}{|}}{\overset{CH_3}{C}}-CH_3}{|}}{\overset{\overset{CH_3}{|}}{\overset{CH_3-CH_2-\overset{CH_3}{C}-CH_3}{|}}}-CH_2-CH_2-\underset{\underset{CH_3}{|}}{CH}-CH_3$$

A. 5, 5-(1,1-Dimethylpropyl)-2-methyldecane
B. 5, 5-Bis(1,1-dimethylpropyl)-2-methyldecane
C. 5, 5-Bis(1,1-dipropylmethyl)-2-methyldecane
D. None of these

Q.37 A well-stopped thermos flask contains ice cubes. This is an example of______.
A. Closed system
B. Open system
C. Isolated system
D. Non-thermodynamic system

Q.38 The enthalpy change for the reaction of 50.00 ml of ethylene with 50.00 ml of H_2 at 1.5 atm pressure is $\Delta H- = -0.31$ kJ. The value of ΔE will be
A. -0.3024 kJ
B. 0.3024 kJ
C. -2.567 kJ
D. -0.0076 kJ

Q.39 An ideal gas expands in volume from 1×10^{-3} to 1×10^{-2} m^3 at 300 K against a constant pressure of 1×10^5 Nm^{-2}. The work done is
A. 270 kJ
B. −270 kJ
C. −900 J
D. 900 kJ

Q.40 In a process a system does 140 J of work on the surroundings and only 40 J of heat is added to the system, hence change in internal energy is
A. 180 J
B. -180 J
C. -23.92 Cal
D. +180 J

General Awareness

Q.41 Which of the following dance is a Manipuri martial dance?
A. Pung Cholom
B. Thang Ta
C. Kartal Cholom
D. Sankirtana

Q.42 The Book 'Bookless in Baghdad' has been written by?
A. Ashish Ray
B. Shashi Tharoor
C. Pablo Neruda
D. Shobha De

Q.43 'One Stop Centres' Schemes are formulated by which Ministry of the Central Government & which is the first state to have these centres in its every district?
A. Ministry of Environment and Forest, Gujarat
B. Ministry of Women and Child Development, Chhattisgarh
C. Ministry of Statistics and Programme Implementation, Tamil Nadu
D. Ministry of Social Justice and Empowerment, Gujarat

Q.44 Who among the following was honoured with Ramon Magsaysay Award, 2018?
A. Bharat Vatwani
B. Nandan Nilekani
C. Azim Premji
D. Brij Bhushan Pandey

Q.45 Which of the following elements do not fall under the category of Paramagnetic Elements?
A. Barium
B. Rhodium
C. Thallium
D. Thorium

Q.46 Who among the following was not a founder member of Madras Mahajan Sabha?
A. M. Veeraraghavachariar,
B. Gazulu Lakshminarasu Chetty
C. G. Subramania Iyer
D. P. Anandacharlu

Q.47 How many times Indian Presidents have used an absolute veto power?
A. 0
B. 1
C. 2
D. 3

Q.48 Balance of trade in context of economy is____________
A. Exports-Imports
B. Expenditure- savings
C. Record of all transactions
D. Scheme of Special Economic Zones

Q.49 Which of the following is the national animal of United Kingdom?
A. Kangaroo
B. Kiwi
C. Lion
D. Tiger

Q.50 Who among the following clinched Men's singles China Open, 2018 badminton title held in Changzhou?
A. Kento Momota
B. Kidambi Srikanth
C. Chou Tien Chen
D. Anthony Sinisuka Ginting

// Smart Answer Sheet //

Correct — Indicates percentage of students who answered questions correctly.

Skipped — Indicates percentage of students who skipped questions.

Q.	Ans.	Correct / Skipped
1	C	41.7 % / 18.27 %
2	B	39.23 % / 24.37 %
3	B	24.8 % / 26.6 %
4	A	15.4 % / 30.5 %
5	B	22.73 % / 31.7 %
6	B	23.03 % / 30.0 %
7	B	20.3 % / 31.0 %
8	D	16.73 % / 30.44 %
9	D	14.27 % / 32.56 %
10	B	19.3 % / 30.63 %
11	B	23.17 % / 27.43 %
12	B	20.73 % / 30.7 %
13	B	21.47 % / 22.86 %
14	A	14.83 % / 27.74 %
15	C	23.07 % / 28.8 %
16	B	22.3 % / 26.37 %
17	A	16.53 % / 29.84 %
18	B	22.73 % / 32.27 %
19	B	30.4 % / 21.2 %
20	B	33.9 % / 18.5 %
21	D	6.4 % / 27.67 %
22	C	20.67 % / 30.96 %
23	A	10.2 % / 29.7 %
24	B	18.23 % / 31.94 %
25	D	12.87 % / 32.1 %
26	D	10.93 % / 30.04 %
27	B	17.37 % / 31.6 %
28	D	7.87 % / 31.2 %
29	B	21.8 % / 32.37 %
30	B	16.9 % / 30.4 %
31	D	12.0 % / 28.63 %
32	B	14.97 % / 29.76 %
33	B	19.53 % / 26.47 %
34	C	19.37 % / 30.16 %
35	C	17.1 % / 29.67 %
36	B	20.1 % / 28.93 %
37	C	26.6 % / 30.7 %
38	A	10.57 % / 32.96 %
39	C	14.67 % / 27.36 %
40	C	16.17 % / 27.0 %
41	B	27.13 % / 19.17 %
42	B	28.73 % / 20.27 %
43	B	26.63 % / 20.54 %
44	A	18.4 % / 21.53 %
45	C	21.93 % / 21.57 %
46	B	23.73 % / 21.1 %
47	C	25.77 % / 20.23 %
48	A	26.63 % / 20.64 %
49	C	26.4 % / 19.67 %
50	D	9.87 % / 21.63 %

Performance Analysis

Avg. Score (%)	7.33%
Toppers Score (%)	100.0%
Your Score	

//Hints and Solutions//

1. $456 \div 24 \times 38 - 958 + 364 = ?$

$19 \times 38 - 958 + 364 = \mathbf{128}$

2. $5616 \div 18 \div 18 = ?$
$312 \div 8 = ?$
$? = \mathbf{39}$

3. First Cow   Second cow

CP x $(750 - x)$

SP $\dfrac{122x}{100}$ $\dfrac{92}{100}(750 - x)$

$3000 = \dfrac{122x}{100} + \dfrac{92}{100}(3000 - x)$

$\therefore 3000 = \dfrac{122x}{100} + \dfrac{92}{100}(3000) - \dfrac{92}{100}x)$

$x = 800$

$\therefore CP$ of second Cow $= 3000 - 800$

$= 2200 Rs$

$\therefore$ Required $S.P. = \dfrac{92}{100} \times 2200$

$= 2024 Rs$

4. First cow   :   Second cow
Let CP- 10x7 : 10x6
  SP- 12x7 : 14x6
Ratio of their cost price = 7 : 6

$\therefore 130 => 39000$

$\Rightarrow 1 ----> 300$

$\Rightarrow 10 -----> 3000$ Rs.

Hence, the correct option is (A).

5. Since both trains are moving in opposite direction so their speed must be added.

As we know, speed $= \dfrac{\text{distance}}{\text{time}}$ (Where distance will be the train of the length)

Time taken by man sitting in second train to pass the first train

$= \dfrac{200}{(60+100)\times\frac{5}{18}} = 4.5 sec$

Note- To convert km/hours to m/sec we have to multiply it by $5/18$

6. 80% of the distance $= VT\ km$

$\therefore$ Total distance $= \dfrac{VT}{80} \times 100 = \dfrac{5}{4}VT\ km$

Remaining distance $= \dfrac{5}{4}VT - VT = \dfrac{1}{4}VT\ km$

Remaining time $= \dfrac{VT}{4S}$ hour Total time $= T + \dfrac{VT}{4S}$

Average speed $= \dfrac{\text{Total Distance}}{\text{Total Time}}$

$= \dfrac{\frac{5}{4}VT}{T+\frac{VT}{4S}} = \dfrac{5VS}{4S+V}km/h$

7. Sister = x; Brother = x+2; Father = 29+x+2; Mother = 25+x
Present age – 4x+58

After 6 years
4x+58+30 = 4x+88
4x+88 = 100
x = 3
Mothers age = 25+x = 28.

8. M/D = 6/7
L- M =7
L+8 = 51, L = 43
M = 36
D = 42
D-M = 42-36 = 6

9. $A = P\left(1 + \dfrac{r}{100}\right)^3$

$266200 = 200000\left(1 + \dfrac{r}{100}\right)^3$

$\dfrac{1331}{1000} = \left(1 + \dfrac{r}{100}\right)^3$

$1 + \dfrac{r}{100} = \dfrac{11}{10}$

$\dfrac{r}{100} = \dfrac{1}{10}$

$r = 10\%$

Hence, the correct option is (D).

10. Balance to be paid in installments $= 8000 - 2000 = 6000$
$(6000 + 6000 * r*3/12*100) = 1020*6 + 1020r/12*$
$100(1 + 2 + 3 + 4 + 5)$
$r = 6.95\%$

11. 108x/100 = 1404
1.08x = 1404
x = 1300
The reduction of the price of the watch = 104

12. Commission up to $10000 = 10000 * 8/100 = 800$
Ratio $= 2x : x$; Commission $= 2x$, Bonus $= x$;
Bonus $= 950 - 800 \times 1/3 = 150 * 1/3 = 50$

13. X/(7+X+5) =2/5
X =8
Bag B = 5 R, 4 Y, 6 G
Probability = 5/15*4/14 = 2/21

14. In the first draw, he picks anyone sock. Now he is left with 5 socks he has to pick one from them of the same color so 1/5,

15. Since each desired number is divisible by 5, so we must have 5 at the unit place. So, there is 1 way of doing it.
The tens place can now be filled by any of the remaining 5 digits (2, 3, 6, 7, 9). So, there are 5 ways of filling the tens place.
The hundreds place can now be filled by any of the remaining 4 digits. So, there are 4 ways of filling it.
$\therefore$ Required number of numbers = (1 x 5 x 4) = **20**

16. Vowels = E, E and A. They can be arranged in 3!/2! Ways
so total ways = 6!*(3!/2!) = 2160

17. The price of the chocolate is equal to Rs. 4.

The ratio of the coins returned by the shopkeeper is given by 50 paise : 1 rupee : 2 rupees = 4:2:1.

Total money returned by the shopkeeper = 4 × 0.5 + 2 × 1 + 1 × 2 = Rs. 6

Cost of the chocolate = 10 - 6 = Rs. 4

If we consider another ratio , eg - 8:4:2.

Total money returned by the shopkeeper = 8 × 0.5 + 4 × 1 + 2 × 2 = Rs. 12

This is not possible as the maximum possible amount is Rs. 10.

18. $R_1 = 4n^2$
$R_2 = 4(n-1)^2$
$R_1-R_2 = 28$
$4n^2-4(n-1)^2=28$
$8n-4= 28$
$n =4$

19. It is given that, 60% of $A = 50\%$ of B

Therefore,

$$\Rightarrow \frac{60}{100} \times A = \frac{50}{100} \times B$$

$$\Rightarrow B = \frac{6}{5} \times A$$

$$\Rightarrow B = [\left(\frac{6}{5}\right) \times 100]\% \times A = 120\% \text{ of } A$$

So, the value of x is 120.

Hence, the correct option is (B).

20. It is given that, two numbers are in the ratio 5 : 6 and the product of their H. C. F and L. C. M is 3000.

We know that, First number × Second Number = L. C. M × H. C. F

Let the first number be $5x$ and the second number be $6x$.

Therefore, according to the question,

$$\Rightarrow 5x \times 6x = 3000$$

$$\Rightarrow x^2 = 100$$

$$\Rightarrow x = \sqrt{100}$$

$$\Rightarrow x = 10$$

So, the first number $= 5x = 5 \times 10 = 50$

The second number $= 6x = 6 \times 10 = 60$

Sum of two numbers $= 50 + 60 = 110$

∴ The sum of two numbers is 110.

Hence, the correct option is (B).

21. $\Delta G° = -nE°F$
$Fe^{2+} + 2e^- \rightarrow Fe \quad ......(i)$

$\Delta G° = -2 \times F \times (-0.440V) = 0.880F$
$Fe^{3+} + 3e^- \rightarrow Fe$
$\Delta G° = -3 \times F \times (-0.036) = 0.108F$

On substracting equation (i) from (ii) $Fe^{3+} + e^- \rightarrow Fe^{2+}$

$\Delta G° = 0.108F - 0.880F = -0.772F$

$E°$ for the reaction $= -\dfrac{\Delta G°}{nF} = -\dfrac{(-0.772F)}{1 \times F} = +0.772V$

22. A motor is a machine that converts electrical energy into mechanical energy. The motor works on "Fleming's left-hand rule".

Fleming's left-hand rule: When current flows through a conducting wire, and an external magnetic field is applied across that flow, the conducting wire experiences a force perpendicular both to that field and to the direction of the current flow (i.e. they are mutually perpendicular).

Hence, the correct option is (C).

23. $E°_{ccll} = \dfrac{0.059}{n} \log K$

$\log K = \dfrac{1.10 \times 2}{0.059} = 37.2881 \Rightarrow K = 10^{-37}$

24. Molar mass of urea (NH_2CONH_2) $= 2(1 \times 14 + 2 \times 1) + 1 \times 12 + 1 \times 16 = 60 g mol^{-1}$

0.25 molar aqueous solution of urea means:

$1000g$ of water contains $0.25 mol = (0.25 \times 60)g$ of urea $= 15g$ of urea

That is,

$(1000 + 15)g$ of solution contains $15g$ of urea

Therefore, $2.5kg (2500g)$ of solution contains $= \dfrac{15 \times 2500}{1000 + 15} g$

$= 36.95g$

$= 37g$ of urea (approx.)

Hence, mass of Urea required is $37g$

25. Molecularity can never be zero or fractional.

26. Pseudo Unimolecular reaction. In a chemical reaction if two or more reactants are involved but the rate of reaction depends only upon the concentration of one of the reactant and independent of other reactants then it is said to be pseudo unimolecular reaction.

27. For a second order kinetics of the reaction A → B
we have rate = k[A]².
When conc. of A is doubled the rate of the reaction increases by a factor of 2²=4.
Since rate of conversion of A = rate of formation of B.
Hence rate of formation of B also increases 4 times.

28. $t_0 \cdot 5 \propto \dfrac{1}{a^{n-1}}$

Given $t_0 \cdot 5 \propto \dfrac{1}{a^3}$

Hence, $n - 1 = 3$

$\therefore n = 4$

29. PDI (Polydispersity Index) is the ratio of the mass average molecular mass to the number average molecular mass.

$$P.D.I = \frac{\overline{M_W}}{\overline{M_n}} = \frac{40000}{30000} = 1.33$$

Thus, PDI of the polymer is > 1,

30. Buna-S is a copolymer of 1,3 - butadiene and styrene.

$$n\,CH_2 = CH - CH = CH_2 + \underset{\text{Styrene}}{\underset{CH = CH_2}{\bigcirc}} \longrightarrow \left[CH_2 - CH = CH - CH_2 - CH - CH_2 \right]_n$$

1,3-Butadiene   Styrene   Butadiene-styrene co-polymer

31. Addition polymers are formed by the repeated addition of a large number of same or different monomers popssissing doubel and triple bonds e.g

(i) orlon is obtained by addition polymerisation of acrylonitrile in presence of a perovide catalyst.

$$n \underset{}{\overset{CN}{=\!\!\!-\!\!\!/}} \xrightarrow[\text{Peroxides}]{\text{Polymerisation}} \underset{\substack{\text{Orlon}\\ \text{(polyacrylonitrile)}}}{-(CH_2-\underset{\underset{CN}{|}}{CH})_n}$$

(ii) Polystryrene is obtained vby addition polymeriration of sytrene.

$$n \underset{\text{Styrene}}{\bigcirc}{-CH=\!\!=CH_2} \xrightarrow{\text{Polymerisation}} \left[\underset{\text{Polystyrene}}{\bigcirc}{-CH-CH_2} \right]_n$$

32. A' is novolac, 'B' is Bakelite. Novolac is a phenol-formaldehyde resin with a formaldehyde to phenol molar ratio of less than one.

33.

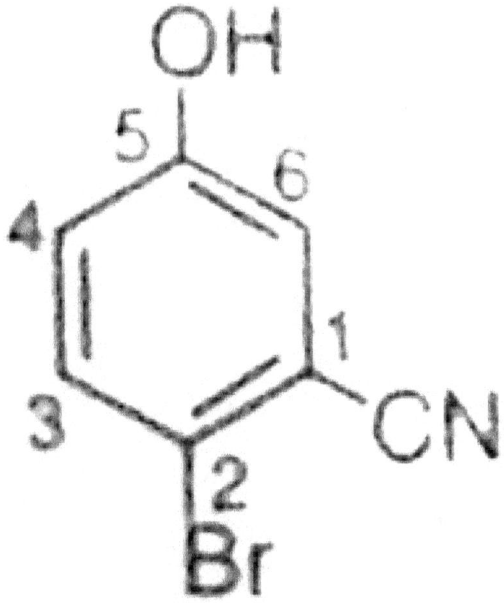

2-Bromo-5-hydroxybenzonitrile

34. C_5H_{12} is of the form CnH_{2n+2}.
Hence it is a saturated alkane. Further, it is given that it has a quaternary carbon. Hence its structure is:

$$\overset{\textcircled{1}}{H_3C} - \overset{\overset{\textstyle CH_3}{|}}{\underset{\underset{\textstyle CH_3}{|}}{\overset{\textcircled{2}}{C}}} - \overset{\textcircled{3}}{CH_3}$$

Longest chain = 3 carbons

$\Rightarrow$ word root = prop

Primary suffix = ane

Secondary prefix = 2,2-Dimethyl

IUPAC name is (c) 2,2-Dimethyl propane

35.

3-chloromethyl-3-methylpentane

Word root = pent

Primary suffix = ane

Lowest locant set = 3,3

Secondary prefixes = 3-(chloromethyl)-3-methyl

IUPAC name is 3-(chloromethyl)-3-methylpentane

36. Decide the parent chain and give the numbering so that more substituted substituent will get the least number.

parent chain

10 carbons $\Rightarrow$ word root $\Rightarrow$ dec

single bond $\Rightarrow$ suffix $\Rightarrow$ ane

substituents at C_5 and C_2

Now,

$\Rightarrow$ 1, 1-dimethyl propyl

Because it's a substituent

There is one more same substituent on C_5

Therefore,

5,5-Bis-(1,1-dimethyl propyl)

Bis $\Rightarrow$ Because two same substituents are there, and a methyl group at $C_2 \Rightarrow$ 2-methyl

Therefore,

5,5-Bis-(1,1-dimethylpropyl)-2-methyldecane

37. The system is subject to surrounding factors such as air temperature and pressure. If we want to study the thermodynamics of the system, we will study the heat exchange between it and the environment surrounding it. On the basis of exchanging criteria of heat and matter, thermodynamics systems are of three types.

Open system: An open system is defined as a system in which there is an exchange of both matter and energy with the surrounding. For example, boiling water above its boiling point without covering the container. This helps the heat generated to escape into the surrounding and there is a transfer of matter in the form of vapours to the surrounding.

Closed system: It is defined as the system which allows only heat to transfer but restricts the moments of matter between the system and the surrounding. Example: Burner transferring its heat to the vessel kept above it. It allows the transfer of energy only, not allowing matter to be transferred.

Isolated System: This system completely restricts any kind of transfer nor of heat neither matter. From the system matter is not

exchanged and also heat transfer takes place. Example: A Thermo flask, which does not allow the exchange of matter as well as energy.

Hence, the correct option is (C).

38. $C_2H_4(g) + H_2(g) \rightarrow C_2H_6(g)$
$\Delta ng = 1 - 2 = -1; \Delta H = -0.31 KJmol^{-1}$
$p = 1.5 atm, \Delta V = -50mL = -0.050L$
$\Delta H = \Delta E + p\Delta V$
$-0.31 = \Delta E - 0.0076;$

$\Delta E = -0.3024 KJ$

39. $P = 1 \times 10^5 N/m^2$
$V_i = 1 \times 10^{-3} m^3$
$V_f = 1 \times 10^{-2} m^3$
$\Delta V = V_f - V_i = 10^{-2} - 10^{-3} = 9 \times 10^{-3} m^3$
As we know that,
$W = -P\Delta V$
$W = -1 \times 10^5 (10^{-2} - 10^{-3})$
$\Rightarrow W = -10^5 \times (9 \times 10^{-3})$
$\Rightarrow W = -9 \times 10^2 = -900J$
The work done is $-900J$.

Hence, the correct option is (C).

40. Given -
$W = -140J$
$q = +40J$
$q = \Delta U - W$
$\Delta U = q + W = +40 - 140J$
$= -100J$

1 calories is equal to 4.184 Joules

So, -23 Cal = -100 Joules

41. Thang Ta is a cultural heritage art of Manipur. Its traditional name is Huyel Langlon. The primary weapons of huyen langlon are the thang (sword) and ta (spear). The spear can be used in its non-missile form while in close or thrown from afar. In this art, movements of sword intended to ward off evil spirits is shown while other dance moves indicate protection.

Sankirtana is a form of performing art involving ritual singing, drumming and dancing performed in the temples and domestic spaces in Manipur State in India.

The Pung Cholom is a unique classical dance of Manipur. This dance may be performed by men or women and is usually a prelude to the Ras Lila.

Kartal Cholom or Cymbal Dance is a characteristic of the Manipuri style of dance and music. The initial movements of this dance are soft and serene, gradually gathering momentum.

42. The Book 'Bookless in Baghdad' has been written by Mr. Shashi Tharoor

Book	Author
One-Day Cricket: The Indian Challenge	Ashish Ray
Fully Empowered	Pablo Neruda
Speed post	Shobha De

43. Ministry of Women and Child Development (MWCD), formulated a Centrally Sponsored Scheme for setting up One Stop Centres (OSC), to be funded from the Nirbhaya Fund. These Centres will be established across the country to provide integrated support and assistance under one roof to women affected by violence, both in private and public spaces in a phased manner. In the first phase, one OSC will initially be established in each State/UT to facilitate access to an integrated range of services including medical, legal, and psychological support. The OSC will be integrated with 181 and other existing helplines. The scheme is being implemented through States/UTs from 1st April 2015.

44. Two Indian nationals, Bharat Vatwani and Sonam Wangchuk, were honored with the Ramon Magsaysay award, popularly known as Asia's Nobel Prize.Cambodian activist Youk Chhang, Filipino Howard Dee, Vietnam's Vo Thi Hoang Yen and East Timore's Maria de Lourdes Martins Cruz were also honoured for their work.

45. Thallium is a chemical element which fall under the category of Diamagnetic Substance with symbol Tl and atomic number 81. It is a grey post-transition metal that is not found free in nature. When isolated, thallium resembles tin, but discolours when exposed to air. Barium, Rhodium & Thorium are Paramagnetic chemical elements.

46. Madras Mahajan Sabha was an Indian nationalist organisation based in the Madras Presidency. Along with the Poona Sarvajanik Sabha, Bombay Presidency Association and the Indian Association, it is a predecessor of the Indian National Congress. In May 1884., M. Veeraraghavachariar, G. Subramania Iyer and P. Anandacharlu established the Madras Mahajan Sabha. The Madras Mahajan Sabha held its first conference between December 29, 1884 and January 2, 1885.

47. An Absolute Veto has been used twice, once by President Rajendra Prasad in 1954 and again by President Ramaswamy Venkataraman in 1991.
Absolute veto- It refers to the power of the President to withhold his assent to a bill passed by the Parliament. The bill then ends and does not become an act.
In 1954, the erstwhile PEPSU (Patiala and East Punjab States Union) was under President's Rule and so the Parliament passed a money appropriation bill on behalf of the state legislature. But by the time the bill reached President Rajendra Prasad, the President's Rule in the state had been revoked. Since the bill was about a subject mentioned under State List, the President rightfully rejected it using Absolute Veto.
In 1991, the Salary, Allowances, and Pensions of Members of Parliament Amendment bill was passed by the Parliament on the last day before the dissolution of the Lok Sabha, without seeking prior recommendation by the President. So, when the bill reached President R. Venkataraman, he invariably rejected it using Absolute Vet

48. The balance of trade (BOT) is the difference between the value of a country's imports and its exports for a given period. The balance of trade is the largest component of a country's balance of payments (BOP).

49. Lion is regarded as the national animal of United Kingdom
Kangaroo- Australia
Kiwi- New Zealand
Tiger- India

50. Indonesia's Anthony Sinisuka Ginting clinched Men's singles China Open, 2018 badminton title beating Japan's Kento Momota in Changzhou. The 2018 China Open was the seventeenth tournament which is been held since 1986. Spain's Carolina Marin beat China's Chen Yufei to take the women's singles title.

Mathematics

Q.1 If one root of the equation $ax^2 + bx + c = 0$ be n times the other root, then

A. $na^2 = bc(n+1)^2$ **B.** $nb^2 = ac(n+1)^2$

C. $nc^2 = ab(n+1)^2$ **D.** $nb^3 = ac(n+1)^2$

Q.2 The coefficient of x in the equation $x^2 + px + q = 0$ was taken as 17 in place of 13, its roots were found to be -2 and -15, the roots of the original equation are

A. 3, 10   **B.** - 3, - 10   **C.** - 5, - 18   **D.** 18,5

Q.3 If the sum of two of the roots of $x^3+px^2+qx+r=0$ is zero, then pq =

A. - r   **B.** r   **C.** 2 r   **D.** - 2 r

Q.4 If α, β, γ are the roots of the equation $x^3+4x+1=0$,then $(\alpha+\beta)^{-1}+(\beta+\gamma)^{-1}+(\gamma+\alpha)^{-1}=$

A. 2   **B.** 3   **C.** 4   **D.** 5

Q.5 If two roots of the equation $x^3-3x+2=0$ are same, then the roots will be

A. 2, 2, 3   **B.** 1, 1, -2   **C.** - 2, 3, 3   **D.** -2, -2, 1

Q.6 In a town of 10,000 families it was found that 40% family buy newspaper A, 20% buy newspaper B and 10% families buy newspaper C, 5% families buy A and B, 3% buy B and C and 4% buy A and C. If 2% families buy all the three newspapers, then number of families which buy A only is

A. 3100   **B.** 3300   **C.** 2900   **D.** 1400

Q.7 Let $n(U) = 700$, $n(A) = 200$, $n(B) = 300$ and $n(A \cap B) = 100$, Then $n(A^c \cap B^c) =$

A. 400   **B.** 600   **C.** 300   **D.** 200

Q.8 If the sets A and B are defined as

$A = \{(x, y) : y = 1x, 0 \neq x \in R\}$

$B = \{(x, y) : y = -x, x \in R\}$, then

A. $A \cap B = A$ **B.** $A \cap B = B$

C. $A \cap B = \emptyset$ **D.** None of these

Q.9 If A and B are two given sets, then $A \cap (A \cap B)^c$ is equal to

A. A   **B.** B

C. $\emptyset$ **D.** $A \cap (B^c)$.

Q.10 In a survey of 200 students from 7 different schools, 50 people do not play NFS, 40 people do not play Dota and 10 people play no online game. Then find the no. of people out of 200 people who do not play both the games provided these are the only two games on offer.

A. 80   **B.** 70   **C.** 60   **D.** 50

Q.11 If A and B are any two sets, then $A \cup (A \cap B)$ is equal to

A. A   **B.** B   **C.** A^c **D.** B^c

Q.12 If $X = \{4^n - 3n - 1 : n \in N\}$ and $Y = \{9(n-1) : n \in N\}$, then $X \cup Y$ is equal to

A. X   **B.** Y

C. N   **D.** None of these

Q.13 Let $A = \{x : x \in R, |x| < 1\}$; $B = \{x : x \in R, |x-1| \geq 1\}$ and $A \cup B = R - D$, then the set D is

A. $[x : 1 < x \leq 2]$ **B.** $[x : 1 \leq x < 2]$

C. $[x : 1 \leq x \leq 2]$ **D.** None of these

Q.14 If a set A has n elements, then the total number of subsets of A is

A. n   **B.** n^2 **C.** 2^n **D.** 2n

Q.15 The set $A = \{x : x \in R, x^2 = 16 \text{ and } 2x = 6\}$ equals

A. $\emptyset$ **B.** $\{14, 3, 4\}$

C. $\{3\}$ **D.** $\{4\}$

Q.16 Which of the following is an empty set

A. $\{ x : x$ is a real number and $x^2-1=0 \}$

B. $\{ x : x$ is a real number and $x^2 + 1=0 \}$

C. $\{ x : x$ is a real number and $x^2 - 9=0 \}$

D. $\{ x : x$ is a real number and $x^2 = x +2 \}$

Q.17 In a city 20 percent of the population travels by car, 50 percent travels by bus and 10 percent travels by both car and bus. Then the percentage of population travelling by car or bus is

A. 80 percent   **B.** 40 percent

C. 60 percent   **D.** 70 percent

Q.18 The number of proper subsets of the set {1, 2, 3} is

A. 8   **B.** 7   **C.** 6   **D.** 5

Q.19 The set of intelligent students in a class is

A. A null set

B. A singleton set

C. A finite set

D. Not a well defined collection

Q.20 If the line $(3x+14y+7)+k(5x+7y+6)=0$ is parallel to the y-axis, then the value of k is

A. 1/3   **B.** -3/5   **C.** -2   **D.** 2

Science

Q.21 The wave length of first member of Balmer series of a hydrogen atom is nearly (The value of Rydberg constant is $1.08 \times 10^7 m^{-1}$)

A. 4400A0   **B.** 5500 A⁰   **C.** 6600 A⁰   **D.** 7700 A⁰

Q.22 The ratio between radii of He^+ ion and H atom is

A. 1:2   **B.** 1:1   **C.** 3:2   **D.** 2:1

Q.23 In an atom, an electron is moving with a speed of 600 m/s with an accuracy of 0.005 %. Certainty with which the position of the electron can be located is

(h = 6.6 × 10^{-34} kg m^2 s^{-1}, mass of electron, em = 9.1 × 10^{-31} kg)

A. 5.10 x 10^{-3} m   **B.** 1.92 x 10^{-3} m
C. 3.84 x 10^{-3} m   **D.** 1.52 x 10^{-4} m

Q.24 Calculate energy of one mole of photons of radiation whose frequency as 5 × 10^{14}Hz.

A. 199.51 kJ mol^{-1} **B.** 299.31 kJ mol^{-1}
C. 399.31 kJ mol^{-1} **D.** 499.31 kJ mol^{-1}

Q.25 The possibility of finding an electron in an orbital was conceived by

A. Rutherford   **B.** Bohr
C. Heisenberg   **D.** Schrodinger

Q.26 The correct order regarding the electronegativity of hybrid orbitals of carbon is?

A. sp < sp^2 < sp^3 **B.** sp < sp^2 > sp^3
C. sp > sp^2 > sp^3 **D.** sp > sp^2 < sp^3

Q.27 Scientific names are writt

A. Capitalised but not printed distinctively, italicised, or underlined
B. Italicised or underlined
C. Capitalised and italicised or underlined
D. Italicised or underlined with the first word capitalised

Q.28 Which of the following is set of rules and recommendations used for animal classification?

A. ICZN   **B.** ICBN   **C.** ICVN   **D.** ICNCP

Q.29 Which of these is NOT the name of a phylum?

A. Annelida   **B.** Echinodermata
C. Tetrapoda   **D.** Arthropoda

Q.30 A scientific name contains information about the

A. Family and Species   **B.** Genus and Species
C. Phylum and Order   **D.** Class and Family

Q.31 Linnaeus is credited with introducing

A. The concept of inheritance
B. The theory of heredity
C. Binomial nomenclature
D. Theory of evolution

Q.32 Which class do birds belong to?

A. Aves   **B.** Amphibia
C. Reptilia   **D.** Felis

Q.33 Genera having similar characters are grouped together in this taxon -

A. Species   **B.** Order   **C.** Phyla   **D.** Family

Q.34 A group of organisms at any particular level in a classification system is called a ____.

A. Species   **B.** Genus   **C.** Taxon   **D.** Phylum

Q.35 In S = a + bt + ct^2 . S is measured in metres and t in seconds. The unit of c is

A. No dimensions   **B.** m
C. ms^{-1} **D.** ms^{-2}

Q.36 If the unit of length and force be increased four times, then the unit of energy is

A. Increased 4 times   **B.** Increased 8 times
C. Increased 16 times   **D.** Decreased 16 times

Q.37 The velocity of a particle depends upon as v = a + bt + ct^2 ; if the velocity is in m/sec, the unit of a will be

A. m/sec   **B.** m/sec^2 **C.** m^2/sec   **D.** m/sec^3

Q.38 Young's modulus of a material has the same units as

A. Pressure   **B.** Strain
C. Compressibility   **D.** Force

Q.39 The equation (P+a/v^2) (v-b) = constant. If P and V are the pressure and volume, the C.G.S units of a is

A. Dyne x cm^5 **B.** Dyne x cm^4
C. Dyne / cm^3 **D.** Dyne / cm^2

Q.40 The pressure on a square plate is measured by measuring the force on the plate and the length of the sides of the plate. If the maximum error in the measurement of force and length are respectively 4% and 2%, The maximum error in the measurement of pressure is

A. 1%   **B.** 2%   **C.** 6%   **D.** 8%

General Awareness

Q.41 Vindhyashakti was founder of which of the following dynasties in ancient India?

A. Vakataka
B. Kakatiya
C. Kalachuri
D. Chalukyas of Badami

Q.42 Which of the following ancient Indian sages did not make substantial contribution to the YOGĀCĀRA (Yogachara) philosophical tradition?

A. Vasubandhu   **B.** Dinnaga
C. Dharmakirti   **D.** Nagarjuna

Q.43 Which of the following rulers were closely associated with Yuehzhi nomadic people?

A. Shaka   **B.** Kushana
C. Pahalva   **D.** None of them

Q.44 Which of the following is not a correct statement about Buddhist Canonical literature?

A. Abhidhamma Pitaka was compiled in third Buddhist Council
B. Digha Nikaya is a part of the Sutta Pitaka
C. Vinaya Pitaka primarily deals with monastic rules for monks and nuns
D. Sutta Pitaka deals with philosophy and psychology and lays down methods for training the mind.

Q.45 Which of the following is a correct statement about Indus Valley Civilization?

A. Both Harappa and Mohejodero are is located on the banks of Indus River

B. Both Chanhudaro and Kalibangan were located within the boundaries of present day Rajasthan.

C. Both Surkotada and Dholavira are located in Katch of Gujarat

D. Lothal site was located on bank of Narmada river

Q.46 In stone age, the Microliths were most commonly found in which of the following ages?

A. Paleolithic

B. Mesolithic

C. Neolithic

D. Chalcolithic

Q.47 Which of the following terms is not associated with a tool tradition of ancient India / World?

A. Mousterian

B. Acheulean

C. Oldowan

D. Grotian

Q.48 The Jorwe culture of ancient India has been named after site of the same name in which of the following states?

A. Rajasthan

B. Gujarat

C. Karnataka

D. Maharashtra

Q.49 Which of the following was most probably the first metal to be used in India?

A. Iron   **B.** Copper   **C.** Gold   **D.** Silver

Q.50 Which of the following is not an event in ancient Indian history in BC era?

A. Foundation of the Indo-Greek empire

B. Beginning of Vikram samvat Era

C. Fourth Buddhist Council

D. Hathigumpha inscription by Kharvela

// Smart Answer Sheet //

Correct — Indicates percentage of students who answered questions correctly.

Skipped — Indicates percentage of students who skipped questions.

Q.	Ans.	Correct / Skipped
1	B	86.49 % / 12.12 %
2	B	87.12 % / 12.49 %
3	B	85.88 % / 13.19 %
4	C	84.12 % / 13.91 %
5	B	85.77 % / 11.22 %
6	B	77.09 % / 18.06 %
7	C	77.57 % / 18.23 %
8	C	78.54 % / 14.57 %
9	D	77.87 % / 15.64 %
10	A	84.47 % / 10.68 %

Q.	Ans.	Correct / Skipped
11	A	77.28 % / 20.51 %
12	B	81.24 % / 13.49 %
13	B	88.4 % / 11.18 %
14	C	84.28 % / 12.58 %
15	A	83.56 % / 15.31 %
16	B	80.2 % / 14.87 %
17	C	87.53 % / 11.56 %
18	B	89.58 % / 10.39 %
19	D	88.18 % / 11.55 %
20	C	89.3 % / 10.17 %

Q.	Ans.	Correct / Skipped
21	C	81.7 % / 17.49 %
22	B	87.4 % / 10.78 %
23	B	79.26 % / 17.73 %
24	A	84.92 % / 13.48 %
25	D	84.7 % / 11.49 %
26	C	84.07 % / 15.27 %
27	D	86.2 % / 10.44 %
28	A	88.64 % / 10.08 %
29	C	89.6 % / 10.08 %
30	B	87.89 % / 10.25 %

Q.	Ans.	Correct / Skipped
31	C	77.97 % / 19.61 %
32	A	89.67 % / 10.01 %
33	D	82.48 % / 10.79 %
34	C	88.69 % / 10.45 %
35	D	88.48 % / 10.11 %
36	C	81.59 % / 12.62 %
37	A	76.65 % / 16.84 %
38	A	83.02 % / 15.36 %
39	B	81.88 % / 14.86 %
40	D	84.05 % / 11.77 %

Q.	Ans.	Correct / Skipped
41	A	87.05 % / 10.9 %
42	D	76.53 % / 11.35 %
43	B	84.24 % / 15.6 %
44	D	85.97 % / 11.57 %
45	C	76.85 % / 18.36 %
46	B	81.7 % / 16.69 %
47	D	80.33 % / 16.42 %
48	D	76.89 % / 18.72 %
49	B	76.8 % / 11.94 %
50	C	83.78 % / 12.45 %

Performance Analysis

Avg. Score (%)	51.33%
Toppers Score (%)	68.0%
Your Score	

//Hints and Solutions//

1. Let the roots be α and $n\alpha$

Sum of roots, $a + n\alpha = -\dfrac{b}{a} \Rightarrow \alpha = -\dfrac{b}{a(n+1)}$

and product, $\alpha.n.\ \alpha = \dfrac{c}{a} \Rightarrow \alpha^2 = \dfrac{c}{na}$

From (i) and (ii). we get

$\Rightarrow \left[-\dfrac{b}{a(n+1)}\right]^2 = \dfrac{c}{na} \Rightarrow \dfrac{b^2}{a^2(n+1)^2} = \dfrac{c}{na}$

$\Rightarrow nb^2 = ac(n+1)^2$

Note: Students should remember this question as a fact.

2. Let the equation (in written form) be $x^2 + 17x + q = 0$.

Roots are -2, -15.

So q = 30,

And correct equation is $x^2 + 13x + 30 = 0$.

Hence roots are -3, -10.

3. Given that, α + β = 0

α + β + γ = -p ⇒ γ = -p

Substituting γ = -p in the given equation

$\Rightarrow -p^3+p^3-pq+r=0 \Rightarrow pq = r$

4. If α, β, y are the roots of the equation
$\alpha + \beta + \gamma = 0, \alpha\beta + \beta\gamma + \gamma\alpha = 4, \alpha\beta\gamma = -1$
therefore $(\alpha + \beta)^{-1} + (\beta + \gamma)^{-1} + (\gamma + \alpha)^{-1}$

$= \dfrac{1}{-\gamma} + \dfrac{1}{-\alpha} + \dfrac{1}{-\beta}$

$= -\left(\dfrac{\alpha\beta+\beta\gamma+\gamma\alpha}{\alpha\beta\gamma}\right)$

$= -\left(\dfrac{4}{-1}\right) = 4$

5. Given equation is $x^3 - 3x + 2 = 0$
$\Rightarrow x^2(x-1) + x(x-1) - 2(x-1) = 0$
$\Rightarrow (x-1)(x^2+x-2) = 0 \Rightarrow (x-1)(x-1)(x+2) = 0$

Hence roots are 1,1,-2

6. n(A) = 40% of 10,000 = 4,000

n(B) = 20% of 10,000 = 2,000

n(C) = 10% of 10,000 = 1,000

n(A ∩ B) = 5% of 10,000 = 500

n(B ∩ C) = 3% of 10,000 = 300

n(C ∩ A) = 4% of 10,000 = 400

n(A ∩ B ∩ C) = 2% of 10,000 = 200

We want to find the number of families which buy only A = n(A) - [n(A ∩ B) + n(A ∩ C) - n(A ∩ B ∩ C)]

=4000 - [500 + 400 - 200] = 4000 - 700 = 3300

7. n(A^c ∩ B^c) = n(U) - n(A ∪ B)

= n(U) - [n(A) + n(B) - n(A ∩ B)]

= 700 - [200 + 300 - 100] = 300.

8. Since y = 1/x, y = -x meet when -x = 1/x ⇒ x^2 = -1,

which does not give any real value of x.

Hence, A ∩ B = ∅.

9.
$$A \cap (A \cap B)^c = A \cap (A^c \cup B^c)$$
$$= (A \cap (A^c)) \cup (A \cap (B^c))$$
$$= \varnothing \cup (A \cap (B^c)) = A \cap (B^c)$$

10. Let the no. of people who do not play NFS be $n(N') = 50$ (Given) Similarly no of people who do not play Dota be $n(D') = 40$ (Given) And the no. of people who do not play any game $n(N' \cap D') = 10$ (Given) We have to find the no. of people who do not play both the games $= n(N \cap D)$
We know from the Demorgan's law
$(A \cap B)' = A' \cup B'$
So. $n(N \cap D)' = n(N') \cup n(D')$
$n(N') \cup n(D') = n(N') + n(D') - n(N' \cap D')$
$n(N') \cup n(D') = 50 + 40 - 10$
$$= 80$$

11. A ∩ B ⊆ A. Hence A ∪ (A ∩ B) = A.

12. since $4^n - 3n - 1 = (3+1)^n - 3n - 1$
$= 3^n +{}^n C_1 3^{n-1} +{}^n C_2 3^{n-2} + \ldots\ldots +{}^n C_{n-1} 3 +{}^n C_n - 3n - 1$
$={}^n C_2 3^2 +{}^n C_3 \cdot 3^3 + \ldots +{}^n C_n 3^n,$
$({}^n C_0 ={}^n C_n, {}^n C_{n-1} ={}^n C_1 \ldots\ldots \text{soon.})$
$= 9[{}^n C_2 +{}^n C_3 (3) + \cdots \ldots +{}^n C_4 3^{n-1}]$
$\therefore 4^n - 3n - 1$ is a multiple of 9 for $n \geq 2$ For $n = 1, 4^n - 3n - 1 = 4 - 3 - 1 = 0$ is a multiple of 9 for all
$n \epsilon N$ For $n = 2, 4^n - 3n - 1 = 16 - 6 - 1 = 9$
$\therefore 4^n - 3n - 1$
$\therefore X$ contains elements, which are multiples of 9, and clearly Y contains all
multiples of 9 $\therefore X \subset Y$ i.e. $, X \cup Y = Y$

13. A = {x: x ∈ R, -1 < x < 1}

B = {x: x ∈ R:x-1 ≤ -1 or x-1 ≥ 1}

= {x : x ∈ R:x ≤ 0 or x ≥ 2}

∴ A ∪ B = R - D, where D = {x : x ∈ R, 1 ≤ x < 2}.

14. Number of subsets of A = $^nC_0 + {}^nC_1$ + ...+ $^nC_n = 2^n$

15. $x^2 = 16 \Rightarrow x = \pm 4$

2x = 6 ⇒x=3

There is no value of x which satisfies both the above equations.

Thus, A = ∅.

16. Since $x^2 + 1 = 0$, gives $x^2 = -1$

⇒ x = ± i

∴ x is not real but x has to be is real (given)

∴ No real value of x is possible in this case.

17. n(C) = 20, n(B) = 50, n(C ∩ B) = 10

Now n(C ∪ B) = n(C) + n(B) - n(C ∩ B)

= 20 + 50 - 10 = 60.

18. Number of proper subsets of the set {1, 2, 3} = 2^3 - 1 = 7.

19. Since, intelligence is not defined for students in a class i.e., Not a well defined collection.

20. Given line is $(3x + 14y + 7) + k(5x + 7y + 6) = 0$

$\Rightarrow (3 + 5k)x + (14 + 7k)y + (7 + 6k) = 0$

If it is parallel to y - axis, then coefficient of $y = 0$

$\Rightarrow 14 + 7k = 0$

$\Rightarrow k = -2$

21. $n_1 = 2 \quad n_2 = 3$

$\frac{1}{\lambda} = R\left[\frac{1}{4} - \frac{1}{9}\right]$

$\lambda = \frac{36}{5R} = \frac{36}{5\times1.08\times10^7}m$

$= \frac{36}{5\times1.08} \times 10^{-7}m$

$\approx 6600A^0$

22. Value of Z for hydrogen $= 1$ Value of Z for helium $= 2$

Value of n for both is $= 1 \; r_H = \frac{0.5\times1^2}{1} r_{He^+} = \frac{0.52\times1^2}{1}$

$\frac{r_H}{r_{He^+}} = 1:1$ or $r_{He^+}:r_H = 1:1$

23. According to Heisenberg uncertainty principle.

$\Delta x.\, m\Delta v = \frac{h}{4\pi}, \Delta x = \frac{h}{4\pi m\Delta v}$

Here $\Delta v = \frac{600\times0.005}{100} = 0.03$

So, $\Delta x = \frac{6.6\times10^{-34}}{4\times3.14\times9.1\times10^{-31}\times0.03}$

$= 1.92 \times 10^{-3}$ meter

24. One thing we have to keep in mind here. 1 mole $= 6.022 \times 10^{23}$

Now the energy of a single photon $E = h\nu = 6.626 \times 10^{-34}Js \times 5 \times 10^{14}s^{-1}$

$= (3.313 \times 10^{-19}J)$

Energy of one mole of photons

$= (3.313 \times 10^{-19}J/6.022 \times 10^{23}mol^{-1})$

$= 199.51kJmol$

25. Solution the Austrian physicist Erwin **Schrödinger** put forward an equation that predicts both the allowed energies of a system as well as the **probability** of finding a particle in a given region of space.

26. With the increase in % of s-character in hybrid orbitals the electronegativity of the hybrid orbitals increases.

sp - 50% s character,

sp² - 33.3 % s character

sp³ - 25% s character.

27. There are some important rules that must be followed to keep all binomial names standardised:

1. The first letter of the name of the genus should always be capitalised.

2. Species name should not be capitalised.

3. When written, the genus and species names should always be underlined separately; when printed it should be italicised. e.g., Pseudomonas syringae

4. The name or abbreviated name of the scientist describing the species first, should be written after the binomial name. The name is not italicised. e.g., Pseudomonas syringae van Hall

5. The year in which the organism was described should be written after the name of the author or scientist. e.g., Pseudomonas syringae van Hall 1902

28. The International Code of Zoological Nomenclature (ICZN) is the set of rules and recommendations used in animal classification. The expansions of the remaining options are as follows:

ICBN - International Code of Botanical Nomenclature

ICVN - International Code of Viral Nomenclature

ICNCP - International Code of Nomenclature for Cultivated Plants

29. Annelida, Arthropoda and Echinodermata are invertebrate phyla in the Kingdom Animalia. Tetrapoda is a superclass of jawed vertebrates (which come under phylum Chordata).

30. Binomial nomenclature is a formal system of naming species of living things by giving each a name composed of two parts, both of which use Latin grammatical forms, although they can be based on words from other languages. Such a name is called a binomial name, a binomen or a scientific name; more informally it is also called a Latin name. The first part of the name identifies the genus to which the species belongs; the second part identifies the respective species within the genus. For example, humans belong to the genus Homo and within this genus, to the species sapiens. The scientific name is thus, Homo sapiens.

31. Linnaeus is famous for introducing binomial nomenclature, which is the scientific system of naming living organisms.

32. Amphibia, Reptilia, Aves and Mammalia are all classes under superclass Tetrapoda, which further, is classified under subphylum Vertebrata. Birds are grouped under the class Aves. Examples for Amphibia, Reptilia and Mammalia are frog, snake, and bear respectively. Felis is a genus of cats.

33. A group of genera having similar characters comprise a family. In biological classification, family is one of the eight major/obligate taxonomic ranks; it is classified between order and genus. A family may be divided into subfamilies, which are intermediate ranks above the rank of genus. In vernacular usage, a family may be named after one of its common members. e.g., Blattidae - The family of common household cockroaches (Blatta is a commonly seen genus of cockroach).

34. A group of organisms at any particular level in a classification system is called as Taxon. The taxon is the fundamental unit of taxonomic classification. The term taxon was coined by Adolf Meyer in 1926 for animals and H.J Lam used this term for plants in 1948.

Taxa are arranged in a hierarchy from kingdom to subspecies, a given taxon ordinarily including several taxa of lower rank. Species, genus and phylum are all specific examples of taxons that have been assigned

35. ct^2 must have dimensions of $L \Rightarrow c$ must have dimensions of L/T^2 i.e.,LT^{-2}

36. Energy = force × distance, so if both are increased by 4 times then energy will increase by 16 times.

37. Quantities of similar dimensions can be added or subtracted so unit of a will be same as that of velocity.

38. Strain has no units due to simply being the ratio between the extension and original length of a material, so Young's Modulus is measured by the same units as stress, i.e. newtons per square metre (Nm^{-2}) or Pascals (Pa).

39. Units of 'a' and' PV^2 are same from the equation.

Units of P =Dyne/cm^2.

Units of $V^2 = cm^{6.}$

Units of a = Units of PV^2 = Dyne ×cm^4

40. $P = \dfrac{P}{A} = \dfrac{F}{l^2}$ So maximum error in pressure (P)

$$\left(\dfrac{\Delta P}{P} \times 100\right)_{max} = \dfrac{\Delta P}{P} \times 100 + 2\dfrac{\Delta l}{1} \times 100$$
$$= 4\% + 2 \times 2\% = 8\%$$

41. Vindhyashakti (c. 250 – c. 270 CE) was the founder of the Vakataka dynasty. His name is derived from the name of the goddess Vindhya.

42. YOGĀCĀRA is a Buddhist philosophical tradition that emphasized idealism. The earliest known text of the school is the Mahāyānasūtrālam kāra attributed to Asanga (c. fifth century CE). Others who contributed to the tradition included Vasubandhu, Dinnāga and Dharmakīrti.

43. The term Yuehzhi refers to nomadic people originally living in northwest China who moved to Central Asia in circa second century BC. The Kushana were a branch of these people, who reached the subcontinent in circa first century BCE.

44. [Sutta Pitaka deals with philosophy and psychology and lays down methods for training the mind.]

Notes: Abhidhamma Pitaka is the third and latest of the Pali canonical texts recognized in the early Buddhist Theravāda tradition. Its compilation is dated to the third Buddhist Council, held during the reign of the Mauryan emperor Asoka, that is, c. third century BCE. The text focuses on philosophy and psychology and lays down methods for training the mind.

45. Mohenjodero was located on banks of river Indus. Harappa on Ravi. Chanhudaro is in Pakistan now. Lothal was on mouth of Gulf of Cambay.

46. Microliths were most commonly found in Mesolithic era.

47. The Mousterian refers to a techno-complex (archaeological industry) of flint lithic tools associated primarily with Neanderthals. Acheulean refers to the ancient industry of stone tool manufacture characterized by distinctive oval and pear-shaped "hand-axes" associated with Homo erectus and related species. Oldowan is the oldest-known stone tool industry and dates back as far as 2.5 million years ago. The term Grotian is related to international law and does not related to ancient stone tool industries.

48. Jorwe Ware Culture is named after site of the same name in Maharashtra. This culture dates between 1600 to 1000 BC. The key features of this culture include red pottery, generally with matt surface bearing paintings in black.

49. The earliest historic evidences of use of metal are of Chalcolithic Age or Stone-Copper Age, which covered the period from 1800 to 800 BC. This period was marked by the use of copper (the first metal to be used in India) as well as stone.

50. Foundation of the Indo-Greek empire by Demetrius in 182 BC. Beginning of Vikram samvat Era in 58BC by Vikramaditya of Ujjain. Fourth Buddhist Council was held in Kundalvana, Kashmir in 72 AD under the patronage of Kushan king Kanishka. The King Kharavela of Kalinga left Hathigumpha inscription in around 50BC. So correct answer would be C.

Mathematics

Q.1 This usual rowing rate, Mohit can travel 12 miles downstream in a certain river in 6 hours less than it takes him to travel the same distance upstream. But if he could double his usual rowing rate for his 24 miles round trip, the downstream 12 miles would then take only one hour less than the upstream 12 miles. What is the speed of the current in miles per hour?

A. 2.5m/hr   **B.** 4 m/hr   **C.** 8/3 m/hr   **D.** 5/3m/hr

Q.2 There is road besides a river. Two friends started from a place P, moved to a shopping mall situated at another place Q and then returned to P again. One of them moves on a cycle at a speed of 12 km/hr, while the other sails on a boat at a speed of 10 km/hr. If the river flows at the speed of 4 km/hr, which of the two friends will return to place P?

A. Both   **B.** Boater
C. Cyclist   **D.** None of these

Q.3 $17 \times 756 \div \sqrt{2916} = ? + 540$

A. 312   **B.** -223   **C.** -302   **D.** -217

Q.4 $\sqrt{[16+(1/21)]} \div \sqrt{[16+(21/84)]} \times 702/27 = ?$

A. 26   **B.** 32   **C.** 43   **D.** 17

Q.5 Deepika buys two bangle set for a total cost of Rs. 600. By selling one bangle set for 4/5 of its cost and the other for 5/4 of its cost, She makes a profit of Rs. 96 on the whole transaction. The cost of the lower priced bangle set is?

A. Rs. 360   **B.** Rs. 320   **C.** Rs. 150   **D.** Rs. 120

Q.6 A milkman buys some milk. If he sells it at rupees 10 a litre, he losses 400 rupees but when he sells it at 12 a litre, he gains 800 rupees. How much milk did he purchase?

A. 400 litre   **B.** 550 litre   **C.** 600 litre   **D.** 650 litre

Q.7 A and B together can do a piece of work in 24 days, which B and C together can do it in 32 days. After A has been working at it for 10 days and B for 14 days, C finishes it in 26 days. In how many days C alone will do the work?

A. 32   **B.** 36   **C.** 44   **D.** 48

Q.8 50 men could complete a work in 200 days. They worked together for 150 days, after that due to bad weather the work is stopped for 25 days. How many more workers should be employed so as to complete the work in time?

A. 25   **B.** 35   **C.** 50   **D.** 60

Q.9 Ajay got married 6 years ago. His present age is 5/4 times his age at the time of his marriage. Ajay's brother was 5 years younger to him at the time of his marriage. What is the present age of Ajay's brother?

A. 22 years   **B.** 11 years   **C.** 25 years   **D.** 19 years

Q.10 Rahul is as much younger than Shyam as he is older than Suresh. If the sum of the ages of Shyam and Suresh is 60 years, what is definitely the difference between Shyam and Rahul's age?

A. 12 years
B. 23 years
C. 19 years
D. Can not be determined

Q.11 A sum of money borrowed at 5% compound interest is to paid in two annual installments of Rs 882 each. What is the sum borrowed?

A. Rs 1650   **B.** Rs 2340   **C.** Rs 2630   **D.** Rs 1640

Q.12 Rs 3903 is to be divided in a way that A's share at the end of 7 years is equal to the B's share at the end of 9 years. If the rate of interest is 4% compounded annually, find A's share.

A. Rs 2475   **B.** Rs 1875   **C.** Rs 2175   **D.** Rs 1935

Q.13 30 litre of solution contains alcohol and water in the ratio 2:3. How much alcohol must be added to the solution to make a solution containing 60% of alcohol?

A. 10   **B.** 12   **C.** 14   **D.** 15

Q.14 2000 sweets need to be distributed equally among the school students in such a way that each student gets sweet equal to 20% of total students. Then the number of sweets, each student gets.

A. 50   **B.** 100   **C.** 120   **D.** 150

Q.15 Find the probability that in a leap year, the numbers of Mondays are 53?

A. 1/7   **B.** 2/7   **C.** 3/7   **D.** 4/7

Q.16 A urn contains 4 red balls, 5 green balls and 6 white balls, if one ball is drawn at random, find the probability that it is neither red nor white.

A. 1/3   **B.** 1/4   **C.** 1/5   **D.** 2/3

Q.17 Two pipes can separately fill the tank in 15hrs and 30hrs respectively. Both the pipe are opened and when the tank is 1/3 full a leak is developed due to which 1/3 water supplied by the pipe leaks out. What is the total time to fill the tank?

A. 20/3 hr   **B.** 35/3 hr   **C.** 40/3 hr   **D.** 50/3 hr

Q.18 Three pipes A, B and C is attached to a cistern. A can fill it in 20 minutes and B can fill it in 30 minutes. C is a waste pipe. After opening both the pipes A and B, Riya leaves the cistern to fill and returns when the cistern is supposed to be filled. But she found that waste pipe C had been left open, she closes it and now the cistern takes 5 minutes more to fill. In how much time the pipe C can empty the full cistern?

A. 26.8 minutes   **B.** 25.8 minutes
C. 27.8 minutes   **D.** 28.8 minutes

Q.19 A town with a population of 1000 has provision for 30days, after 10 days 600 more men added, how long will the food last at the same rate ?

A. 12 days
C. 12 ½ days
B. 14 ½ days
D. 15 days

Q.20 A man spends Rs.2480 to buy lunch box Rs.120 each and bottles at Rs.80 each,What will be the ratio of maximum number of bottles to lunch box are bought ?

A. 13:12   **B.** 11:13   **C.** 9:12   **D.** 7:10

Science

Q.21 The temperature of a body falls from 40°C to 36°C in 5 minutes when placed in a surrounding of constant temperature 16°C . Find the time taken for the temperature of the body to become 32°C.

A. 8.1 min   **B.** 6.1 min   **C.** 5.3 min   **D.** 5.1 min

Q.22 The graph shown in the adjacent diagram, represents the variation of temperature (T) of two bodies, x and y having same surface area, with time (t) due to the emission of radiation. Find the correct relation between the emissivity (e) and absorptivity (a) power of the two bodies.

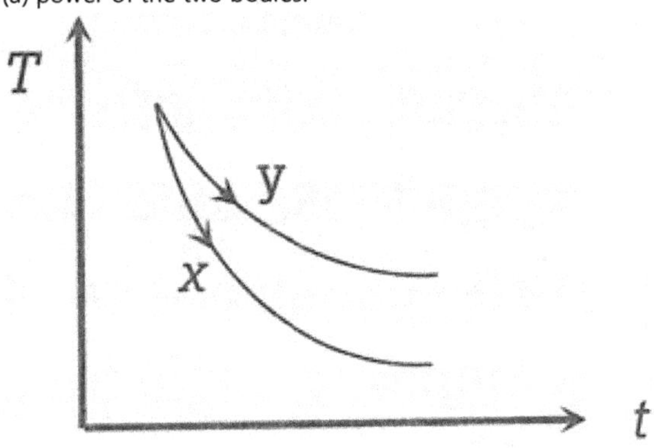

A. ex>ey,ax>ay
B. ex>ey,ay>ax
C. ey>ex,ay>ax
D. ey>ex,ax>ay

Q.23 Variation of radiant energy emitted by sun, filament of tungsten lamp and welding arc as a function of its wavelength is shown in figure. Which of the following option is the correct match?

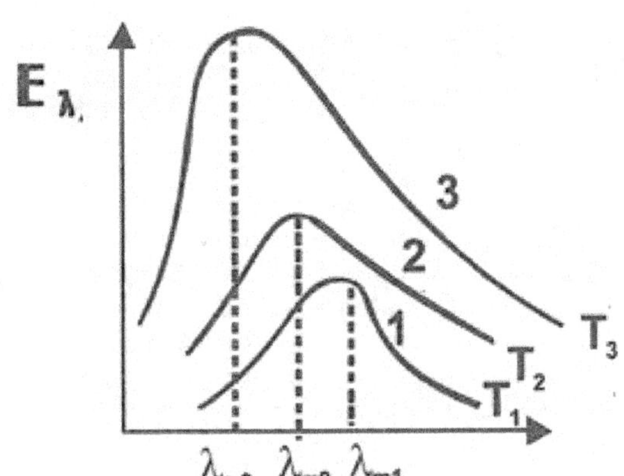

A. Sun - T_3, tungsten filament - T_1, welding are - T_2
B. Sun - T_2, tungsten filament - T_1, welding are - T_3
C. Sun - T_3, tungsten filament - T_2, welding are - T_1
D. Sun - T_1, tungsten filament - T_2, welding are - T_3

Q.24 The Bat Life: What can be said with 100% confidence about the temperatures at point P_1 and P_2?

A. $TP_1 = TP_2$
B. $TP_1 > TP_2$
C. $TP_1 < TP_2$
D. $TP_1 \neq TP_2$.

Q.25 The Bat Life: Batman is undercover, and to prevent anyone from recognizing his voice (or Bruce Wayne's) he inhales a very dilute Helium gas (search YouTube for "voice after helium" to see the effects). The helium is stored ina cylindrical chamber as shown.

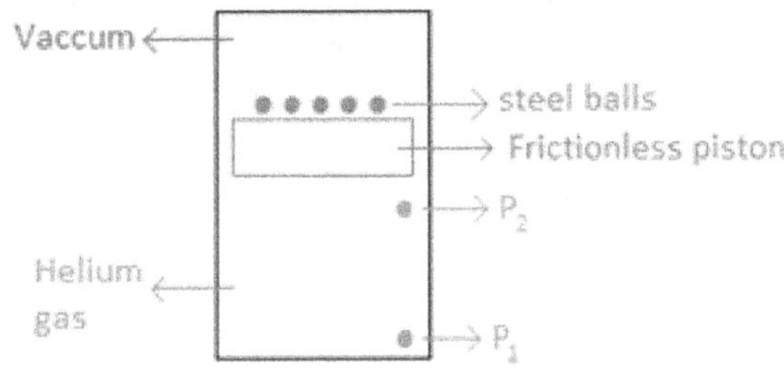

During a fight one of the steel balls gets dislodged. What will happen to the piston?

A. It will move down
B. It will move up
C. It will remain in the same place
D. Not enough information, only Batman will know

Q.26 Which amongst the following graphs represents the V-T graph shown in the figure?

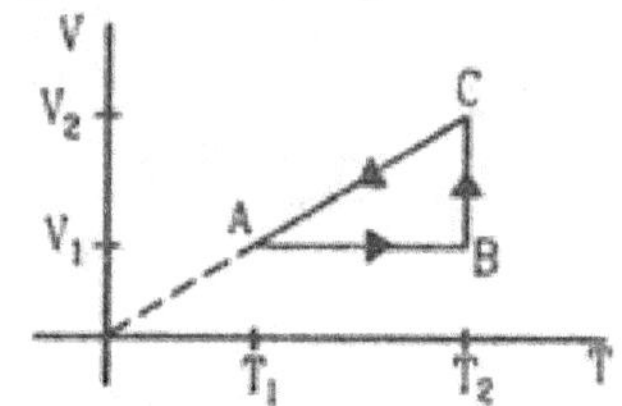

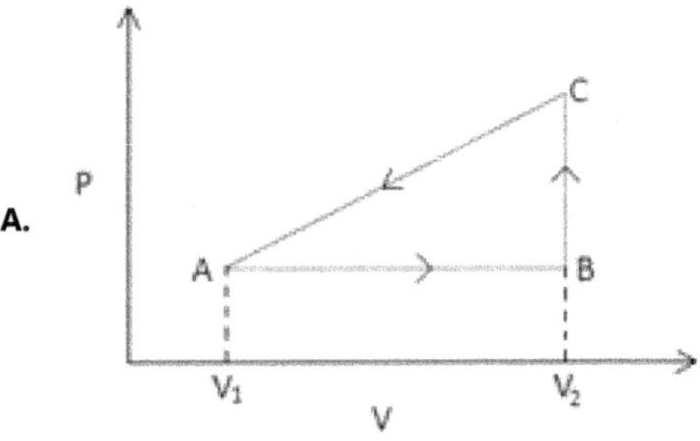

A.

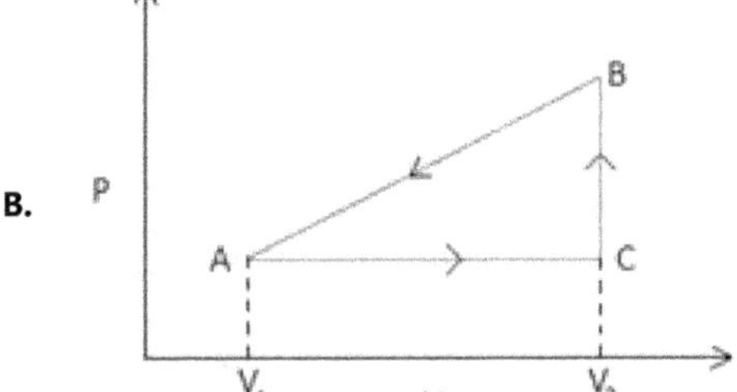

B.

C.

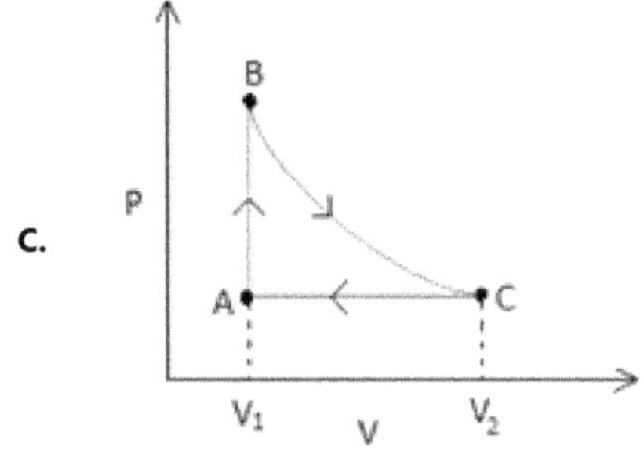

D.

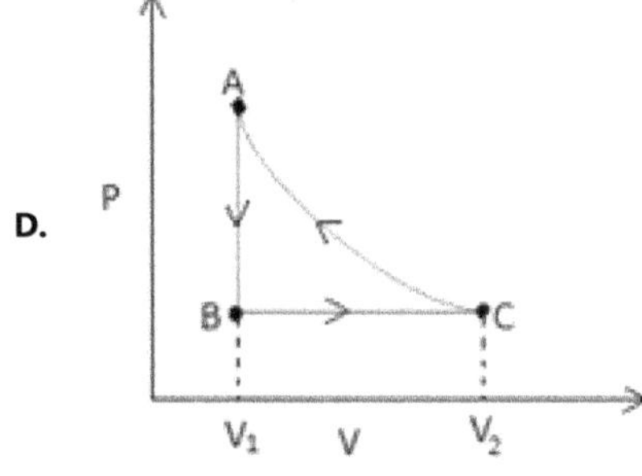

Q.27 Which among the following is a false statement?

A. For a first order reaction $t_{\frac{1}{2}} = \frac{0.693}{k}$

B. Rate of zero order reaction is independent of initial concentration of reactant

C. Half-life of a third order reaction is inversely proportional to the square of initial concentration of the reactant

D. Molecularity of a reaction may be zero or fraction

Q.28 Certain bimolecular reactions which follow first order kinetics are called

A. Bimolecular reactions

B. Unimolecular reactions

C. First order reaction

D. Pseudo unimolecular reactions

Q.29 The conversion of A to B follows second order kinetics. Doubling the concentration of A increases the rate of formation of B by a factor of

A. 2   **B.** 4   **C.** 1/2   **D.** 1/4

Q.30 The mass average molecular weight and number average molecular weight of a polymer are respectively 40000 and 30000. The poly-dispersity index of the polymer will be

A. < 1   **B.** > 1   **C.** 1   **D.** 0

Q.31 Buna-S rubber is which of the following of 1-3-butadiene and styrene

A. Polymers

B. Copolymer

C. Step growth polymer

D. Condensation polymer

Q.32 Which one of the following polymers will not catch fire even at a high temperature of 300°C?

A. $(-CF_2 - CF_2 -)_m$ **B.** $(-CH_2 - CH_2 -)_n$

C. $(-CF_3 - CF_2 -)_m$ **D.** None of the above

Q.33 What is the correct IUPAC name of the compound?
$CH_2=CH-CH_2-C\equiv CH$?

A. 1,4-Pentenyne   **B.** Pent-1-en-4-yne

C. Pent-1-yn-4-ene   **D.** 1, 4-Pentynene

Q.34 The IUPAC name of:-

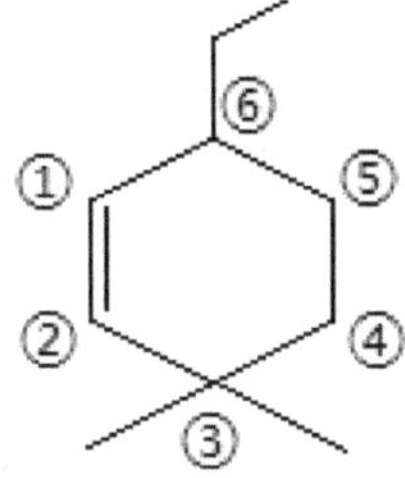

A. 6-Ethyl-3,3-dimethylcyclohex-1-ene

B. 3-Ethyl-6,6-dimethylcyclohex-1-ene

C. Both a and b are accepted

D. Neither a nor b

Q.35 What is the IUPAC name of the following compound?

$$CH_3 - CH_2 - \underset{\underset{CH_3}{|}}{C} = CH - CH_2 - \underset{\overset{|}{CH_3}}{CH} - CH_2 - CH_3$$

A. 3,6-Dimethyl-3-octene

B. 3,6-Dimethyl-5-octene

C. 2-Ethyl-5-methyl-2-heptene

D. None of the above

Q.36 Given standard electrode potentials

$Fe^{++}+2e^-\rightarrow Fe$; $E°=-0.440$ V

$Fe^{+++}+3e^-\rightarrow Fe$; $E°=-0.036$ V

The standard electrode potential ($E°$) for $Fe^{+++}+e^-\rightarrow Fe^{++}$ is

A. - 0.476 V   **B.** - 0.404 V

C. + 0.404 V   **D.** + 0.772 V

Q.37 Calculate standard free energy change for the reaction $\frac{1}{2}Cu(s) + \frac{1}{2}Cl_2(g) \rightleftharpoons \frac{1}{2}Cu^{2+} + Cl$ taking place at in a cell whose standard e.m.f. is 1.02 volts

A. - 98430 J   **B.** 98430 J

C. 96500 J   **D.** - 49215 J

Q.38 $E°$ for the cell is Zn |Zn^{2+} (aq)||Cu^{2+} (aq)| Cu at 25°C, the equilibrium constant for the
reaction $Zn+Cu^{2+}(aq)\rightleftharpoons Cu+Zn^{2+}$ (aq) is of the order of

A. 10^{-37} **B.** 10^{-28} **C.** 10^{+18} **D.** 10^{+17}

Q.39 In both DNA and RNA, heterocyclic base and phosphate ester linkages are at

A. C'_5 and C'_2 respectively of the sugar molecule

B. C'_2 and C'_5 respectively of the sugar molecule

C. C'_1 and C'_5 respectively of the sugar molecule

D. C'_5 and C'_1 respectively of the sugar molecule

Q.40 Molisch's test is done for the detection of?

A. Alkyl halide   **B.** Carbohydrate

C. Alkaloid   **D.** Fat

General Awareness

Q.41 Among the SAARC countries the most densely populated country is?

A. Bangladesh 　　　　**B.** India

C. Pakistan 　　　　**D.** Maldives

Q.42 The Nuclear Non-Proliferation Treaty came into force in

A. 1967 　　**B.** 1970 　　**C.** 1971 　　**D.** 1974

Q.43 Which of the following is a World Bank group of five institution:

A. IMF 　　**B.** IDA 　　**C.** ILO 　　**D.** ITU

Q.44 When did UN General Assembly established UN industrial Development Organization :

A. 1986 　　**B.** 1966 　　**C.** 1967 　　**D.** 1965

Q.45 How many countries are represented in Unrepresented Nations are peoples Organisation:

A. 54 　　**B.** 53 　　**C.** 58 　　**D.** 59

Q.46 SAARC was founded in:

A. New Delhi 　　　　**B.** Dhaka

C. Geneva 　　　　**D.** Thimpu

Q.47 The headquarters of Food and Agriculture Organization is in:

A. Paris 　　　　**B.** Rome

C. Madrid 　　　　**D.** Washington

Q.48 In India FERA has been replaced by?

A. FEMA 　　**B.** FETA 　　**C.** FENA 　　**D.** FELA

Q.49 The first Defence Minister of India was

A. Baldev Singh

B. Gopalaswami Aiyangar

C. Gopalaswami Aiyangar

D. Sardar Patel

Q.50 Who was the Sikh Guru to be slaughtered by Aurangzeb?

A. Ramdas 　　　　**B.** Teg Bahadur

C. Arjundev 　　　　**D.** Gobind Singh

// Smart Answer Sheet //

Correct — Indicates percentage of students who answered questions correctly.

Skipped — Indicates percentage of students who skipped questions.

Q.	Ans.	Correct / Skipped
1	C	78.89 % / 14.91 %
2	C	89.8 % / 10.13 %
3	C	82.31 % / 14.33 %
4	A	80.16 % / 15.78 %
5	D	86.28 % / 12.26 %
6	C	79.22 % / 20.19 %
7	D	85.4 % / 11.98 %
8	C	82.67 % / 12.38 %
9	C	84.32 % / 10.02 %
10	D	89.99 % / 10.0 %
11	D	82.85 % / 16.07 %
12	B	85.12 % / 13.66 %
13	D	86.26 % / 10.14 %
14	B	83.19 % / 10.53 %
15	B	78.73 % / 19.43 %
16	A	84.05 % / 10.88 %
17	C	76.04 % / 23.46 %
18	D	77.27 % / 17.22 %
19	C	86.61 % / 11.34 %
20	A	80.36 % / 13.84 %
21	B	80.41 % / 13.5 %
22	A	88.21 % / 10.74 %
23	A	86.77 % / 10.17 %
24	D	82.82 % / 10.77 %
25	B	82.59 % / 13.43 %
26	C	79.81 % / 13.08 %
27	D	78.3 % / 10.4 %
28	D	82.18 % / 11.53 %
29	B	82.55 % / 11.02 %
30	B	89.04 % / 10.22 %
31	B	85.38 % / 10.63 %
32	A	77.01 % / 22.46 %
33	B	87.7 % / 12.11 %
34	A	83.31 % / 15.3 %
35	A	88.83 % / 11.13 %
36	D	89.72 % / 10.22 %
37	A	83.99 % / 15.8 %
38	A	77.68 % / 13.95 %
39	C	82.92 % / 16.28 %
40	B	88.45 % / 10.08 %
41	A	82.27 % / 14.93 %
42	B	86.27 % / 10.71 %
43	B	78.72 % / 16.12 %
44	B	83.31 % / 11.88 %
45	B	82.0 % / 16.8 %
46	B	79.14 % / 13.9 %
47	B	76.06 % / 11.77 %
48	A	78.97 % / 13.98 %
49	A	78.05 % / 11.98 %
50	B	81.68 % / 18.11 %

Performance Analysis

Avg. Score (%)	64.67%
Toppers Score (%)	66.0%
Your Score	

//Hints and Solutions//

1. Basic Formula:

Speed of the stream = ½ (a-b) km/hr

Explanation:

Let the speed in still water be x m/hr

Speed of stream be y m/hr

Then, speed upstream = x-y m/hr and

Speed downstream = x+y m/hr

12/x-y – 12 / x+y = 6 so,6 (x^2 – y^2) = 24 y

x^2 – y^2 = 4y

x^2 = y^2 + 4y.............1

also

12/ 2x-y – 12/2x +y = 1 4x^2 – y^2 = 24y

x^2 = [24y + y^2] / 4 2

16y + 4y^2 = 24y + y2 [put X^2 value from 1] 3y^2 = 8 y so, y = 8/3

speed of the current = 8/3 m/hr = 2 (2/3) m/hr

2. Explanation:

The cyclist moves both ways at a speed of 12khr so average speed fo the cyclist – 12 km/hr boat sailor moves downstream at 10+4 = 14km/hr and upstream 10-4 = 6km/hr

Average speed of the boat sailor = 2 x 14 x 6 / 14 +6 = 42/ 5 = 8.4km/hr

The average speed of cyclist is greater .so,cyclist comes first and return to place P.

3. 17*756÷54 = ? +540

17*14 = ? +540

238 = ? + 540

? =238-540 = -302

4. = √(337/21)÷ √(1365/84) × 26

= 16÷16 ×26 = 26

5. CP of 1st bangle set = x

CP of 2nd bangle set = 600-x

SP of 1st bangle set = 4x/5

SP of 2nd bangle set=(600-X)5/4

Profit=SP-CP

96=4x/5+(600-X)5/4-600

X = 120

Shortcut:

-20...................25

.............16.....................

9.........................36

1 : 4

5 = 600

1 = 120

6. 10x=s-400

12x=s+800

2x=1200

X=600

7. 1/A + 1/B = 1/24 , 1/B + 1/C = 1/32

10/A + 14/B + 26/C = 1

10(1/A + 1/B) + 4(1/B + 1/C) + 22/C = 1

10/24 + 4/32 + 22/C = 1, we get C = 48 days

8. Let additional workers be P,

(50*150)/(50*200) = 3/4 of the work is already completed and now only 1/4 of the work is to be done. So,

1/4 = ((50 + P) * 25)/50*200, solve for p, we get P = 50

9. Present age of Ajay = x ; Present age of Ajay's sister = y

x = (x-6)(5/4)

x = 30

present age of Ajay's brother = 30 – 5 = 25

10. Shyam's age – Rahul's age = Rahul's age – Suresh's age

Suresh's age + Shyam's age = 2 Rahul's age

Shyam's age + Suresh's age = 60

Rahul's age = 30; We can not find the difference between Shyam and Rahul's age

11. The general formulae for installments in case of compound interest is

$$P = x/(1 + r/100) + x/(1 + r/100)^\wedge 2 \ldots . x/(1 + r/100)^\wedge n$$

Here we have to find P given $x = 882 r = 5$ and $n = 2$
On substituting the values we get

$$P = 882/(1 + 5/100) + 882/(1 + 5/100)^\wedge 2$$
$$P = 882^* 20/21 + 882^* 400/441$$
$$P = 840 + 800 => p = 1640$$

12. Let B's present share $= Rs. X. \therefore \quad (3903 -$

$$x)\left(1 + \frac{4}{100}\right)^7 = x\left(1 + \frac{4}{100}\right)^9$$
$$\Rightarrow (3903 - x) = x\left(\frac{26}{25}\right)^2 = \frac{676x}{625}$$
$$\Rightarrow 3903 \times 625 - 625x = 676x$$
$$\Rightarrow 1301x = 3903 \times 625$$
$$\Rightarrow \quad x = \frac{3903 \times 625}{1301} = Rs. 1875$$

13. alcohol = 30*2/5 = 12 and water = 18 litres

(12 + x)/(30 +x) = 60/100, we will get x = 15

14. (20/100)*t*t = 2000

$t^2 * \dfrac{1}{5} = 2000$

$t^2 = 5 * 2000$

$t^2 = 100 * 100$

t= 100

15. In a leap year there are 52 complete weeks i.e. 364 days and 2 more days. These 2 days can be SM, MT, TW, WT, TF, FS, and SS.

So P = 2/7

16. Probability of any event is the number of favourable events by the number of Total events:

Since there are only three colours of balls here, neither red nor white refers to green balls.

Therefore, the number of favourable events is 5

And the number of Total events is:

4+5+6=15

Therefore, the probability of a randomly drawn ball being neither red nor white is 5/15=1/3

17. (1/15 + 1/30)*T1 = 1/3, T1 = 10/3 hr

Now after leak is developed, [(1/15 + 1/30) – (1/3)*(1/15 + 1/30)]*T2 = 2/3

T2 = 10 hr. So total time = 10 + 10/3 = 40/3 hr

18. The tank supposed to be filled in (30*20)/50 = 12 minutes

so, (1/20 + 1/30)*12 – 12/C + (1/20 + 1/30)*5 = 1 (A and B work for 12 minutes and also C work for 12 minutes and then A and B takes 5 more minutes to fill the tank)

solve for C, we will get C = 144/5 = 28.8

19. 1000*20/1600

=12 ½ days

20. 120×12=1440 for lunch box

80×13 = 1040 for bottels

13:12

21. As the temperature differences are small, we can use Newton's law of

cooling. $\dfrac{d\theta}{dt} = -k(\theta - \theta_0)$

$\dfrac{dg}{\theta\theta_0} = -kdt$

Where k is a constant, θ is the temperature of the body at time t and $\theta_0 = 16°C$ is the temperature of the surrounding. We

have. $\int_{40°e}^{35°e} \dfrac{d\theta}{\theta-\theta_0} = -k(5\text{min})$

$In\dfrac{36°e-16°e}{40°e-16°e} = -k(5\text{min})$

or, $k = -\dfrac{\ln(5/6)}{\sin^{11}n}$

or, If t be the time required for the temperature to fall from $36°C$ to $32°C$ then by (1)

$\int_{36'e}^{32°c} \dfrac{d\theta}{\theta-\theta_0} = -kt$

$In\dfrac{32°c-16^c}{36^6c-16^0} = -\dfrac{In(5/6)t}{senin}$

$t = \dfrac{\ln(4/5)}{\ln(5/6)} \times 5\text{min} = 6.1\text{min}$

22. From the graph it is clear that initially both the bodies are at same temperature but after that at any instant temperature of body x is less than the temperature of body y. It means body x emits more heat i.e., emissivity of body x is more than body y $\therefore e_x > e_y$ and according to Kirchhoff's law good emitter are also good absorber so $a_x > a_y$.

23. According to Wein's displacement law λm×T = Constant

Here **λm<λm2<λm1** ⇒T₃>T₂>T₁

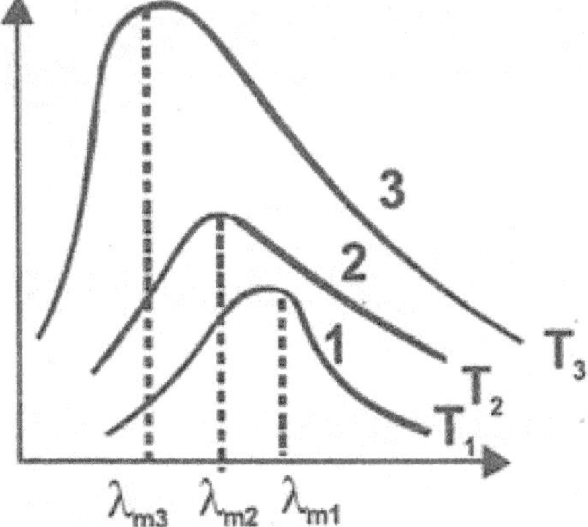

The temperature of Sun is higher than that of welding arc which in turn is greater than tungsten filament.

Therefore **T₃** is the Sun's temperature, **T₂** the welding arc's and **T₁** the tungsten filament's.

24. Just like a single macroscopic pressure being undefined for a gas which is not in equilibrium, a single macroscopic temperature is also undefined. So the temperature at **P₁ and P₂** need not necessarily be the same, and most likely wouldn't be the same.

25. Initial free body diagram -

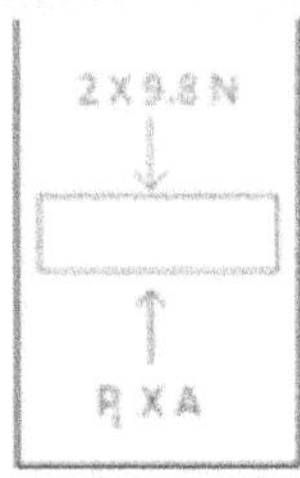

When the system was in equilibrium, the force applied by the steel balls

on the piston was offset by the force applied by the gas on the piston.

Just after removing the ball -

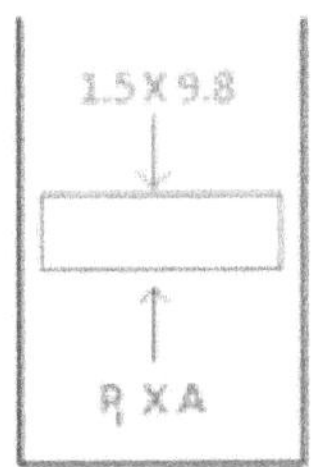

The instant the ball is dislodged the downward force acting on the piston reduces from $19.6N(\text{i.e.,},2 \times 9.8N)$ to $14.7N(1.5 \times 9.8N)$

However the pressure of the helium gas has not changed. Hence there is an unbalanced force in the upward direction. This upward force will push the piston up. After some time, the weight of the balls would equal the force exerted by the hellum gas and the system would eventually

come to rest

26. Let us analyse each process separately. BC is an isothermal process, which implies that the P-C graph would be represented by a rectangular hyperbola. (Since PV = constant).

This rectangular hyperbola starts at a lower volume **V₁** and goes to a higher volume as represented in the figure below -

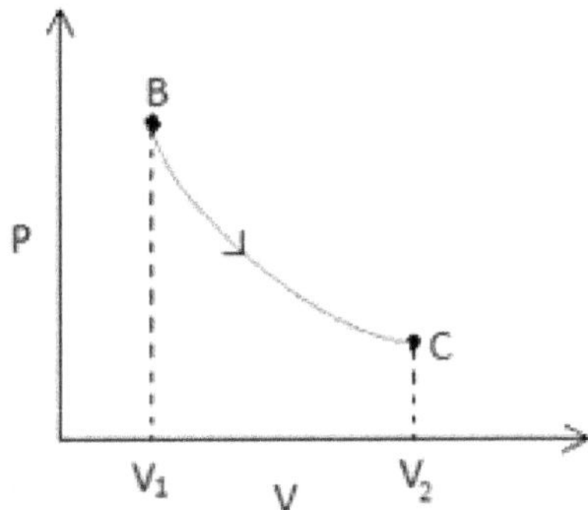

Process AB is an isochoric process, which in a P-V graph would be a vertical line. Also we notice that the temperature drops in this process, whichimplies that the pressure will also drop (since PV=nRT, when V is constant **P∝T**). Therefore point Acan be anywhere on the line represented in blue in the figure below.

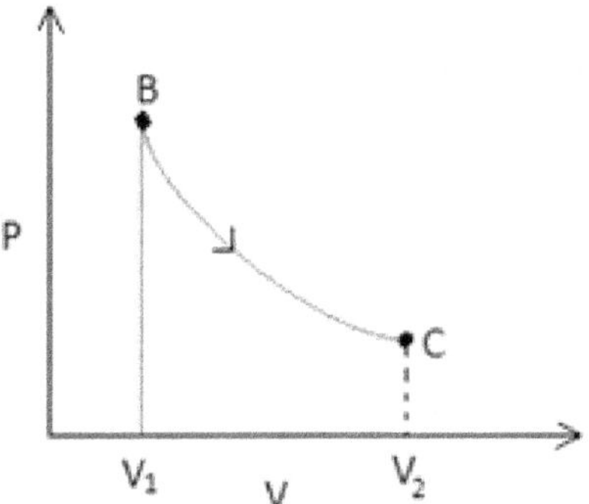

This process is an isobaric process since it represents a curve where **V∝T** (this is possible only when pressure is a constant, remember Charles' law?). So the process can be represented by a horizontal line in a P-Vgraph. The point where the line joining process A-Band C-Ameet is the point A

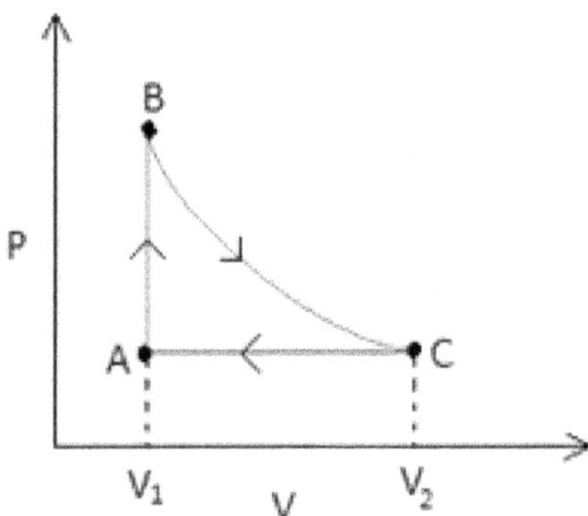

27. Molecularity can never be zero or fractional.

28. Certain bimolecular reactions that follow the first-order kinetics are called. It is the characteristic of pseudo-unimolecular reactions.

29. For a second order kinetics of the reaction A → B we have rate = **k[A]²**. When conc. of A is doubled the rate of the reaction increases by a factor of **2²(=4)**. Since rate of conversion of A = rate of formation of B. Hence rate of formation of B also increases 4 times.

30. $P.D.I = \dfrac{\overline{M_W}}{M_n} = \dfrac{40000}{30000} = 1.33$

31.

Buna-*S* is a copolymer of 1, 3- butadiene and styrene.

32. Teflon ($-CF_2 - CF_2-$)ₙ is stable upto 598K.

33. While naming, the double bond gets a lower number than the triple bond.

$$\underset{1}{C}H_2 = \underset{2}{C}H - \underset{3}{C}H_2 - \underset{4}{C} \equiv \underset{5}{C}H$$

Wort root = pent

Pent-1-en-4-yne

Not 4-Penten-1-yne

Because, if there is a choice in numbering, the double bond is always given preference over the triple bond.

34. The parent hydrocarbon is a 6 member ring with one carbon-carbon double bond.

Hence, it is called cyclohex-1-ene.

One ethyl group at sixth carbon atom and two methyl groups at third carbon atoms are present.

Hence, the IUPAC name of the compound is 6-ethyl-3,3-dimethyl cyclohex-1-ene.

35. Parent chain is

$$\overset{1}{CH_3} - \overset{2}{CH_2} - \overset{3}{\underset{\underset{CH_3}{|}}{C}} = \overset{4}{CH} - \overset{5}{CH_2} - \overset{6}{\underset{\underset{CH_3}{|}}{CH}} - \overset{7}{CH_2} - \overset{8}{CH_3}$$

Word root $\Rightarrow$ oct

Double bond $\Rightarrow$ sufffix $\Rightarrow$ ene

Two methyl groups at C_3 and C_5 $\Rightarrow$ 3,6 -dimethyl

Therefore, 3,6-Dimethyl-3-octene

36. $\Delta G^\circ = -nE^\circ F$
$Fe^{2t} + 2e^- \rightarrow Fe$
$\Delta G^\circ = -2 \times F \times (-0.440V) = 0.880F$
$Fe^{3+} + 3e^- \rightarrow Fe$
$\Delta G^\circ = -3 \times F \times (-0.036) = 0.108F$
On substracting equation (i) from (i i) $Fe^{3+} + e^- \rightarrow Fe^{21}$
$\Delta G^\circ = 0.108F - 0.880F = -0.772F$
E° for the reaction $= -\dfrac{\Delta G^\circ}{nP} = -\dfrac{(-0.772F)}{1 \times P} = +0.772V$

37. $\Delta G = -nFE^\circ$
$\Rightarrow \Delta G = -1 \times 96500 \times 1.02 \Rightarrow \Delta G = -98430$

38. $E^o_{ccll} = \dfrac{0.059}{n} \log K$

$\log K = \dfrac{1.10 \times 2}{0.059} = 37.2881 \Rightarrow K = 10^{-37}$

39.

(a)

(b)

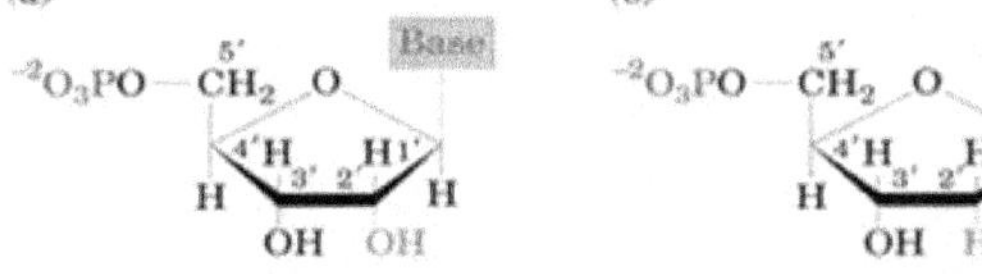

Ribonucleotides   **Deoxyribonucleotides**

You can see that the base is at the C'$_1$ carbon and the phosphate linkage is at the C'$_5$ carbon.

40. Molisch's test is done for the detection of carbohydrate bond formation.

41. Bangladesh has a population of 159.86 million people and a population density of 1238 persons per square kilometers, the highest among the world's larger countries.

42. The nuclear Nonproliferation Treaty (NPT), which entered into force in March 1970, seeks to inhibit the spread of nuclear weapons.

43. Its five organizations are the International Bank for Reconstruction and Development (IBRD), the International Development Association (IDA), the International Finance Corporation (IFC), the Multilateral Investment Guarantee Agency (MIGA) and the International Centre for Settlement of Investment Disputes (ICSID).

44. Subsequently, the United Nations General Assembly created the UNIDO in November 1966 as a special organ of the United Nations. In January 1967, the Organization was formally established with Headquarters in Vienna, Austria.

45. 53 countries are represented in Unrepresented Nations are peoples Organisation.

46. The South Asian Association for Regional Cooperation (SAARC) was established when its Charter was formally approved on 8 December 1985 by the Heads of State or Government of Bangladesh, Bhutan, India, Maldives, Nepal, Pakistan and Sri Lanka.

47. The FAO Headquarters is located in the city centre of Rome, near the Circo Massimo and close to the Colosseum. It's a lofty white building that is easy to recognize.

48. This was done in order to relax the controls on foreign exchange in India. FERA was repealed in 1998 by the government of Atal Bihari Vajpayee and replaced by the Foreign Exchange Management Act, which liberalised foreign exchange controls and restrictions on foreign investment.

49. The first defence minister of independent India was Baldev Singh, who served in Prime Minister Jawaharlal Nehru's cabinet during 1947–52. Rajnath Singh is the current defence minister of India.

50. In 1675 Guru Tegh Bahadur was executed in Delhi on 11 November under the orders of the Mughal Emperor Aurangzeb. According to J.S. Grewal, a scholar of Sikh history, Guru Tegh Bahadur decided to confront the religious persecution of Kashmiri Brahmins by the Mughal officials.

Mathematics

Q.1 36 * 1.75 + 24 * 3.25 = ?
A. 142 **B.** 141 **C.** 162 **D.** 182

Q.2 5.8 * 2.5 + 0.6 * 6.75 + 139.25 = ?
A. 139.80 **B.** 157.80 **C.** 156.70 **D.** 170.70

Q.3 The ratio selling prices three articles A, B, and C is 29:27:32., the ratio of percentage profit is 4:2:5, respectively. If the cost price of article A is equal to B and the cost price of article C is Rs. 480. Then what is the overall gain?
A. 10% **B.** 12% **C.** 15% **D.** 18%

Q.4 Swati went shopping to buy a watch with some money. She selected a watch, which is marked Rs.400 higher price than the money she had. But shopkeeper gave two successive discounts of 10% and 15% respectively on the marked price of the watch. Then she could buy that watch and also another watch worth ₹540 with all the money she had. Then what is the marked price on the first watch?
A. ₹3060 **B.** ₹3600 **C.** ₹4000 **D.** ₹4200

Q.5 A Boat takes 128 min less to travel to 48 Km downstream than to travel the same distance upstream. If the speed of the stream is 3 Km/hr. Then Speed of Boat in still water is?
A. 6 Km/hr **B.** 9 Km/h
C. 12 Km/hr **D.** 15 Km/hr

Q.6 The speed of Boat in Still water is 40 Km/hr and speed of the stream is 20 Km/hr. The distance between Point A and Point B is 480 Km. The boat started traveling downstream from A to B, in the midway, it is powered by an Engine due to which speed of the Boat increased. Now Boat reached Point B and started back to point A with help of the same engine. It took 19 hours for the entire journey. Then with the help of the engine, the speed of the boat increased by how many Km/hr?
A. 10 Km/hr **B.** 15 Km/hr
C. 20 Km/hr **D.** 24 Km/hr

Q.7 Two Cars started at same time, same place and towards same direction. First Car goes at uniform speed of 12Km/hr. Second Car goes at speed of 4 Km/hr in first hour and increases it speed by 1 Km/hr for every hour. Then what is the distance traveled by car B when the both the Cars meet for the first time?
A. 196 Km **B.** 198 Km **C.** 200 Km **D.** 204 Km

Q.8 A man traveled 100 km by Bike in 2 hours. He then traveled in Bus for 8 hrs and then Train in 9 hrs. Ratio of Speeds of Bus to Train is 4:5. If speed of train is 4/5 of Bike speed then the entire journey covered by him in Km is?
A. 516 Km **B.** 616 Km **C.** 716 Km **D.** 816 Km

Q.9 Eight years ago Ravi's mother was five times older than her daughter. After Eight years Ravi's mother will be twice older than her daughter. Find the present age of Ravi?
A. 18.33 years **B.** 12.5 years
C. 16.7 years **D.** 13.33 years

Q.10 The ratio of Arun's and Varun's ages is 4:5. If the difference between the present age of Varun and the age of Arun 5 years hence is 3 years, then what is the total of present ages of Arun and Varun?
A. 73 years **B.** 72 years **C.** 75 years **D.** 69 years

Q.11 Leela takes a loan of ₹ 8400 at 10% p.a. compounded annually which is to be repaid in two equal annual installments. One at the end of one year and the other at the end of the second year. The value of each installment is?
A. 4200 **B.** 4140 **C.** 4840 **D.** 5640

Q.12 A sum of money lent at compound interest for 2 years at 20% per annum would fetch ₹723 more, if the interest was payable half yearly than if it was payable annually. The sum is
A. ₹ 20000 **B.** ₹ 15000 **C.** ₹ 30000 **D.** ₹ 45000

Q.13 Ankita is 25 years old. If Rahul's age is 25% greater than that of Ankita then how much percent Ankita's age is less than Rahul's age
A. 40% **B.** 35% **C.** 10% **D.** 20%

Q.14 Mr.Ravi's salary was reduced by 25% for three months. But after the three months, his salary was increased to the original salary. What is the percentage increase in salary of Mr.Ravi?
A. 33.33% **B.** 42.85% **C.** 28.56% **D.** 16.66%

Q.15 A committee of five persons is to be chosen from a group of 10 people. The probability that a certain married couple will either serve together or not at all is?
A. 54/199 **B.** 52/195 **C.** 53/186 **D.** 51/126

Q.16 Out of 14 applicants for a job, there are 6 women and 8 men. It is desired to select 2 persons for the job. The probabilty that atleast one of selected persons will be a Woman is?
A. 77/91 **B.** 54/91 **C.** 45/91 **D.** 40/91

Q.17 An amount of money is to be distributed among P, Q and R in the ratio of 7:4:5 respectively. If the total share of P and R is 4 times the share of Q, what is definitely Q's share?
A. 2000 **B.** 4000
C. 6000 **D.** Data inadequate

Q.18 Two candles of same height are lighted at the same time. The first is consumed in 3 hours and second in 2 hours. Assuming that each candles burns at a constant rate, in how many hours after being lighted, the ratio between the first and second candles becomes 2:1?

A. 2 hour **B.** 2.5 hour **C.** 4 hour **D.** 4.5 hour

Q.19 Two Inlet Pipes A and B together can fill a Tank in 'X' minutes. If A and B take 81 minutes and 49 minutes more than 'X' minutes respectively, to fill the Tank. Then They can fill the 5/7 of that Tank in how many minutes?

A. 45 Minutes **B.** 49 Minutes
C. 63 Minutes **D.** 81 Minutes

Q.20 Pipe A can fill a Tank in 18 Hours, Pipe B can empty a Tank in 12 Hours, Pipe C can fill Tank in 6 Hours. The Tank is already filled up to 1/6 of its capacity. Now Pipe A is opened in the First Hour alone, Pipe B is opened in the Second Hour alone and Pipe C is opened in the Third Hour alone. This cycle is repeated until the Tank gets filled. Then in How many Hours does the rest of Tank gets filled?

A. 15 Hours **B.** 18 Hours
C. 20 Hours **D.** 24 Hours

Science

Q.21 The solubility of lower alcohols in water is due to -

A. Formation of hydrogen bond between alcohol and water molecules
B. Hydrophobic nature of carbon chain
C. Increases in boiling points
D. None of these

Q.22 The IUPAC name of tert-butyl alcohol is

A. 2-metylpropan-2-ol **B.** 2-methylbutan-1-ol
C. Propan-2-ol **D.** Butan-2-ol

Q.23 In the following reaction

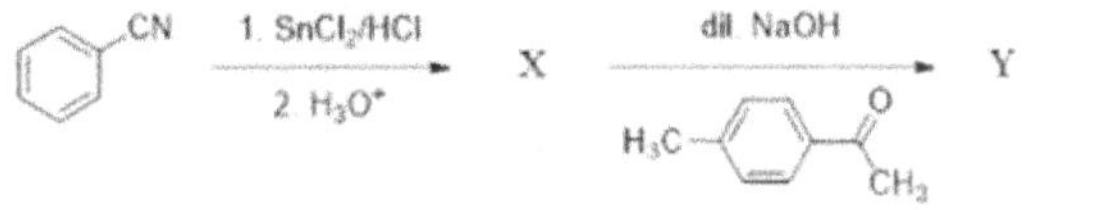

A. 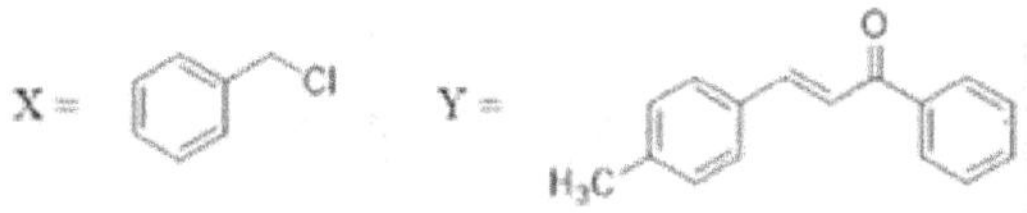 X =   Y =

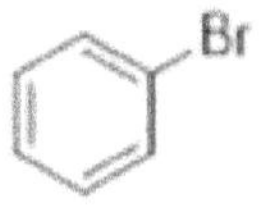

B. 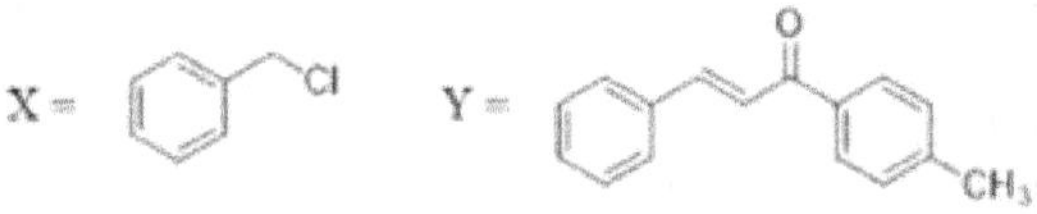 X =   Y =

C. 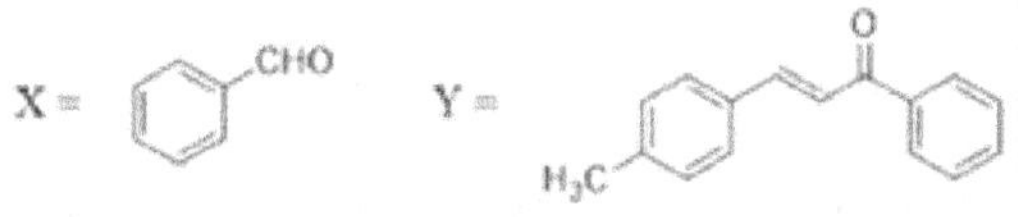 X =   Y =

D. 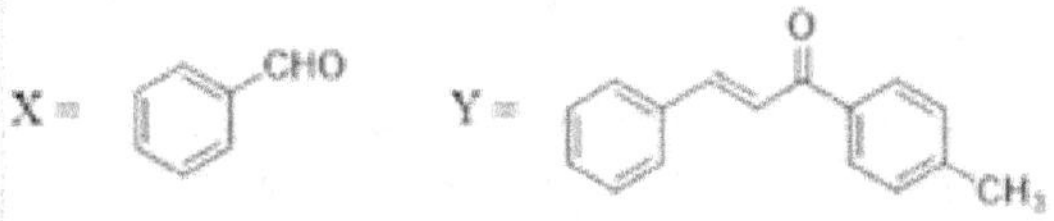 X =   Y =

Q.24 In the following reaction

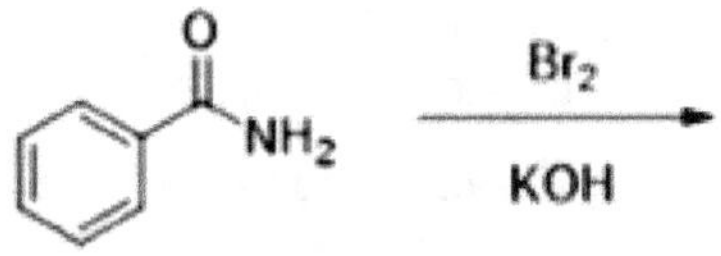

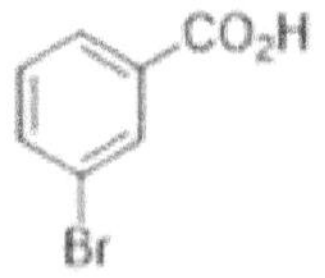

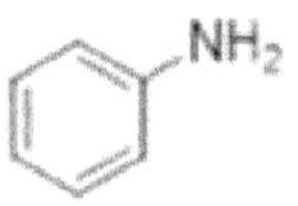

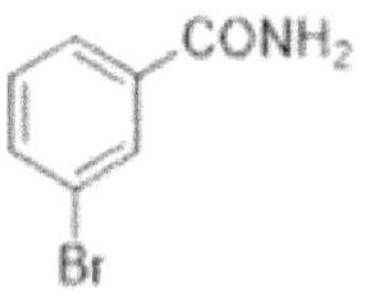

Q.25 Which of these will not result in formation of alcohol on reaction with nitrous acid?

A. Methyl amine
B. Ethyl amine
C. N, N Dimethyl phenyl amine
D. None of these

Q.26 In a protein molecule various amino acids are linked together by

A. β-glycosidic bond **B.** peptide bond
C. dative bond **D.** α-glycosidic bond

Q.27 The secondary structure of a protein refers to

A. α-helical backbone
B. hydrophobic interactions
C. sequence of α-amino acids
D. fixed configuration of the polypeptide backbone

Q.28 $[NH(CH_2)_6NHCO(CH_2)_4CO]_n$ is a :

A. co-polymer
B. addition polymer
C. thermo-setting polymer
D. homopolymer

Q.29 A polymer commercially called 'SYNTHETIC WOOL' also called orlon is a homopolymer. Identify the polymer.

A. Terylene **B.** Dacron
C. Polyacrylonitrile **D.** Polythene

Q.30 The formation of amide linkage and ester linkage occurs through the condensation mechanism. Both reaction loses same substance during polymerisation. Identify the substance:

A. Alcohol **B.** Water
C. Aldehyde **D.** Ester

Q.31 Starch is not a single compound but is a mixture of two components – amylose (10 to 20%) and amylopectin (20 to 80%). Both amylose and amylopectin are polymers of α-D-glucose. Specify the carbons in which this polymerization occurs.

A. c1-c4 bond **B.** c1-c6 bond
C. c2-c4 bond **D.** c2-c6 bond

Q.32 A circuit is charged with the help of a 16 V battery as shown in the figure, if Vs is a 28 V sinusoidal source, the maximum amount of diode current and reverse- bias voltage that appear across the diode is

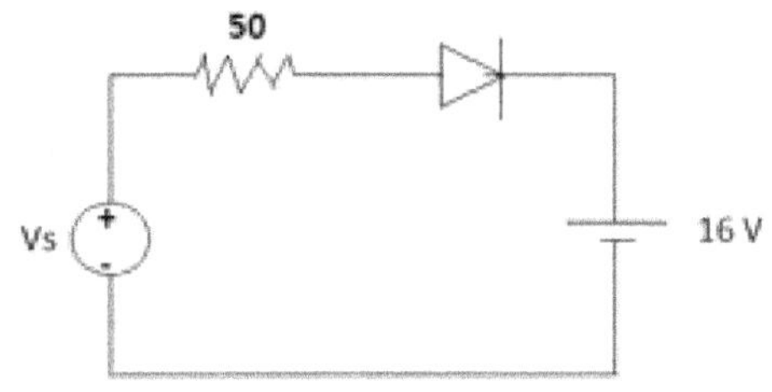

A. 0.12 A, 36 V   B. 0.24 A, 44 V

C. 0.16 A, 42 V   D. 0.36 A, 58 V

Q.33 A 2V battery is connected across AB as shown in the figure. The value of the current supplied by the battery when in one case battery's positive terminal is connected to A and in other case when positive terminal of battery is connected to B will respectively be:

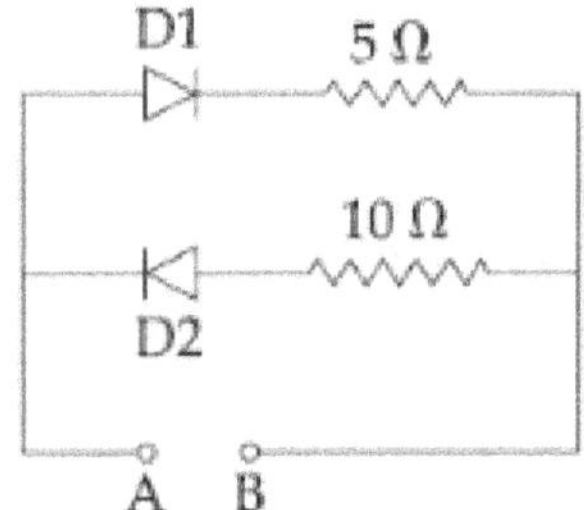

A. 0.2 A and 0.1 A   B. 0.4 A and 0.2 A

C. 0.1 A and 0.2 A   D. 0.2 A and 0.4 A

Q.34 The reading of the ammeter for a silicon diode in the given circuit is :

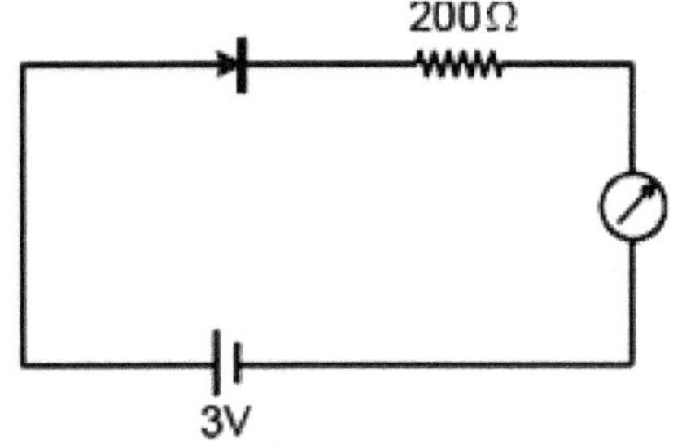

A. 13.5 mA   B. 0   C. 15 mA   D. 11.5 mA

Q.35 When a transistor is connected in common base mode, the current gain is found to be $\alpha = 0.98$ and the reverse saturation current for the collector-base junction is found to be 0.6 μA. On connecting the same transistor in common-emitter mode as an amplifier the base current is found to be 20 μA, the magnitude of the collector current in this case is

A. 2020 µA   B. 1010 µA   C. 2400 µA   D. 1200 µA

Q.36 This circuit in figure represents which LOGIC Gate

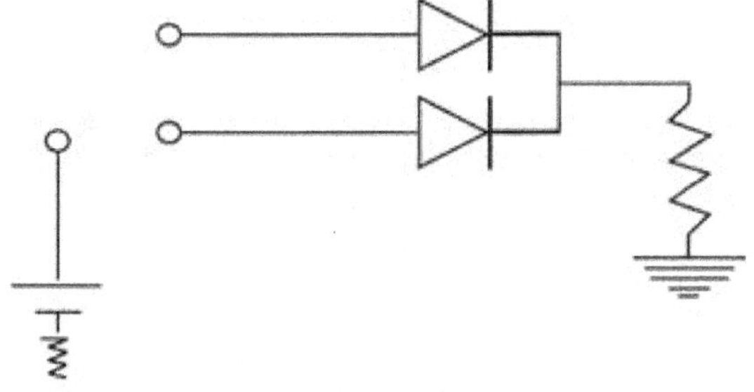

A. AND   B. NAND   C. OR   D. XOR

Q.37 Mobilities of electrons and holes in a sample of intrinsic germanium a room temperature are $0.36 m^2V^{-1}s^{-1}$ and $0.17 m^2V^{-1}s^{-1}$. The electron and hole densities are each equal to $2.5 \times 10^{19} m^3$. The electrical conductivity of germanium is

A. 4.24 Sm⁻¹   B. 2.12 Sm⁻¹

C. 1.09 Sm⁻¹   D. 0.47 Sm⁻¹

Q.38 A gamma-ray photon breaks a deuteron into a proton and a neutron (photon disintegration). Find the minimum possible energy of the gamma ray in MeV. Given

$$m_H = 1.00785 amu, m_n = 1.008665 amu \text{ and } m_D = 2.014102 amu$$

A. 2.548MeV   B. 2.248MeV

C. 1.248MeV   D. 1.648MeV

Q.39 A 60 mg radioactive element Y was found to have become 30 mg after 4.5 days. Then, how much of 40 mg of that radioactive element will remain after 90 days?

A. 0.38 mg   B. 0.038 mg

C. 0.38 µg   D. 0.038 µg

Q.40 Which of the following spectral series of hydrogen atom is lying in visible range of electromagnetic wave?

A. Lyman series   B. Paschen series

C. Balmer series   D. Pfund series

General Awareness

Q.41 Whom does the Vice-President submit his resignation to?

A. President

B. Prime Minister

C. Speaker of Lok Sabha

D. Deputy Chairman of Rajya Sabha

Q.42 Which of the following is not a feature of the Early Vedic Period?

A. The king was given 'Bali' or presents by the people

B. Women played some part in the productive process

C. Prajapati was the most important God

D. In 'yajnas', the 'purohita' was the intermediate between the clansmen and God

Q.43 Since which year did Gandhiji permit women to participate fully in the national movements?

A. 1920   B. 1927   C. 1930   D. 1935

Q.44 Consider the following characteristics of a crop –

1. The suitable climate for growing is warm and wet climate

2. Temperatures ranging from 70–100 °F and relative humidity of 70%–90%

3. Requires 2–3 inches of rainfall weekly

Which of the following crops is being talked about?

A. Rice   **B.** Wheat   **C.** Jute   **D.** Cotton

Q.45 Consider the following statements about the art and architecture of a dynasty:-

1. Shiva is represented in the greater variety than anywhere else in India like Bhiksatana, Dakshinamurti, Kankalamurti etc.

2. There was a boom of temple-building

3.The Nageshvara at Kumbakonam stands out

Which of the following dynasties is being talked about?

A. Pallavas   **B.** Chalukyas

C. Rashtrakutas   **D.** Cholas

Q.46 What is the name of the first fully India-made train that was flagged off recently?

A. Medha   **B.** Chanchala

C. Megha   **D.** Chanchal

Q.47 About how many minutes is the period of the sidereal day less than the mean period of solar day?

A. 3   **B.** 4   **C.** 5   **D.** 6

Q.48 Consider the following features of a Mahajanapada:-

1. It was situated at the confluence of the Ganges and Yamuna rivers

2. It's capital Kausambi is now a small town in Uttar Pradesh called Kosam

Which of the following Mahajanapadas is being talked about?

A. Kosala   **B.** Vatsa   **C.** Kashi   **D.** Malla

Q.49 The Ames Test refers to a test -

A. Performed on a bacterium to determine the carcinogenicity of chemicals

B. Performed on laboratory animals to determine the carcinogenicity of chemicals

C. To determine the pathogenicity of a bacterium

D. To determine the effectiveness of an antibiotic

Q.50 Which of the following is a bacterial disease among crops?

A. Bunt of rice   **B.** Paddy blight

C. Leaf curl   **D.** Potato mosaic

// Smart Answer Sheet //

Correct   Indicates percentage of students who answered questions correctly.

Skipped   Indicates percentage of students who skipped questions.

Q.	Ans.	Correct / Skipped	Q.	Ans.	Correct / Skipped	Q.	Ans.	Correct / Skipped	Q.	Ans.	Correct / Skipped	Q.	Ans.	Correct / Skipped
1	B	76.28 % / 17.62 %	11	C	78.21 % / 14.5 %	21	A	89.31 % / 10.14 %	31	A	87.55 % / 11.15 %	41	A	81.29 % / 17.94 %
2	B	83.51 % / 13.59 %	12	C	80.95 % / 15.47 %	22	A	87.66 % / 11.68 %	32	B	84.29 % / 10.66 %	42	C	80.36 % / 16.88 %
3	C	76.72 % / 17.23 %	13	D	83.92 % / 14.7 %	23	D	79.64 % / 18.05 %	33	B	85.71 % / 11.22 %	43	C	79.66 % / 12.27 %
4	C	76.48 % / 10.44 %	14	A	78.25 % / 12.35 %	24	C	79.21 % / 19.59 %	34	D	83.42 % / 15.62 %	44	C	78.99 % / 16.72 %
5	C	76.24 % / 17.62 %	15	D	86.42 % / 11.56 %	25	C	87.23 % / 12.73 %	35	B	81.19 % / 14.73 %	45	D	89.87 % / 10.08 %
6	C	82.95 % / 16.53 %	16	A	84.7 % / 12.3 %	26	B	79.52 % / 10.84 %	36	C	84.3 % / 11.83 %	46	A	80.49 % / 18.94 %
7	D	80.69 % / 18.02 %	17	D	79.68 % / 18.33 %	27	A	77.43 % / 19.35 %	37	B	81.96 % / 12.08 %	47	B	76.81 % / 11.4 %
8	C	83.73 % / 15.3 %	18	D	80.26 % / 18.97 %	28	A	89.67 % / 10.02 %	38	B	83.56 % / 12.0 %	48	B	76.3 % / 21.07 %
9	D	86.94 % / 10.05 %	19	A	86.49 % / 13.23 %	29	C	78.7 % / 19.28 %	39	D	87.75 % / 10.87 %	49	A	89.65 % / 10.08 %
10	B	87.9 % / 10.25 %	20	B	85.21 % / 12.16 %	30	B	79.09 % / 12.11 %	40	C	80.04 % / 12.43 %	50	B	79.86 % / 18.12 %

Performance Analysis

Avg. Score (%)	32.0%
Toppers Score (%)	60.0%
Your Score	

//Hints and Solutions//

1. 36 * 1.75 + 24 * 3.25 = 63 + 78 = 141

2. 5.8 * 2.5 + 0.6 * 6.75 + 139.25 = 157.80

3. 29y/27y = (100+4x/100+2x)

x = 4

% are 16%,8%,20%

32y = 480(120/100)

y =18

SP's are 522,486,576

CP of A

29*18 = CP (116/100)

CP =450

CP's are 450,450 and 480

Overall gain =

1584 =1380(100+g/100)

g =15%

4. (x+400)*90/100*85/100+540 =x

x = 3600

MP = 3600+400 = 4000

5. 32/15 = 48(1/s-3 − 1/s+3)

s= 12

6. 19 = 240/60 + 240/60+x + 480/20+x

x = 20

7. 12*x = x/2(2*4+(x-1)*1)

X= 17

D = 17*12 =204

8. Speed of train = 50

Bus = 32

Train = 40

Distance = 100+32*8+40*9 = 716

9. Eight years ago, Ravi's age = x

Eight years ago, Ravi's Mother age = 5x

2(x+16) = 5x+16

2x+32 = 5x+16

x=16/3

Present age of Ravi = 16/3 + 8 = 13.33 years

10. Arun's age = x

Varun's age = y

x/y = 4/5

y − (x + 5) = 3

y − x = 8

y = 8 + x

x/8 + x = 4/5

x = 32 years

y = 40 years.

x + y = 72 years.

11. 8400 = x*(210/121) => 4840

12. sum − Rs.x

C.I. compounded half yearly = (4641/10000)x

C.I. compounded annually = (11/25)x

(4641/10000)x − (11/25)x = 723

x = 30000

13. Percentage decrease = 25/125 * 100 = 20%

14. Percentage increase = 25/75 * 100 = 33.33%

15. Five persons is to be chosen from a group of 10 people = 10C5 = 252

Couple Serve together = 8C3 * 2C2 = 56

Couple does not serve = 8C5 = 56

Probability = 102/252 = 51/126

16. Man only = 8C2 = 14

Probability of selecting no woman = 14/91

Probability of selecting atleast one woman = 1 − 14/91 = 77/91

17. Total sum not given

18. Height of both candles are same i.e. h

First one takes 6 hours to burn completely, so in one hour = h/3

Similarly second one will burn in one hour = h/2

Let after t time, ratio between their height is 2:1

so, remaining height of first candle = h − t*(h/3)

similarly for second candle = h − t*(h/2)

ratio given 2:1,

h − t*(h/3) / h − t*(h/2) = 2/1

Solving we get t = 9/2 = 4.5

19. Time taken by two pipes to fill full Tank is = √ab min = 63 min

5/7 Tank = 63*5/7 = 45 min

20. In First Hour Tank filled = 1/6+1/18

Second Hour = 1/6+1/18-1/12

Third Hour = 1/6+1/18-1/12+1/6 = 11/36 is filled

25/36 is left

From then 3 hours work = 1/18-1/12+1/6 = 5/36

5*3 Hours = 5*5/36 = 25/36

Total = 5*3+3 = 18 Hours

21. It is due to the hydroxyl group in the alcohol which is able to form hydrogen bonds with water molecules. Alcohols with smaller hydrocarbon chain are very soluble. As the length of the hydrocarbon chain increases, the solubility in water decreases.

22. Tert-butyl alcohol has the structure-

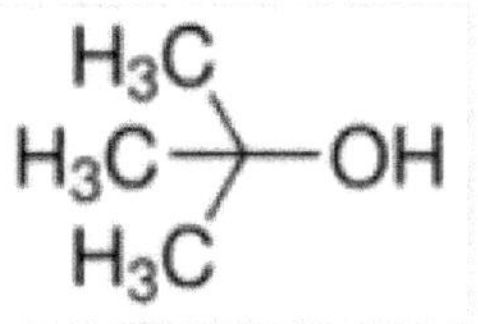

$$
\begin{array}{c}
H_3C \\
H_3C{-}\!\!\!\!\!\overset{\textstyle |}{\underset{\textstyle |}{C}}\!\!\!\!\!{-}OH \\
H_3C
\end{array}
$$

23.

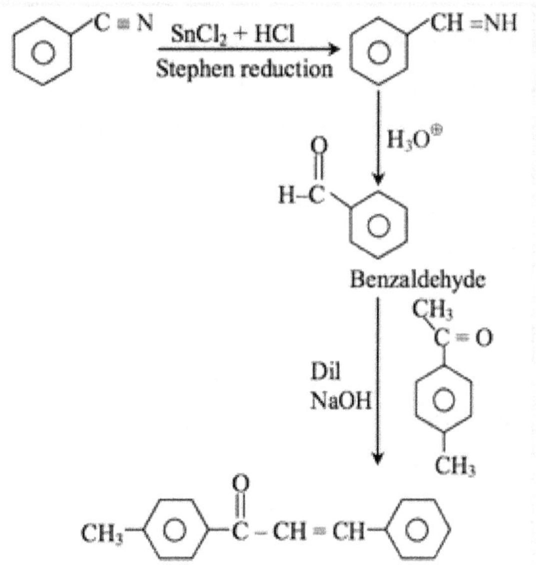

24. This is a Name Reaction to prepare 1 ° amine.

Its name is Hoffmann bromamide reaction.

25.

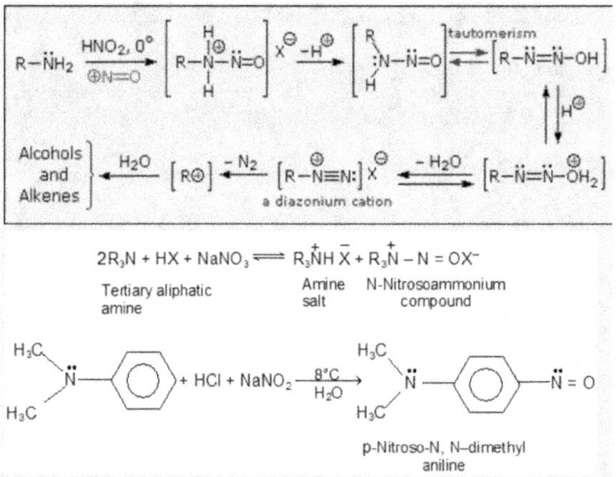

26. Two amino acids in a protein are linked by a peptide bond.

e.g. When carboxylic group of glycine combines with the amino group of alanine glycylalanine is formed.

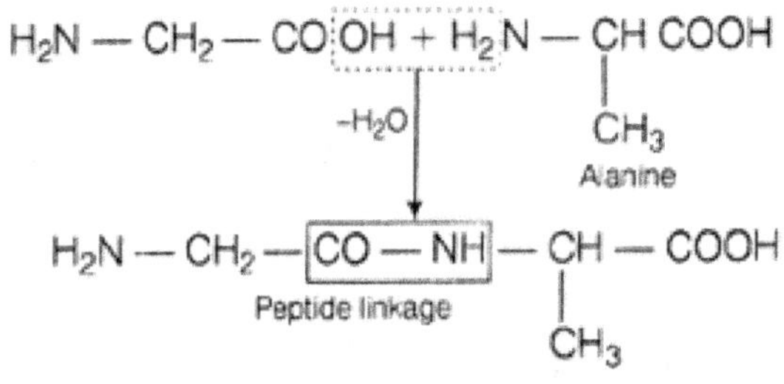

Glycylalanine (Gly-Ala)

27. Primary structure involves sequence of α-amino acids polypeptide chain. Secondary structure involves α-helical and β-pleated sheet like structure.

28. $[NH(CH_2)_6NHCO(CH_2)_4CO]_n$ is a copolymer because repeating structural units are derived from two or more types of monomer. Here,

$nH_2N(CH_2)_6NH_2 + nHOOC(CH_2)_4COOH \rightarrow$
$[NH(CH_2)_6NHCO(CH_2)_4CO]_n$

29. The addition polymerisation of acrylonitrile in presence of a peroxide catalyst leads to the formation of polyacrylonitrile. The polymer is a substitute for wool.It is called synthetic wool. The monomer is acrylonitrile and hence called polyacrylonitrile.

30. Both the formation of amide and ester linkage occurs due to the loss of water. For amide linkage, Amine and carboxylic acid reacts and releases water, but in thecase of ester linkage, alcohol and carboxylic acid reacts and loses water.

31. In starch glucose units which are linked to one another through α-linkage involving C1 of one glucose unit with C4. The structure is

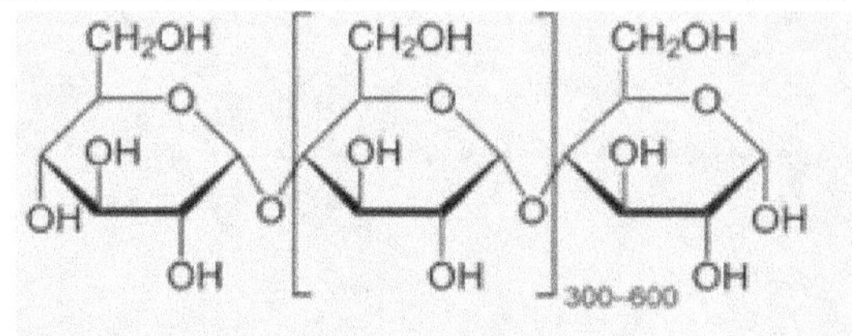

A	B	C
0	0	0
0	1	1
1	0	1
1	1	1

Therefore, it will represent OR Gate

32. Peak value of diode current is

$$Id = \frac{28-16}{50} = 0.24A$$

Maximum reverse voltage across the diode occurs when Vs is at its negative peak,

= 28+16 = 44V

33. When a positive terminal connected to A then diode D_2 is in reverse biased and diode D_1 is in forward biased.
The current will not flow throw diode D_2 only Diode D_1 works.
So current flows through the diode D_1 is

$$I = \frac{V}{R}$$
$$I = \frac{2}{5}$$
$$I = 0.4A$$

When a positive terminal connected to B then diode D_1 is in reverse biased and diode D_2 is in forward biased. The current will not flow throw diode D_1 only Diode D_2 works. So current flows through the diode D_2 is $I = \frac{V}{R}$

$$I = \frac{2}{10}$$
$$I = 0.2A$$

34. As given in the circuit silicon diode is in forward bias. Therefore, the potential drop across is 0.7 V that is the barrier potential of silicon diode.

Current in the circuit is $I = \frac{V - \Delta V}{R}$

$$I = \frac{3-0.7}{200}$$
$$I = 11.5mA$$

35. The common base current amplification factor, $a = 0.98$
Reverse saturation current, $I_{CO} = 0.6\mu A$ When the transistor is connected in common emitter mode the collector current is given by:

$$l_l = \beta_{l_l} + (1+\beta)_{l_0}$$

Where, β is the current amplification factor for the common-emitter mode, that is given by:

$$\beta = \frac{\alpha}{1-\alpha} = \frac{0.98}{1-0.98} = 49$$

Thus, the collector current can be calculated as:

$$4 = 49 \times 20 + 50 \times 0.6 = 1010\mu A$$

36. This circuit will give this truth table

37. Electrical conductivity. $\sigma = \frac{1}{\rho} = \rho(\mu_a n_3 + \mu_n n_n)$

$$= 1.6 \times 10^{-19}[0.36 + 0.17](2.5 \times 10^{19})] = 2.12sm^{-1}$$

38. $\gamma + {}_1^2H \rightarrow p + n$
The energy of photon will be minimum when it is just enough to break deuteron without providing any kinetic energy.
$E_{\sin For}$ % photon is $E_{\min} = (m_p + m_n - m_D)c^2$
$E_{\min} = (1.00785 + 1.008665 - 2.014102) \times 931.5$
$= 2.248MeV$

39. The half-life $= 4.5$ days

Therefore, 90 day $\frac{90}{4.5} = 20$

Hence, mass of the element remaining $= \frac{40}{20}$

$$= 0.038\mu g$$

40. The Balmer series lies in the visible region. The Lyman series is in the ultraviolet region, and Paschen and Pfund series are in the infrared region.

41. The Vice-President submits his resignation to the President

42. In early Vedic Culture, Indra and Agni were the most important Gods. It was in the later Vedic Period that Prajapati or the Creator became the most important God, while Indra and Agni relegated to the background

43. Gandhiji had not allowed women to participate fully in the national movements; this decision had disappointed the women. However, he had permitted their full participation from the Dandi March in the year 1930.

44. The crop being talked about is jute.
Jute is a long, soft, shiny Bast fiber that can be spun into coarse, strong threads. It is produced primarily from plants in the genus Corchorus, which was once classified with the family Tiliaceae. The primary source of the fiber is Corchorus olitorius, but it is considered inferior to Corchorus capsularis. "Jute" is the name of the plant or fiber used to make burlap, hessian or gunny cloth.

45. It was under the Cholas that the Dravida style of Architecture reached its apex. Temple building saw a boom.

46. The first fully India-made 12-coach train "Medha" has flagged off between Dadar to Borivali at Lokmanya Tilak Terminus in Mumbai, Maharashtra.

47. The sidereal day is the time required for a 360° rotation of the earth, while the mean solar day is the average time period for the successive passages of the Sun over a given meridian and it is exactly 24 hours.

On Earth, a sidereal day lasts for 23 hours 56 minutes 4.091 seconds, which is slightly shorter than the solar day measured from noon to noon. Our usual definition of an Earth day is 24 hours, The Sidereal Day is 4 minutes shorter than the Mean Solar Day,

48. The Vatsa Mahajanapada is being talked about. It was earlier a branch of the Kuru Dynasty

49. The Ames Test refers to a test performed on a bacterium to determine the carcinogenicity of chemicals

50. Paddy blight affects rice and is caused by Xanthomonas oryzae

Mathematics

Q.1 The speed of a Boat in standing water is 10km/hr. It traveled Down Stream from point A to B in certain time. After reaching B the Boat is powered by Engine then Boat started to return from Point B to A. The time taken for Forward journey and Backward journey are same. Then what is the speed of the stream?

A. 2 Km/hr
B. 3 Km/hr
C. 5 Km/hrr
D. Cannot be determined

Q.2 A boat running upstream takes 8 hours 48 minutes to cover a certain distance, while it takes 4 hours to cover the same distance running downstream. What is the ratio between the speed of the boat and speed of the water current respectively?

A. 3:8   **B.** 9:5   **C.** 9:6   **D.** 8:3

Q.3 A boat takes 19 hours for travelling downstream from point A to point B and coming back to a point C which is at midway between A and B. If the velocity of the stream is 4 kmph and the speed of the boat in still water is 14 kmph, what is the distance between A and B ?

A. 30 Km   **B.** 90 Km   **C.** 100 Km   **D.** 180 Km

Q.4 555.55 + 55.55 + 15 + 0.55 + 0.05 = ?

A. 626.50   **B.** 626.70   **C.** 625.50   **D.** 626.70

Q.5 (3080 + 6160) ÷ ? = 330

A. 24   **B.** 23   **C.** 28   **D.** 27

Q.6 Rahim went shopping to buy a Mobile, the shopkeeper asked him to pay 18% Tax if he wants a bill. If not you can get 7% discount on the actual price of the mobile. Then Rahim decided not to take the bill and paid Rs. 4650. By this how much money could Rahim saved on purchasing mobile?

A. Rs.250   **B.** Rs.650   **C.** Rs.850   **D.** Rs.1250

Q.7 A seller bought 2750 Mangoes and 1210 Apples at the same price. He sells in such a way that he can buy 406 Mangoes with the sale of 322 Mangoes and he can buy only 289 Apples with the sale of 391 Apples. Then what is the overall profit percentage made by him?

A. 0%   **B.** 2%   **C.** 5%   **D.** 6%

Q.8 A car started from Indore to Bhopal at a certain speed. The Car missed an accident at 40Kms away from Indore, then the driver decided to reduce Car speed to 4/5 of the original speed. Due to this, he reached Bhopal by a late of 1hr 15min.Suppose if he missed an accident at 80Km away from Indore and from then he maintained 4/5 of original speed then he would reach Bhopal by a late of 1hour. Then what is the original speed of the Car?

A. 20 km/hr   **B.** 40 km/hr   **C.** 60 km/hr   **D.** 80 km/hr

Q.9 Two places A and B are at a certain distance. Ramu started from A towards B at a speed of 40 kmph. After 2 hours Raju started from B towards A at a speed of 60 kmph. If they meet at a place C then ratio of ratio of time taken by Raju to Ramu to reach Place C is 2:3. Then what is the distance between A and B?

A. 300 Km   **B.** 400 Km   **C.** 480 Km   **D.** 600 Km

Q.10 Ramu started from A towards B at a speed of 20Km/hr and Raju started from B towards A. They crossed each other after one hour. Raju reached his destination 5/6 hour earlier than Ramu reached his destination.Then what is the distance between A and B?

A. 40 Km   **B.** 50 Km   **C.** 60 Km   **D.** 80 Km

Q.11 The sum of the present ages of a Suresh and his son is 60 years. Five years ago, Suresh's age was four times the age of his son. What will be the age of Suresh's son?

A. 15   **B.** 17   **C.** 18   **D.** 19

Q.12 In a college, the average age of students of a class is 15.8 years. The average age of boys in the class is 16.4 years and that of the girls is 15.4 years. The ratio of number of boys to the number of girls in the class is

A. 3:5   **B.** 2:3   **C.** 2:1   **D.** 2:7

Q.13 The compound interest on a certain sum for 2 years is Rs. 786 and S.I. is Rs. 750. If the sum is invested such that the S.I. is Rs. 1296 and the number of years is equal to the rate per cent per annum, Find the rate of interest?

A. 4%   **B.** 5%   **C.** 6%   **D.** 8%

Q.14 Hari took an educational loan from a nationalized bank for his 2 years course of MBA. He took the loan of Rs.5 lakh such that he would be charged at 7% p.a. at CI during his course and at 9% CI after the completion of the course. He returned half of the amount which he had to be paid on the completion of his studies and remaining after 2 years. What is the total amount returned by Hari?

A. Rs. 626255   **B.** Rs. 626277
C. Rs. 616266   **D.** Rs. 626288

Q.15 A card from a pack of 52 cards is lost. From the remaining cards of the pack, two cards are drawn and are found to be both hearts. Find the Probability of the lost card being a heart?

A. 12/50   **B.** 8/50   **C.** 11/50   **D.** 9/50

Q.16 There are three boxes each containing 3 Pink and 5 Yellow balls and also there are 2 boxes each containing 4 Pink and 2 Yellow balls. A Yellow ball is selected at random. Find the probability that Yellow ball is from a box of the first group?

A. 42/61   **B.** 45/61   **C.** 51/61   **D.** 52/61

Q.17 In how many ways can 5 boys and 4 girls can be seated in a row so that they are in alternate position.

A. 2780   **B.** 2880   **C.** 2800   **D.** 2980

Q.18 In how many ways 5 African and five Indian can be seated along a circular table, so that they occupy alternate position.

A. 5! 5!   **B.** 4! 5!   **C.** 5! 4!   **D.** 4! 4!

Q.19 An amount of money is to be divided between P, Q and R in the ratio of 3:7:12. If the difference between the shares of P and Q is Rs.X, and the difference between Q and R's share is Rs.3000. Find the total amount of money?

A. 11000   **B.** 12400   **C.** 13200   **D.** 14300

Q.20 If a certain amount X is divided among A, B, C in such a way that A gets 2/3 of what B gets and B gets 1/3 of what C gets, which of the following is true

A. C's Share = 1053 and X = 1666
B. A's Share = 238 and X = 1638
C. B's Share = 234 and X = 1666
D. C's Share = 1053 and X = 1638

Science

Q.21 Current in the circuit will be

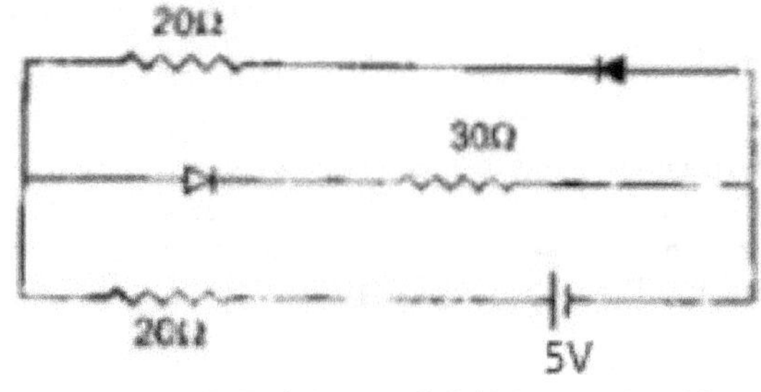

A. 5/40 A   **B.** 5/50 A   **C.** 5/10 A   **D.** 5/20 A

Q.22 The condition of a semiconductor diode can be determined quickly using

A. a digital display meter (DDM)
B. a curve tracer
C. both (A) and (B)
D. None of the above

Q.23 The ratio of change in collector current to corresponding change in base-emitter voltage depends upon

A. Geometry   **B.** Doping level
C. Biasing of transistor   **D.** All of the above

Q.24 An experiment is performed to determine the I-V characteristics of a Zener diode, which has a protective resistance of R=100 Ω, and a maximum power of dissipation rating of 1 W. The minimum voltage range of the DC source in the circuit is:

A. 0.5 V   **B.** 0- 8 V   **C.** 0-12 V   **D.** 0-24 V

Q.25 A high energy gamma ray while passing through the strong electric field of the nucleus sometimes gives rise to a particle and antiparticle. This phenomenon is called

A. Pair production   **B.** Annihilation
C. Radioactivity   **D.** Compton scattering

Q.26 Let Fpp, Fpn and Fnn denote the magnitude of the net force by a proton on a proton, by a proton on a neutron and by a neutron on a neutron respectively. Neglect gravitational force. When the separation is 1 fm, -

A. Fpp> Fpn= Fnn   **B.** Fpp = Fpn = Fnn
C. Fpp> Fpn> Fnn   **D.** Fpp< Fpn= Fnn

Q.27 Assuming that about 200 MeV of energy is released per fission of $92U235$ nuclei, then the mass of $U235$ consumed per day in a fission reactor of power 1 megawatt will approximately be -

A. 10–2g   **B.** 1 g   **C.** 100 g   **D.** 10000 g

Q.28 In one model of the electron, the electron of mass m_e is thought to be uniformly charged shell of radius R and total charge e, whose electrostatic energy E is equivalent to its mass m_e via Einstein's mass energy relation $E = m_e c^2$. In this model, R is approximately electron charge $= 1.6 \times 10^{-19} C$

A. 1.4x10-15m   **B.** 2x10-13m
C. 5.3x10-11m   **D.** 2.8x10-35m

Q.29 In a nuclear reactor 400 MeV is generated due to fission of one atom of $92U235$. Suppose we want to produce power equivalent to 3kW then what will be the number of fissions required?

A. 4.68 X 1014   **B.** 4.68 X 1012
C. 4.68 X 1011   **D.** 4.68 X 1013

Q.30 The radius of $29Cu64$ nucleus in Fermi is (given R0=1.2×10-15 m)

A. 4.8   **B.** 1.2   **C.** 7.7   **D.** 9.6

Q.31 Nuclear reactor in which uranium-235 is used as fuel, uses 2 kg of uranium-235 in 30 days. Then power output of the reactor will be (given: Energy released per fission = 185 MeV)

A. 43.5 MW   **B.** 58.5 MW
C. 69.6 MW   **D.** 73.1 MeV

Q.32 Addition polymerisation reaction mainly follows the formation of a reactive intermediate, which consist of one unpaired electron. Identify the intermediate:

A. Carbocation   **B.** Carbanion
C. Free Radical   **D.** Benzyne

Q.33

$$H_2N - \overset{\overset{\displaystyle H}{|}}{\underset{\underset{\displaystyle H}{|}}{C}} - COOH$$

glycine

The given amino acid reacts with:

A. Acid   **B.** Base
C. Both   **D.** Does not react

Q.34 The shown figure represents polymerization of a compound. Identify the polymerization reaction.

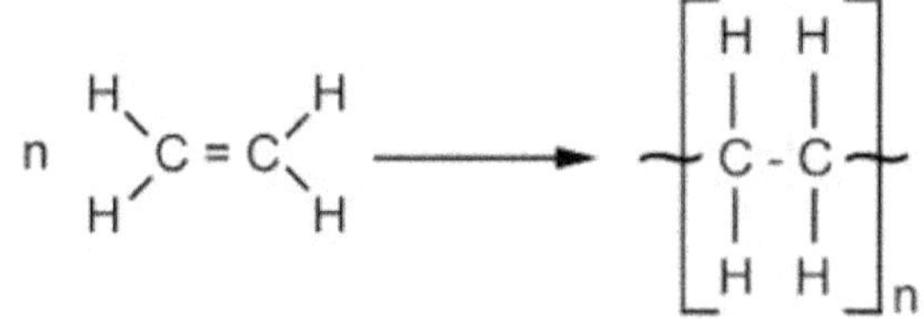

A. Condensation polymerization
B. Addition polymerization
C. Substitution
D. None of theabove

Q.35 A polymer commercially called 'SYNTHETIC WOOL' also called orlon is a homopolymer. Identify the polymer.

A. Terylene	B. Dacron
C. Polyacrylonitrile	D. Polythene

Q.36 In Zeiger Natta polymerization of ethylene, the active species is

A. AlCl3	B. Et3Al
C. CH2CH2	D. Ti3+

Q.37 Which of the following is an elastomer?

A. Vulcanized rubber	B. Dacron
C. Polystyrene	D. Malamine

Q.38 In a protein molecule various amino acids are linked together by

A. β-glycosidic bond	B. peptide bond
C. dative bond	D. ∝-glycosidic bond

Q.39 The acid that reacts with aniline in order to produce diazonium salt is:

A. Nitric acid	B. Nitrous acid
C. Nitroxide acid	D. Hydrochloric acid

Q.40 The reaction of aniline with bromine water results in formation of:
A. Bromo phenol
B. 2-bromo aniline
C. 4-bromo aniline
D. 2,4,6-tribromo aniline

General Awareness

Q.41 Which of the following country has co-sponsored 'Cobra Gold') an annual multilateral military exercise along with Thailand?

A. India	B. Indonesia
C. USA	D. China

Q.42 Takshashila University was located between which two rivers?

A. Indus and Jhelum	B. Jhelum an d Ravi
C. Beas and Indus	D. Satluj and Indus

Q.43 Which Indian sportsperson has been selected as Barbie role model?

A. Saina Nehwal	B. Dipa Karmakar
C. Mithali Raj	D. Mary Kom

Q.44 Lakshya Sen is related to which sport?

A. Badminton	B. Table Tennis
C. Hockey	D. Cricket

Q.45 Which key is used to move to next line in a Ms-Word document?

A. Enter key	B. Escape key
C. Shift key	D. Return key

Q.46 Who was the pioneer of Chipko movement of 1973?
A. Sambaji
B. Baba Amte
C. Sunderlal Bahuguna
D. Medha Patkar

Q.47 In computer terminology, what is the full form of FTP?
A. Final Transfer Position
B. File Transfer Posit ion
C. File Transfer Packet
D. File Transfer Protocol

Q.48 Which among the following is also called as 'power house of the cell'?

A. Plastids	B. Mitochondria
C. Golgi bodies	D. Cell wall

Q.49 Which company was the official sponsor for the Men's Cricket World Cup 2019?

A. VIVO	B. Apple
C. GoDaddy	D. Pepsi

Q.50 Which of the following pair is INCORRECT?
I. Parsec – Distance
II. Barrel – Liquid
III. Light year – Time

A. Only III	B. Only I and III
C. Only II	D. All are correct

// Smart Answer Sheet //

Correct Indicates percentage of students who answered questions correctly.

Skipped Indicates percentage of students who skipped questions.

Q.	Ans.	Correct / Skipped	Q.	Ans.	Correct / Skipped	Q.	Ans.	Correct / Skipped	Q.	Ans.	Correct / Skipped	Q.	Ans.	Correct / Skipped
1	D	78.75 % / 17.0 %	11	A	88.53 % / 10.21 %	21	B	77.52 % / 16.66 %	31	B	88.45 % / 10.1 %	41	C	86.57 % / 10.54 %
2	D	79.19 % / 20.19 %	12	B	80.06 % / 17.44 %	22	C	80.19 % / 15.84 %	32	C	83.85 % / 11.1 %	42	A	88.21 % / 11.71 %
3	D	79.37 % / 14.14 %	13	C	88.37 % / 10.89 %	23	D	88.9 % / 10.09 %	33	D	88.43 % / 10.99 %	43	B	84.56 % / 10.65 %
4	D	88.78 % / 10.31 %	14	D	85.31 % / 10.53 %	24	B	85.35 % / 12.16 %	34	B	88.19 % / 11.16 %	44	A	80.14 % / 14.76 %
5	C	83.14 % / 15.33 %	15	C	85.99 % / 13.75 %	25	A	85.54 % / 13.38 %	35	C	86.64 % / 13.34 %	45	A	85.98 % / 13.62 %
6	D	78.3 % / 12.62 %	16	B	85.72 % / 13.06 %	26	B	77.38 % / 15.12 %	36	D	78.85 % / 16.2 %	46	C	76.04 % / 13.56 %
7	A	81.98 % / 16.94 %	17	B	78.95 % / 12.85 %	27	B	83.75 % / 10.14 %	37	A	88.18 % / 11.1 %	47	D	82.99 % / 10.23 %
8	B	84.76 % / 13.6 %	18	B	84.88 % / 12.61 %	28	A	88.52 % / 11.05 %	38	B	89.72 % / 10.19 %	48	B	80.35 % / 10.82 %
9	C	77.01 % / 14.74 %	19	C	81.21 % / 18.32 %	29	D	87.05 % / 12.84 %	39	B	84.46 % / 12.46 %	49	C	83.54 % / 13.01 %
10	B	83.02 % / 14.7 %	20	D	79.6 % / 18.49 %	30	A	76.29 % / 14.01 %	40	D	80.22 % / 12.32 %	50	A	80.34 % / 11.97 %

Performance Analysis

Avg. Score (%)	**47.33%**
Toppers Score (%)	**72.0%**
Your Score	

//Hints and Solutions//

1. Cannot be determined

S+R = D/t ; S-R+x = D/t

S+R = S-R+x

R =x/2

2. Let the man's rate upstream be $xkmph$ and that downstream be $ykmph$. Then, distance covered upstream in 8 hrs 48 min $=$ Distance covered downstream in 4 hrs. $\Rightarrow$

$$x \times 8\frac{4}{5} = y \times 4$$
$$\Rightarrow \frac{44}{5}x = 4y$$
$$\Rightarrow y = \frac{11}{5}x$$

$\therefore$ Required ratio $= \frac{y+x}{2} : \frac{y-x}{2}$
$$= \left(\frac{16x}{5} \times \frac{1}{2}\right) : \left(\frac{6x}{5} \times \frac{1}{2}\right)$$
$$= \frac{8}{5} : \frac{3}{5}$$
$$= 8:3$$

3. Speed in downstream = (14 + 4) km/hr = 18 km/hr;

Speed in upstream = (14 – 4) km/hr = 10 km/hr.

Let the distance between A and B be x km.

Then, x/18 + (x/2)/10 = 19 $\Leftrightarrow$ x/18 + x/20 = 19 $\Rightarrow$ x = 180 km.

4. 555.55 + 55.55 + 15 + 0.55 + 0.05 = 626.70

5. 3080 + 6160 = 9240

9240 / 330 = 28

6. SP*93/100 = 4650

SP = 5000

Including tax= 5000+900

= 5900

Saving = 5900-4650

= 1250

7. Cost of 2750 Mangoes = 1210 Apples

Total cost = 2420 Apples

Given: 406 = 322(100+x/100)

x = 6/23%

Given: 289 = 391(100+y/100)

y = 6/23% loss

Overall profit:

2750 Mangoes*(100+6/23/100) +1210 Apples*(100-6/23/100) = 2420*Apples (100+P/100)

1210 Apples*(100+6/23/100) +1210 Apples*(100-6/23/100) = 2420*Apples (100+P/100)

P = 0%

8. (x+40/s) + 5/4 = 40/s + 5x/4s $—$ $—$ $—$ 1

(x+40/s) + 1 = 80/s + 5(x-40)/4s $—$ $—$ $—$ 2

s = 40 km/hr

Alternative solution :

Let, Original Speed =5x km/hr

Reduced Speed =4x km/hr

V=D/T

=> T=D/V

=> (80-40)/4x -(80-40)/5x =15/60

=> 40/4x -40/5x =1/4

=> 40/20x =1/4

=> X=8

Original Speed =5x km/hr

=40 km/hr

9. v_1 = speed of ramu = 40 km/h

v_2 = speed of raju = 60 km/h

t_1 = time of travel for ramu

t_2 = time of travel for raju

d = distance between A and B

distance between A and B is given as

d = distance traveled by ramu + distance traveled by raju

d = $v_1 t_1$ + $v_2 t_2$ eq-1

raju start after 2 hours

hence t_1 - t_2 = 2

t_1 = t_2 + 2 .... eq-2

also , ratio of times taken is given as , t_2 /t_1 = 2/3

using eq-2

$t_2 /(t_2 + 2)$ = 2/3

t_2 = 4 h

using eq-2

t_1 = t_2 + 2

t_1 = 4 + 2

t_1 = 6 h

using eq-1

d = $v_1 t_1$ + $v_2 t_2$

inserting the values

d = (40) (6) + (60)(4)

d = 480 km

so distance between A and B is 480 km

10. Total distance = AB = d+20

Ramu's speed = 20 km/hr

Ramu and Raju meet after an hour => Raju's speed = d km/hr.

Time taken by Ramu to cover d+20 km = (d+20)/20 hours

Time taken by Raju to cover d+20 km = (d+20)/d hours

Raju reaches 5/6 hrs earlier than Ram so,

(d+20)/20 - (d+20)/d = 5/6

=> 6 x (d^2 - 400) = 5 x 20d,

=> 6d^2 - 2400 = 100d;

=> 6d^2 - 100d - 2400 = 0;

=> Solving the above we get d = 30 km.

Therefore Raju's speed is 30 km/hr.

The total distance from A to B = 20+30 = 50 km.

11. Present ages of son and Suresh be x and (60 -x) years respectively.

(60 − x) − 5= 4(x − 5)

55 − x = 4x − 20

5x = 75

x = 15

12. Number of boys = x

Number of boys = y

(x*16.4 + y*15.4)/x + y = 15.8

16.4x + 15.4y = 15.8x + 15.8y

0.6x = 0.4y

x:y = 2:3

13. CI for 2 years = Rs. 786

SI for 2 years = Rs. 750

36/360 * 100 = 10%

P for first year = 3600

P*x*x/100 = 1296

x = 6%

14. 5,00,000 * (1.07)² = 572450

Returned amount = 286225

After two years = 286225 * (1.09)²

= 340063

Total amount = 286225 + 340063

= 626288

15. Total cards = 52

Drawn cards(Heart) = 2

Present total cards = total cards-drawn cards =52-2=50

Remaining Card 13-2 = 11

Probability = 11/50

16. Probability = (3/5 * 5/8)/([3/5 * 5/8] + [2/5 * 1/3]) = 45/61

17. First boys are seated in 5 position in 5! Ways, now remaining 4 places can be filled by 4 girls in 4! Ways, so number of ways = 5! 4! = 2880

18. First 5 African are seated along the circular table in (5-1)! Ways = 4!. Now Indian can be seated in 5! Ways, so 4! 5!

19. 12a-7a = 3000

5a = 3000

a = 600

7a-4a = x

3a = x

x = 1800

22*600 = 13200

20. A= 2/3 B; B= 1/3C;

A:B = 2:3 ; B:C = 1:3;

A:B:C = 2:3:9

C = 9/14 * 1638 = 1053

21. The diode in lower brance is forward and diode in upper branch is resversed biased, so

I = 5/ 20+30 = 5/50A

22. On a digital display meter with a diode checking capability appears, the small diode symbol as the bottom option of the rotating dial to check functionality of diode. The curve tracer of can display the characteristics of a host of devices, including the semiconductor diode. By properly connecting the diode to the test panel at the bottom center of the unit and adjusting the controls, the display can be obtained.

23. The trans conductance is defined as the ratio of change in collector current to corresponding change in base-emitter voltage.

$$g_m = \frac{\Delta i_c}{\Delta v_{BE}}$$

It depends upon, geometry, doping level and the biasing of transistor.

24. Zener diode or Breakdown diode is a special type of semiconductor diode which also works in reverse biased mode. When the reverse voltage applied across the zener diode is exceeds the rated voltage of the diode then Avalanche Breakdown occurs and a large amount of current flows through it. Zener diode also works as a voltage regulator.

we know that the maximum power of the circuit is

$$P_{\max} = \frac{V^2}{R}$$
$$V^2 = RP_{\max}$$

For the minimum voltage of DC source is $V_{\min} \leq \sqrt{RP_{\max}}$

$$V_{\min} \leq \sqrt{1 \times 100}$$
$$V_{\min} \leq 10$$

So the minimum voltage range of the DC source in the circuit is $0 - 8V$

25. high energy γ-ray photon while passing through strong $E^{\rightarrow}$ of nucleus

hυ →e⁺ + e⁻

positron electron

Phenomenon is pair production.

26. The nuclear forces within the given range will be charge independent and same for all three. Hence, Fpp= Fpn= Fnn

27. $200MeV = 200 \times 1.6 \times 10^{-13}J$
$= 3.2 \times 10^{-11}J/$ fission
or 3.2×10^{-11} J/Atom
power required $= 1$ Mega Watt $= 10^6 J/s$
no. of atoms required per second $\dfrac{10^6}{3.2 \times 10^{-11}}$
$= 3.125 \times 10^{16}$ atoms/sec.
no. of atoms per day $= 3.125 \times 10^6 \times 8.64 \times 10^4$
$= 2.7 \times 10^{21}$ atoms/day.
Mass consumed per day $= \dfrac{235}{6 \times 10^{23}} \times \dfrac{2.7 \times 10^{21}}{1} =$
$1.05 gram$

$= 1$ gram

28. the Einstein's mass-energy relation $E = mc^2$ the total energy of the element of the electron $= KE + PE =$
$KQ^2/2R = mc^2$
$= 9 \times 10^9 \times (1.6 \times 10^{-19})^2$
$= 9.1 \times 10^{-31} \times (3 \times 10^8)^2$
so the radius of the electron,
$R = 9 \times 10^9 \times \left(1.6 \times 10^{-19}\right)^2 / 2 \times 9.1 \times 10^{-31} \times \left(3 \times 10^8\right)^2$
$= 1.4 \times 10^{-15}$

29. The energy released per fission $= 400 \times 10^6 \times 1.6 \times 10^{-19} = 6.4 \times 10^{-11}J$
The number of fissions required per second to produce power of
$3kW$ $\dfrac{\text{Total power}}{\text{Energy released per fission}}$ $\dfrac{3000}{6.4 \times 10^{-11}}$
$= 4.68 \times 10^{13}$

30. Nuclear radius R = R0A1/3

Where R0 is a constant and A is the mass number

RCu = (1.2×10-15 m) (64)1/3

= (1.2×10-15 m) (43)1/3

= 4.8×10-15 m = 4.8 fm (∵ 1 fm=10-15 m)

31. No. of atoms in $2kg$ of uranium $= \dfrac{6.02 \times 10^{23}}{235} \times$
$2000 = 5.12 \times 10^{24}$
Energy obtained $= 5.12 \times 10^{24} \times 185MeV$
Time spent $= 30$ days $= 30 \times 24 \times 60 \times 60$sec
Energy obtained/sec $= \dfrac{5.12 \times 10^{24} \times 185 \times 10^6 \times 1.6 \times 10^{-19}}{30 \times 24 \times 60 \times 60}W$
$= 58.47 \times 10^6 watt = 58.47MW$

32. A variety of alkenes or dienes and their derivatives are polymerised in the presence of a free radical generating initiator (catalyst) like benzoyl peroxide, acetyl peroxide, tert-butyl peroxide, etc. This generates free radicals as intermediates.

33. The given amino acid is glycine. It is a neutral amino acid which does not react with both acid and base. Hence the correct answer is D.

34. The addition polymers are formed by the repeated addition of monomer molecules possessing double or triple bonds, e.g., the formation of polythene from ethene.The given molecule is ethene.

35. The addition polymerisation of acrylonitrile in presence of a peroxide catalyst leads to the formation of polyacrylonitrile. The polymer is a substitute for wool.It is called synthetic wool. The monomer is acrylonitrile and hence called polyacrylonitrile.

36. $(C_2H_5)_3Al + TiCl_4 \rightarrow$ Active species. Ti^{3+} has one active site vacant and thus accommodate one alkyl group.
$[as(C_2H_5)_3 \text{ Al reduces } TiCl_4 \text{ to } TiCl_3]$

37. Vulcanized rubber is an elastomer.

So option A is correct.

38. Two amino acids in a protein are linked by a peptide bond.

e.g. When carboxylic group of glycine combines with the amino group of alanine glycylalanine is formed.

Glycylalanine (Gly-Ala)

39. Benzenediazonium chloride is prepared by the reaction of aniline with nitrous acid at 273-278K. Nitrous acid is produced in the reaction mixture by the reaction of sodium nitrite with hydrochloric acid. The conversion of primary aromatic amines into diazonium salts is known as diazotization.

40. The reaction of bromine water with aniline is an electrophilic reaction.Since the ortho-para positions of aniline is activated, bromination results in formation of 2,4,6 tribromo aniline.

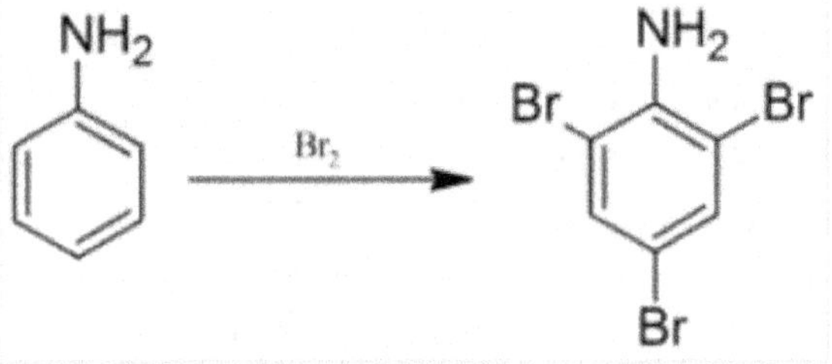

41. Cobra Gold is an Asia-Pacific military exercise held in Thailand every year. It is the largest Asia-Pacific military exercise held each year, and is among the largest multinational military exercise in which the United States participates.

Cobra Gold was first held in 1982. It served as military training exercise to improve coordination between the armed forces of the United States and Thailand in both hostile military and humanitarian efforts.

42. World's first university was established in Takshila. Taxila also known as Takshashila, flourished from 600 BC to 500 AD, in the kingdom of Gandhar. 68 subjects were taught at this university and the minimum entry age, ancient texts show, was 16. The panel of masters at the university included legendary scholars like Kautilya, Panini, Jivak and Vishnu Sharma. Thus, the concept of a full-fledged university was developed in India.

43. In celebration of International Women's Day (IWD-2019) and its 60th anniversary, American toymaker Mattel has released a new range of barbies to honor 20 female role models across 18 countries speaking 14 different languages. Indian gymnast Dipa Karmakar has been selected as a Barbie Role Model to help inspire the next generatio

44. Young Indian shuttlers Lakshya Sen and Riya Mookerjee broke into the top-100 among Men's and Women's singles players in the latest World Badminton Rankings. Making a massive jump of 28 places, Lakshya Sen is placed 76th. Riya Mookerjee climbed up 19 spots to be placed 94th. In the women's singles rankings, P V Sindhu and Saina Nehwal are static with Sindhu at sixth and Saina at ninth position. Among men, B Sai Praneeth also moved up three places to 19th. Kidambi Srikanth remains static and is the best placed Indian in the men's rankings at seventh.

45. On computer keyboards, the enter key in most cases causes a command line, window form, or dialog box to operate its default function. This is typically to finish an "entry" and begin the desired process, and is usually an alternative to pressing an OK button.

46. Sunderlal Bahuguna (born 9 January 1927) is a noted Garhwali environmentalist, Chipko movement leader and a follower of Mahatma Gandhi's philosophy of Non-violence and Satyagraha. This idea of chipko movement was of his wife and the action was taken by him. For years he has been fighting for the preservation of forests in the Himalayas, first as a member of the Chipko movement in the 1970s, and later spearheaded the Anti-Tehri Dam movement starting 1980s, to early 2004.

47. The File Transfer Protocol (FTP) is the standard network protocol used for the transfer of computer files between a client and server on a computer network.

FTP is built on a client-server model architecture and uses separate control and data connections between the client and the server.[

The first FTP client applications were command-line programs developed before operating systems had graphical user interfaces, and are still shipped with most Windows, Unix, and Linux operating systems.

48. The mitochondrion (plural mitochondria) is a double membrane-bound organelle found in all eukaryotic organisms. Some cells in some multicellular organisms may however lack them (for example, mature mammalian red blood cells). A number of unicellular organisms, such as microsporidia, parabasalids, and diplomonads, have also reduced or transformed their mitochondria into other structures.

The most prominent roles of mitochondria are to produce the energy currency of the cell, ATP (i.e., phosphorylation of ADP), through respiration, and to regulate cellular metabolism. The central set of reactions involved in ATP production are collectively known as the citric acid cycle, or the Krebs cycle.

49. The website hosting company GoDaddy was the official sponsor of the Men's Cricket World Cup along with the International Cricket Council (ICC).
England were declared winners of the Cricket World Cup 2019 after a tied match and Super Over against New Zealand on account of the superior number of boundaries hit by the hosts.

50. The light-year is a unit of length used to express astronomical distances. It is about 9.5 trillion kilometers or 5.9 trillion miles. As defined by the International Astronomical Union (IAU), a light-year is the distance that light travels in vacuum in one Julian year (365.25 days). Because it includes the word "year", the term light-year is sometimes misinterpreted as a unit of time.

The light-year is most often used when expressing distances to stars and other distances on a galactic scale, especially in non-specialist and popular science publications.

Mathematics

Q.1 A man can row 30km upstream and 44km downstream in 10 hrs. It is also known that he can row 40km upstream and 55km downstream in 13 hrs. Find the speed of the man in still water.

A. 7.5 km/h   **B.** 8 km/h   **C.** 7 km/h   **D.** 8.5 km/h

Q.2 A boat, while going downstream in a river covered a distance of 50 miles at an average speed of 60 miles per hour. While returning, because of the water resistance, it took 1 hr 15 minutes to cover the same distance. What was the average speed during the whole journey?

A. 45 miles/h   **B.** 52 miles/h
C. 48 miles/h   **D.** 46 miles/h

Q.3 $184 \div 46 \div 0.008 \div 12.5 = ?$

A. 30   **B.** 40   **C.** 60   **D.** 80

Q.4 $(4270 \div 122) + ? = 200$

A. 165   **B.** 155   **C.** 175   **D.** 185

Q.5 A shopkeeper marks up his goods by 20% and then gives a discount of 20%. Besides he cheats both his supplier and customer by 100 g, i.e., he takes 1100 g from his supplier and sells only 900 g to his customer. What is his net profit percentage? (Rounded off to two decimal points)

A. 24.5%   **B.** 17.33%   **C.** 25%   **D.** 32.5%

Q.6 Some mangoes are purchased at the rate of 8 mangoes/Rs and some more mangoes at the rate of 6 mangoes/Rs, investment being equal in both the cases. Now, the whole quantity is sold at the rate of 3.5 mangoes/Rs What is the net percentage profit/loss?

A. 100% profit   **B.** 60% loss
C. 80% loss   **D.** no profit/no loss

Q.7 A train travelling at 48 kmph crosses another train, having half of its length and travelling in opposite direction at 42 kmph, in 12 seconds. It also passes a railway platform in 45 seconds. The length of railway platform is:

A. 400 m   **B.** 500 m
C. 660 m   **D.** None of these

Q.8 The train traveling at 50 km/h overtakes a motorbike traveling at 32 km/h in 80 s. What is the length of the train in meters?

A. 400   **B.** 800   **C.** 777   **D.** 111

Q.9 Leena's age is 5 years more than twice Gayathri's age. Vijay's age is 13 years less than 10 times Gayathri's age. If Vijay is 3 times as old as Leena, how old is Leena?

A. 17   **B.** 16   **C.** 12   **D.** 19

Q.10 8 years ago, Geeta was half as old as Saina. Saina is now 20 years older than Geeta. How old will Geeta be in 10 years?

A. 45   **B.** 40   **C.** 35   **D.** 38

Q.11 A man gave 50% of his savings of Rs. 168200 to his wife and divided the remaining sum among his sons Abid and Bisth of 15 and 13 years of age respectively. He divided it in such away that each of his sons when they attain the age of 18 years, would receive the same amount of 5% compound interest per annum. The share of Bisth was:

A. Rs. 50,000   **B.** Rs. 42,000
C. Rs. 40,000   **D.** Rs. 48,000

Q.12 A certain sum is interested at compound. The interest accrued in the first two years is Rs. 544 and that in the first three years is Rs. 868. Find the rate per cent.

A. 12 .5%   **B.** 7 .5%   **C.** 17 .5%   **D.** 25%

Q.13 Initially, Suresh has Rs.200 in his paytm wallet then he increased it by 20%. Once again he increased his amount by 25%. The final value of money in his wallet will be how much % greater than the initial amount?

A. 40%   **B.** 50%   **C.** 80%   **D.** 60%

Q.14 Mr.Ramesh gives 10% of some amount to his wife and 10% of the remaining to hospital expenses and again 10% of the remaining amount to charity. Then he has only Rs.7290 with him. What is the initial sum of money with that person

A. Rs.8000   **B.** Rs.9000
C. Rs.10000   **D.** Rs.20000

Q.15 Suppose children like three types of chocolates Perk, Munch, and 5Star. If they are asked to choose to pick chocolate they have their own preference, one-sixth of children population preference is Perk>Munch>5star. One-sixth of children population preference is Munch>5star>Perk. Similarly remaining four-sixths children preferences follows as per above combinations. If you met a random child and give him chance to pick a chocolate between Munch and Perk. He picked Munch. Now you offer Munch and 5star, what is the probability that he chooses again Munch?

A. 1/6   **B.** 1/2   **C.** 2/3   **D.** 3/4

Q.16 A bag contains 100 tickets, numbered from 1 to 100. If three tickets are picked at random and with replacement, what is the probability that sum of three numbers on the tickets will even number?

A. 1/2   **B.** 3/4   **C.** 1/8   **D.** 3/8

Q.17 There are 6 players in a cricket which is to be sent to Australian tour. The total number of members is 12.

If 2 particular member is always included

A. 210   **B.** 270   **C.** 310   **D.** 420

Q.18 There are 6 players in a cricket which is to be sent to Australian tour. The total number of members is 12.

If 3 particular player is always excluded

A. 76   **B.** 82   **C.** 84   **D.** 88

Q.19 Four friends A, B, C, and D have some money among them, they decided to equate the money, so first A gave B what B had initially, now B gave C what C had initially. Again C gave D what D had initially and finally, D gave what A had now. Thus each of them had an equal sum of Rs.48. Then what amount does A have initially?

A. 48   **B.** 60   **C.** 69   **D.** 72

Q.20 A,B,C, and D are four numbers if B is more than A, D is 10 more than B, C is 5 less than D, A is 10 less than C. Then ratio of A: B: C: D is?

A. 1:2:3:4
B. 1:2:4:5
C. 1:3:4:1
D. Cannot be determined

Science

Q.21 The spectrum of He is expected to be similar to that of

A. H   **B.** Na   **C.** He^+ **D.** Li^+

Q.22 What will be the geometry of a molecule with dsp^2 or sp^2d hybridisation?

A. Octahedral
B. Square planar
C. Tetrahedral
D. Trigonal bipyramidal

Q.23 Which of the following is correct for Hydrochloride gas?

A. It is an ionic compound
B. It is a covalent compound.
C. Both 1 and 2
D. None of these

Q.24 Methane is a/an

A. ionic compound   **B.** covalent compound
C. Both 1and 2   **D.** None of these

Q.25 Which of the following is mostly used as a reference electrode?

A. $ZnCl_2$ **B.** $CuSO_4$ **C.** Na_2SO_3 **D.** Hg_2Cl_2

Q.26 During the measurement of EMF of a half cell using a reference electrode and a salt bridge, if the salt bridge is removed, then the voltage

A. remains unchanged
B. decreases to half the previous value
C. increases to its maximum value
D. drops to zero or becomes negative

Q.27 Equilibrium constant of a reaction is related to

A. pressure
B. standard free energy change Δ G°
C. volume
D. None of the above

Q.28 For the reaction: $N_2O_4(g) \rightleftharpoons 2NO_2(g)$, the vapour density of the mixture at 1 atmospheric pressure is 34.5 The degree of dissociation is:

A. 0.5   **B.** 0.25   **C.** 0.53   **D.** 0.75

Q.29 Which of the following polymers contains nitrogen?

A. PVC   **B.** Teflon
C. Nylon   **D.** Polyester

Q.30 Write the chemical name of melamine.

A. 1,3,5-triazine-2,4,6-triamine
B. 2,4,6-triamine-1,3,5-triazine
C. Acrylonitrile
D. Benzene-1,3,5-triamine

Q.31 The monomers used to synthesize proteins are called:

A. Nucleotides   **B.** Fatty acids
C. Amino acids   **D.** Sugars

Q.32 A nucleoside does not contains

A. Nitrogenous base   **B.** Phosphate group
C. Pentose sugar   **D.** None of these

Q.33 Cannizzaro reaction is not given by

A. trimethylacetaldehyde
B. acetaldehyde
C. benzaldehyde
D. formaldehyde

Q.34 Benzene reacts with CH_3COCl in the presence of anhydrous $AlCl_3$ to give

A. $C_6H_5CH_3$ **B.** C_6H_5Cl
C. C_6H_5OCl **D.** $C_6H_5COCH_3$

Q.35 The half-life of ^{131}I is 8 days. Given a sample of ^{131}I at time t=0, we can assert that

A. no nucleus will decay before t = 4 days
B. no nucleus will decay before t = 8 days
C. all nuclei will decay before t = 16 days
D. a given nucleus may decay any time after t = 0

Q.36 A radioactive nuclide can decay simultaneously by two different processes, which have individual decay constants λ_1 and λ_2 . The effective decay constant of the nuclide (λ) is given by

A. $\lambda_p = \lambda_1 + \lambda_2$ **B.** $\frac{1}{\lambda} = \frac{1}{\lambda_1} + \frac{1}{\lambda_2}$
C. $\lambda = \frac{1}{2}(\lambda_1 + \lambda_2)$ **D.** none of above

Q.37 The binding energies for nuclei $_1H^1$, $_2He^4$, $_{26}Fe^{56}$ and $_{92}U^{235}$ are 2.22, 28.4, 492 and 17.86 MeV, respectively. The most stable nucleus is

A. $_1H^1$ **B.** $_2He^4$ **C.** $_{26}Fe^{56}$ **D.** $_{92}U^{235}$

Q.38 The binding energy per nucleon of $_1H^2$ is 1.1 MeV and binding energy per nucleon of $_2He^4$ is 7 MeV. The energy released when two $_1H^2$ combine to form $_2He^4$ is

A. 6.8 MeV   **B.** 30.2 MeV
C. 23.6 MeV   **D.** None of these

Q.39 The pressure and density of a diatomic gas $\left(\gamma = \frac{7}{5}\right)$ change adiabatically from (P_1, ρ_1) to (P_2, ρ_2) If $\frac{\rho_2}{\rho_1} = 32$, then $\frac{P_2}{P_1}$ should be

A. 16　　　　**B.** 32　　　　**C.** 64　　　　**D.** 128

Q.40 If there is a straight line parallel to volume axis in a P-V diagram, then it is an ___ graph.

A. isochoric

B. isobaric

C. isothermal

D. None of these

General Awareness

Q.41 What could be the main reason that the sun never 'rises' on 22 December at the Arctic Circle?

1. Earth's inclination to the plane of the ecliptic

2. Earth's rotation about its axis

3. Earth's revolution around the Sun

Which of the statements given above is/are correct in this context?

A. Only 1

B. Only 1 and 2

C. Only 1 and 3

D. Only 2 and 3

Q.42 The Matatilla Multipurpose Project is on the river -

A. Krishna　　**B.** Sutlej　　**C.** Rihand　　**D.** Betwa

Q.43 Who was the Viceroy of India when the University Commission was appointed?

A. Lord Ripon

B. Lord Curzon

C. Lord Wavell

D. Lord Irwin

Q.44 In which state is the Jaldapara Sanctuary located?

A. Assam

B. Odisha

C. West Bengal

D. Jharkhand

Q.45 Consider the following features of an image being formed on a convex lens –

1. Image is real and inverted

2. Image is enlarged

Where is the object placed?

A. Between Optical Centre and F

B. At F

C. Between F and 2F

D. Beyond 2F

Q.46 Which of the following will have the highest pH?

A. Gastric juice

B. Sea water

C. Saliva

D. Pancreatic juice

Q.47 The Government has recently launched an Online Film Certification System. Choose the option/s that are correct:-

A. Now a short-film of 15 minutes won't need to be examined at the Examining Theatre

B. However, even a 2 minute trailer of a full-length feature film will have to be taken to the Examining Theatre

C. The applicant will be informed status of their application by SMS/e-mail

D. All of the above

Q.48 What are the organisms called which change their body temperature according to the surrounding?

A. Sphygothermic

B. Poikilothermic

C. Homeothermic

D. Hypothermic

Q.49 When the Portugese first arrived in India, what was the place that they had chosen to be their capital/headquarter?

A. Calicut

B. Cannanore

C. Goa

D. Cochin

Q.50 From which country's Constitution has the rule of nominating members to the Rajya Sabha by the President been taken into the Indian Constitution?

A. Britain　　**B.** USA　　**C.** Canada　　**D.** Ireland

// Smart Answer Sheet //

| Correct | Indicates percentage of students who answered questions correctly. |

| Skipped | Indicates percentage of students who skipped questions. |

Q.	Ans.	Correct / Skipped	Q.	Ans.	Correct / Skipped	Q.	Ans.	Correct / Skipped	Q.	Ans.	Correct / Skipped	Q.	Ans.	Correct / Skipped
1	B	84.91 % / 12.97 %	11	C	88.47 % / 10.02 %	21	D	81.1 % / 13.45 %	31	C	82.88 % / 15.94 %	41	C	76.7 % / 12.03 %
2	C	78.95 % / 12.24 %	12	A	77.57 % / 21.15 %	22	B	80.43 % / 11.83 %	32	B	89.56 % / 10.11 %	42	D	87.75 % / 11.14 %
3	B	76.25 % / 21.31 %	13	B	89.04 % / 10.91 %	23	B	79.89 % / 18.55 %	33	B	86.48 % / 12.28 %	43	B	77.12 % / 19.15 %
4	A	86.7 % / 10.34 %	14	C	80.1 % / 13.12 %	24	B	87.18 % / 12.57 %	34	D	79.18 % / 16.61 %	44	C	79.87 % / 15.02 %
5	B	85.25 % / 13.82 %	15	C	80.93 % / 18.98 %	25	D	76.73 % / 10.36 %	35	D	81.7 % / 12.52 %	45	C	89.75 % / 10.21 %
6	A	78.04 % / 12.71 %	16	A	78.39 % / 15.87 %	26	D	83.82 % / 15.66 %	36	A	79.39 % / 10.07 %	46	D	76.52 % / 11.67 %
7	A	81.38 % / 13.62 %	17	A	81.82 % / 10.03 %	27	D	76.45 % / 17.53 %	37	C	86.67 % / 10.76 %	47	C	81.12 % / 13.43 %
8	A	78.01 % / 12.3 %	18	C	87.52 % / 11.01 %	28	C	76.21 % / 12.44 %	38	C	81.37 % / 18.39 %	48	B	79.05 % / 14.7 %
9	D	82.88 % / 16.05 %	19	C	83.46 % / 15.7 %	29	C	82.47 % / 10.54 %	39	D	78.23 % / 20.91 %	49	D	82.41 % / 13.09 %
10	D	77.58 % / 16.47 %	20	D	79.62 % / 13.9 %	30	A	80.57 % / 11.71 %	40	B	82.22 % / 15.55 %	50	D	81.65 % / 17.7 %

Performance Analysis

Avg. Score (%)	71.33%
Toppers Score (%)	72.67%
Your Score	

//Hints and Solutions//

1. ATQ

$$\frac{30}{a-r} + \frac{44}{a+r} = 10 \dots (i)$$

$$\frac{40}{(a-r)} + \frac{55}{a+r} = 13 \dots (ii)$$

Solving (i) $\&(ii), a = 8, r = 3$

Hence, speed of man in still water $= 8km/hr$

2. Average speed $= \frac{50+50}{\frac{50}{60}+\frac{75}{60}} = \frac{100\times60}{125} = 48miles/hr$

3. $184 \div 46 = 4; 4 \div 0.008 = 500; 500 \div 12.5 = 40$

4. $4270 \div 122 = 35$

$200 - 35 = 165$

5. Let initial $CP = 100Rs$

When the shopkeeper cheats from manufacturer then he will get 110 units in the price of 100 units

$\therefore$ profit $\% = \frac{10}{100} \times 100 = 10\%$

$\therefore$ New price $= Rs.\,110Rs$ Now $MP = 132$

$SP = 132 - 26.4 = 105.60$

Now the shopkeeper cheats from the customer If he sells 100 units then he will get a profit of 10 units

. profit $\% = \frac{10}{90} \times 100 = \frac{100}{90}$

$\therefore$ New $SP = \left(100 + \frac{100}{30}\right) \times \frac{1}{100} \times 105.60$

$= \frac{10}{9} \times 105.60 = \frac{1056}{9}$

$-117.33Rs$

$\therefore$ his net profit $\% = 17.33\%$

6. Let 1 Rs. invested in both the cases

$\therefore$ in 2 Rs. no. of mangoes Purchased $= 8 + 6 = 14$

SP of 14 mangoes $= 14 \times \frac{1}{3.5} = 4Rs$

$\therefore$ 100% profit.

7. Let the length of the train traveling at 48 kmph be $2x$ meters. And length of the platform is y meters. Relative speed of train

$= (48 + 42)kmph$

$= \frac{90\times5}{18}$

$= 25m/sec$

And $48kmph$

$= \frac{48\times5}{18}$

$= \frac{40}{3}m/sec$

According to the question, $\frac{2x+x}{25} = 12$

Or, $3x = 12 \times 25 = 300$

Or, $x = \frac{300}{3} = 100m$

Then, length of the train

$= 2x$

$= 100 \times 2 = 200m$

$\frac{200+y}{\frac{40}{3}} = 45$

$600 + 3y = 40 \times 45$

Or, $3y = 1800 - 600$

$= 1200$

$Or, 3y = 1800 - 600$

$= 1200$

$Or, y = \frac{1200}{3} = 400m$

Length of the platform

$= 400m$

8. since both are moving in same direction so their speed must be subtracted.

As we know, speed $= \frac{distance}{time}$ (where distance will be the train of the length)

Length of train $= (50 - 32) \times \frac{5}{18} \times 80$

$-400m$

9. given l = 2g+5

v = 10g-13

v=3l

from v=3l

=> 10g-13 = 6g+15

g = 7

l= 2g+5 = 19

10. Saina is now 20 years older than Geeta –> S=G+20 –> Saina 8 years ago was G+20-8=G+12 years old.

(G-8)*2=G+12 –> G=28. 28+10=38 years.

11. Total share of Abid and Bisth $= 84100$ Rs

Let share of Abid $= x$ Share of Bisth $= 84100 - x$

$$x \times \left(1 + \frac{5}{100}\right)^3 = (84100 - x)\left(1 + \frac{5}{100}\right)^5$$

$x = 44100$

Share of $Bisth = 84100 - 44100 = Rs \cdot 40000$

12. $544 = P\left[\left(1 + \frac{R}{100}\right)^2 - 1\right]$

$868 = P\left[\left(1 + \frac{R}{100}\right)^3 - 1\right]$

$(2) \div (1)$

$\frac{q^3-1}{q^2-1} = \frac{868}{544}, q = \left(1 + \frac{R}{100}\right)$

$\frac{q^2+q+1}{q+1} = \frac{217}{136}$, solving the eq^n

$q = \frac{9}{8}, 1 + \frac{R}{100} = \frac{9}{8}$

$R = 12.5\%$

13. $200 + 20\%$ of $200 = 240$

$240 + 25\%$ of $240 = 300$

Required percentage = 300 – 200/200 * 100 = 50%

14. Remaining amount = x * 0.9 * 0.9 * 0.9

0.729x = 7290

x = 10000

15. Possible preferences

P>M>5

M>5>P

P>5>M

M>P>5

5>P>M

5>M>P

Child picks Munch over Perk P(M5P), P(MP5) or P(5MP)

Then child prefers Munch over 5star P(M5P) P(MP5)

Probability = (1/6+1/6)/(1/6+1/6+1/6) =2/3

16. P(odd) = P(even) = 1/2

Sum of three numbers to be even cases

Even+ even+ even = 1/2*1/2*1/2

Even+ odd+ odd = 1/2*1/2*1/2

Odd+ odd + even = 1/2*1/2*1/2

Odd+ even + odd = 1/2*1/2*1/2

Probability = 1/8+1/8+1/8+1/8 = 1/2

17. If 2 particular member is always included,
So, Only 4 players to select from 10 players, So it can be done in
$^{10}C_4$ = 210

18. 6 players to be selected from remaining 9 players in $^9C_6$ = 84 ways

19. A B C D

A-B B+B C D

A-B B+B-C C+C D

A-B 2B-C 2C-D 2D

2(A-B) 2B-C 2C-D 2D-(A-B)

48 48 48 48

2(A-B) =48

A-B =24

2D-(A-B) =48

2D = 72 D =36

2C-D = 48 C = 42

2B-C = 48 B =45

A-B = 24 A =69

20. From the above values of A, B, C and D cannot be determined

21. No. of electrons in $Li^+ \& He = 2$. Therefore the spectrum will be same for both of them with same no. of electrons.

22. A molecule with dsp² or sp²d hybridization will have a square planar geometry.

The dsp² hybrid orbitals are inner orbital complexes in which the electrons get paired up due to the presence of a strong field ligand. So, the electron pairs of the ligands occupy one d orbital, one s orbital and then 2 p orbitals in a square planar geometry. Xef₂ is linear, but it is sp³ hybridization.

23. HCl is not an ionic compound it is a **covalent bond**. This is because **chlorine** and hydrogen share an electron in HCl making it a **covalent bond**

24. Carbon atom has four electrons in its valence shell. In order to complete its octet, it shares four electrons one each with hydrogen atoms and thus covalent bond is formed

25. The saturated calomel **electrode** (SCE) is a **reference electrode** based on the reaction between elemental mercury and mercury(I) chloride. ... The aqueous phase in contact with the mercury and the mercury(I) chloride (Hg₂Cl₂, "calomel") is a saturated solution of potassium chloride in water

26. If you remove the salt bridge, the circuit of the voltaic cell will be cut and the voltage will go to zero instantly. Opening or cutting the circuit by removing the salt bridge stops all Galvanic chemical reactions instantly

27. Equilibrium constant depends on temperature and is independent of the actual quantities of reactants and products, the presence of a catalyst and the presence of inert material. It is also independent of concentrations, pressures and volumes of reactants and products.
Definition of equilibrium constant. : a number that expresses the relationship between the amounts of products and reactants present at equilibrium in a reversible chemical reaction at a given temperature.

28. The relationship between molar mass and vapour density is
Molar mass $= 2 \times$ vapour density
$$= 2 \times 30 \quad = 60$$
$$N_2O_4 \qquad NO_2$$
Moles at equilibrium $1 - \alpha, \qquad 2\alpha$ Mole fraction
$$\left(\frac{1-\alpha}{1+\alpha}\right)\left(\frac{2\alpha}{1+\alpha}\right)$$
Thus $92\left(\frac{1-\alpha}{1+\alpha}\right) + 46\left(\frac{2\alpha}{1+\alpha}\right) = 60$
$$\alpha = 0.533$$

29.

- Nylon is made when the appropriate monomers (the chemical building blocks which make up polymers) are combined to form a long chain via a condensation polymerisation reaction.

- The monomers for nylon 6-6 are adipic acid and hexamethylene diamine. The two molecules are combined to create the polymer and water (H2O) is produced as a by-product.

- The water is removed from the production process as its continued presence stops the creation of more polymer.
- The polymer chain can be made up of over 20,000 monomer units, connected together via an amide group, which contains a nitrogen atom.

30. 1,3,5-Triazine-2,4,6-triamine is the chemical name for melamine.

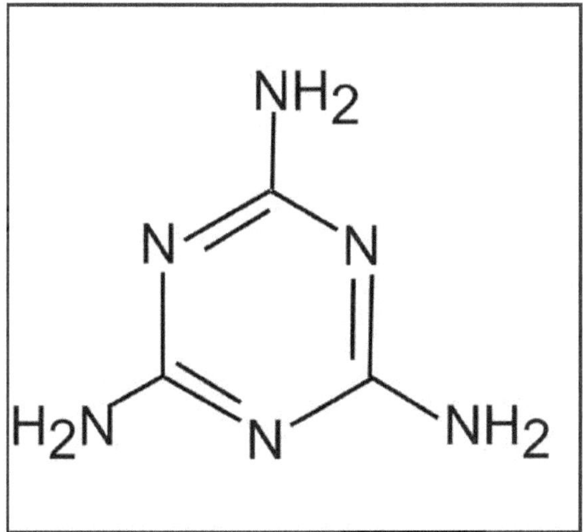

31. For proteins, the monomers are amino acids. Polymerization occurs at ribosomes. Usually about 20 types of amino acid monomers are used to produce proteins.

32. A nucleoside is a compound that contains a nitrogenous-base bound to a deoxyribose or a ribose sugar.It does not contain phosphate group. It occurs when nucleic acids are hydrolyzed or broken down.

33. The **Cannizzaro reaction is not given** by Acetaldehyde. Aldehydes that contains alpha hydrogen atoms are not involved in Cannizzaro reaction and aldehyde like acetaldehyde contains alpha hydrogen in it. So, that's why it can't participate or involve in this reaction.

34. The given reaction is Friedel-Craft's acylation reaction. In this reaction, the acyl group substitutes one of the hydrogen atoms on benzene to form acetophenone.

35. At time t=0 the nuclei starts to decay and at any time after that some of the nuclei may have decayed. Up to time t=8 days, about half the initial number of the nucleus have decayed and up to 16 days, only one-fourth of the initial number of the nucleus are left undecayed.

36. Equation for parallel disintegration can be written as

$$-\frac{dN_X}{dt} = \lambda_1 N_X + \lambda_2 N_X$$

$$\Rightarrow -\frac{dN_X}{dt} = (\lambda_1 + \lambda_2)N_X$$

Effective decay in parallel disintegration is given by $\lambda_p = \lambda_1 + \lambda_2$

37. Binding energy/nucleon is maximum for e^{56}, hence it is most stable element.

$$_2He^4 \rightarrow{}_1 H^2 +{}_1 H^2$$

No. of nucleon $=$ No of protons $+$ No of neutrons

Mass of $_2He^4 = 4 \times 7$

Mass of $_1H^2 = 2 \times 1.1$

38. Energy released $= 4 \times 7 - 2(2 \times 1.1) = 23.6 MeV$

39. For an adiabatic process,

$PV^\gamma = $ constant

$P\rho^{-\gamma} = $ constant

$$\frac{P_2}{P_1} = \left(\frac{\rho_1}{\rho_2}\right)^{-\gamma} = \left(\frac{1}{32}\right)^{-7/5} = (32)^{7/5} = 128$$

Hence Option D is correct option.

40. It is an Isobaric graph

An Isobaric process is a thermodynamic process in which the pressure stays constant: ΔP = 0. The heat transferred to the system does work, but also changes the internal energy of the system. Using this convention, by the first law of thermodynamics, where W is work, U is internal energy, and Q is heat.

41. The earth is tilted with respect to the plane of the ecliptic. As the earth revolves around the Sun, on 22 December, the earth tilts in such a way that the North Pole is at the farthest from the Sun and thus the Sun never 'rises' on 22 December at the Arctic Circle.

42. The Matatilla Multipurpose Project is on the river Betwa in the states of Uttar Pradesh and Madhya Pradesh

43. Lord Curzon was the Viceroy of India when the University Commission was appointed in 1902. It was formed to study the universities and introduce reforms.

44. The Jaldapara Sanctuary is in West Bengal and is famous for its tigers, leopards, sambhers, chitals.

45. For a convex lens the image is enlarged only when the object is placed either between Optical Centre and F or between F and 2F. However in the former case, the image formed is virtual and erect, hence the object is in between F and 2F

46. Pancreatic juice will have the highest pH out of these.

47. Examining short-films/trailers etc. having duration of less than 2 minutes can be done online. It needn't be sent to the Examining Theatre

48. Poikilothermic are organisms which change their body temperature according to the surrounding.

49. Vasco da Gama reached the port of Calicut in May 17, 1498. However Cochin was selected as the headquarters for their trade.

50. The rule of nominating members to the Rajya Sabha by the President was taken from the Constitution of Ireland

Mathematics

Q.1 What value should replace the question mark (?) in the following question?

12.5 × 14 ÷ 8.75 + 12 = 20 + ?

A. 14 **B.** 11 **C.** 12 **D.** 18

Q.2 What value should replace the question mark (?) in the following question?

? * (523.5 + 687.5) = 24220

A. 10 **B.** 15 **C.** 17 **D.** 20

Q.3 A boat went down the river for a distance of 20 km. It then turned back and returned to its starting point, having travelled a total of 7 hours. On its return trip, at a distance of 12 km from the starting point it encountered a log which had passed the starting point at the moment at which the boat had started downstream. The downstream speed of the boat is

A. 10.5 km/h **B.** 12 km/h

C. 8 km/h **D.** 10 km/h

Q.4 Two boats go downstream from point X to point Y. The faster boat covers the distance from X to Y 1.5 times as fast as the slower boat. It is known that for every hour the slower boat lags behind the faster boat by 8 km. However if they go upstream then the faster boat covers the distance from Y to X in half the time as the slower boat. Find the speed of the slower boat in still water?

A. 8 km/h **B.** 10 km/h **C.** 14 km/h **D.** 12 km/h

Q.5 A seller calculated his intended selling price at 6% profit on the cost of a product. However, owing to some mistake while selling, the units and tens digits of the selling price got interchanged. This reduced the profit by Rs. 180 and profit percentage to 2.4%. What is the cost price of the product?

A. Rs. 4500 **B.** Rs. 5000 **C.** Rs. 4750 **D.** Rs. 6000

Q.6 Jim sells a book to Carrey at a profit of 20% and Carrey sells this book to Sid at a profit of 25%. Now Sid sells this book at a loss of 10% to Simba. At what percentage loss should Simba sells this book now so that his SP becomes equal to Jim's CP?

A. 26.68%

B. 25.92%

C. 58.66

D. Cannot be determined

Q.7 Train X starts at 7.00 a.m. from a certain station with A Km/h and train Y starts at 9.30 a.m. from the same station at B km/h. If B > A, then how many hours will train Y take to overtake train X?

A. 5A/(2(B-A)) hrs **B.** 2A/(5(B-A)) hrs

C. (2(B-A))/5A hrs **D.** (5(B-A))/2A hrs

Q.8 The average speed of a train is 20% less on the return journey than on the onward journey. The train halts for an hour at the destination station before starting on the return journey. If the total time taken for the to and fro journey is 46 hrs, covering a distance of 2000 km, the speed of the train on the return journey is:

A. 50 km/h **B.** 40 km/h **C.** 60 km/h **D.** 65km/h

Q.9 Mr. X has three sons namely P, Q and R. P is the eldest son of Mr. X while R is the youngest one. The present ages of all three of them are square numbers. The sum of their ages after 5 years is 44. What is the age of P after three years?

A. 1 **B.** 19 **C.** 9 **D.** 16

Q.10 Sum of the twice the age of Surya and his Father age is 79. Sum of the twice the age of Father and Surya's age is 104. The average of Surya, his Father and his Mother is 32. Then what is the age of his Mother?

A. 32 **B.** 33 **C.** 34 **D.** 35

Q.11 Rs. 12200 was partly invested in Scheme A at 10% p.a. compound interest (compounded annually) for 2 years and partly in Scheme B at 10% p.a. simple interest for 4 years. Both the schemes give equal interests. How much was invested in Scheme A ?

A. Rs. 7500 **B.** Rs. 9000 **C.** Rs. 8000 **D.** Rs. 6050

Q.12 A man borrows Rs. 8000 at 20% compound rate of interest. At the end of each year he pays back Rs. 3000. How much amount should he pay at the end of the third year to clear all his dues?

A. Rs. 5492 **B.** Rs. 5552 **C.** Rs. 5904 **D.** Rs. 6933

Q.13 In a library 60% of the books are in Hindi, 60% of the remaining books are in English rest of the books are in Malayalam. If there are 4800 books in English, then the total number of books in Malayalam are?

A. 3400 **B.** 3500 **C.** 3100 **D.** 3200

Q.14 80% of a small number is 4 less than 40% of a larger number. The larger number is 125 greater than the smaller one. The sum of these two numbers is

A. 325 **B.** 345 **C.** 355 **D.** 365

Q.15 Anil placed a deck of 52 cards. If you pick two cards what is the probability that both are aces?

A. 1/169 **B.** 1/221 **C.** 1/338 **D.** 4/663

Q.16 Continuation of question of 5: if Anil fails to draw aces in two chances. Now he is given ten more chances to pick aces, again he failed. Then his friend Ramesh picks two cards from remaining cards, then what is the probability that he exactly draws one ace?

A. 0.075 **B.** 0.0923 **C.** 0.15 **D.** 0.1846

Q.17 There are 15 points in a plane out of which 6 are collinear. Find the number of lines that can be formed from 15 points.

A. 105 **B.** 90 **C.** 91 **D.** 95

Q.18 In how many ways 4 Indians, 5 Africans and 7 Japanese be seated in a row so that all person of same nationality sits together

A. 4! 5! 7! 3!

B. 4! 5! 7! 5!

C. 4! 6! 7! 3!

D. can't be determined

Q.19 In the year 2013, in a company the ratio of employees in three different departments HR, MT and TA are 2:3:4 respectively. In the year 2014 in each department if 'n' number of employees left then the ratio becomes 3:5:7. In the year 2015 in each department 5 employees left then the ratio became 1:2:3. Then what is the total number of employees in the year 2014?

A. 70

B. 72

C. 75

D. 78

Q.20 In a horse racing, there are three horses, A, B and C. The Payoffs at A is 3:7, at B, is 4:9, at C, is 5:11. Sharif bets Rs. 693 on a horse which would fetch maximum amount. Luckily his horse has won. Then what is the total amount won by him?

A. Rs.990

B. Rs.1001

C. Rs.1008

D. Rs.1011

Science

Q.21 Which of the following statements is incorrect?

A. The charge on an electron and that on a proton are equal and opposite.

B. The neutron has no charge.

C. The electrons and protons have the same weight.

D. The mass of a proton is nearly identical to that of a neutron.

Q.22 The radius of the first Bohr's orbit for hydrogen is 0.53A°. The radius of the third Bohr's orbit is

A. 4.77 A°

B. 3.18 A°

C. 159 A°

D. None of these

Q.23 Which of the following statements is correct?

A. Double bond is stronger than single bond.

B. Double bond is weaker than single bond.

C. Double bond is equal to single bond.

D. Double bond is stronger than triple bond.

Q.24 How many double bonds are present in a carbon dioxide molecule?

A. Three

B. One

C. Two

D. Four

Q.25 In a cell that utilizes the reaction

$$Zn_{(s)} + 2H^{+}_{(aq)} \rightarrow Zn^{2+}_{(aq)} + H_{2(g)}$$

addition of H_2SO_4 to cathode compartment, will

A. lower E and shift the equilibrium to the left

B. lower E and shift the equilibrium to the right

C. increase E and shift the equilibrium to the right

D. increase E only

Q.26 Calculate the emf of the cell. $Zn|Zn^{2+}(0.001M)$ ∥ $Cu^{2+}(0.1M)|Cu$ The standard potential of Cu/Cu^{2+} half-cell is +0.34 and Zn/Zn^{2+} is 0.76 V.

A. 2.041 V

B. 1.041 V

C. 3.041 V

D. 5.041 V

Q.27 What current strength in ampere will be required to liberate 10 g of chlorine from sodium chloride solution in one hour?

A. 7.55 ampere

B. 8.55 ampere

C. 9.55 ampere

D. 6.55 ampere

Q.28 A positive charge q exerts a force of magnitude - 0.20 N on another charge - 2q. Find the magnitude of each charge if the distance separating them is equal to 50 cm.

A. -3.23 x 10⁻⁶ C

B. -3 x 10⁻⁶ C

C. -4.23 x 10⁻⁶ C

D. None of above

Q.29 19 g of molten $SnCl_2$ is electrolysed for some time using inert electrodes until 0.119 g of Sn is deposited at the cathode. No substance is lost during electrolysis. Find the ratio of the masses of $SnCl_2$: $SnCl_4$ after electrolysis.

A. 71.34: 1

B. 71.34: 2

C. 81.34: 1

D. 81.34: 2

Q.30 In Haber's process for the manufacture of:-

A. SO_2

B. NH_3

C. NO

D. NO_2

Q.31 Which of the following combinations is/are correct?

A. PVC : –(CH₂ - CHCl)ₙ–

B. Teflon : –(CF₂ - CF₂)ₙ–

C. Polystyrene : –[CH₂ - CH(C₆H₅)]ₙ–

D. All of the above

Q.32 In which of the following polymers are the repeating units joined by glycosidic bonds?

A. Polynucleotide

B. Protein

C. Polysaccharides

D. Fats

Q.33 The coagulation of protein is called:

A. dehydration

B. decay

C. denaturing

D. none of the above

Q.34 Nucleic acid i.e.DNA & RNA is a polymer of:-

A. Monosaccharides

B. Nucleotide

C. Amino acids

D. Fatty acids

Q.35 A current of 2.68 ampere is passed for one hour through an aqueous solution of copper sulphate using copper electrodes. Calculate the change in mass of cathode and that of the anode. (At. mass of copper = 63.5).

A. 3.0 g

B. 4.174 g

C. 3.174 g

D. None of these

Q.36 Which of the following reagents will produce CCl_2F_2, commonly called as Freon 12?

A. $C + F_2 + Cl_2 \rightarrow$

B. $CH_3Cl_4 + HF \rightarrow$

C. $CCl_4 + HF \xrightarrow{SbCl_5}$

D. None of these

Q.37 The ground state energy of hydrogen atom is − 13.6 eV. (i) What is the kinetic energy of an electron in the 2ⁿᵈ excited state?

A. +1.51 eV

B. +3.4 eV

C. +6.8 eV

D. +13.4 eV

Q.38 A beam of 35.0 keV electrons strikes a molybdenum target, generating the X-rays. What is the cutoff wavelength?

A. 35.5 pm

B. 40.0 pm

C. 15.95 pm

D. 18.2 pm

Q.39 During adiabatic expansion of 2 moles of gas the internal energy is found to decrease by 2 joules. The work done is

A. zero

B. - 1J

C. 2 J

D. None of the above

Q.40 A system goes from A to B via two processes I and II as shown in the figure. If ΔU_1 and ΔU_2 are the changes in internal energies in processes I and II, respectively, then

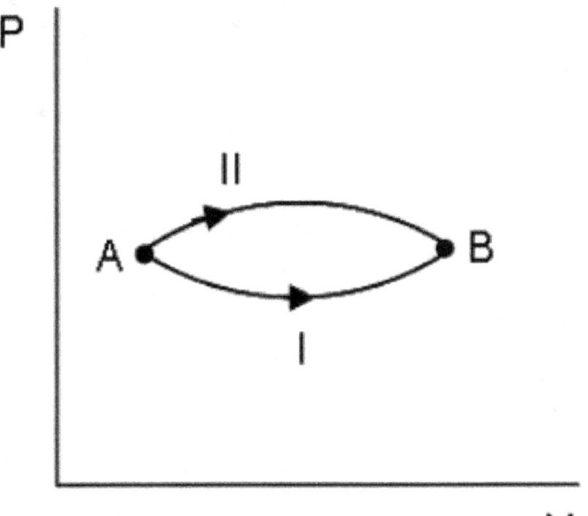

A. $\Delta U_1 = \Delta U_2$

B. relation between ΔU_1 and ΔU_2 cannot be determined

C. $\Delta U_2 > \Delta U_1$

D. $\Delta U_2 < \Delta U_1$

General Awareness

Q.41 Which among the following is an affected organ when a person is suffering from Diphtheria?

A. Lungs

B. Urinary Path

C. Respiratory Tube

D. Nervous System

Q.42 Which of the following is a name of operating system developed by Sun Microsystems?

A. Solaris

B. SOX

C. Venix

D. COSIX

Q.43 Balance of trade in context of economy is____________

A. Exports-Imports

B. Expenditure- savings

C. Record of all transactions

D. Scheme of Special Economic Zones

Q.44 Which of the following is the national animal of New Zealand?

A. Kangaroo

B. Kiwi

C. Lion

D. Tiger

Q.45 Who is the winner of the US Open 2019 Men's title?

A. Roger Federer

B. Rafael Nadal

C. Daniil Medvedev

D. Novak Djokovic

Q.46 Which type of radiations helps in observing an object through a telescope?

A. Canal radiation

B. Electromagnetic radiation

C. Alpha radiation

D. Beta radiation

Q.47 What is the total number of parallels of Latitude?

A. 180

B. 181

C. 182

D. 183

Q.48 What is the base year of Wholesale price index?

A. 2012-13

B. 2011-12

C. 2015-16

D. 2017-18

Q.49 Which among the following cell organelle is referred to as Suicidal bags of the cell?

A. Ribosomes

B. Lysosomes

C. Endoplasmic Reticulum

D. Cytoplasm

Q.50 Which among the following term is used for the Biome where Fresh Water & Salt Water meet?

A. Taiga

B. Estuary

C. Coral reefs

D. Savanna

// Smart Answer Sheet //

Correct   Indicates percentage of students who answered questions correctly.

Skipped   Indicates percentage of students who skipped questions.

Q.	Ans.	Correct / Skipped
1	C	37.84 % / 24.32 %
2	D	32.43 % / 45.95 %
3	D	8.11 % / 56.75 %
4	D	13.51 % / 56.76 %
5	B	21.62 % / 54.06 %
6	B	10.81 % / 56.76 %
7	A	8.11 % / 54.05 %
8	B	16.22 % / 56.75 %
9	B	24.32 % / 51.36 %
10	D	8.11 % / 56.75 %
11	C	16.22 % / 48.64 %
12	C	16.22 % / 54.05 %
13	D	18.92 % / 54.05 %
14	C	18.92 % / 51.35 %
15	B	21.62 % / 54.06 %
16	D	8.11 % / 56.75 %
17	C	21.62 % / 54.06 %
18	A	13.51 % / 54.06 %
19	C	18.92 % / 54.05 %
20	C	18.92 % / 54.05 %
21	C	32.43 % / 35.14 %
22	A	13.51 % / 51.35 %
23	A	35.14 % / 32.43 %
24	C	32.43 % / 35.14 %
25	C	16.22 % / 51.35 %
26	B	16.22 % / 54.05 %
27	A	24.32 % / 48.65 %
28	A	21.62 % / 51.35 %
29	A	5.41 % / 56.75 %
30	B	21.62 % / 48.65 %
31	D	29.73 % / 40.54 %
32	C	32.43 % / 45.95 %
33	C	13.51 % / 48.65 %
34	B	24.32 % / 37.84 %
35	C	24.32 % / 51.36 %
36	C	13.51 % / 43.25 %
37	A	10.81 % / 48.65 %
38	A	10.81 % / 51.35 %
39	C	16.22 % / 51.35 %
40	A	27.03 % / 43.24 %
41	C	32.43 % / 29.73 %
42	A	21.62 % / 35.14 %
43	A	48.65 % / 27.03 %
44	B	54.05 % / 27.03 %
45	B	16.22 % / 29.73 %
46	B	21.62 % / 40.54 %
47	B	10.81 % / 35.14 %
48	B	24.32 % / 37.84 %
49	B	32.43 % / 29.73 %
50	B	18.92 % / 37.84 %

Performance Analysis

Avg. Score (%)	10.67%
Toppers Score (%)	62.0%
Your Score	

//Hints and Solutions//

1. 12.5 × 14 ÷ 8.75 + 12 = 20 + ?
12.5 × 1.6+12 = 20+?
20 + 12 – 20 = ?
?=12

2. ?× (523.5 + 687.5) = 24220

24220 / 1211 = ?

? = 20

3. Let the speed of the boat in still water $= x\,km/h$
Let the speed of the stream $= y\,km/h$
According to the question, $\dfrac{20}{x+y} + \dfrac{8}{x-y} = \dfrac{12}{y}$
While solving we get, $\dfrac{x}{y} = \dfrac{7}{3}$
Now speed of boat in still water $= 7a$
Speed of stream $= 3a$
According to the question again, $\dfrac{20}{x+y} + \dfrac{20}{x-y} = 7$
$\Rightarrow \dfrac{20}{7a+3a} + \dfrac{20}{7a-3a} = 7$
Solving we get $a = 1$
Required answer $= 7a + 3a = 10a$
$= 10\,km/hr$

4. Ratio of downstream speed of faster boat to the downstream speed of slower boat $= 3:2$
ATQ, $3x - 2x = 8$ or, $x = 8$
Hence, downstream speed of faster boat $= 24\,km/hr$
Hence, downstream speed of slower boat $= 16\,km/hr$
Let, speed of faster boat in still water be 'a" km/hr.
Then, speed of slower boat in still water is 'a $-8'\,km/hr$
Also, Let the speed of stream be 'b' km/hr.
So, we have $= a + b = 24 \dots (i)$ Also $a-b = \dfrac{1}{2}\left(\dfrac{D}{a-8-b}\right)$
or, $2a - 16 - 2b = a - b$
or $a - b = 16 \dots (11)$
from (i) and (ii), $a = 20\,km/hr$

Hence, speed of slower boat $= a - 8 = 12\,km/h$

5. Profit % reduced $= 6 - 2.4 = 3.6\%$
$\therefore$ Required $CP = \dfrac{180}{3.6} \times 100$
$= 5000\,Rs$

6. Let Jim $C.P = 100x$
Carrey $C.P = 100x \times \dfrac{120}{100} = 120x$
Sid $C.P = 120x \times \dfrac{125}{100} = 150x$
Simba $C.P = 150x \times \dfrac{90}{100} = 135x$
Change $= \dfrac{135-100}{135} = \dfrac{35}{135} \times 100 = 25.92\%$

7. Let train y overtakes train x after t hours

ATQ
Time $gap = 2\dfrac{1}{2}$ hours $= \dfrac{5}{2}$ hours
Now, Distance covered by train $=$ Distance covered by train Y

$Bt = A\left(t + \dfrac{5}{2}\right)$ $(As,\ \text{distance} = \text{speed} \times \text{time})$
$\Rightarrow t = \dfrac{5A}{2(B-A)}$

8. Let the speed of train on onward journey be x km/h
then, speed of train on return journey $= 0.8x\,km/h$
ATQ Total Time $= 46 - 1 = 45$
$\dfrac{1000}{x} + \dfrac{1000}{0.8x} = 45$
$x = 50\,km/h$
Speed of train on return journey $= 0.8 \times 50 = 40\,km/hr$

9. $P = 16$ Years (4^2)
$Q = 9$ Years (3^2)
$R = 4$ Years (2^2)
Age after 5 Years
$P = 16 + 5 = 21$ Years
$Q = 9 + 5 = 14$ Years
$R = 4 + 5 = 9$ Years
Total $= 21 + 14 + 9 = 44$
Age of P after 3 Years $= 16 + 3 = 19$ Years

10. 2S+F = 79

2F+S = 104

S =18 F = 43

18+43+M/3 = 32

M =35

11. Let amount invested Scheme $A = x$ Rs

Amount invested in Scheme $B = (12200 - x)$

i.e, $x\left[\left(1 + \dfrac{10}{100}\right)^2 - 1\right] = \dfrac{(12200x)\times 10\times 4}{100}$

$21x = 488000 - 40x$

$61x = 488000 = 8000$

12. At end of 1st year $8000 + 1600 = 9600$

Amount $9600 - 3000 = 6600$

At the end of 2nd year $6600 + 1320 = 7920$

Amount $7920 - 3000 = 4920$

Amount to be paid at the end of third year $= 4920 + 984 = 5904$

13. Let there are X books in the library.

Hindi books = 60% of X = 60X /100 = 0.6X

Remaining Books = X – 0.6X = 0.4X

English books = 40% of reaming books = 60% of 0.4X = 0.24X.

Malayalam Books = X-0.6X -0.24X = 0.16X

Given,

0.24X = 4800

X = 4800/0.24 = 20000

Malayalam Books = 0.16X = 0.16*20000 = 3200.

14. smaller number = x; larger number = y

0.8x + 4 = 0.4y

4y – 8x = 40

y – x = 125

x = 115; y = 240

x + y = 355

15. There are 4 aces in 52 cards.
Therefore, probability that first card is ace =4/52

Now, the card has 3 aces and 51 cards in total as you have already picked one ace.

Thus, probability of second picked card is ace is =3/51

Now, these two events have to occur together.

Thus, required probability =(4/52)×(3/51) =1/221

16. 4/40*36/39 + 36/40*4/39 = 0.1846

17. From 15 points number of lines formed = $^{15}C_2$

6 points are collinear, number of lines formed by these = $^6C_2$

So total lines = $^{15}C_2 - ^6C_2 + 1 = 91$

18. Taking all person of same nationality as one person, then we will have only three people.

These three person can be arranged themselves in 3! Ways.

4 Indians can be arranged themselves in 4! Way.

5 Africans can be arranged themselves in 5! Ways.

7 Japanese can be arranged themselves in 7! Ways.

Hence, required number of ways = 4! 5! 7! 3! Ways.

19. The total number of employees in the year 2014 is 75 .
Step-by-step explanation:
In the year 2013 the ratio of employees are $= 2:3:4$
=2 x: 3 x: 4 x
in the year 2014 in each department 'n' number of employees left, then the ratio becomes $= 3:5:7$
=3 y: 5 y: 7 y
In the year 2015 in each department 5 employees left, then the ratio became $= 1:2:3$

$$(3y - 5):(5y - 5):(7y - 5) = 1:2:3$$

$$\frac{3y - 5}{5y - 5} = \frac{1}{2}$$
$$(3y - 5) \times 2 = 1 \times (5y - 5)$$
$$6y - 10 = 5y - 5$$
$$y - 10 = -5$$
$$y = 5$$

Therefore, the number of employees in $2014 =$
$$(3 \times 5):(5 \times 5):(7 \times 5)$$
=15,25,35
Employees in 2013
$$2x - n = 15$$

$$3x - n = 25$$
$$x = 10$$
Therefore, the number of employees in $2013 =$
$$(2 \times 10):(3 \times 10):(4 \times 10)$$
=20,30,40
5 employees left in $2015 = (15 - 5)(25 - 5)(35 - 5)$
=10,20,30
then the ratio became 1: 2: 3
Hence the total number of employees in the year 2014
$$= 15 + 25 + 35$$
$$= 75 \text{ employees}$$
The total number of employees in the year 2014 is 75 .

20. If he bets on horse A: 693×3/7 = 297

If he bets on horse B: 693×4/9 = 308

If he bets on horse C: 693×5/11 = 315

So he bets on horse C and he wins 315

Total = 693+315 = 1008

21. Protons and neutrons have approximately the same mass, about 1.67 × 10^{-24} grams. Scientists define this amount of mass as one atomic mass unit (amu) or one Dalton. Although similar in mass, protons are positively charged, while neutrons have no charge. Therefore, the number of neutrons in an atom contributes significantly to its mass, but not to its charge.

Electrons are much smaller in mass than protons, weighing only 9.11 × 10^{-28} grams, or about 1/1800 of an atomic mass unit. Therefore, they do not contribute much to an element's overall atomic mass. When considering atomic mass, it is customary to ignore the mass of any electrons and calculate the atom's mass based on the number of protons and neutrons alone.

22. Radius of bhors 3rd orbit is 4.761A°
it is actual as compare to the above information the radius is 4.77A°

Formula: $\dfrac{0.53 \times n^2}{z}$

$\Rightarrow \dfrac{0.53 \times (3)^2}{1}$

=0.53×9
=4.77A°

23. $E_{cell} = E_C - E_A$

Given, $E^{\circ}_{Ag^+/Ag} = 0.80V$

$H_2|H^+ \| Ag^+|Ag$

Hydrogen is anode and silver is cathode.

$E_{cell} = E_C - E_A$

$= 0.80 - 0 \quad \left(\because E^{\circ}_{H^+/H} = 0\right)$

$= 0.80V$

24. Carbon dioxide could be drawn (without making any assumptions about the shape) as

O = C = O

The carbon originally had 4 electrons in its outer level (group 4). Each oxygen contributes 2 electrons - 1 for each bond. That means there are a total of 8 electrons around the carbon, in 4 pairs. Because there are 4 bonds, these are all bond pairs. Each double bond uses 2 bond pairs - which are then thought of as a single unit. Those two double bond units will try to get as far apart as possible, and so the molecule is linear. The structure we've drawn above does in fact represent the shape of the molecule.

25. $Zn_{(s)} + 2H^+(aq) \rightleftharpoons Zn^{2+}(aq) + H_2(g)$

$E_{cell} = E^{\circ}_{cell} - \dfrac{0.059}{2}\log\dfrac{[Zn^{2+}]\times p_{H_2}}{[H^+]^2}$

On adding H_2SO_4 the $[H^+]$ will increase therefore E cell will also Increase and the equtlbrlum will shift towards the right

$Zn_{(s)} + 2H^+(aq) \rightleftharpoons Zn^{2+}(aq) + H_2(g)$

$E_{cell} = E^{\circ}_{cell} - \dfrac{0.059}{2}\log\dfrac{[Zn^{2+}]\times p_{H_2}}{[H^+]^2}$

On adding H_2SO_4 the $[H^+]$ will increase therefore

E cell will also Increase and the equtlbrlum will shift towards the right.

26. Given $Zn|Zn^{2+}(0.001M) \| Cu^{2+}(0.1M)|Cu$

Overall cell reaction:

$Zn \rightarrow Zn^{2+} + 2e^-$

$Cu^{2+} + 2e^- \rightarrow Cu$

$\overline{Zn + Cu^{2+} \rightarrow Zn^{2+} + Cu}$

E^O_{cell} = standard reduction potential of cathode + standard oxidation potential of anode

$E^O_{cell} = 0.34$ to $0.76V$

$E^O_{cell} = 1.1V$

$K_C = \dfrac{[Zn^{2+}]}{[Cu^{2+}]} = \dfrac{10^{-3}}{10^{-1}} = 10^{-2}$

EMF of the cell at any electrode concentration is:

$E = E^O - \dfrac{0.059}{n}\log(K_C)$

$= 1.1 - \dfrac{0.059}{2}\log\left(10^{-2}\right) = 1.1 - \dfrac{0.059}{2} \times (2) = 1.1$

$- 0.059 = 1.041V$

27. Applying E = Z × 96500 (E for chlorine = 35.5)

35.5 = Z × 96500

or Z = 35.5/96500 g

Now, applying the formula

W = Z × I × t

Where W = 10 g, Z= 35.5/96500

t = 60×60 =3600 second

$I = \dfrac{10}{\frac{35.5}{96500}\times 3600} = 7.55\ ampere$

28. The force that q exert on $2q$ is given by Coulomb's law.

$F = k(q)(-2q)/r^2,\ r = 0.5m, F = -0.20N$

$-0.2 = -2q^2 k/0.5^2$

$q^2 = 0.2 \times 0.5^2/(2k)$

$q = \sqrt{[(0.2 \times 0.5^2/(2 \times 9 \times 10^9)]} = 1.66 \times 10^{-6}C$

$q = 1.66 \times 10^{-6}C, -2q = -3.23 \times 10^{-6}C$

29. The chemical reaction occurring during electrolysis is:

$$\underset{2\times190g}{2SnCl_2} \rightarrow \underset{261g}{SnCl_4} + \underset{119g}{Sn}$$

119 g of Sn is deposited by the decomposition of 380 g of SnCl₂. So, 0.119 g of Sn is deposited by the decomposition of

$\dfrac{380}{119} \times 0.119 = -0.380g$ of $SnCl_2$

Remaining amount of $SnCl_2 = (19 - 0.380) = 18.62g$

$380g$ of $SnCl_2$ produce $= 261g$ of $SnCl_4$

So, $0.380g$ of $SnCl_2$ produce $= \dfrac{261}{380} \times 0.380 = 0.261g$ of $SnCl_4$

Thus, the ratio $SnCl_2 : SnCl_4 = \dfrac{18.62}{0.261}$, i.e., $71.34 : 1$

30. On an industrial scale, ammonia is prepared by Haber's process. The constituents of ammonia N_2 and H_2 combine in a ratio of 1: 3

$N_2 + 3H_2 \rightleftharpoons 2NH_3$

The reaction proceeds in the forward direction with a remarkable decrease in volume and thus the reaction is exothermic. In accordance with Le Chatelier's principle, high pressure would favour the formation of ammonia. The optimum conditions for the production of ammonia are a pressure of approx 200 atm, a temperature of approx $700K$ and the use of a catalyst such as iron oxide with small amounts of K_2O and Al_2O_3 to increase the rate of attainment of equilibrium.

31. All of these combinations are correct.

32. Polysaccharides are long chains of carbohydrate molecules, specifically polymeric carbohydrates composed of monosaccharide units bound together by glycosidic linkages. This carbohydrate can react with water using amylase enzymes at catalyst, which produces constituent sugars

33. The coagulation of protein is called denaturing. Denaturation of proteins involves the disruption and possible destruction of both the secondary and tertiary structures.

34. Nucleic acids are basically the polymer molecules of nucleotides which are essentially made up of three basic components, a heterocyclic nitrogenous base, a pentose sugar and a phosphate group. Both of the nucleic acids i.e. DNA and RNA contain adenine, guanine and cytosine

35. The electrode reactions are:

$$\underset{1\,mole}{Cu^{2+}} + \underset{2\times96500\,C}{2e^-} \rightarrow Cu \text{ (Cathode)}$$

$$Cu \rightarrow Cu^{2+} + 2e^- \text{ (Anode)}$$

Thus, cathode increases in mass as copper is deposited on it and the anode decreases in mass as copper from it dissolves.

Charge passed through cell = 2.68 × 60 × 60 coulomb

Copper deposited or dissolved $= \dfrac{63.5}{2\times96500} \times 2.68 \times 60 \times 60$ =3.174 g

Increase in mass of cathode = Decrease in mass of anode = 3.174 g

36. $CCl_4 + HF \xrightarrow{\ SbCl_5\ } CCl_2F_2 + 2HCl$

Dichlorodifluoromethane is a direct contact freezing agent for foods. Refrigerant, aerosol propellant Dichlorodifluoromethane (R-12), usually sold under the brand name Freon-12, is a chlorofluorocarbon halomethane (CFC), used as a refrigerant and aerosol spray propellant. Complying with the Montreal Protocol, its manufacture was banned in the United States along with many other countries in 1994 due to concerns about damage to the ozone layer. It is soluble in many organic solvents.

37. 2nd excited state means 3rd normal state or $n = 3$ state

total energy of nth level is $E_n = E_0/n^2$

given that $E_0 = -13.6eV$

So total energy for 3 rd state will be $E_3 = -13.6/9 = -1.51eV$

We know that total energy=-kinetic energy

So kinetic energy=- $(-1.51eV) = 1.51eV$

38. The cut-off wavelength λ min corresponds to an electron transferring (approximately) all of its energy to an X-ray photon, thus producing a photon with the greatest possible frequency and least possible wavelength.
From relation

$$\lambda_{\min} = \frac{hc}{K_0} = \frac{(4.14\times10^{-5})(3\times10^8)}{35.0\times10^3}$$
$$= 3.55 \times 10^{-11} = 35.5\text{pm}$$

39. There is no transfer of heat and matter take place during adiabatic expansion.

So,

dQ=0

According to first law,

dQ= dU + dW

0= -2J + dW (As internal energy decreases by 2 J)

dW= -2J

Therefore, work done on the gas is -2 J and work done by the gas is 2 J.

40. Change in internal energy do not depend upon the path followed by the process. It only depends on initial and final states i.e., $\Delta U_1 = \Delta U_2$

41. Diphtheria is a serious bacterial infection that affects the mucous membranes of the Respiratory Tube I.e. Throat and Nose, it is an infection caused by the bacterium Corynebacterium diphtheriae and usually spread between people by direct contact or through the air. It may also be spread by contaminated objects. Diphtheria vaccine is effective for prevention and available in several formulations.

Disease	Affected Organ
Gonorrhoea	Urinary Path
Pneumonia	Lungs
Tetanus	Nervous system

42. Solaris is a Unix operating system originally developed by Sun Microsystems. It superseded their earlier SunOS in 1993. In 2010, after the Sun acquisition by Oracle, it was renamed Oracle Solaris.

Solaris is known for its scalability, especially on SPARC systems, and for originating many innovative features such as DTrace, ZFS and Time Slider. Solaris supports SPARC and x86-64 workstations and servers from Oracle and other vendors. Solaris is registered as compliant with the Single UNIX Specification.

Operating System	Developer
SOX	Cobra Tecnologia, Brazil
Venix	Interval Zero, Inc., USA
COSIX	China National Computer Software & Technology Service Corporation (CS&S)

43. The balance of trade (BOT) is the difference between the value of a country's imports and its exports for a given period. The balance of trade is the largest component of a country's balance of payments (BOP).

44. Kiwi is regarded as the national animal of New Zealand.

Kangaroo- Australia

Lion- United Kingdom

Tiger- India

45. US Open 2019 Men's title was won by Rafael Nadal. Rafael Nadal defeated Daniil Medvedev of Russia in the final. This is Nadal's 19th Grand Slam singles titles.

46. Telescope is an optical instrument that aids in the observation of remote objects by collecting electromagnetic radiation (such as visible light). As wavelengths become longer, it becomes easier to use antenna technology to interact with electromagnetic radiation (although it is possible to make very tiny antenna). The near-infrared can be collected much like visible light, however in the far-infrared and submillimetre range, telescopes can operate more like a radio telescope

47. The total number of parallels of latitude is 181. 90 in north, 90 in south and one equator. Latitude is an angle which ranges from 0° at the Equator to 90° (North or South) at the poles. Lines of constant latitude, or parallels, run east - west as circles parallel to the equator. Latitude is used together with longitude to specify the precise location of features on the surface of the Earth.

48. The base year of All-India Whole sale price index (WPI) has been revised from 2004-05 to 2011-12 on 12 May 2017 to align it with the base year of other macroeconomic indicators like the Gross Domestic Product (GDP) and Index of Industrial Production (IIP).

49. Lysosomes are known as suicidal bags of the cell, these cellular organelles contain digestive enzymes that break down waste materials, foreign materials and foreign particles that entered cell. It helps the cell to process its nutrients and is responsible for destroying the cell after it has died. It is bounded by only one single membrane. It break-down the structures within the cells. However, in certain circumstances may be in case of diseases or some conditions lysosomes begin to break-down living cells.

50. The place where fresh and salt-water meet is called an estuary, it is a place Where the Ocean Meets Fresh Water, Estuaries form a unique marine biome that occurs where a source of fresh water, such as a river, meets the ocean. Therefore, both fresh water and salt water are found in the same vicinity. Mixing results in a diluted (brackish) saltwater. Estuaries form a transition zone between river environments and maritime environments. They are subject both to marine influences - such as tides, waves, and the influx of saline water - and to riverine influences - such as flows of fresh water and sediment. The mixing of sea water and fresh water provide high levels of nutrients both in the water column and in sediment, making estuaries among the most productive natural habitats in the world.

Mathematics

Q.1 The cost of three liquids A, B and C per kg is Rs. 200, Rs. 150 and Rs. 180. These liquids are used in a ratio of 3 : 5 : 4 to make a mixture. What will be the selling price if the seller wants to earn 10% profit?

A. Rs. 160   **B.** Rs. 172.5
C. Rs. 178.5   **D.** Rs. 189.75

Q.2 In a triangle ABC, angle bisector of $\angle A$, $\angle B$ & $\angle C$ cuts circumcircle at X, Y, Z respectively. If $\angle CZY = 40$ & $\angle A = 50$, then, find $\angle BYZ$?

A. 30 degree   **B.** 25 degree
C. 20 degree   **D.** 60 degree

Q.3 If the cost price of an article is 80% of its selling price, the profit per cent is :

A. 20 %   **B.** $22\frac{1}{2}$ %   **C.** 24%   **D.** 25%

Q.4 Find the value of $4^9 + 4^9 - (8\sqrt{2})^6$?

A. 2×2^{19} **B.** 3×2^{19} **C.** -3×2^{19} **D.** 2^{19}

Q.5

$$\frac{\cos A \sin A}{\cos ecA - \cot A}\left(\frac{\sin^2 A}{1 + \cos A}\right) = \left(a + b\right)\cos A - \left(2b - 3a\right)\cos 3 A$$

If , then. Fin dthe value of a and b respectively.

A. a = 1/20 ; b= 1/15   **B.** a = 1/10 ; b= 1/5
C. a = 1/20 ; b= 1/5   **D.** a = 1/15 ; b= 1/5

Q.6 The difference between a number and its two-fifth is 510. What is 50% of 10% of that number?

A. 425   **B.** 42.5   **C.** 85   **D.** 8.50

Q.7 Section A and section B of 7th class in a school contain total of 285 students. Which of the following can be a ratio of the number of boys and the number of girls in the class?

A. 10 : 6   **B.** 10 : 9   **C.** 10 : 11   **D.** 10 : 12

Q.8 The percentage of profit, when an article is sold of ₹ 78, is twice than when it is sold for ₹ 69. The cost price of the articls is :

A. ₹ 49   **B.** ₹ 51   **C.** ₹ 57   **D.** ₹ 60

Q.9 Consider ∆ABC shown in the following figure where BC = 12cm, DB = 9cm, CD = 6cm and $\angle BCD = \angle BAC$. What is the ratio of the perimeter of the triangle ADC to the perimeter of the triangle BDC?

A. 7 : 9   **B.** 5 : 9   **C.** 9 : 5   **D.** 9 : 7

Q.10 If there are coins of three denomination 1-rupee, 50-paise and 25-paise in the ratio of 7 : 8 : 20. Their total value is Rs. 400. The total number of coins is how much?

A. 1200   **B.** 961   **C.** 744   **D.** 875

Q.11 Find the ratio between compound interest at 6% p.a. and simple interest at 5% p.a. earned on 2000$ after 3 years.

A. 191:150   **B.** 150:191   **C.** 201:150   **D.** 150:201

Q.12 If $5\sqrt{5} \times 5^3 \div 5^{\frac{3}{2}} = 5^{a+2}$ then find the value of a.

A. 1   **B.** 2   **C.** 3   **D.** 4

Q.13 A's pocket money is 20% more than that of B and B's pocket money is 15% less than that of C then how much is A's pocket money more than that of C?

A. 2%   **B.** 15%   **C.** 17%   **D.** 20%

Q.14 The perimeters of ∆LMN and ∆XYZ are 36 cm and 48 cm respectively and LM = 15 cm. If both are similar triangles, then what is the value of the side XY?

A. 25 cm   **B.** 30 cm   **C.** 20 cm   **D.** 35 cm

Q.15 What is the value of x in the equation
$$\frac{x\,cosec^2 30° sec^2 45°}{8\cos^2 45° \sin^2 60°} = \tan^2 60° - \tan^2 30°.$$

A. $x = 1$ **B.** $x = 2$ **C.** $x = 3$ **D.** $x = 4$

Science

Q.16 What is the SI unit of pressure?

A. Newton   **B.** Weber   **C.** Henry   **D.** Pascal

Q.17 Which one of the following is the SI Unit of Power?

A. Joule   **B.** Watt
C. Newton Metre   **D.** Kilowatt hour

Q.18 Electropositive atoms tend to form __________.

A. Negative ions   **B.** Positive ions
C. Covalent bonds   **D.** Metallic bonds

Q.19 The atoms of the elements having same difference between mass number and atomic number are called _____.

A. Isobar
B. Isotopes
C. Isotones
D. No option is correct.

Q.20 Which of the following is not true about Frictional force?

A. Friction is the force which opposes the relative motion of two surfaces in contact.
B. The force of friction that acts when a body is moving (sliding) on a surface is called sliding friction
C. Friction in machines Wastes energy and also causes wear and tear.
D. Rolling friction is much more than sliding friction, the use of ball bearings in a machine considerably reduces friction

Q.21 The moment of force measures?

A. Moment of inertia of body about any axis
B. The tendency of rotation of the body along an axis

C. Work done by force on the body
D. None of these

Q.22 Calculate the electricity that would be required to reduce 12.3 g of nitrobenzene to aniline, if the current efficiency for the process is 50 percent. If the potential drop across the cell is 3.0 volt, how much energy will be consumed?

A. 347.4 kJ   **B.** 447.4 kJ   **C.** 367.4 kJ   **D.** 547.4 kJ

Q.23 Number of RBC increases if one lives at higher altitude because _____?
A. There is less oxygen on mountains
B. More heat is required in body for producing body warmth
C. There are no germs in mountain air
D. There is more oxygen on mountains

Q.24 Soil erosion can be prevented by-
A. Increasing bird population
B. Afforestation
C. Removal of vegetation
D. Overgrazing

Q.25 Red data book contains data of which of the following?
A. Only plant species
B. Only animal species
C. All endangered species
D. None of the above

Q.26 An organism capable of reproducing by two asexual reproduction methods one similar to the reproduction in yeast and the other similar to the reproduction in Planaria is:-
A. Hydra   **B.** Bryophyllum
C. Paramecium   **D.** Microcrondiea

Q.27 According to Mendeleev's periodic law, the physical and chemical properties of the elements are the periodic function of their:
A. Atomic number   **B.** Atomic masses
C. Atomic radii   **D.** Ionization Potential

Q.28 Curie point is the temperature at which ---------------
A. Matter becomes radioactive
B. A metal loses magnetic properties
C. A metal loses conductivity
D. Transmutation of metal occurs

Q.29 Which is the lightest metal on earth?
A. Silver   **B.** Gold   **C.** Lithium   **D.** Lead

Q.30 Who determined the absolute value of charge on electron?
A. R.A. Millikan   **B.** J.J. Thomson
C. Chadwick   **D.** Rutherford

General Awareness

Q.31 The Governor-General was given power to issue ordinances by the act of
A. 1858   **B.** 1861   **C.** 1860   **D.** 1871

Q.32 Which of the following is one of the causes for the passing of the Act of 1773?
A. Failure of Double Government
B. Success of Double Government
C. Agitation in India
D. Desire of the Indian Merchants

Q.33 Pitt's India Bill was introduced by _______ in 1784.
A. Prime Minister Pitt
B. Governor-General of India
C. Senior Merchants
D. East India Company

Q.34 Who among the following Governor General created the Covenanted Civil Service of India which later came to be known as the Indian Civil Service?
A. Warren Hastings   **B.** Wellesley
C. Cornwallis   **D.** William Bentinck

Q.35 Under which article, President of India can proclaim constitutional emergency?
A. Article 32   **B.** Article 349
C. Article 356   **D.** Article 360

Q.36 How many members of upper house (RajyaSabha) can be nominated by President of India?
A. 10   **B.** 12   **C.** 14   **D.** 16

Q.37 Who was the Defence Minister of India during the Indo China War of 1962?
A. R.N. Thapar
B. V.K. Krishna Menon
C. Govind Ballabh Pant
D. Jagjivan Ram

Q.38 When was the States Reorganization Commission constituted?
A. 1953   **B.** 1952   **C.** 1951   **D.** 1954

Q.39 The Ghatampur thermal power plant approved by Cabinet is to be setup in –
A. Rajasthan   **B.** Uttar Pradesh
C. Karnataka   **D.** Madhya Pradesh

Q.40 What process takes place during the youthful stage of a river?
A. Valley widening   **B.** River rejuvenating
C. Valley deepening   **D.** Meandering

Basic English

Q.41 I **must** remember my key.
What does the underlined auxiliary 'must' suggest?
A. Necessity   **B.** Determination
C. Promise   **D.** Obligation

Q.42 Which of the following sentences is correct ?
A. He reached the station before the train started.
B. I arrived at the station after the train started.
C. He was seeing the sea.

D. The nightingale as well as the cuckoo is a singing bird.

Q.43 Passengers **must** switch off their mobile phones. What does the underlined auxiliary 'must' suggest?

A. expectation   **B.** compulsion
C. obligation   **D.** None of these

Q.44 Choose the **odd** one out

A. Left   **B.** Milkshake
C. Right   **D.** Forward

Q.45 Direction: Read the each sentence to find out whether there is any grammatical error in it. The error, if any will be in one part of the sentence. The letter of that part is the answer. If there is no error, the answer is 'D'. (Ignore the errors of punctuation, if any.)

Block of Residential flats (A)/ are coming up (B)/ near our house. (C)/ No error (D)

A. A   **B.** B   **C.** C   **D.** D

Q.46 Direction : In the following questions, choose the word opposite in meaning to the given word.
VACILLATING

A. fascinating   **B.** fanaticism
C. indolence   **D.** resolute

Q.47 Direction : In the following questions, choose the word opposite in meaning to the given word.
RECKLESS

A. modest   **B.** awkward
C. celebrated   **D.** cautious

Ques (48-50):Direction : Read the following passage carefully and answer the questions given below it.

In May 1996, The World Health Organization was authorized to initiate a global campaign to eradicate smallpox. The goal was to eradicate the disease in one decade. Because similar projects for malaria and yellow fever had failed, few believed that smallpox could actually be eradicated but eleven years after the initial organization of the campaign, no cases were reported in the field. The strategy was not only to provide mass vaccination but also to isolate patients with active smallpox in order to contain the spread of the disease and to break the chain of human transmission. Rewards for reporting smallpox assisted in motivating the public to aid health workers. One by one, each smallpox victim was sought out, removed from contact with others and treated. At the same time, the entire village where the victim had lived was vaccinated. Today smallpox is no longer a threat to humanity. Routine vaccinations have been stopped worldwide.

Q.48 Which of the following is the best title for the passage ?

A. The World Health Organisation
B. The Eradication of Smallpox
C. Smallpox Vaccinations
D. Infectious Diseases

Q.49 What was the goal of the campaign against smallpox ?

A. To decrease the spread of smallpox worldwide.
B. To eliminate smallpox worldwide in ten years.

C. To provide mass vaccination against smallpox worldwide
D. To initiate worldwide projects for smallpox, malaria and yellow fever at the same time

Q.50 According to the paragraph what was the strategy used to eliminate the spread of small pox ?

A. Vaccination of the entire village
B. Treatment of individual victims
C. Isolation of victims and mass vaccinations
D. Extensive reporting of outbreaks

// Smart Answer Sheet //

Correct — Indicates percentage of students who answered questions correctly.

Skipped — Indicates percentage of students who skipped questions.

Q.	Ans.	Correct / Skipped
1	D	25.0 % / 19.32 %
2	B	21.97 % / 22.22 %
3	D	23.48 % / 22.86 %
4	C	21.72 % / 25.0 %
5	C	16.41 % / 28.92 %
6	B	33.71 % / 27.65 %
7	C	16.67 % / 27.4 %
8	D	22.47 % / 27.4 %
9	A	11.49 % / 27.9 %
10	D	19.44 % / 27.28 %

Q.	Ans.	Correct / Skipped
11	A	20.2 % / 24.88 %
12	A	26.14 % / 25.38 %
13	A	24.62 % / 22.6 %
14	C	26.64 % / 22.85 %
15	A	26.77 % / 26.26 %
16	D	52.4 % / 16.41 %
17	B	48.36 % / 16.03 %
18	B	32.95 % / 16.92 %
19	B	34.85 % / 16.03 %
20	D	20.45 % / 18.94 %

Q.	Ans.	Correct / Skipped
21	B	27.27 % / 19.19 %
22	A	22.1 % / 19.06 %
23	A	48.11 % / 18.43 %
24	B	61.87 % / 18.18 %
25	C	49.75 % / 18.94 %
26	A	28.03 % / 18.69 %
27	B	38.13 % / 17.17 %
28	B	26.52 % / 18.56 %
29	C	60.61 % / 15.4 %
30	A	18.69 % / 17.93 %

Q.	Ans.	Correct / Skipped
31	B	31.94 % / 17.05 %
32	A	21.72 % / 16.03 %
33	A	23.48 % / 17.3 %
34	C	33.84 % / 15.65 %
35	C	39.39 % / 17.3 %
36	B	53.54 % / 16.91 %
37	B	34.09 % / 17.43 %
38	A	22.73 % / 18.18 %
39	B	25.88 % / 17.3 %
40	C	24.37 % / 17.93 %

Q.	Ans.	Correct / Skipped
41	A	48.74 % / 11.36 %
42	D	18.06 % / 11.86 %
43	C	18.18 % / 12.63 %
44	B	59.6 % / 12.5 %
45	A	20.71 % / 13.89 %
46	D	15.66 % / 14.39 %
47	D	17.68 % / 14.01 %
48	B	28.16 % / 14.9 %
49	B	22.85 % / 15.41 %
50	C	27.53 % / 15.9 %

Performance Analysis

Avg. Score (%)	14.67%
Toppers Score (%)	100.0%
Your Score	

//Hints and Solutions//

1. It is given that,

The cost of liquid A = Rs. 200

The cost of liquid B = Rs. 150

The cost of liquid C = Rs. 180

The ratio in which liquids are used to form a mixture = 3 : 5 : 4

We know that,

$$SP = CP \times \frac{(100+P)}{100}$$

Here, SP = Selling Price, CP = Cost Price and P = Profit

Let the amount of liquids used be 3 kg, 5 kg, 4 kg respectively.

So, average cost of mixture $= \frac{(200\times3+150\times5+180\times4)}{(3+5+4)} = \frac{2070}{12}$ = Rs. 172.5 per kg

Therefore, SP $= 172.5 \times \frac{(100+10)}{100}$ = Rs. 189.75

∴ Selling price of the mixture is Rs. 189.75.

Hence, the correct option is (D).

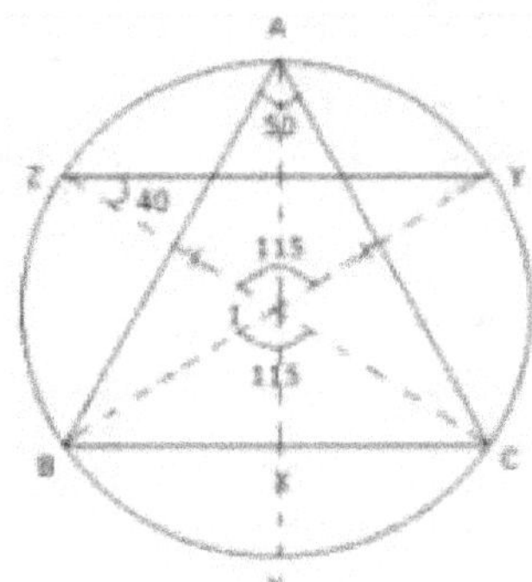

2.
Because I is the intersection point of all angle bisectors so I will be in centre, hence
∠BIC = 90 +∠A/2 = 115
∠ZIY = ∠BIC = 115 (Vertical opposite angles)
In ΔZIY,
∠BYZ = 180 – 115 – 40 = 25.
∴ ∠BYZ is 25⁰

3. Let S.P. = Rs. 100
C.P. = Rs. 80
∴ Gain = Rs. 20
∴ Gain per cent = 20/80*100 = 25%

4. Given that,
Let a = 4³
b = 4³
c = - (8√2)²
Then, a+b+c=4³ + 4³ - (8√2)² = 64 + 64 - 128 = 0
a³ + b³ + c³= 3abc
⇒4⁹ + 4⁹ - (8√2)⁶ = 3 x 4³ x 4³ x (-(8√2)²)
⇒-3 x 46 x 128 = -3 x 2¹² x 2⁷

=-3 x 2¹⁹

∴ -3 x 2¹⁹ is the required answer

5. Solve the LHS, $LHS = \frac{cosAsinA}{cosecA-cotA}\left(\frac{sin^2A}{1+cosA}\right)$

$\Rightarrow \operatorname{cosec} A = 1/\sin A; \cot A = \cos A/\sin A; \sin^2 A = 1 - \cos^2 A$

$= \frac{sin2A}{2\left(\frac{1}{sinA}-\frac{cosA}{sinA}\right)}\left(\frac{1-cos^2A}{1+cosA}\right)$

$= \frac{sin2AsinA}{2(1-cosA)}\left(\frac{(1+cosA)(1-cosA)}{1+cosA}\right)$

$= \frac{sin2AsinA}{2} = \frac{2sin2AsinA}{4}$

We know, $2sinCsinD = \cos(C-D) - \cos(C+D)$

$\frac{2sin2AsinA}{4} = \frac{\cos(2A-A)}{4} - \frac{\cos(2A+A)}{4}$

$\Rightarrow \frac{cosA}{4} - \frac{cos3A}{4}$

Comparing LHS and RHS $\frac{cosA}{4} - \frac{cos3A}{4} = (a+b)cosA - (2b-3a)cos3A$

We get, $\Rightarrow a+b = 1/4$

$\Rightarrow 2b - 3a = 14$

Solving (1) and (II), we get, $\Rightarrow a = 1/20; b = 1/5$

6. Let number be x
= x-2x/5 = 510
x = 850
10% of 850 = 85
50% of 85 = 42.5

7. B) 10 : 9

Explanation:

The number of boys and girls cannot be in decimal values, so the denominator should completely divide number of students (285).

Check each option:

6+5 = 11, and 11 does not divide 285 completely.

10+9 = 19, and only 19 divides 285 completely among all.

8. Let the C.P. of article be Rs. x.

$\left(\frac{78-x}{x}\right) \times 100$

$= 2 \times \left(\frac{69-x}{x}\right) \times 100$

$\Rightarrow 78 - x = 2 \times 69 - 2x$

$\Rightarrow 2x - x = 138 - 78 \Rightarrow x = 60$

9.

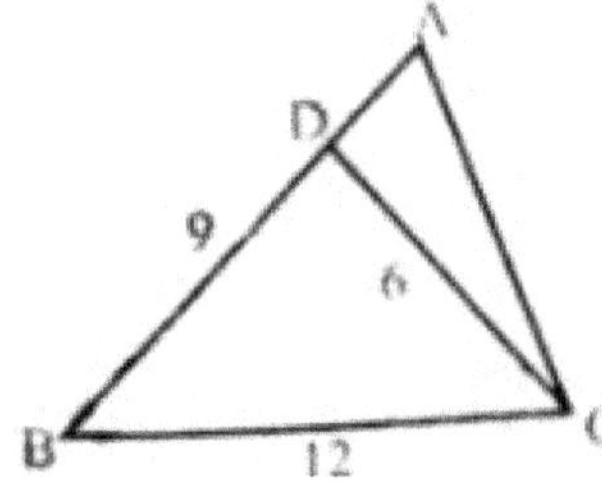

In $\triangle BAC$ and $\triangle BCD, \angle BCD = \angle BAC, \angle B$ is common

$$\angle BDC = \angle BCA$$

Therefore, the two triangles are similar. $\dfrac{AB}{BC} = \dfrac{AC}{CD} = \dfrac{BC}{BD}$

$$\Leftrightarrow AB = \dfrac{BC^2}{BD} = 16$$

$$\Leftrightarrow AD = 7$$

Similarly, $AC = \dfrac{BC \times CD}{BD} = 8$

Perimeter of $\triangle ADC = 7 + 6 + 8 = 21$

Perimeter of $\triangle BDC = 27$

Therefore, Ratio $= \dfrac{21}{27} = \dfrac{7}{9}$

Required ratio is 7: 9

10. Number of coin of
1 rupee = 7x
50 paise = 8x
25 paise = 20x
⇒Total money = (7x × 1) + (8x × 1/2) + (20x × 1/4)
⇒7x + 4x + 5x = 400
⇒16x = 400
⇒x = 400/16
= 25
Total number of coins = 7x + 8x + 20x
= 175 + 200 + 500
= 875

11. Simple Interest = 2000*5*3/100 = 300$
Compound interest = 2000 * [1+0.06]3 - 2000= 2382 – 2000$ = 382$
Required ratio = 382: 300 = 191: 150

12. The given equation is,

$$5\sqrt{5} \times 5^3 \div 5^{\frac{3}{2}} = 5^{a+2}$$

We can write the above equation as,

$$\Rightarrow 5 \times 5^{\frac{1}{2}} \times 5^3 \div 5^{\frac{3}{2}} = 5^{a+2}$$

$$\Rightarrow 5^{1+\frac{1}{2}+3-\frac{3}{2}} = 5^{a+2}$$

$$\Rightarrow 5^3 = 5^{a+2}$$

By comparing the powers,

$$\Rightarrow a + 2 = 3$$

$$\Rightarrow a = 1$$

Hence, the correct option is (A).

13. Let pocket money of C = 100
Of B = 100 - 15% of 100 = 85
Of C = 85 + 20% of 85 = 102
Diff b/w A and C pocket money = 2
Required %= 2/100 × 100% = 2%

14. It is given that, both the triangles are similar. Therefore, the ratio of the similar sides is equal.

So, we can write,

$$\Rightarrow \dfrac{LM}{XY} = \dfrac{MN}{YZ} = \dfrac{LN}{XZ} = k \quad ---- (1)$$

Also, their perimeter is in the same ratio.

$$\therefore \dfrac{\text{Perimeter of } \triangle LMN}{\text{Perimeter of } \triangle XYZ} = \dfrac{36}{48} = k$$

$$\Rightarrow k = \dfrac{3}{4}$$

$$\Rightarrow \dfrac{LM}{XY} = k \quad \text{[From equation (1)]}$$

$$\Rightarrow \dfrac{15}{XY} = \dfrac{3}{4}$$

$$\therefore XY = 20 \text{ cm}$$

Hence, the correct option is (C).

15. Given:

$$\dfrac{x \cdot \text{cosec}^2 30° \sec^2 45°}{8\cos^2 45° \sin^2 60°} = \tan^2 60° - \tan^2 30°$$

$$\Rightarrow \dfrac{x \times (2)^2 \times (\sqrt{2})^2}{8 \times \left(\frac{1}{\sqrt{2}}\right)^2 \times \left(\frac{\sqrt{3}}{2}\right)^2} = \left(\sqrt{3}^2\right) - \left(\dfrac{1}{\sqrt{3}}\right)^2$$

$$\Rightarrow \dfrac{x \times 4 \times 2 \times 4}{8 \times \frac{1}{2} \times 3} = 3 - \dfrac{1}{3}$$

$$\Rightarrow \dfrac{8x}{3} = \dfrac{8}{3}$$

$$\Rightarrow x = 1$$

Hence, the correct option is (A).

16. The SI unit for pressure is the pascal (Pa), equal to one newton per square meter (N/m²).

17. • Power is the rate of doing work, the amount of energy transferred per unit time.
• The SI unit of power is Watt (W).

18. • Electropositive Atoms having a positive electric charge (of an atom, group, molecule etc.) tending to release electrons and form positive ions or polarized bonds compare to electronegative.

• Electropositive elements tend to lose electrons and form positive ions (e.g. the univalent alkali metals Li+, Na+, k+ etc ., and the divalent alkaline-earth metals).

19. The atoms of the elements having same difference between mass number and atomic number are called Isotones. Two nuclides are isotones if they have the same neutron number , but different proton number.

20. Rolling friction is much more than sliding friction, the use of ball bearings in a machine considerably reduces friction is not true about Frictional force. Frictional force is a contact force that acts in the opposite direction to the motion of an object. This

force can cause objects in motion to come to rest, as they act in the opposite direction to its motion.

21. Moment of force measures the affinity of rotation of body about any axis , the axis may be centroid or any other axis along the body

22. The reduction reaction is

$$C_6H_5NO_2 + 3H_2 C_6H_5NH_2 + 2H_2O$$

Hydrogen required for reduction of $12.3/123$ or 0.1 mole of nitrobenzene $= 0.1 \times 3 = 0.3$ mole

Amount of charge required for liberation of 0.3 mole of hydrogen $= 2 \times 96500 \times 0.3 = 57900$ coulomb

Actual amount of charge required as efficiency is $50\% = 2 \times 57900 = 115800$ coulomb

Energy consumed $= 115800 \times 3.0 = 347400J = 347.4kJ$

23. When traveling to an altitude much higher than usual RBCs are kicked into circulation early, in a less mature and hence less competent, form by the Reticuloendothelial System (RES) in response to a sudden demand for more oxygen than had been usual at the lower elevation.

24. Soil erosion can be prevented by Afforestation. Overgrazing and removal of vegetation causes deforestation.

25. The Red Data Book is a type of a public document, which is created for the recordings of rare and endangered species including animals, plants and fungi as well as some local subspecies, which are present within the region of the state or country.

26. Hydra like planaria, too can reproduce by regeneration. It can be cut into any number of pieces and each piece grows into a complete organism.

27. According to Mendeleev's periodic law, the physical and chemical properties of the elements are the periodic function of their atomic masses. Mendeleev's arranged all the elements known at that time in increasing order of atomic mass and this arrangement become periodic table.

28. Curie point, also called Curie Temperature, is the temperature at which certain magnetic materials undergo a sharp change in their magnetic properties.

29. The lightest metal on Earth is Lithium which has the lowest density of all metals, which is nearly 2 times lower than that of water.

30. Robert Andrews Millikan was an American experimental physicist honoured with the Nobel Prize for Physics in 1923 for the measurement of the elementary electronic charge and for his work on the photoelectric effect.

31. The Indian Councils Act 1861 was passed by British Parliament in 1861 to make substantial changes in the composition of the Governor General's council for executive & legislative purposes. The most significant feature of this Act was the association of Indians with the legislation work.

32. The key objectives of the Regulating Act of 1773 included addressing the problem of management of company in India address the problem of dual system of governance instituted by Lord Clive to control the company, which had morphed from a business entity to a semi-sovereign political entity.

33. Pitt's India Act (1784), named for the British prime minister William Pitt the Younger, established the dual system of control by the British government and the East India Company, by which the company retained control of commerce and day-to-day administration.

34. Charles Cornwallis is known as 'the father of civil service in India'. Cornwallis introduced two divisions of the Indian Civil service—covenanted and uncovenanted. The covenanted civil service consisted of only Europeans (i.e., British personnel) occupying the higher posts in the government.

35. Underarticle 356, its Provisions allow President to proclaim constitutional emergency in case of failure of constitutional machinery in States.

36. Under article 80 of the Constitution, the Council of States (RajyaSabha) is composed of 250 members, of whom 12 are nominated by the President of India from amongst persons who have special knowledge or practical experience in respect of such matters as literature, science, art and social service.

37. Vengalil Krishnan Krishna Menon was defence minister during Indo china war of 1962.

38. The States Reorganisation Commission (SRC) was a body constituted by the Central Government of India in 1953 to recommend the reorganisation of state boundaries.

39. Ghatampur Thermal Power Station is an upcoming coal-based thermal power plant located in Ghatampur in Kanpur district, Uttar Pradesh.

40. During the youthful stage river cuts vertically and leads to headward erosion because of its high velocity. This leads to valley deepening. Hence, we find many V-shaped valleys at the initial course of river. It has very less or no time for lateral erosion.

41. Underlined word 'must' suggest Necessity because 'must' used to express necessity or strong recommendation, although native speakers prefer the more flexible form "have to." "Must not" can be used to prohibit actions, but this sounds very severe; speakers prefer to use softer modal verbs such as "should not" or "ought not" to dissuade rather than prohibit.

42. 'The nightingale as well as the cuckoo is a singing bird.' is the correct sentence.

43. 'Must' implies mandatory which shows obligation. Because, also use 'must' to express a strong obligation.

44. Left, Right and Forward these are direction.

45. There should be 'Blocks' instead of 'Block' . So correct sentence is 'Blocks of Residential flats are coming up near our house.'

46. Vacillating is fluctuating. Therefore the answer is Resolute as it means admirably purposeful, determined, and unwavering.

Fanaticism is the quality of being fanatical.
Fascinating: Extremely interesting.

47. Reckless means careless or rash or heedless.
Cautious on the other hand means aware.

48. It can be inferred from the given first line of the passage "In May 1996, The World Health Organization was authorized to initiate a global campaign to eradicate smallpox." that the best title for the passage is **the eradication of smallpox**.

Hence, the correct option is (B).

49. The answer is in the first line of the passage i.e. "The goal was to eradicate the disease in one decade. "

50. The answer is in the first few lines of the second paragraph of the passage i.e. "The strategy was not only to provide mass vaccination, but also to isolate patients with active smallpox in order to contain the spread of the disease and to break the chain of human transmission. "

Mathematics

Q.1 A sum doubles itself in 6 yr at compound interest. The sum will be eight times at the same rate of interest in

A. 15 yr   **B.** 12 yr   **C.** 18 yr   **D.** 10 yr

Q.2 Mohan and Ramesh working together do a piece of work in 20 days. Mohan alone can do it in 28 days. Ramesh alone will do the work in

A. 20 days   **B.** 40 days   **C.** 50 days   **D.** 70 days

Q.3 ABC is an equilateral triangle. Find the ratio of its circumradius and the side of largest square inside it.

A. $2 : \sqrt{3}$ **B.** $(\sqrt{3} + 2) : 3$

C. $3 : (\sqrt{3} + 2)$ **D.** $2 : 3$

Q.4
If $(1 + \sin\alpha)(1 + \sin\beta)(1 + \sin\gamma) = (1 - \sin\alpha)(1 - \sin\beta)(1 - \sin\gamma)$

,then each side is equal to

A. $\pm\cos\alpha.\cos\beta.\cos\gamma$

B. $\pm\sin\alpha\sin\beta\sin\gamma$

C. $\pm\sin\alpha\cos\beta\cos\gamma$

D. $\pm\sin\alpha\sin\beta\cos\gamma$

Q.5 A vendor sells lemons at the rate of 5 for ₹ 14, gaining thereby 40%. For how much did he buy a dozen lemons ?

A. ₹ 20   **B.** ₹ 21   **C.** ₹ 24   **D.** ₹ 28

Q.6 If a car cover 350m, then how aproximately many times does the tyre of radius 28 inches rotate? (1 inch = 2.54cm)

A. 74   **B.** 76   **C.** 78   **D.** 80

Q.7 A, B and C three pipes are attached in a tank. All are opened together then A and B filled of tank and A and C filled of tank. If A can fill it alone in 12 hrs then A, B and C can fill it together in:

A. $4\frac{1}{2}$ hrs   **B.** $3\frac{1}{2}$ hrs   **C.** $2\frac{1}{4}$ hrs   **D.** 5hrs

Q.8 If 2z=3y=6-zthen$\left(\dfrac{1}{x} + \dfrac{1}{y} + \dfrac{1}{z}\right)$is equal to

A. 0   **B.** 1   **C.** 3/2   **D.** -1/2

Q.9 The angles of elevation of the top of a tower from two points A and B lying on the horizontal line through the foot of the tower are respectively 15° and 30°. If A and B are on the same side of the tower and AB = 48 metre, then the height of the tower is

A. $24\sqrt{3}$ metre   **B.** 24 metre

C. $24\sqrt{2}$ metre   **D.** 96 metre

Q.10 The population of a village is 1,00,000. If the population increases at 10% per annum, then the population at the start of the third year is

A. 1,33,100   **B.** 1,21,000   **C.** 1,20,000   **D.** 1,10,000

Q.11 Rs 6300 is divided among three friends in the ratio of $\dfrac{1}{3} : \dfrac{1}{5} : \dfrac{1}{6}$ respectively what is the share of each person?

A. 3000,1600,1800   **B.** 3500,1500,1300

C. 2000,2500,1800   **D.** 3000,1800,1500

Q.12 In a triangle PQR, A is the midpoint of side PQ. There is any point M on side QR. A line RN is drawn parallel to AM which intersects PQ at N. If area of ΔPQR is 2 square unit then, find the area of ΔNQM?

A. 1   **B.** 2   **C.** 1/2   **D.** 4

Q.13 The average marks obtained by a student in 6 subjects is 88. On subsequent verification it was found that the marks obtained by him in a subject was wrongly copied as 86 instead of 68. The correct average of the marks obtained by him is

A. 86   **B.** 87   **C.** 85   **D.** 84

Q.14 Find the value of

$$\left(\sqrt{42 + \sqrt{42 + \sqrt{42 + \ldots\ldots\infty}}}\right) X \left(\sqrt{42 - \sqrt{42 - \sqrt{42 - \ldots\ldots\infty}}}\right)$$

A. 48   **B.** 40   **C.** 42   **D.** 7

Q.15 At a point on a horizontal line through the base of a monument, the angle of elevation of the top of the monument is found to be such that its tangent is 1/5 . On walking 138 metres towards the monument the secant of the angle of elevation is found to be $\sqrt{193}/12$. The height of the monument (in metre) is

A. 35   **B.** 49   **C.** 42   **D.** 56

Science

Q.16 After electrolysis of a sodium chloride solution with inert electrodes for a certain period of time, 600 mL of the solution was left which was found to be 1 N in NaOH. During the same period 31.75 g of copper was deposited in the copper voltameter in series with the electrolytic cell. Calculate the percentage theoretical yield of NaOH obtained.

A. 60   **B.** 90   **C.** 61   **D.** 91

Q.17 A circular loop of radius R, carrying current I, lies in x-y plane with its centre at origin. The total magnetic flux through x-y plane is

A.   directly proportional to I

B.   directly proportional to R

C.   inversely proportional to R

D.   zero

Q.18 What is the composition of Gun metal?

A.   Copper (70%) + Zinc (30%)

B.   Copper (88%) + (8-10%) tin+ (2-4%) Zinc

C.   Copper (90%) + tin (10%)

D.   Copper (60%) + Zinc (40%)

Q.19 'Kelp' is .

A. Sulphide mineral of iron
B. Partially decomposed vegetation
C. Sea weed rich in iodine content
D. An aluminum silicate mineral

Q.20 The number of protons in a heavy stable nucleus is:

A. Larger than that of neutrons
B. Less than that of neutrons
C. The same as that of neutrons
D. Half the number of neutrons

Q.21 The most important ore of Aluminium is–

A. Bauxite
B. Calamine
C. Calcite
D. Galena

Q.22 .A charged particle is released from rest in a region of steady and uniform electric and magnetic fields which are parallel to each other. The particle will move in a :-

A. circle
B. helix
C. straight line.
D. cycloid

Q.23 Which among the following determines the pitch of a sound?

A. Amplitude
B. Frequency
C. Loudness
D. Wavelength

Q.24 The Newton's First Law is also called as-

A. Law of moment
B. Law of inertia
C. Law of energy
D. Law of momentum

Q.25 On a clean glass plate a drop of water spreads to form a thin layer whereas a drop of mercury remains almost spherical because _______

A. Mercury is a metal
B. Density of mercury is greater than that of water
C. Cohesion of water is greater than its adhesion with glass
D. Cohesion of mercury is greater than its adhesion with glass

Q.26 Foreign materials entering the cell, such as bacteria or food, as well as old organelles end up in the ___________.

A. Vacuoles
B. Mitochondria
C. Plastids
D. Lysosomes

Q.27 Which is the process of killing diseases producing micro-organism in food items by heat-

A. Pasteurisation
B. Sterlisation
C. Disinfection
D. Autoclave

Q.28 Respiratory pigment in human body is:

A. Chlorophyll
B. Water
C. Blood
D. hemoglobin

Q.29 Full form of DNA is_____

A. DI Nitro Acid
B. Dioxide Nucleic Acid
C. Deoxyribo Nuclear Acid
D. Deoxyribo Nucleic Acid

Q.30 Consider the following :

1. Birds
2. Dust blowing
3. Rain
4. Wind blowing

Which of the above spread plant diseases?

A. 1 and 3 only
B. 3 and 4 only
C. 1, 2 and 4 only
D. 1, 2, 3 and 4

General Awareness

Q.31 What type of electromagnetic radiation is used in the remote control of a television ?

A. Infrared
B. Ultraviolet
C. Visible
D. None of these

Q.32 The halogen being used as analgesic is

A. Chlorine
B. Bromine
C. Iodine
D. Fluorine

Q.33 Which state has launched new higher education model named "RACE" ?

A. Haryana
B. Madhya Pradesh
C. Maharashrta
D. Rajasthan

Q.34 National Handloom Day is celebrated on _________

A. 4 August
B. 5 August
C. 6 August
D. 7 August

Q.35 Lichen is a composite combination of which of the following two organisms?

A. Fungi and Bryophyta
B. Fungi and Fer
C. Algae and Bryophyta
D. Algae and Fungi

Q.36 Which one of the following trees is considered to be an environmental hazard?

A. Babool
B. Amaltas
C. Neem
D. Eucalyptus

Q.37 Which of the following bears naked seeds?

A. Angiosperms
B. Gymnosperms
C. Bryophytes
D. Pteridophytes

Q.38 Which one of the following European trading companies adopted the "Blue Water Policy" in India?

A. Dutch company
B. French company
C. Portuguese company
D. British East India company

Q.39 Who of the following led the army of the East India Company in the battle of Buxar in 1764?

A. Hector Munro
B. Watson
C. Warren Hastings
D. Lord Clive

Q.40 What does the 'Judicial Review' function of the Supreme Court mean?

A. Review its own judgment
B. Review the functioning of judiciary in the country

C. Examine the constitutional validity of the constitution

D. Examine the judicial amendments

Basic English

Ques (41-44):Direction : Read the following passage and answer the questions that follow the passage. Your answers to these items should be based on the passage only.

The object underlying the rules of natural justice "is to prevent miscarriage of justice" and secure "fair play in action". As pointed out earlier the requirement about recording of reasons for its decision by an administrative authority exercising quasi-judicial functions achieves his object by excluding changes of arbitrariness and ensuring a degree of fairness in the process of decision making. Keeping in view the expanding horizon of the principle of natural justice which governs exercise of power by administrative authorities. The rules of natural justice are not embodied rules. The particularly statutory framework where under jurisdiction has been conferred on the administrative authority. With regard to the exercise of particular power by an administrative authority including exercise of judicial or quasi-judicial functions the legislature, while conferring the said power, may feel that it would not be in the larger public interest that the reasons for the order passed by the administrative authority be recorded in the order and be communicated to the aggrieved party and it may dispense with such a requirement.

Q.41 "The rules of the natural justice are not embodied rule" means that these rules.

A. are left deliberately vague

B. cannot be satisfactorily interpreted

C. are flexible

D. cannot be visualised

Q.42 From the passage it is clear that it is the legislature that-

A. invests the administrative authority with enormous powers

B. embodies rules

C. has the larger interests of public welfare

D. leaves administrative authority enough discretion to interpret rules.

Q.43 According to the passage, there is always a gap between-

A. Rules of natural justice and their application

B. Conception of a rule and its concretisation

C. Demand for natural justice and its realisation

D. Intention and execution

Q.44 "To dispense with a requirement" means

A. to do without the demand

B. to drop the charge

C. to cancel all formal procedure

D. to alter the provisions of the case

Q.45 Direction : In the following questions, choose the word opposite in meaning to the given word.

COUNTERFEIT

A. Fake

B. dual

C. Genuine

D. Transient

Q.46 Direction : In the following questions, choose the word opposite in meaning to the given word.

CURB

A. Encourage

B. Endure

C. abstain

D. Purge

Ques (47-50):Direction : In the following questions a part of sentence is bold. Below are given alternatives to the bold part at (A), (B) and (C) and (D) which may improve the sentence. Choose the correct alternative. In case no improvement , your answer is (E).

Q.47 He has not and can never be in the good books of his employer because he lacks honesty.

A. has not and cannot be

B. has not and can never been

C. has not been and can never be

D. No Improvement

Q.48 When the examinations were over Anil and me went to our native town.

A. me and Anil

B. Anil and I

C. I and Anil

D. No Improvement

Q.49 Our office clock is not so correct as it should be it is usually five minutes fast.

A. right

B. regular

C. accurate

D. No Improvement

Q.50 I shall be grateful to you if you are of help to me now.

A. help

B. would help

C. helped

D. No Improvement

// Smart Answer Sheet //

Correct   Indicates percentage of students who answered questions correctly.

Skipped   Indicates percentage of students who skipped questions.

Q.	Ans.	Correct / Skipped
1	C	83.09 % / 10.16 %
2	D	86.18 % / 10.93 %
3	B	85.92 % / 12.94 %
4	A	78.64 % / 10.97 %
5	C	83.59 % / 14.08 %
6	C	81.18 % / 18.05 %
7	A	78.59 % / 12.81 %
8	A	77.93 % / 11.4 %
9	B	79.16 % / 16.55 %
10	B	77.17 % / 17.01 %

Q.	Ans.	Correct / Skipped
11	D	85.47 % / 10.6 %
12	A	87.57 % / 12.12 %
13	C	76.95 % / 10.03 %
14	C	84.91 % / 12.92 %
15	C	85.98 % / 10.98 %
16	A	81.74 % / 15.67 %
17	D	77.44 % / 16.63 %
18	B	89.29 % / 10.37 %
19	C	80.63 % / 14.28 %
20	B	88.71 % / 10.78 %

Q.	Ans.	Correct / Skipped
21	A	78.39 % / 11.21 %
22	C	82.7 % / 16.65 %
23	B	77.65 % / 19.97 %
24	B	88.28 % / 10.19 %
25	D	84.86 % / 15.03 %
26	D	84.75 % / 10.44 %
27	A	81.82 % / 13.05 %
28	D	80.29 % / 11.88 %
29	D	80.33 % / 11.72 %
30	D	81.5 % / 14.68 %

Q.	Ans.	Correct / Skipped
31	A	88.23 % / 11.37 %
32	B	82.61 % / 10.69 %
33	D	88.54 % / 11.39 %
34	D	81.85 % / 15.57 %
35	D	78.86 % / 16.17 %
36	D	86.48 % / 10.36 %
37	B	87.63 % / 11.87 %
38	C	85.84 % / 10.62 %
39	A	77.23 % / 16.74 %
40	B	77.24 % / 11.83 %

Q.	Ans.	Correct / Skipped
41	B	80.0 % / 10.08 %
42	A	78.22 % / 18.89 %
43	A	84.15 % / 11.02 %
44	A	80.91 % / 16.61 %
45	C	89.57 % / 10.06 %
46	A	76.72 % / 21.99 %
47	C	85.22 % / 10.14 %
48	B	85.65 % / 10.72 %
49	D	86.86 % / 12.01 %
50	B	78.14 % / 12.25 %

Performance Analysis	
Avg. Score (%)	34.67%
Toppers Score (%)	56.0%
Your Score	

//Hints and Solutions//

1. sum doubles itself in 6 yr at compound interest.

it will double itself again in another 6 years and so on..

We know that

23 = 8

∴Required time = 6 × 3 = 18 yr

2. Mohan alone can do a work in 28 days

∴ Part of work done by Mohan in 1 day = 1/28

Let, Ramesh alone can do a work in 'x' days

∴ Part of work done by Ramesh in 1 day = 1/x

∵ Mohan and Ramesh working together do the work in 20 days

∴ (1/28) × 20 + (1/x) × 20 = 1

⇒ (20/28) + (20/x) = 1

⇒ (20x + 560)/28x = 1

⇒ 20x + 560 = 28x

⇒ 8x = 560

⇒ x = 70 days

3.

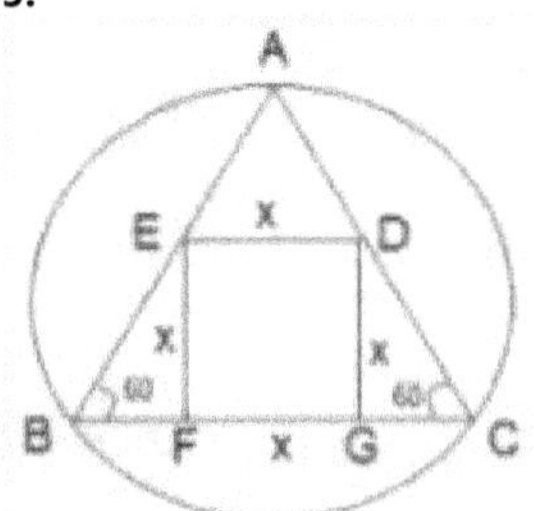

Let a be the side of the triangle ABC, and r be its circumradius.
Then, $r = \dfrac{a}{\sqrt{3}}$

$a = r\sqrt{3}$

Now let x be the side of the largest possible square inside ΔABC. In ΔEBF

$\tan 60 = \dfrac{x}{BF}$

$BF = \dfrac{x}{\sqrt{2}}$

Similarly, In $\triangle DCG$ $GC = \dfrac{x}{\sqrt{3}}$

Now, $BC = BF + FG + GC$

$\Rightarrow a = \dfrac{x}{\sqrt{2}} + x + \dfrac{x}{\sqrt{3}}$

$\Rightarrow r\sqrt{3} = x\left(1 + \dfrac{2}{\sqrt{3}}\right)$

$\dfrac{r}{x} = \dfrac{\sqrt{3}+2}{3}$

the required ratio is $\left(\sqrt{3} + 2\right) : 3$

4. $(1 + \sin\alpha)(1 + \sin\beta)(1 + \sin\gamma) = (1 - \sin\alpha)(1 - \sin\beta)(1 - \sin\gamma) = x$

$\therefore x \cdot x = (1 + \sin\alpha)(1 - \sin\alpha)(1 + \sin\beta)(1 - \sin\beta)(1 + \sin\gamma)(1 - \sin\gamma)$

$= (1 - \sin^2\alpha)(1 - \sin^2\beta)(1 - \sin^2\gamma)$

$= \cos^2\alpha \cdot \cos^2\beta \cdot \cos^2\gamma$

$\therefore x = \pm\cos\alpha \cdot \cos\beta \cdot \cos\gamma$

5. C.P. of 5 lemons

100/140x14=Rs.10

∴ C.P. of 12 lemons

10*12/5 =24

6. Distance covered by tyre in one rotation = 2πr = 2*22*28/7 inches = 176inches

Distance covered by car = 350m = 350 * 100/2.54 inches = 13780 inches

Number of rotations = 13780/176 = 78 rotations

7. Work completed by A, B and C together = 1

Work completed by C = $1 - \dfrac{5}{8} = \dfrac{3}{8}$

Work completed by B = $1 - \dfrac{3}{4} = \dfrac{1}{4}$

Work completed by A = $1 - \left(\dfrac{3}{8} + \dfrac{1}{4}\right) = \dfrac{3}{8}$

Working ratio of A : B : C = $\dfrac{3}{8} : \dfrac{1}{4} : \dfrac{3}{8} :: = 3 : 2 : 3$

Required time = $\dfrac{12x3}{8} = \dfrac{9}{2} = 4\dfrac{1}{2}$ hrs

8. $2^x = 3^y = 6^{-2} = k$

$2 = k^{\frac{1}{x}}; 3 = k^{\frac{1}{y}}; 6 = k^{\frac{1}{z}}$

$\because 2 \times 3 = 6$

$k^{\frac{1}{x}} \times k^{\frac{1}{y}} = k^{-\frac{1}{z}}$

$k^{\frac{1}{x}+\frac{1}{y}} = k^{\frac{1}{z}}$

$\dfrac{1}{x} + \dfrac{1}{y} = -\dfrac{1}{z}$

$\dfrac{1}{x} + \dfrac{1}{y} + \dfrac{1}{z} = 0$

9.

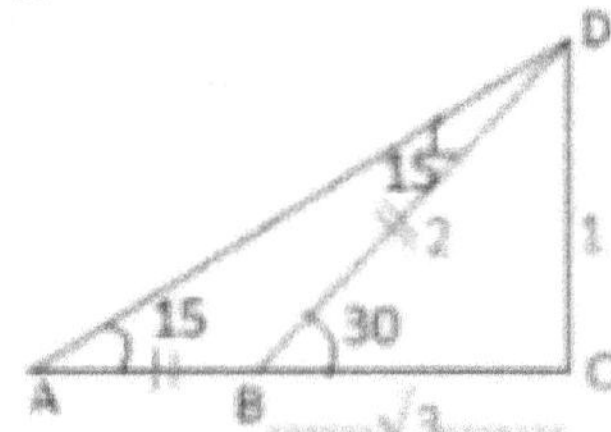

using external angle theore

$\angle ADB = \angle DBC - \angle DAC$

$\angle ADB = 30 - 15 = 15°$

Now in triangle ADB.

$\angle DAB = \angle ADB = 15°$

SO $AB = BD = 48$

Now in triangle DBC
using ratios

2 unit $= BD = 48$

1 unit $= DC = 24$

$h = 24$

10. 100000==10%↑(1st year)==>110000

110000==10%↑(2nd year)==>121000

Population at the end of 2 years is same as the population at the starting of 3rd year.

Hence Population at starting of 3rd year = 121000.

11. $A:B:C = \dfrac{1}{3}:\dfrac{1}{5}:\dfrac{1}{6}$

L. $C.M$ of A, B and $C = 30$ Let total salary be $= 30x$

Share of $A = \dfrac{1}{3} \times 30 = 10x$

Share of $B = \dfrac{1}{5} \times 30 = 6x$

Share of $C = \dfrac{1}{6} \times 30 = 5x$

A.T.Q $10x + 6x + 5x = 6300$

$x = 300$

Hence Share of $A = 10 \times 300 = Rs3000$

Share of $B = 6 \times 300 = Rs1800$

Share of $C = 5 \times 300$ Rs 1500

12.

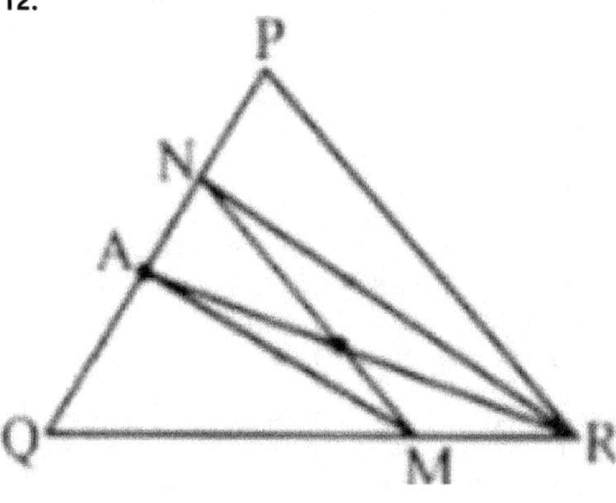

$\because A$ is the mid-point of PQ, then, AR is the median of $\triangle PQR$.

$\therefore$ Area of $\triangle AQR =$ Area of $\triangle APR = \dfrac{1}{2}$ area of $\triangle PQR (i)$

$\because AM$

A Area of $\triangle AMR =$ Area of $\triangle AMN$

Area of $\triangle AQR =$ Area of $\triangle AQM +$ Area of $\triangle AMR$

$\Rightarrow$ Area of $\triangle AQM +$ Area of $\triangle AMN$

$\Rightarrow$ Area of $\triangle AQR =$ Area of $\triangle NQM$

From equation

2 area of $\triangle PQR =$ Area of $\triangle NQM$

2

Area of $\triangle NQM = \dfrac{1}{2} \times 2 = 1$

Area of ANQM is $1cm$ sq.

13. Required average

$= \dfrac{88x6 - 86 + 68}{6}$

$= \dfrac{510}{6} = 85$

14. Given

$(\sqrt{42 + \sqrt{42 + \sqrt{42 +}}}\ldots\infty) \times ($

$\sqrt{42 - \sqrt{42 - \sqrt{42 -}}}\ldots\infty)$

$\sqrt{42 + \sqrt{42 +}\cdots\infty} = x(\text{ say })$

Squaring $42 + \sqrt{42 + \sqrt{42 +}\cdots\infty} = x^2 \Rightarrow x^2 = 42 + x$

$\Rightarrow (x - 7)(x + 6) = 0 \Rightarrow [x = 7, -6]$ As $x > 0 \Rightarrow x = 7$

similarly, $\sqrt{42 - \sqrt{42 -}\cdots\infty} = x(\text{ say })$

Squaring $42 - sqrt42 - \sqrt{42 -}\cdots\infty = x^2 \Rightarrow x^2 = 42 - x$

$\Rightarrow (x + 7)(x - 6) = 0 \Rightarrow [x = -7, 6]$ As $x > 0 \Rightarrow x = 6$

$= 7 \times 6$

$= 42$

15.

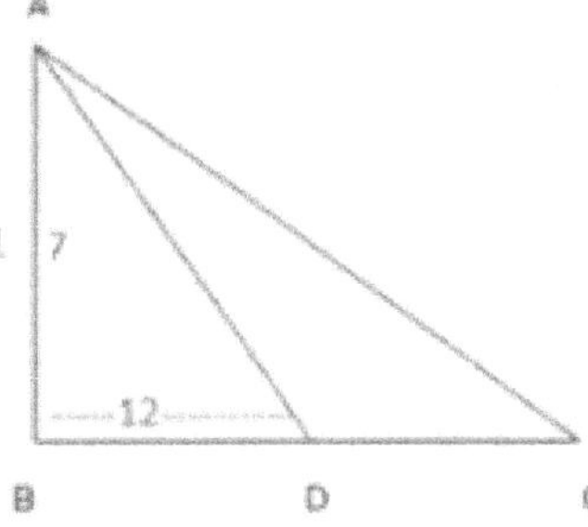

From first condition,

$tanC = 1/5$

$AB:BC = 1:5$

for second

$secD = \sqrt{193/12}$

$tan2D = sec2D - 1$

$tan2D = 193/144 - 1$

$tan2D = 49/144$

$tanD = 7/12$

$AB:BD = 7:12$

after scaling we get

$AB \cdot BD = 7:12$

$AB:BC = 7:35$

$AB = 7$ units

$BD = 12$ units

$BC = 35$ units

$DC = 35 - 12 = 23$ units

23 units $= 138m$

1 unit $= 6m$

$AB = 7$ unit $= 42m$

Basic Method:

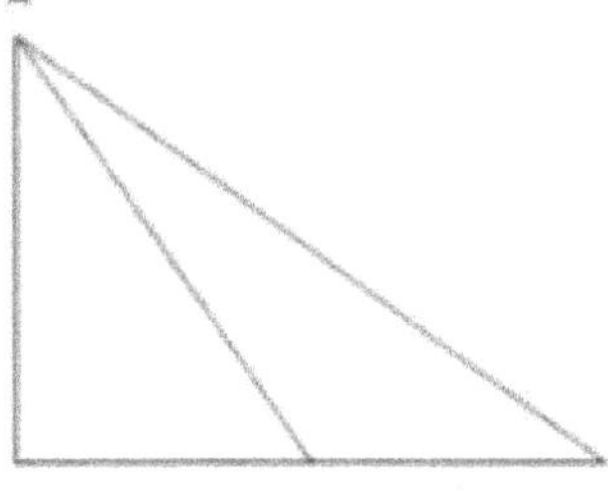

$AB =$ monument $= h$ metre $DC = 138$ metre

$BD = x$ metre $\tan\alpha = \dfrac{1}{5}$

$\sec\beta = \dfrac{\sqrt{193}}{12}$

$\therefore \tan\beta = \sqrt{\sec^2\beta - 1}$

$= \sqrt{\dfrac{193}{144} - 1}$

$= \sqrt{\dfrac{193-144}{144}}$

$= \sqrt{\dfrac{49}{144}} = \dfrac{7}{12}$

$\therefore$ From $\triangle ABC$

$\tan\alpha = \dfrac{AB}{BC}$

$\dfrac{1}{5} = \dfrac{h}{x+138}$

$h = \dfrac{x+138}{5}$

$h = \dfrac{x+138}{5}$

$5h = x + 138$

From $\triangle ABD$ $\tan\beta = \dfrac{h}{x}$

$\dfrac{7}{12} = \dfrac{h}{x}$

$x = \dfrac{12h}{7}$

$\therefore 5h = \dfrac{12h}{7} + 138$

$5h \times 7 = 12h + 138 \times 7$

$35h - 12h = 138 \times 7$

$23h = 138 \times 7$

$h = \dfrac{138 \times 7}{23} = 42$ metre

16. Equivalent mass of NaOH = 40/1000 × 600 = 24 g

Amount of NaOH formed = 40/1000 × 600 = 24 g

31.75 g of Cu = 1 g equivalent of Cu.

During the same period, 1 g equivalent of NaOH should have been formed.

1 g equivalent of NaOH = 40 g

% yield = 24/40 × 100 = 60

17. Total magnetic flux passing through whole of the x — y plane will be zero.The magnetic lines form a closed loop. The number of lines moving downwards in x — y plane will be same in number to that coming upwards from the x-y plane. Net flux will therefore be zero.

18. Gunmetal, also known as red brass in the United States, is a type of bronze – an alloy of copper, tin, and zinc. Proportions vary by approximation but 88% copper, 8–10% tin, and 2–4% zinc is an approximation. Originally used chiefly for making guns, it has largely been replaced by steel.

19. Kelps are large seaweeds (algae) beloging to the brown algae in the order laminariales. Because of its high concentration of iodine, kelp has been used to treat goiter, an enlargement of the thyroid gland caused by a lack of iodine.

20. If there are more protons then there will be more repulsions in the nucleus due to more positive charges.

The arrangement of neutrons with protons is in such a way that repulsions are reduced to a minimum extent.

An increase in neutrons will lead to an increase in mass ratio and a decrease in repulsions between protons, resulting in instability of the nucleus.

Thus, the number of protons in a heavy stable nucleus is less than the number of neutrons.

Hence, the correct option is (B).

21. Bauxite is an ore of aluminum. This is the main source of aluminum in the world. It contained GibSite Al(OH)3, boehmite γ-AlO (OH) and diaspora α-AlO (OH), and two iron oxides of goethite and Hematite and anatase TiO2. is.

22. Uniform electric and magnetic fields are parallel to each other.The electric field will accelerate or decelerate the charged particle parallel to itself. The charged particle will move parallel to electric field and so parallel to magnetic field. The magnetic force on such charged particle will be zero. Path of particle will be a straight line.

23. Pitch is determined by the frequency of a wave, and frequency is the combination of wavelength and speed at which the wave is travelling.

24. Newton's first law of motion - sometimes referred to as the law of inertia. An object at rest stays at rest and an object in motion stays in motion with the same speed and in the same direction unless acted upon by an unbalanced force.

25. On a clean glass plate a drop of water spreads to form a thin layer whereas a drop of mercury remains almost spherical because cohesion of mercury is greater than its adhesion with glass.

26. Lysosomes are basically a class of waste disposal system of the cell that helps to maintain the cleanness of the cell by digesting any strange material as well as useless cell organelles.

27. Pasteurization is the application of heat to a food product in order to destroy pathogenic (disease-producing) microorganisms, to inactivate spoilage-causing enzymes, and to reduce or destroy spoilage microorganisms.

28. A respiratory pigment is a molecule, such as hemoglobin in humans and other vertebrates, that increases the oxygen-carrying capacity of the blood. The four most common invertebrate respiratory pigments are hemoglobin, hemocyanin, hemerythrin and chlorocruorin.

29. DNA is known as Deoxyribo Nucleic Acid. DNA is a thread-like chain of nucleotides carrying the genetic instructions used in the growth, development, functioning and reproduction of all known living organisms and many viruses.

30. Plant diseases can be infectious (transmitted from plant to plant) or noninfectious. Common plant disorders are caused by deficiencies in plant nutrients, by waterlogged or polluted soil, and by polluted air. Too little (or too much) water or improper nutrition can cause plants to grow poorly. Plants can also be stressed by weather that is too hot or too cold, by too little or too much light, and by heavy winds. Pollution from automobiles and industry, and the excessive application of herbicides (for weed control) can also cause noninfectious plant disorders.

31. Most remote controls send signals using infrared radiation (which is a kind of invisible red light that hot objects give off and halogen hobs use to cook with), though some use radio waves instead.

32. Compounds of bromine have been used as sedatives, hypnotics, and analgesics.

33. Minister of State for Higher Education Bhanwar Singh Bhati inaugurated the new higher education model, titled Resource Assistance for Colleges with Excellence(RACE) in Rajasthan.

34. The National Handloom Day is observed annually on August 7 since 2015. The objective of the day is to generate awareness about the importance of the handloom industry to the socio economic development of the country.

35. Lichens are composite organisms composed of fungus and alga. Fungus is a saprophyte and alga is an autotroph. The Fungus supplies water and minerals to the cells of the alga while the alga supplies food; prepared by photosynthesis.

36. Eucalyptus is considered to be an environmental hazard as it depletes ground water table. Eucalyptus species consume more water than others, less productive species.

37. Gymnosperm are the plants which bear naked seeds.

38. Portuguese trading company adopted the "Blue Water Policy" in India. Francisco de Almeida became the 1st Portuguese viceroy in India initiated the Blue Water Policy, which aimed at the Portuguese Mastery of the Sea and confined Portuguese relationship with India only for the purpose of trade and commerce.

39. The Battle of Buxar was fought on 23 October 1764 between the forces of the British East India Company led by Hector Munro and the combined army of Mughal rulers. The Mughal forces were drawn from 2 princely states, whose rulers were Mir Qasim, the Nawab of Bengal, and the Mughal King Shah Alam II.

40. A Judicial review is the power of the Supreme Court of the United States to review actions taken by the legislative branch (Congress) and the executive branch (president) and decide whether or not those actions are legal under the Constitution

41. Embody means "be an expression of or give a tangible or visible form to (an idea, quality, or feeling)." Therefore, the rules are flexible as they are not embodied.

42. These lines from the last part of the passage answer the question- "With regard to the exercise of particular power by an administrative authority including exercise of judicial or quasi-judicial functions the legislature, while conferring the said power".

43. the answer is in the first few lines of the passage- "The object underlying the rules of natural justice "is to prevent miscarriage of justice" and secure "fair play in action". As pointed out earlier the requirement about recording of reasons for its decision by an administrative authority exercising quasi-judicial functions achieves his object by excluding changes of arbitrariness and ensuring a degree of fairness in the process of decision making."

44. It can be concluded from the given lines of the passage "while conferring the said power, may feel that it would not be in the larger public interest that the reasons for the order passed by the administrative authority be recorded in the order and be communicated to the aggrieved party and it may dispense with such a requirement."

45. Counterfeit: made in exact imitation of something valuable with the intention to deceive or defraud.

Transient is to last for short time.

Genuine: truly what something is said to be; authentic.

46. Curb is a check or restraint on something. Therefore, encourage is the opposite.

Endure is to remain in existence.

Purge is to get rid of unwanted feeling or condition.

47. Has/have/had + past participle

Here, past participle is missing, therefore "been" is to be used as third form of verb.

48. "Anil and I" is the appropriate answer as a reference is made to the subject. When used as a subject 'Anil and I' will be correct and when used as an object 'Anil and me' will be correct.

49. Accurate is correct in all details or precise. This is a better word as per the context.

50. As per the context "would help" is appropriate as some sort of request is being made.

Mathematics

Q.1 The cost price of 24 apples is the same as the selling price of 18 apples. The percentage of gain is:

A. 53.3%   **B.** 36.3%   **C.** 43.3%   **D.** 33.3%

Q.2 8 men and 12 boys can complete a work in 15 days, whereas 10 men can complete the same work in 18 days. How many days will be 15 boys take to complete the same work?

A. 36   **B.** 18   **C.** 27   **D.** 12

Q.3 If $x = 5 - \sqrt{21}$, then the value of is $\dfrac{\sqrt{x}}{\sqrt{32-2x}-\sqrt{21}}$

A. $\frac{1}{\sqrt{2}} \times (\sqrt{3}-\sqrt{7})$

B. $\frac{1}{\sqrt{2}} \times (\sqrt{7}-\sqrt{3})$

C. $\frac{1}{\sqrt{2}} \times (\sqrt{7}+\sqrt{3})$

D. None of the above

Q.4 A certain sum of money amounts to Rs. 2300 in 2 years and Rs. 2700 in 4 years using simple interest. How much the sum will amount to, in 7 years?

A. 2900   **B.** 3100   **C.** 3300   **D.** 3500

Q.5 In a triangle ABC, ∠B = 2∠C. AD & BP are bisectors of angle ∠BAC and ∠ABC. If AB = CD, then, find angle ∠ABC?

A. 60 degree   **B.** 80 degree

C. 72 degree   **D.** 65 degree

Q.6 Ankit has a specific average for 8 innings. In the ninth innings, he scores 113 runs in this manner his average increases by 11 runs. His new average is:

A. 17   **B.** 14   **C.** 21   **D.** 25

Q.7 If $\tan\theta = \sqrt{3}$, find the value of given equation $\dfrac{6\sin^2\theta+3\cos^2\theta}{8\sin^4\theta-6\cos^3\theta}$ is

A. 24/5   **B.** 23/5   **C.** 21/5   **D.** 7/5

Q.8 A candidate who gets 20% marks in an examination fails by 30 marks but another candidate who gets 32% gets 42 marks more than the pass marks. Then, the percentage of pass marks is

A. 52%   **B.** 50%   **C.** 33%   **D.** 25%

Q.9 $\left(999 + \dfrac{998}{999}\right) \times 999$ is equals to:

A. 998999   **B.** 999899   **C.** 989999   **D.** 999989

Q.10 An employer reduce the no. of his employee in the ratio 9:4 and increase the wage 2:5. His bill of total wage increase or decrease and in what ratio

A. Increase 100/9 %   **B.** Decrease 100/3%

C. Increase 100/7%   **D.** Decrease 100/7%

Q.11 A team of 39 persons can repair a road in 12 days working 5 hours a day, then in how many days will 30 persons working 6 hours a day complete the work?

A. 10   **B.** 13   **C.** 14   **D.** 15

Q.12 The true discount on ₹1,860 due after a certain time at 5% is ₹60. Find the time after which it is due

A. 10 months   **B.** 8 months

C. 9 months   **D.** 1 year

Q.13 ABCD is a rectangle. There are two points P & Q on side AB and AD such that area of ΔPAQ, ΔCDQ & ΔPBC are equal. If the length of BP is 2 cm, find the length of AP?

A. $\sqrt{5}$ **B.** $1/\sqrt{5}$ **C.** $1 + \sqrt{5}$ **D.** $1 - \sqrt{5}$

Q.14 The number obtained by interchanging the digits of a two digit number is less than the original number by 18. If sum of the digits is 6, what was the original two digit number?

A. 51   **B.** 24   **C.** 42   **D.** 15

Q.15 If 5 men or 8 women can do a piece of work in 12 days, how many days will be taken by 2 men and 4 women to do the some work?

A. 15 days   **B.** $13\frac{1}{3}$ days

C. $13\frac{1}{2}$ days   **D.** 10 days

Science

Q.16 A particle of charge q and mass m moves in a circular orbit of radius r with angular speed uj . The ratio of the magnitude of its magnetic moment to that of its angular momentum depends on:

A. w and q   **B.** w, q and m

C. q and m   **D.** w and m

Q.17 A particle of mass m and charge q moves with a constant velocity v along the positive x direction. It enters a region containing a uniform magnetic field B directed along the negative z direction, extending from x = a to x = b. The minimum value of v required so that the particle can just enter the region:

A. q(b+a)2B/m   **B.** q(b-a)B/m

C. q(b+a)B/m   **D.** q(b-a)2B/m

Q.18 .A mass m is moving with a constant velocity along a line parallel to the x axis, away from the origin. Its angular momentum with respect to the origin.

A. goes on increasing   **B.** goes on decreasing.

C. Zero   **D.** Constant

Q.19 A cubical block of side L rests on a rough horizontal surface with coefficient of friction p. A horizontal force F is applied on the block as shown. If the coefficient of friction is sufficiently high so that the block does not slide before toppling, the minimum force required to topple the block is :

A. mg/2   **B.** mg/4

C. 2mg   **D.** none of the above

Q.20 Kinetic theory of gases proves:-

A. Only Charles' law
B. Only Avogadro's law
C. Only Boyle's law
D. All of these

Q.21 What is the freezing point of C_2H_5OH?

A. -114.1^{0}C   **B.** -95^{0}C   **C.** -50^{0}C   **D.** -145^{0}C

Q.22 What is the name of the acid in our blood?

A. Lactic acid   **B.** Formic acid
C. Acetic acid   **D.** Tartaric acid

Q.23 In gas welding, which of the following gas is used to generate light?

A. Oxalic acid   **B.** Ethylene
C. Acetylene   **D.** Acetic acid

Q.24 _____________is an organic compound that contains only carbon, chlorine and fluorine, produced as a volatile derivative of methane and ethane.

A. UV radiation   **B.** CFC
C. Hydrocarbons   **D.** Benzopyrene

Q.25 The heat required to raise the temperature of body by 1 K is called :

A. specific heat   **B.** thermal capacity
C. water equivalent   **D.** none of these

Q.26 Na and Mg crystallize in BCC and FCC type crystals respectively. Then the number of atoms of Na and Mg present in the unit cell of their respective crystal is :

A. 4 and 2   **B.** 8 and 4   **C.** 2 and 8   **D.** 2 and 4

Q.27 According to the kinetic theory of gases, in an ideal gas, between two successive collisions a gas molecule travels :

A. straight-line path   **B.** in a wavy path
C. in a circular path   **D.** in a helix path

Q.28 As the temperature is raised from 20°C to 40°C, the average kinetic energy of neon atoms changes by a factor of which of the following?

A. 1   **B.** 0.83   **C.** 0.93   **D.** 2

Q.29 Cadmium amalgam is prepared by electrolysis of a solution of CdCl2 using a mercury c0thode. Find how long a current of 5 ampere should be passed in order to prepare 12% Cd-Hg amalgam on a cathode of 2 g mercury. At mass of Cd = 112.40.

A. 93.75   **B.** 93   **C.** 83.75   **D.** 83

Q.30 In Van der Waals equation of state of the gas law, the constant 'b' is a measure of:-

A. The volume occupied by the molecules
B. Intermolecular collisions per unit volume
C. Intermolecular attraction
D. None of the above

General Awareness

Q.31 Bharat ratna and Padma vibhushan awards in India were instituted in the year ___ .

A. 1958   **B.** 1968   **C.** 1964   **D.** 1954

Q.32 Guru Gobind Singh commanded Sikhs to wear five items all the time. Which of the following is NOT one of these five items?

A. Kesh   **B.** Kila   **C.** Kara   **D.** Kangha

Q.33 The Sepoy Mutiny of 1857 took place when ___ was the Governor General of India.

A. Lord Bentick   **B.** Lord Wellesley
C. Lord Canning   **D.** Lord Dalhousie

Q.34 Which of the following instruments measures electromagnetic radiation?

A. Pyrheliometer   **B.** Cathetometer
C. Bolometer   **D.** Phenograph

Q.35 Twelfth Film London Jarman Award is won by ____

A. Hetain Patel   **B.** Nik Thakkar
C. Rahul Potluri   **D.** Lucian Freud

Q.36 When was NABARD established?

A. 1986   **B.** 1980   **C.** 1982   **D.** 1984

Q.37 Who is the author of the book, 'The Google Story'?

A. Frederick Forsyth   **B.** Daved A. Vise
C. Shobha Dey   **D.** Vikram Seth

Q.38 A minor planet is named after which of the following legends?

A. Viswanathan Anand   **B.** Milkha Singh
C. A.R. Rehman   **D.** Sachin Tendulkar

Q.39 Which among the following state cricket associations has become the first state cricket association to announce contracts for its first class cricketers?

A. Uttar Pradesh   **B.** Karnataka
C. Maharashtra   **D.** Uttarakhand

Q.40 Where was the sanskriti kumbh, a 29 days cultural exravaganza, held in January 2019?

A. Chandrashila   **B.** Sonprayag
C. Agastramuni   **D.** Prayagraj

Basic English

Ques (41-45):Direction : Read the following passage carefully and answer the questions given below it.

How many really suffer as a result of labor market problems? This is one of the most critical yet contentious social policy questions. In many ways, our social statistics exaggerate the degree of hardship. Unemployment does not have the same dire consequences today as it did in the 1930's when most of the unemployed were primary breadwinners, when income and earnings were usually much closer to the margin of subsistence, and when there were no countervailing social programs for those failing in the labor market. Increasing affluence, the rise of families with more than one wage earner, the growing predominance of secondary earners among the unemployed, and improved social welfare protection have unquestionably mitigate the consequences of joblessness. Earnings and income data also overstate the dimensions of hardship. Among the millions with hourly earnings at or below the minimum wage level, the overwhelming majority are from multiple-earner, relatively affluent families. Most of those counted by the poverty statistics are elderly or handicapped or have family responsibilities which keep them out of the labor force, so the poverty statistics are by no means an accurate indicator of labor market pathologies.

Yet there are also many ways our social statistics underestimate the degree of labor-market-related hardship. The unemployment counts exclude the millions of fully employed workers whose wages are so low that their families remain in poverty. Low wages and repeated or prolonged unemployment frequently interact to undermine the capacity for self-support. Since the number experiencing joblessness at some time during the year is several times the number unemployed in any month, those who suffer as a result of forced idleness can equal or exceed average annual unemployment, even though only a minority of the jobless in any month really suffers. For every person counted in the monthly unemployment tallies, there is another working part-time because of the inability to find full-time work, or else outside the labor force but wanting a job. Finally, income transfers in our country have always focused on the elderly, disabled, and dependent, neglecting the needs of the working poor, so that the dramatic expansion of cash and in-kind transfers does not necessarily mean that those failing in the labor market are adequately protected.

As a result of such contradictory evidence, it is uncertain whether those suffering seriously as a result of labor market problems number in the hundreds of thousands or the tens of millions, and, hence, whether high levels of joblessness can be tolerated or must be countered by job creation and economic stimulus. There is only one area of agreement in this debate—that the existing poverty, employment, and earnings statistics are inadequate for one their primary applications, measuring the consequences of labor market problems.

Q.41 What is the main theme of the passage?

A. The causes of labor market pathologies which lead to suffering.

B. The reason for the imprecise income measures in determining rate of poverty.

C. The way by which social figures provide a vague picture of the extent of hardship due to low wages and inadequate job opportunities.

D. The areas of agreement among employment, income figures and poverty.

Q.42 The words "labor market problems" used by the author in the passage refer to:

A. All the factors responsible for poverty.

B. Inefficiency in the training of the work force.

C. Trade links between producers of goods and commodities.

D. Scarcity of jobs that provide sufficient income.

Q.43 The author of the passage compares the 1930s with the modern day to prove that:

A. There was more redundancy in the 1930s.

B. Redundancy now has less rigorous effects.

C. More social and employment programs are required to be

implemented.

D. Poverty has decreased since the 1930s.

Q.44 The author mentions that the justifying effect of social programs concerning transfers of income on the level of income of low-income people is usually not realized by:

A. Retired people

B. Full time workers who turn jobless

C. Reliant children in single-earner families

D. The employed poor

Q.45 A factor that leads to unemployment and earnings figures to over expect the extent of economic hardship is the:

A. Dominance, among low-income earners and the jobless, of members of families in which are working

B. Repetition of periods of redundancy for a group of low-income earners

C. Probability that income might be received from more than one job per worker

D. Setting up of a system of record-keeping which makes it feasible to pile up poverty statistics

Ques (46-47):Direction : In the following questions a part of sentence is bold. Below are given alternatives to the part of sentence given in bold, which may improve the sentence. Choose the alternative which makes the sentence grammatically and contextually correct. In case the sentence is correct as it is, choose 'No Improvement' as your option.

Q.46 It was announced that the economy grew during the third quarter at a 6% annual rate, while inflation eased when it might have been expected for it to rise

A. It might have been expected to rise

B. It might have been expected that it should rise

C. Its rise has been expected

D. No correction

Q.47 An important figure in the Scottish explanation, Adam Smith's two major books are to democratic capitalism what Marx's Das Kapital is to socialism.

A. Adam Smith's two major books are to democratic capitalism like

B. Adam Smith's two major books are to democratic capitalism just as

C. Adam Smith wrote two major books that are to democratic capitalism what

D. No correction

Q.48 Direction : In the following questions, choose the word opposite in meaning to the given word.

CULPRIT

A. Witness   **B.** Accused

C. Victim   **D.** Spectator

Q.49 Direction : In the following questions, choose the word opposite in meaning to the given word.

UNCOUTH

A. Rude   **B.** Courteous

C. Hungry   **D.** Impolite

Q.50 Direction : In the following questions out of the four/five alternatives, choose the one which is best express the meaning of the given word.

PESTER

A. Carefree   **B.** Bother   **C.** Relaxed   **D.** Gratify

// Smart Answer Sheet //

Correct Indicates percentage of students who answered questions correctly.

Skipped Indicates percentage of students who skipped questions.

Q.	Ans.	Correct / Skipped
1	D	76.67 % / 12.02 %
2	A	84.89 % / 13.18 %
3	B	85.93 % / 10.22 %
4	C	85.13 % / 10.11 %
5	C	87.7 % / 10.34 %
6	D	79.77 % / 14.06 %
7	D	85.74 % / 10.12 %
8	D	89.52 % / 10.14 %
9	A	86.93 % / 12.31 %
10	A	87.31 % / 10.49 %

Q.	Ans.	Correct / Skipped
11	B	80.94 % / 16.34 %
12	B	79.31 % / 10.84 %
13	C	76.75 % / 22.12 %
14	C	88.69 % / 10.69 %
15	B	79.36 % / 15.63 %
16	C	80.12 % / 17.59 %
17	B	88.47 % / 10.29 %
18	D	84.05 % / 13.35 %
19	A	85.69 % / 13.54 %
20	D	76.66 % / 23.06 %

Q.	Ans.	Correct / Skipped
21	A	88.65 % / 10.74 %
22	A	78.55 % / 18.09 %
23	C	81.78 % / 14.16 %
24	B	77.7 % / 18.18 %
25	B	85.57 % / 13.54 %
26	D	77.73 % / 18.65 %
27	A	80.4 % / 14.35 %
28	C	78.68 % / 10.76 %
29	A	86.95 % / 10.3 %
30	A	87.11 % / 10.03 %

Q.	Ans.	Correct / Skipped
31	D	87.2 % / 11.47 %
32	B	81.54 % / 11.28 %
33	C	78.93 % / 19.48 %
34	C	87.9 % / 11.74 %
35	A	89.58 % / 10.12 %
36	C	81.55 % / 10.12 %
37	B	84.85 % / 11.62 %
38	A	81.39 % / 18.33 %
39	D	83.49 % / 12.62 %
40	D	87.79 % / 10.65 %

Q.	Ans.	Correct / Skipped
41	C	86.9 % / 12.87 %
42	D	89.99 % / 10.01 %
43	B	84.7 % / 13.7 %
44	D	82.09 % / 15.04 %
45	A	88.34 % / 11.62 %
46	A	82.32 % / 14.81 %
47	C	84.68 % / 11.91 %
48	C	84.79 % / 14.71 %
49	B	86.99 % / 12.03 %
50	B	82.08 % / 12.49 %

Performance Analysis

Avg. Score (%)	38.67%
Toppers Score (%)	58.67%
Your Score	

//Hints and Solutions//

1. Let the CP of 1 apple = ₹1

CP of 18 apples = ₹18

SP of 18 apples = ₹24

Gain per cent =

$$\frac{6}{8} x 100 = \frac{100}{3} = 33.3\%$$

2. $8men + 12$ boys complete a work in 15 days

∴ 8 men's +12 boys's 1 day's work $= \dfrac{1}{15}$

Now, Also, 10 men complete the same work in 18 days

∴ 10 men's 1 day's work $= \dfrac{1}{18}$

∴ 1 man's 1 day's work $= \dfrac{1}{18 \times 10}$

∴ 8 men's 1 day's work $= \dfrac{8}{18 \times 10} = \dfrac{2}{45}$

∴ 12 boys' 1 day's work $= \dfrac{1}{15} - \dfrac{2}{45} = \dfrac{3-2}{45} = \dfrac{1}{45}$

∴ 1 boy's 1 day's work $= \dfrac{1}{45 \times 12}$

∴ 15 boy's 1 day's work $= \dfrac{15}{45 \times 12} = \dfrac{1}{36}$

∴ Required number of days $= 36$ days

3. $x = 5 - \sqrt{21}$

$$\frac{\sqrt{x}}{\sqrt{32-2x-\sqrt{21}}}$$

$$= \frac{\sqrt{5-\sqrt{21}}}{\sqrt{32-10+2\sqrt{21}-\sqrt{21}}}$$

$$= \frac{\sqrt{5-\sqrt{21}}}{\sqrt{22+2\sqrt{21}-\sqrt{21}}}$$

$$= \frac{\left(\sqrt{10-2\sqrt{21}}\right)/\sqrt{2}}{\sqrt{21+1+2\sqrt{21}}} - \sqrt{21}$$

$$= \frac{\left(\sqrt{7+3-2\sqrt{7\times3}}\right)\sqrt{2}}{\sqrt{21+1+2\sqrt{21}-\sqrt{21}}}$$

$$= \frac{\left(\sqrt{\left(\sqrt{7}-\sqrt{3}\right)^2}\right)\sqrt{2}}{\sqrt{\left(\sqrt{21}+1\right)^2-\sqrt{21}}}$$

$$= \frac{\sqrt{7}-\sqrt{3}}{\sqrt{2}\left(\sqrt{21}+1-\sqrt{21}\right)} = \frac{\sqrt{7}-\sqrt{3}}{\sqrt{2}}$$

4. Let the principal be P

Amount after 2 years = 2300

Amount after 4 years = 2700

Simple Interest for 2 years = Amount after 4 years - Amount after 2 years

= 2700 – 2300 = 400

Initial amount = 2300 – 400 = 1900

Amount after 7 years = 1900 + 200*7 = 3300

5.

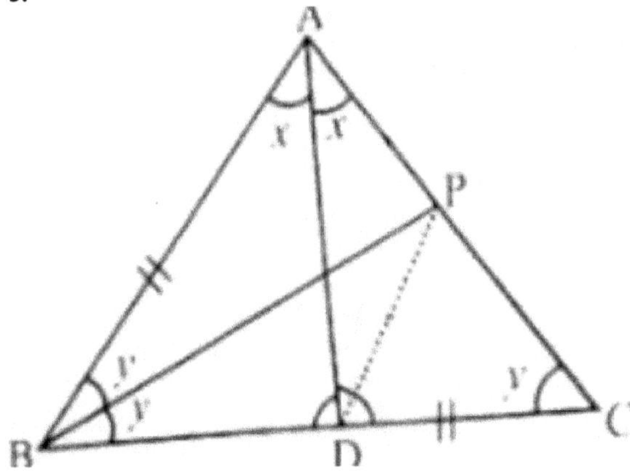

In ΔABC,

∠B = 2∠C or, ∠B = 2y where, ∠C = y

AD is bisector of ∠BAC.

∠BAD = ∠CAD = x (let)

Let BP be the bisector of ∠ABC. Join PD.

In ΔBPC,

∠CBP = ∠BCP = y

So, BP = PC

In ΔABP and ΔDCP,

∠ABP = ∠DCP = y

AB = DC (given)

And BP = PC

By SAS congruency

ΔABP ≅ ΔDCP

∠BAP = ∠CDP and AP = DP

∠CDP = 2x and ∠ADP = ∠DAP = x

[∵∠A = 2x]

In ΔABD,

ΔADC = ΔABD + ∠BAD

x + 2x = 2y + x

⇒ x = y

In ΔABC,

∠A + ∠B + ∠C = 180

2x + 2y + y = 180

⇒ 5x = 180

⇒ x = 36

⇒∠BAC = 2x = 72

∴ ∠BAC is 72º

6. Let's Assume Ankit's average be x for 8 innings.

So, Ankit scored 8x run in 8 innings.

In the 9th inning, he scored 113 runs then average become (x+11). And he scored (x+11)*9 runs in 9 innings.

Now,

$\Rightarrow$ 8x+113 = 9*(x+11)

Or, 8x+113 = 9x+99

Or, x = 113-99

Or, x = 14

New average = (14+11) = 25 runs.

7. $\tan\theta = \sqrt{3} = \tan 60° \Rightarrow \theta = 60°$

Required

$$\frac{6\sin^2 60° + 3\cos^2 60°}{8\sin^2 60° - 6\cos^3 60°} = \frac{6\times\left(\frac{\sqrt{3}}{2}\right)^2 + 3\times\left(\frac{1}{2}\right)^2}{8\times\left(\frac{\sqrt{3}}{2}\right)^4 - 6\times\left(\frac{1}{2}\right)^3} = \frac{6\times\frac{3}{4}+3\times\frac{1}{4}}{8\times\frac{9}{16}-6\times\frac{1}{8}}$$

$$= \frac{\frac{18}{4}+\frac{3}{4}}{\frac{72}{16}-\frac{6}{8}} = \frac{\frac{21}{4}}{\frac{60}{16}} = \frac{7}{5}$$

8. Difference of percentages of maximum marks obtained by two candidates = 32% – 20% = 12%

Difference of scores between two candidates

= 30 + 42 = 72

$\therefore$12% of maximum marks = 72

$\therefore$Maximum marks = 72 x 100/12 =600

$\therefore$Pass marks = 20% of 600 + 30

= 120 + 30 = 150

$\therefore$Required percentage = 150/600 x 100 =25%

9. Given:

$$\left(999 + \frac{998}{999}\right) \times 999$$

$$= \left(999 + \frac{998}{999}\right) \times 999$$

$$= 999^2 + 998$$

$$= (1000 - 1)^2 + 998$$

$$= 1000000 - 2000 + 1 + 998$$

$$= 998999$$

Hence, the correct option is (A).

10. If the employees ratio is decreased in the ratio 9 : 4

and wage per employee is increased in the ratio 2 : 5

Then the total wage ratio is

(9 × 2 : 4 × 5) = (18 : 20) = 9 : 10

Which means total wage is increased from 9 to 10. so increase is 1 over 9.

Hence, Percentage is $\frac{1}{9}x100 = \frac{100}{9}\%$

11. By using formula: $\frac{M_1 D_2 H_1}{W_1} = \frac{M_2 D_2 H_2}{W_2}$

$M_1 = 39$ persons, $D_1 = 12$ days, $H_1 = 5$ hours per day
$M_2 = 30$ persons, $D_2 = ?, H_2 = 6$ hours per day $D_2 = \frac{M,D,H,W_2}{M_2 H_2 W_1}$

$\Rightarrow D_2 = \frac{39\times12\times5\times W}{30\times6\times W}$

$\Rightarrow D_2 = 13$ days

12. Short Trick:

payment due after some time = 1860

payment if done now is 1800

so 60 rs interest on 1800 at 5% rate

for 1 year interest would have been = 1800*5/100 = 90

for 12 months interest = 90

for 8 months interest = 60

Hence answer is 8 months.

Basic Method:

True discount $-\frac{A\times R\times T}{100+(R\times T)}$

$\Rightarrow 760 \cdot \frac{r 1860\times 5\times T}{100+5T}$

$\therefore 100 + 5T = 1557$

$\Rightarrow T = \frac{2}{3}years = 8 months$

13. Let $AP = X, AO = Y \& OD = Z$

$SO, BC + y \cdot Z \& CD = x \cdot 2$

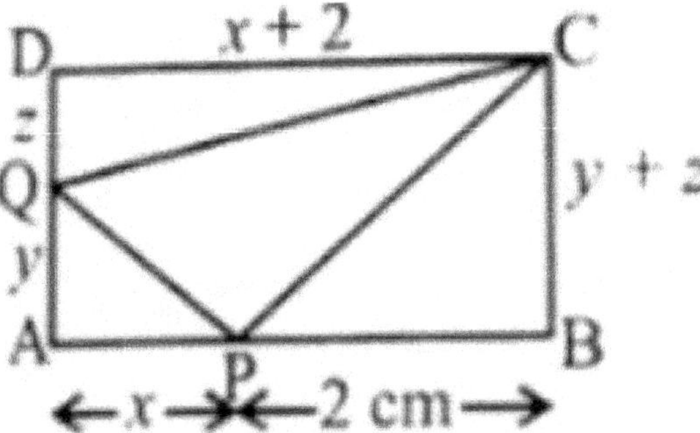

Area of ΔPAQ = Area of ΔPBC = Area of ΔCDQ

$\frac{1}{2}xy = \frac{1}{2}\cdot 2(y + z) = \frac{1}{2}z(x + 2)$

$xy = 2y + 2z = zx + 2z$

From last two relations $(2y + 2z = zx + 2z) \Rightarrow z = \frac{2y}{x}$

From first & last relation $\{xy = z(x + 2)\}$ Put the value of

z in above relation $xy = \frac{2y}{x}(x + 2) \Rightarrow x^2 = 2(x + 2)$

$x^2 - 2x - 4 = 0$

$$x = \frac{2 \pm \sqrt{4+16}}{2} = 1 + \sqrt{5}$$
$$AP = 1 + \sqrt{5}$$

14. Let the original number be 10x+y.

Number obtained by interchanging the digits=10y+x

10x+y-10y-x=18

9x-9y=18

X - y =2....................(i)

Again, x + y = 6 ....(ii)

From Eqs. (i) and (ii),

x=4 and y=2

Original number = 10 x 4 + 2 = 42

15. According to the question
$$5men = 8 \text{ women}$$
$$\therefore 2men = \frac{8}{5} \times 2 = \frac{16}{5} \text{ women}$$
$$\therefore \text{Total women } = \frac{16}{5} + 4 = \frac{36}{5} \text{ women}$$
$$\therefore \text{Number of days to do the same work } = \frac{8 \times 12}{\frac{36}{5}} =$$
$$\frac{8 \times 12 \times 5}{36} = \frac{40}{3} = 13\frac{1}{3} days$$

16. Angular momentum= L
$$L = mr^2\omega = 2\pi n m r^2 \text{ where } n = \text{frequency}$$
Magnetic moment $= M$
$$M = i \times \text{area} = (qn)(\pi r^2)$$
$$\therefore \frac{M}{L} = \frac{qn \times \pi r^2}{2\pi n m r^2} \text{ or } \frac{M}{L} = \frac{q}{2m}$$

17. Ans.
(b) The uniform magnetic field B is perpendicular to motion of charged particle.

$\therefore$ Magnetic force $=$ Centripetal force $Bqv = \frac{mv^2}{r}$ or $r = \frac{mv}{Bq}$

The magnetic field extends from $x = a$ to $x = b$. $\therefore r = (b - a)$

$\therefore (b - a) = \frac{mv_m}{Bq}$ where $v_m = $ minimum speed. or $v_m = \frac{(b-a)Bq}{m}$

18. Angular moment of particle w.r.t origin $=$ linear momentum x perpendicular distance on line of action of linear momentum from origin. $= mv \times a = mva =$ constant.

19. The block will topple if, $(F \times L) > mg \times \frac{L}{2}$ or, $F > \frac{mg}{2}$

Thus, the least force, $F_{\min} = \frac{mg}{2}$

20. Postulates of kinetic theory explain all gas laws.

21. Freezing point of alcohol is -114.1^0C

while freezing point of mercury is -39^2C

Hence, to measure below -39^2C

Ethanol is a chemical compound, a simple alcohol with the chemical formula C_2H_6O. Its formula can be also written as CH_3-CH_2-OH or C_2H_5OH, and is often abbreviated as EtOH. Ethanol is a volatile, flammable, colorless liquid with a slight characteristic odor.

22. Lactic acid, or lactate, is a chemical byproduct of anaerobic respiration — the process by which cells produce energy without oxygen around. Bacteria produce it in yogurt and our guts. Lactic acid is also in our blood, where it's deposited by muscle and red blood cells.

23. Acetylene is used to generate light, to weld metals. Oxygen and Acetylene are the gases used to produce the welding flame. The flame will only melt the metal. A flux is used during welting to prevent oxidations and to remove impurities. Metals 2mm to 50mm thick are welded by gas welding.

24. A Chloro Fluoro Carbon (CFC) is an organic compound that contains only carbon, chlorine and fluorine, produced as a volatile derivative of methane and ethane. The manufacture of CFC has been phased out (and replaced with products such as R-410 A) by the montreal protocol because they contribute to ozone depletion in the upper atmosphere.

25. The heat required to raise the temperature of body by IK is called thermal capacity or heat capacity.

26. Ans.
(4) In BCC lattice, 8 points are at corners and one in the centre of the unit cell. Number of atoms per unit cell $= 8 \times \frac{1}{8} + 1 \times 1 = 2$ In FCC lattice, $8 -$ points are at the corners and 6 in centre of the six faces of each cell.

Number of atoms per unit cell $= 8 \times \frac{1}{8} + 6 \times \frac{1}{2} = 4$

27. Ans. According to kinetic theory the gas, molecules travel in a straight line path but show haphazard motion. This is due to collisions.

28. Ans.
(3) Kinetic energy is directly propertional to absolute temperature. $\frac{E_1}{E_2} = \frac{T_1}{T_2}$

Substitution of the values gives the ratio of energy as $= \frac{293}{313} = 0.93$

29. 2 g Hg require Cd to prepare 12% amalgam = 12/88 × 2 = 0.273 g

1 mole 2 × 96500C

112.40g

Charge required to deposit 0.273 g of Cd = 2*96500/112.40 × 0.273 coulomb

Charge = ampere × second

Second = 2*96500*0.273/112.40*5 = 93.75

30. In van der Waals equation, 'b' is the excluded volume. Excluded volume is the volume occupied by the molecules of gas.

31. The Padma Vibhushan is the second-highest civilian award of the Republic of India, second only to the Bharat Ratna. Instituted on 2 January 1954, the award is given for "exceptional and distinguished service".

32. The five Ks are:Kesh (uncut hair),Kara (a steel bracelet),Kanga (a wooden comb),Kaccha – also spelt, Kachh, Kachera (cotton underwear) and Kirpan (steel sword)

33. The governor general at the time of 1857 revolt was Lord Canning.

34. A bolometer is a device for measuring the power of incident electromagnetic radiation via the heating of a material with a temperature-dependent electrical resistance. It was invented in 1878 by the American astronomer Samuel Pierpont Langley.

35. Hetain Patel, whose practice encompasses moving image works, sculpture, photography, and performance, has won the 2019 Film London Jarman Award. He was presented with the award, which is named after the late British director Derek Jarman.Now in its twelfth year, the annual $12,000 prize recognizes the spirit of imagination and innovation in the work of UK-based artists and filmmakers.

36. NABARD was established on the recommendations of B. Sivaraman Committee on 12 July 1982 to implement the National Bank for Agriculture and Rural Development Act 1981.

37. The Google Story is a book by David Vise and Mark Malseed.

38. Viswanathan Anand, the Chess Grand Master of India now has a planet named after him, called, '4538 Vishyanand'.

39. Uttarakhand cricket association is the first cricket association to announce contracts to its first class cricketers and scholarships for both under 16 and under 19 men and women cricketers.

40. Sanskriti Kumbh is a 29 days Cultural extravaganza being held at Kumbh Mela Area, Prayagraj, Uttar Pradesh.

41. The main theme of the passage is the way by which social figures provide a vague picture of the extent of hardship due to low wages and inadequate job opportunities.

42. The words "labor market problems" used by the author in the passage refer to the scarcity of jobs that provide sufficient income and it can be concluded from the given lines of the passage "Unemployment does not have the same dire consequences today as it did in the 1930's when most of the unemployed were primary breadwinners, when income and earnings were usually much closer to the margin of subsistence, and when there were no countervailing social programs for those failing in the labor market."

43. The author of the passage compares the 1930s with the modern day to prove that redundancy now has less rigorous effects.

This can be concluded from the given lines of the passage "Unemployment does not have the same dire consequences today as it did in the 1930's when most of the unemployed were primary breadwinners, when income and earnings were usually much closer to the margin of subsistence, and when there were no countervailing social programs for those failing in the labor market."

44. The author mentions that the justifying effect of social programs concerning transfers of income on the level of income of low-income people is usually not realized by the employed poor.

45. A factor that leads to unemployment and earnings figures to over expect the extent of economic hardship is the dominance, among low-income earners and the jobless, of members of families in which are working.

46. Option (a) is correct because 'expected to rise' makes a meaningful sense in the sentence. The correct idiom usage is X is expected to Y. Moreover, the main issue here is lack of parallelism. 'Inflation' is a plain noun - and we're continuing to talk about inflation - so it's most logically parallel to continue the sentence in a manner that continues to address 'inflation' itself (or the equivalent pronoun 'it', which is what the correct answer does). Choice D unnecessarily switches the subject to 'its rise', creating a nonparallel construction that's also (arguably) more difficult to understand.

47. The beginning modifier (in technical jargon, it's called appositive) "A leading figure" must modify Adam Smith, not his two books. This cancels A and B.The sentence presents a similarity using the structure "x is to y what a is to b" making C as the right option.

48. 'Culprit' is used to refer to a 'wrongdoer, one responsible for the crime'. Thus, the antonym for 'culprit' is 'victim' which means a person harmed, injured, or killed as a result of a crime, accident, or other event or action.

Witness: a person who sees an event, typically a crime or accident, take place.

Accused: charge (someone) with an offense or crime.

Spectator: a person who watches at a show, game, or other events.

49. 'Uncouth' means 'uncivilized' or 'rude'. Thus, the antonym for 'uncouth' is 'courteous' which refers to polite, respectful, or considerate in manner.

50. 'Pester' means to 'annoy', or 'harass'. Therefore, the synonym for 'pester' is 'bother.'

Gratify refers to giving (someone) pleasure or satisfaction.

Mathematics

Q.1 Two trains start from stations A and B and travel towards each other at the same time at speeds of 50 kmph and 60 kmph respectively. At the time of their meeting, the second train has travelled 120 km more than the first. The distance between A and B is ?

A. 1200 km   **B.** 1440 km   **C.** 1320 km   **D.** 990 km

Q.2 In a ΔABC, P, Q & R are three points on side BC, such that BP = 3x, QR = 2x, PQ = 4x and RC = 5x. If G is centroid then, find the ratio of area of ΔPGR to area of ΔABC?

A. 2:7   **B.** 3:5   **C.** 1:7   **D.** 7:1

Q.3 If $x = \dfrac{\sqrt{m+3n}+\sqrt{m-3n}}{\sqrt{m+3n}-\sqrt{m-3n}}$, then

A. $3nx^2 - 2mx + 3n = 0$

B. $2nx^2 - 2mx + 3n = 0$

C. $3nx^2 - 2mx - 3n = 0$

D. $3nx^2 + 2mx + 3n = 0$

Q.4 Find the minimum value of
$$\frac{\sin^2(90-\theta)+\cos^2(90-\theta)}{cosec^2(90-\theta)} + \frac{\cot^2(90-\theta)-cosec^2(90-\theta)}{\sec^2(90-\theta)}$$

A. 1   **B.** 2   **C.** 0   **D.** -1

Q.5 The average age of ten members of a committee is the same as it was 2 years ago, as an old member has been replaced by a young member. How much younger is the new member to the old member?

A. 20 years   **B.** 15 years   **C.** 10 years   **D.** 2 years

Q.6 In a book store house, the ratio of English to hindi books is 7:2. If there are 1512 English books and due to increase in demand of English books, few English books are added by the shopkeeper and the said ratio become 15:4. The number of English books added is:

A. 432   **B.** 1620   **C.** 3034   **D.** 108

Q.7 Points D, E and F divide the sides of triangle ABC in the ratio 1 : 3, 1 : 4 and 1 : 1 as shown in figure. What fraction of the area of triangle ABC is the area of triangle DEF?

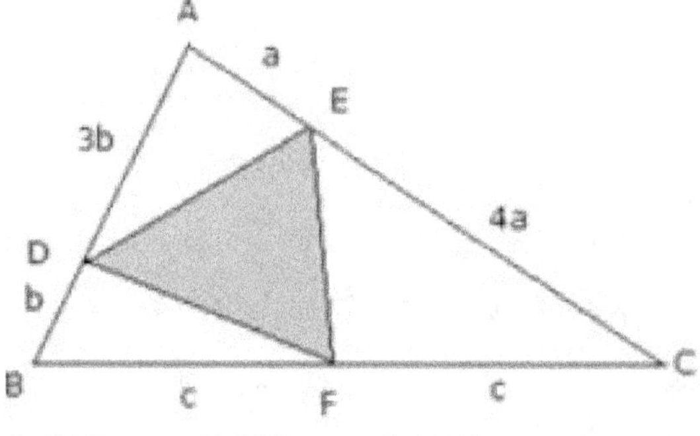

A. 13/40   **B.** 3/40   **C.** 11/40   **D.** 15/40

Q.8 When the price of cloth was reduced by 25%, the quantity of cloth sold increased by 20%. What was the effect on gross receipt of the shop?

A. 5% increase   **B.** 5% decrease

C. 10% increase   **D.** 10% decrease

Q.9 A does half as much work as B in one sixth of the time. If together they take 10 days to complete a work, how much time shall B take to do it alone?

A. 70 days   **B.** 30 days   **C.** 40 days   **D.** 50 days

Q.10 ABCD is a square with side length 10. A circle is drawn through A and D so that it is tangent to BC?

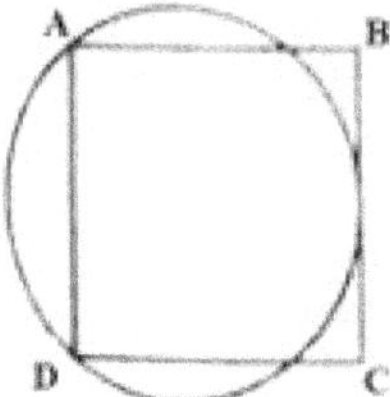

What is the radius of circle?

A. 6 cm   **B.** 5.5 cm   **C.** 5 cm   **D.** 6.25 cm

Q.11 A man purchases milk for three consecutive years. In the first year, he purchases milk at the rate of ₹ 7.50 per litre, in the second year, at the rate of ₹ 8.00 per litre and in the third year, at ₹8.50 per litre. If he purchases milk worth ₹4,080 each year, the average price of milk per litre for the three years is

A. ₹7.68   **B.** ₹7.98   **C.** ₹7.54   **D.** ₹7.83

Q.12 ₹ 3,000 is divided between A, B and C such that A receives 1/3 of the amount received by B and C together. And B receives 2/3 of the amount received by A and C together. Then the share of C is

A. 600   **B.** 525   **C.** 1625   **D.** 1050

Q.13 If sin $\dfrac{\pi x}{2} x^2 - 2x +$ $2\ then\ the\ value\ of\ x\ is$

A. 0   **B.** 1

C. -1   **D.** None of these

Q.14 Find the area of a quadrilateral whose vertices are (2, 0), (6, 0), (0, 6) and (0, 5).

A. 17   **B.** 15   **C.** 13   **D.** 19

Q.15 Respective ratio of the present age of Reena and Beena is 2: 3. 4 years hence the resepective ratio of their ages will be 5: 7 then what is the difference between their ages?

A. 8 years   **B.** 6 years   **C.** 4 years   **D.** 5 years

Science

Q.16 An electric current of 100 ampere is passed through a molten liquid of sodium chloride for 5 hours. Calculate the volume of chlorine gas liberated at the electrode at NTP.

A. 208.91 L   **B.** 108.91 L   **C.** 208 L   **D.** 208.01 L

Q.17 How much charge is required to reduce (a) 1 mole of Al^{3+} ?

A. 289500 coulomb   **B.** 289508 coulomb
C. 287500 coulomb   **D.** 189500 coulomb

Q.18 How much electric charge is required to oxidise 1 mole of H_2O to O_2

A. 193800 C   **B.** 192974 C
C. 192784 C   **D.** 14000 C

Q.19 0.2964 g of copper was deposited on passage of a current of 0.5 ampere for 30 minutes through a solution of copper sulphate. Calculate the atomic mass of copper. (1 faraday = 96500 coulomb)

A. 62.56   **B.** 63
C. 63.56   **D.** None of the above

Q.20 The sun radiates energy in all directions. The average radiations received on the earth surface from the sun is 1.4 kilowatt/m ^{2}. The average earth-sun distance is $1.5 \times 10^{11} m$. The mass lost by the sun per day is (1 day $3/4864$ seconds).

A. 3.8 x 10^{14} kg   **B.** 4.8 x 10^{14} kg
C. 3.8 x 10^{15} kg   **D.** 3.8 x 10^{16} kg

Q.21 An ideal gas expands in volume from $1 \times 10^{-3} m^3$ to $1 \times 10^{-2} m^3$ at $300K$, against a constant pressure of $1 \times 10^5 Nm^{-2}$. The work done is

A. -900J   **B.** 900J   **C.** -900KJ   **D.** 900KJ

Q.22 An ionic compound has a unit cell consisting of A ions at the corners of a cube and B ions on the centers of the faces of the cube. The empirical formula for this compound would be :-

A. AB$_3$ **B.** A$_2$B$_3$
C. AB   **D.** None of these

Q.23 What is the boiling point of propyl acetate?

A. 102°C   **B.** 78.3°C   **C.** 62°C   **D.** 46°C

Q.24 In a hydrogen atom, if energy of an electron in the ground state is $13.6eV$, then that in the $2nd$ excited state is:-

A. 1.4 eV   **B.** 1.3 eV   **C.** 1.6 eV   **D.** 1.5 eV

Q.25 Equal masses of methane and oxygen are mixed in an empty container at $25°C$. The fraction of the total pressure exerted by oxygen is:

A. 1/3   **B.** 1/2   **C.** 1/5   **D.** 2/3

Q.26 In Bohr series of lines of hydrogen spectrum, the third line from the red end corresponds to which one of the following inter-orbit jumps of the electron for Bohr orbits in an atom of hydrogen :-

A. 2 ----->5   **B.** 5 ---->2   **C.** 3---->2   **D.** 2---->3

Q.27 Consider the ground state of Cr atom (Z=24).The number of electrons with the azimuthal quantum numbers 1 =1 and 2 are respectively':-

A. 12 and 4   **B.** 16 and 5
C. 16 and 4   **D.** 12 and 5

Q.28 Which of the following statements in relation to the hydrogen atom is correct?

(1)3s orbital is lower in energy than 3p orbital

(2)3p orbital is lower in energy than 3d orbital

(3)3s and 3p orbitals are of lower energy than 3d orbital

(4)3s, 3p and 3d orbitals all have the same energy

A. Only 1   **B.** Only 2   **C.** Only 3   **D.** Only 4

Q.29 The ammonia evolved from the treatment of 0.30 g of an organic compound for the estimation of nitrogen was passed in 100 mL of 0.1 M sulphuric acid. The excess of acid required 20 mL of 0.5M sodium hydroxide solution hydroxide solution for complete neutralization. The organic compound is:-

A. benzamide   **B.** acetamide
C. Urea   **D.** thiourea

Q.30 A compound with molecular mass 180 is acylated with CH₃COC/ to get a compound * with molecular mass 390. The number of amino groups present per molecule of the former compound is

A. 2   **B.** 5   **C.** 3   **D.** 1

General Awareness

Q.31 Article 35A was incorporated into the constitution of India in ______by an order of the then President Rajendra Prasad on the advice of the Jawaharlal Nehru cabinet.

A. 1959   **B.** 1950   **C.** 1954   **D.** 1956

Q.32 Which of the following is the vector of Malaria?

A. Aedes Mosquito
B. Fleas
C. Anopheles Mosquito
D. Sand fly

Q.33 In January 2019, ________cargo craft departed from the International Space after its successful mission to deliver scientific equipment and other supplies.

A. SpaceX   **B.** SpaceY   **C.** SpaceM   **D.** SpaceZ

Q.34 Which ruler constructed the highest and biggest gateway of Victory, Buland Darwaja?

A. Aurangzeb   **B.** Akbar
C. Jahangir   **D.** Mohammed Ghori

Q.35 Jahangir, the ______ Mughal emperor ruled India from 1605 until his death in 1627 .

A. fifth   **B.** third   **C.** second   **D.** fourth

Q.36 Who has been appointed by RBI as the PMC Bank's administrator?

A. R.N. Mishra   **B.** Naveen Chadha
C. Jai Bhagwan Bhoria   **D.** Saket Singh

Q.37 From which city did Jeevan Rekha, the world's first hospital train start its journey on July 16, 1991?

A. Bangalore
B. New Delhi
C. Bombay
D. Varanasi

Q.38 Prime minister Narendra Modi released a commemorative coin and stamp dedicated to ___ to mark his 350th birth anniversary on 5th January 2019.

A. Guru Amar Das
B. Guru Arjun Dev
C. Guru Ram Das
D. Guru Gobind Singh

Q.39 In which city of India was the first ever Formula One race held?

A. Mumbai
B. Greater Noida
C. Faridabad
D. Pune

Q.40 As of February 2019, who is the Governor of Tamil Nadu?

A. BD Mishra
B. Jagdish Mukhi
C. OP Kohli
D. Banwarilal Purohit

Basic English

Q.41 Direction : In the following questions, some of the sentences have errors and some have none. Find out which part of the sentence has an error. The number of that part is your answer. If there is no error, the answer would be (D).

The Bhagavad Gita is more than a religious or philosophical text (A)/ its 700 plus verses offer insight into (B)/ every aspect of life and are universal relevant. (C)/ No Error (D)

A. A
B. B
C. C
D. D

Q.42 Direction : Sentences are given with blanks to be filled in with an appropriate Preposition.Some alternatives are suggested for each question.Choose the correct alternative out of given alternatives.

He has to be motivated to exercise restraint, change lifestyle and comply_______ medical advice.

A. to
B. with
C. for
D. from

Q.43 Direction : In the following questions out of the four/five alternatives, choose the one which is best express the meaning of the given word.

Flinch

A. forge
B. plunder
C. slovenly
D. blench

Q.44 Direction : In the following questions, choose the word opposite in meaning to the given word.

Charlatan

A. Swindler
B. Hoaxer
C. Exponent
D. Cajole

Q.45 Direction : In the following questions, four/five alternatives are given for the meaning of the given Idiom/Phrase. Choose the alternative which best express the meaning of the Idiom/Phrase.

To hang fire

A. to give false hope
B. to do the dangerous task

C. remain unsolved
D. repeat the arguments

Ques (46-49):Direction : In the following passage some of the words have been left out. First read the passage over and try to understand what it is about. Then fill in the blanks with the help of the alternatives given.

India is not new to the phenomenon called ------------------ inflicting cruelty on animals for personal amusement. A cat, being run over by a car or a dog being attacked by a bunch of - ---------------------- are some of the sights that urban India witnesses quite often. However, Army personnel cooking chinkara meat and superstars of Indian film industry ------------ -----------------endangered deers and owning tusks are some of the news stories that frequently do the rounds.

According to the Wildlife Protection Act of 1972,_______________for the protection of wild animals, birds, and plants, the act of hunting constitutes "capturing, killing, poisoning, snaring, or trapping any wild animal". In fact, injuring, damaging or stealing body part of any animal also constitutes hunting. For wild birds and reptiles, "disturbing or damaging the eggs or nests" is________to hunting.

Q.46 India is not new to the phenomenon called________inflicting cruelty on animals for personal amusement.

A. Bio semiotics
B. Zoosadism
C. Zoosadism
D. Zoo semiotics

Q.47 a bunch of____are some of the sights that urban India witnesses.

A. Urchins
B. Youngster
C. Dandy
D. Zombie

Q.48 Indian film industry___________endangered deers.

A. Are poaching
B. Poaching
C. Poached
D. Had poached

Q.49 ___________for the protection of wild animals, birds, and plants.

A. Enacted
B. Enacts
C. Had enacted
D. Enacting

Q.50 In the following question, out of the four alternatives, select the word opposite in meaning to the given word.

Enslave

A. Emancipate
B. Grasp
C. Enthrall
D. Pragmatic

// Smart Answer Sheet //

Correct — Indicates percentage of students who answered questions correctly.

Skipped — Indicates percentage of students who skipped questions.

Q.	Ans.	Correct / Skipped
1	C	78.78 % / 19.34 %
2	C	86.59 % / 11.08 %
3	A	81.81 % / 12.8 %
4	D	88.68 % / 11.32 %
5	A	79.13 % / 19.4 %
6	D	76.29 % / 22.37 %
7	A	89.44 % / 10.13 %
8	D	80.99 % / 13.66 %
9	C	81.7 % / 16.63 %
10	D	79.91 % / 19.99 %
11	B	88.15 % / 11.22 %
12	D	76.55 % / 20.11 %
13	B	77.46 % / 13.32 %
14	C	81.18 % / 18.0 %
15	A	81.57 % / 16.86 %
16	A	79.39 % / 16.24 %
17	A	76.94 % / 15.98 %
18	B	87.52 % / 10.48 %
19	C	76.69 % / 22.88 %
20	A	80.06 % / 13.84 %
21	A	78.13 % / 15.56 %
22	A	84.12 % / 15.36 %
23	A	88.43 % / 10.0 %
24	D	87.88 % / 11.87 %
25	A	88.17 % / 11.5 %
26	B	79.02 % / 15.5 %
27	D	79.15 % / 14.64 %
28	D	86.69 % / 11.89 %
29	C	89.59 % / 10.33 %
30	B	78.48 % / 12.87 %
31	A	80.89 % / 18.31 %
32	C	85.5 % / 13.0 %
33	A	88.21 % / 11.04 %
34	B	76.07 % / 18.21 %
35	D	76.44 % / 14.28 %
36	C	78.74 % / 15.01 %
37	C	81.54 % / 17.12 %
38	D	78.54 % / 21.0 %
39	B	85.76 % / 14.08 %
40	D	81.15 % / 15.6 %
41	C	81.1 % / 11.22 %
42	B	84.91 % / 10.78 %
43	D	87.83 % / 10.76 %
44	C	76.99 % / 13.26 %
45	C	81.48 % / 16.76 %
46	B	83.08 % / 13.26 %
47	A	82.19 % / 16.77 %
48	B	84.53 % / 12.28 %
49	A	87.93 % / 10.22 %
50	A	86.55 % / 11.58 %

Performance Analysis

Avg. Score (%)	41.33%
Toppers Score (%)	58.0%
Your Score	

//Hints and Solutions//

1. Let the distance travelled by first train be x. Then, the distance travelled by second train $= x + 120$ Time taken by first train $= x/50$ Time taken by second train $= x + 120/60$ A/Q.

$$\frac{x}{50} = \frac{x+120}{60}$$
$$\Rightarrow x = 600$$

Distance travelled by first train $= 600$ Distance travelled by second train $= x + 120 = 720$ The distance between A and $B = 600 + 720 = 1320$

2. Height of ∆GBP, ∆GPQ, ∆GQR & ∆GRC are equal, so area of ∆GBP, ∆GPQ, ∆GQR & ∆GRC will be divided in the ratio of their base. Hence area of ∆GBP, ∆GPQ, ∆GQR & ∆GRC will be in the ratio 3 : 4 : 2 : 5.

Let area of these triangle ∆GBP, ∆GPQ, ∆GQR & ∆GRC is 3, 4, 2 and 5 respectively, then, area of ∆BGC is equal to 14. Area of triangle ∆AGB, ∆BGC & ∆AGC are equal. Hence, area of triangle ABC will be equal to 42.

$$\Rightarrow \frac{\text{Area of } \Delta PGR}{\text{Area of } \Delta 4BC} = \frac{6}{42} = \frac{1}{7}$$

required ratio is 1: 7

3. $\dfrac{x}{1} = \dfrac{\sqrt{m+3n}+\sqrt{m-3n}}{\sqrt{m+3n}-\sqrt{m-3n}}$

By componendo and dividend rule,

$\frac{x+1}{x-1} = \frac{\sqrt{m+3n}+\sqrt{m-3n}+\sqrt{m+3n}-\sqrt{m-3n}}{\sqrt{m+3n}+\sqrt{m-3n}-\sqrt{m+3n}+\sqrt{m-3n}} \Rightarrow \frac{x+1}{x-1} = \frac{\sqrt{m+3n}}{\sqrt{m-3n}}$

Squaring both sides, $\dfrac{(x+1)^2}{(x-1)^2} = \dfrac{m+3n}{m-3n}$

Applying componendo and dividend rule, $\dfrac{(x+1)^2+(x-1)^2}{(x-1)^2-(x-1)^2} = \dfrac{m+3n+m-3n}{m+3n-m+3n}$

$$\Rightarrow \frac{2(x^2+1)}{2(2x)} = \frac{2m}{2(3n)}$$
$$\Rightarrow \frac{x^2+1}{2x} = \frac{m}{3n}$$
$$\Rightarrow 3n(x^2+1) = 2mx$$
$$\Rightarrow 3nx^2 - 2mx + 3n = 0$$

4. $\dfrac{\sin^2(90-\theta)+\cos^2(90-\theta)}{\csc^2(90-\theta)} + \dfrac{\cot^2(90-\theta)-\csc^2(90-\theta)}{\sec^2(90-\theta)}$

$= \dfrac{\cos^2(\theta)+\sin^2(\theta)}{\sec^2(\theta)} + \dfrac{\tan^2(\theta)-\sec^2(\theta)}{\csc^2(\theta)}$

$\Rightarrow \dfrac{1}{\sec^2(\theta)} + \dfrac{-1}{\csc^2(\theta)}$

$\Rightarrow \cos^2(\theta) - \sin^2(\theta)$

$\Rightarrow \cos 2\theta$

We know that minimum value of $\cos\alpha = -1$
Hence, required answer is -1

5. let the sum of nine member (total) $=x$

and the age of old one$= z$

so its average 2 yrs before=(x+z)/10.

after 2 yrs let z be replaced by y.

so now avg=(x+2*10+y)/10

now (x+z)/10=(x+20+y)/10

so after solving it found

z=y+20.

so old person is 20yrs older than young one.

6. Ratio of English books/hindi books

7:2 = 1512:hindi books

hindi books=432

let x books are added

15:4=(1512+x):432

on sol we get x=108

7. $\dfrac{\text{Area of } \Delta ADE}{\text{Area of } \Delta ABC} = \dfrac{\frac{1}{2}\times a \times 3b \times \sin A}{\frac{1}{2}\times 5a \times 4b \times \sin A} = \dfrac{3}{20}$

$\dfrac{\text{Area of } \Delta BDF}{\text{Area of } \Delta ABC} = \dfrac{\frac{1}{2}\times b \times c \times \sin B}{\frac{1}{2}\times 4b \times 2c \times \sin B} = \dfrac{1}{8}$

$\dfrac{\text{Area of } \Delta CFE}{\text{Area of } \Delta ABC} = \dfrac{\frac{1}{2}\times 4a \times c \times \sin C}{\frac{1}{2}\times 5a \times 2c \times \sin C} = \dfrac{2}{5}$

Therefore, $\dfrac{\text{Area of } \Delta DEF}{\text{Area of } \Delta ABC} = 1 - \left(\dfrac{3}{20}+\dfrac{1}{8}+\dfrac{2}{5}\right) = \dfrac{13}{40}$

8. Required per cent effect

$$= \left(20 - 25 - \frac{20\times25}{100}\right)\%$$
$$= (-5 - 5) = -10\%$$

Negative sign shows decrease.

9. Let B does the whole work in x days Work done by B in 1 day $= \dfrac{1}{x}$ According to question,

A does the $\dfrac{1}{2}$ work in days $\dfrac{x}{6}$

A does the whole work in $\dfrac{2x}{6}$ days $= \dfrac{x}{3}$ days Work done by A in one day $= (3/x)$

∴ Work done by A and B together in one day $= \dfrac{1}{x}+\dfrac{3}{x}=\dfrac{4}{x}$

Time taken to complete the whole work by A and B together $= \dfrac{1}{4} = \dfrac{x}{4}$ days

Again, given that $\dfrac{\frac{x}{4}}{\frac{4}{x}} = 10$

$x = 40$ days

10.

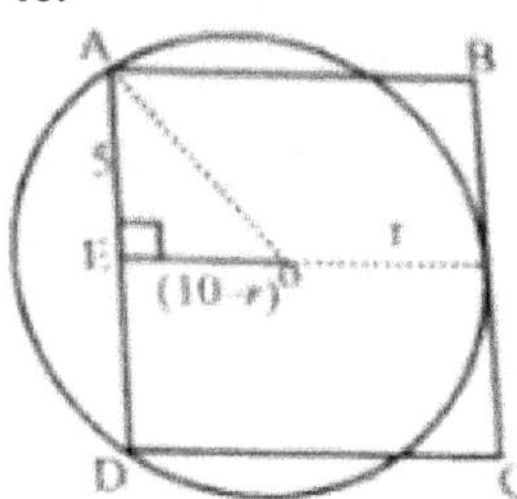

Let 0 is the centre of circle.

$$OE \perp AD$$

$$AE = ED = 5$$

Let r be the radius of circle.

Hence, $OE = (10 - r)$

In $\triangle AEO$

$$AE^2 + EO^2 = AO^2$$

$$5^2 + (10 - r)^2 = r^2$$

On solving.

$$\therefore r = 6.25$$

11. Quantity of milk:

First year $\Rightarrow \dfrac{4080}{7.5} = 544$ litres   Second year $\Rightarrow \dfrac{4080}{8} = 510$ litres

Third year $\Rightarrow \dfrac{4080}{8.5} = 480$ litres

Required average $= \dfrac{12240}{1534}$

$= Rs\,7.98$ per litre

12. Let X, Y and Z be the shares of A, B and C.

X+Y+Z= 3000 ....(1)

X = 1/ 3(Y+Z) => 3X –Y –Z =0 ....(2)

Y = 2/3 (X+Z) => 2X – 3Y + 2Z =0 ....(3)

From (1) and (2)

4X = 3000 => X= 750

Y+ Z = 2250 .... (4)

By (3)

3Y- 2Z = 1500 .... (5)

{eqn.(4)×3 – eqn.(5)}

5Z = 5250

Z = 1050

Hence C's share = 1050

13. For $x = 1$

since, $\sin\left(\dfrac{\pi}{2}\right) = 1$

$$\sin\dfrac{\pi x}{2} x^2 - 2x + 2 = x^2 - 2x + 2$$

put $x = 1$

$$1^2 - 2 += 1$$

14. Area of quadrilateral = area of $\triangle OBC$ − area of $\triangle OAD$

$$\Rightarrow \dfrac{1}{2} \times 6 \times 6 - \dfrac{1}{2} \times 2 \times 5 = 18 - 5 = 13 \text{ unit}$$

: the required are is 13

15. Let present age of Reena and Beena be 2x and 3x years respectively

According to the question

$$\dfrac{2x+4}{3x+4} = \dfrac{5}{7}$$

$$14x + 28 = 15x + 20 \quad \therefore x = 8$$

Required difference = 3 x 8 - 2 x 8 = 8 years

16. The reaction taking place at anode is $2CI^- \rightarrow Cl_2 + 2e-$

$Q = 1 \times t = 100 \times 5 \times 600$ coulomb

The amount of chlorine liberated by passing $100 \times 5 \times 60 \times 60$ coulomb of electric charge. $= 1/(2 \times 96500) \times 100 \times 5 \times 60 \times 60 = 9.3264$ mole

Volume of Cl_2 liberated at $NTP = 9.3264 \times 22.4 = 208.91 L$

17. (a) The reduction reaction is $Al^{3+} + 3e- \rightarrow Al$

Thus, 3 mole of electrons are needed to reduce 1 mole of $Al3 +$

$Q = 3 \times F = 3 \times 96500 = 289500$ coulomb

18. We have $1 mol$ of H_2O

$1 mol$ of H_2O will give one atom of 0 $H_2O \rightarrow H_2 + \dfrac{1}{2} O_2$

Electricity required for the oxidation of 1 mole of H_2O to $O_2 = nF$

(Here, $n = 2$) $= 2 \times 96487$ Coulombs

$= 192974$ Coulombs

$= 1.93 \times 10^5$ Coulombs

19. Quantity of charge passed

0.5 × 30 × 60 = 900 coulomb

900 coulomb deposit copper = 0.2964 g

96500 coulomb deposit copper = 0.2964/900×96500=31.78 g

Thus, 31.78 is the equivalent mass of copper.

At. mass = Eq. mass × Valency = 31.78 × 2 = 63.56

20. (D) Energy radiated $3/41.4 kW/m^2$

$$= 1.4 kJ/sec m^2 = \dfrac{1.4 kJ}{\frac{1}{86400} \text{day } m^2} = \dfrac{1.4 \times 86400}{\text{day } m^2}$$

Total energy radiated/day

$$= \dfrac{4\pi \times (1.5 \times 10^{l1}) \times 1.4 \times 86400}{1} \dfrac{kJ}{day} = E$$

$$\therefore E = mc^2 \Rightarrow m = \frac{E}{c^2}$$
$$= \frac{4\pi(1.5 \times 10^{11})^2 \times 1.4 \times 86400}{(3 \times 10^9)^2} = 3.8 \times 10^{14} kg$$

21. Ans.(1):- Work done $= -P(\Delta V) =$
$-1 \times 10^5[10^{-2} - 10^{-3}] = -900J$

22. At the corners, $A = \frac{1}{8} \times 8 = 1$ At the centre of the faces, $B = \frac{1}{2} \times 6 = 3$ Atoms of A and B based on the given date are in the ratio, $1 : 3$.

23. The boiling point of propyl acetate is 102°c.

24. (1) 2nd excited state will be the 3 rd energy level $E_n = \frac{13.6}{n^2}eV$ or $E = \frac{13.6}{9}eV = 1.5eV$

25. Let us assume the mass of methane and oxygen is each, w

Mole fraction of oxygen $= \frac{\frac{w}{32}}{\frac{w}{32}+\frac{w}{16}} = \frac{\frac{1}{32}}{\frac{1}{32}+\frac{1}{16}} = \frac{\frac{1}{32}}{\frac{3}{32}} = \frac{1}{3}$

Let the total pressure be P The pressure exerted by oxygen

$P_{O_2} = X_{O_2} \times P_{\text{total}} = \frac{1}{3}$

26. The lines falling in the visible region comprise Balmer series. Hence the third line would be $n_1 = 2$ $n_2 = 5$. The transition is, $5 \rightarrow 2$

27. Ans. 4) Configuration of $Cr(Z = 24)$ is
$Is^2 2s^2 2p^6 3s^2 3p^6 3d^5 4s^*$
$1 = 1,$ denotes p-electrons $(2p^6, 3p^6)$ $1 = 2,$ denotes d-electrons $(3d^5)$

28. Ans.4) Auf-bau principle is not applicable for H atom. Hence option D is correct.

29. Ans.(3) Urea has C and N atoms in the ratio 1:2. Hence option C is correct.

30. Mol mass difference $= 390 - 180 = 210$
Increased molar mass of $CH_3 - CO -$ is 43
Number of acetyl groups $= \frac{210}{43} = 5$
Number of Amino groups $= 5$

31. Article 35A was incorporated into the Constitution in 1954 by the orders of the then president Rajendra Prasad on the advice of the Jawaharlal Nehru Cabinet.

32. Malaria is caused by Plasmodium parasites. The parasites are spread to people through the bites of infected female Anopheles mosquitoes, called "malaria vectors."

33. The SpaceX cargo craft departed from the International Space Station after its successful mission to deliver scientific equipment and other supplies.

34. Buland Darwaza or the "Gate of victory", was built in 1601 A.D. by Mughal emperor Akbar to commemorate his victory over Gujarat. It is the main entrance to the Jama Masjid at Fatehpur Sikri.

35. Jahangir, was the fourth Mughal Emperor, who ruled from 1605 until his death in 1627. His imperial name, means 'conqueror of the world', 'world-conqueror' or 'world-seizer'.

36. The Reserve Bank of India (RBI) has appointed Jai Bhagwan Bhoria as the PMC bank's administrator.

➤ The Reserve Bank of India (RBI) has superseded the Board of Punjab and Maharashtra Cooperative Bank Limited, Mumbai.

➤ According to an official release, the amount of withdrawal from the bank allowed to depositors has been increased

from one thousand to ten thousand rupees.

➤ The RBI's directives will remain in force for a period of six months

37. On board the Lifeline Express, world's first hospital train. On July 16, 1991, the world's first hospital on a train chugged out of Mumbai's Chhatrapati Shivaji Terminus on its maiden journey.

38. PM Modi introduces commemorative coin of Rs 350 to mark birth anniversary of Guru Gobind Singh.

39. The Indian Grand Prix was a Formula One race in the calendar of the FIA Formula One World Championship, which was held at the Buddh International Circuit in Noida.

40. Banwarilal Purohit is an Indian politician who is the current and 21st Governor of Tamil Nadu.

41. Universally should be used in place of universal, as an adverb is required here and to modify a verb, an adverb is used.

42. The standard form for that phrasal verb is "comply with", which means "to act or be in accordance with a wish, request, demand, requirement, or condition".

43. Flinch: make a quick, nervous movement

Blench: a sudden movement out of fear and pain

Forge: make something from scratch

Plunder: obtain goods and money illegally

Slovenly: Messy or untidy

44. Charlatan: a person falsely claiming to have a special knowledge or skill

Exponent: someone who is very good at a particular skill or activity and is an example to other people

Swindler: one who cheats a person out of money or other assets

Hoaxer: a person who trick or deceive someone by means of a hoax

Cajole: persuade someone

45. The problem of unemployment has been a hanging fire for the last many years.

46. Zoosadism means a pleasure which an individual gains from the cruelty to animals.

Ethology: Study of animal behaviour

Bio semiotics: deals with sign processes in nature in all dimensions

Zoo semiotics: the study of animal communication.

47. Urchins means mischievous children

Dandy means a man unduly concerned with looking stylish and fashionable.

48. Poaching: illegal hunting or capturing of wild animals.

The part 'Army personnel cooking chinkara meat' will be followed by an equivalent form of verb after the conjunction, making 'poaching' as the suitable choice.

49. Enact means to establish by legal and authoritative act and is an action of past, therefore, enacted is the most appropriate answer.

50. 'Enslave' means to cause (someone) to lose their freedom of choice or action.

'Grasp' means to seize and hold something firmly.

'Emancipate' means to set free, especially from legal, social, or political restrictions.

'Enthrall' means to capture the fascinated attention of something.

'Pragmatic' is the person who thinks logically and practically.

Mathematics

Q.1 From 2008 to 2009, the sale of a book decreased by 80%. If the sale in 2010 were the same as in 2008, by what per cent did it increase from 2009 to 2010?

A. 80% **B.** 100% **C.** 120% **D.** 400%

Q.2 A and B together can do a piece of work in 36 days, B and C together can do it in 24 days. A and C together can do it in 18 days. The three working together can finish the work in

A. 8 days **B.** 16 days **C.** 30 days **D.** 32 days

Q.3 A godown is 15 m long and 12 m broad. The sum of the areas of the floor and the celling is equal to the sum of areas of the four walls. The volume (in m3) of the godown is:

A. 900 **B.** 1200 **C.** 1800 **D.** 720

Q.4 If q is the mean proportional between p and r the $\dfrac{p^2-q^2+r^2}{p^{-2}-q^{-2}+r^{-2}}$ is equal to

A. p^2q^3 **B.** q^3 **C.** q^4 **D.** $p^2r^2q^4$

Q.5 A training plane flies along the four sides of a rectangle at the speeds of 400, 400, 1200 and 800 km/h, starting from the longer side. The length and breadth of the rectangle are in the ratio 2 : 1. Find the average speed of the plane around the field.

A. 824 km/hr **B.** 748 km/hr
C. 576 km/hr **D.** 816 km/hr

Q.6 In triangle ABC, D and E are any points on AB and AC such AD = AE. The bisector of ∠C meets ED at F. It is known that ∠B = 60.What is the degree measure of ∠ EFC?

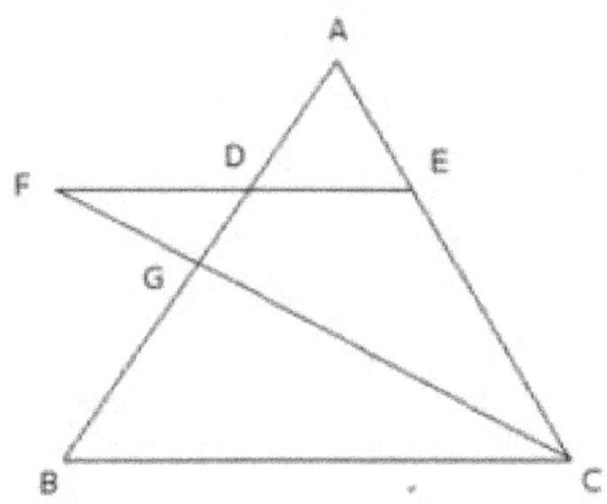

A. 45 **B.** 30 **C.** 35 **D.** 55

Q.7 What number must be added to the expression $16a^2 - 12a$ to make it a perfect square?

A. 9/4 **B.** 11/2 **C.** 13/2 **D.** 16

Q.8 A man invested Rs. 3500, part of it at a yearly interest rate of 4% and the rest at 5%. He received a total annual interest of Rs. 153. How much did he invest at rate 5%?

A. Rs. 2200 **B.** Rs. 1300 **C.** Rs. 2000 **D.** Rs. 1800

Q.9 Rs. 3480 is divided among P, Q, R; the division is such that 1/3 of P's money = 1/4 of Q's money = 1/5 of R's money. Who will receive the highest money and how much?

A. R, Rs. 1450 **B.** R, Rs. 1160
C. Q, Rs. 1160 **D.** Q, Rs. 1450

Q.10 The length of three medians of a triangle are 9cm, 12cm and 15cm. The area (in cm²) of the triangle is:

A. 24 **B.** 72 **C.** 48 **D.** 144

Q.11 Let α and β be the roots of quadratic equation x2 - 3x - 1 = 0, then find the value of $\alpha^7 + \beta^7$.

A. 4567 **B.** 4287 **C.** 3500 **D.** 4200

Q.12 If a partnership business, B's capital was half of A's. If after 8 months, B withdrew half of his capital and after 2 more months, A withdrew (1/4)th of his capital, then what will be the profit ratio of A and B after completion of one year?

A. 5:2 **B.** 10:23 **C.** 2:5 **D.** 23:10

Q.13 In a ΔABC, AB = 5cm, BC = 6cm and AC = 7 cm. If AD is perpendicular to BC, find the length of BD?

A. 4 cm **B.** 2.5 cm **C.** 3 cm **D.** 1 cm

Q.14 The price of 2 pens, 3 pencils and 4 notebooks is 11Rs and the price of 3 pens, 5 pencils and 2 notebooks is 17Rs. Find the price of 3 pens, 4 pencils and 10 notebooks?

A. Rs.16 **B.** Rs.15 **C.** Rs.18 **D.** Rs.20

Q.15 A shopkeeper gives a discount of 20% on cost priceof rice but uses 900gm weight instead of 1kg weight while selling. Find his overall profit/losspercent?

A. 12.5% loss **B.** 11.11% profit
C. 12.5% profit **D.** 11.11% loss

Science

Q.16 Complete hydrolysis of cellulose gives:-

A. D-ribose **B.** D-glucose
C. D-fructose **D.** L-glucose

Q.17 The reason for double-helical structure of DNA is operation of:-

A. dipole – dipole interaction
B. hydrogen bonding
C. electrostatic attractions
D. van der Waal's forces

Q.18 Which of the following is a polyamide?

A. Teflon **B.** Nylon – 6,6
C. Terylene **D.** Bakelite

Q.19 Bakelite is obtained from phenol by reacting with:-

A. $(CH_2OH)_2$ **B.** HCHO
C. CH_3COCH_3 **D.** None of the above

Q.20 The pyrimidine bases present in DNA are:-
A. cytosine and adenine
B. cytosine and guanine
C. cytosine and thymine
D. cytosine and uracil

Q.21 According to Modern periodic law, the physical and chemical properties of the elements are the periodic function of their:
A. Atomic number   **B.** Atomic masses
C. Atomic radii   **D.** Ionization Potential

Q.22 A non-conducting ring of radius $0.5m$ carries a total charge of $1.11 \times 10^{-10} C$ distributed non-uniformly on its circumference, producing an electric field E every where in space. The value of the integral $\int_{t=\infty}^{t=0} \vec{E} \cdot \vec{d\ell}(l = 0$ being centre of the ring) in volt is :-
A. 2   **B.** -2   **C.** zero   **D.** 1

Q.23 A parallel combination of 0.1 $M\Omega$ resistor and a 10μ F capacitor is connected across a $1.5V$ source of negligible resistance. The time required for the capacitor to get charged up to $0.75V$ is approximately (in seconds)
A. infinity   **B.** ln2   **C.** 1   **D.** zero

Q.24 .A hollow metal sphere of radius 5 cm is charged such that the potential on its surface is 10 volt. The potential at the centre of the sphere is:-
A. 10   **B.** 1
C. zero   **D.** None of the above

Q.25 Two identical metal plates are given positive charges Q1 and Q2 (<Q1) respectively. If they are now brought close together to form a parallel plate capacitor with capacitance C, the potential difference between them is:-
A. (Q1+Q2)/(2C)   **B.** (Q1-Q2)/(2C)
C. (Q1-Q2)/C   **D.** (Q1+Q2)/C

Q.26 Three positive charges of equal value q are placed at the vertices of an equilateral triangle. The resulting lines of force should be sketched as in :-

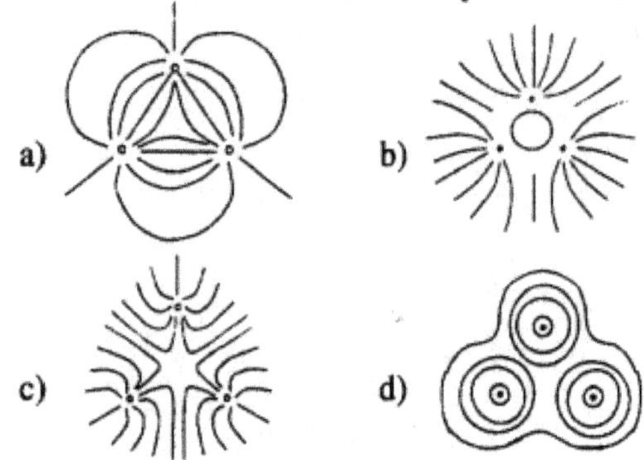

A. Only A   **B.** Only B
C. Only C   **D.** Either C or A

Q.27 Which of the following compounds can be detected by Molish's test ?

A. Nitro compounds   **B.** Sugars
C. Amines   **D.** None of these

Q.28 The half life of radioactive radon is 3.8 day. The time at the end of which (l/20)th of the radon sample will remain undecayed is (given log₁₀e= 0.4343).
A. 10.5 days   **B.** 16.5 days
C. 12.5 days   **D.** 13.5 days

Q.29 Beta rays emitted by a radioactive material are:-
A. electromagnetic radiations
B. the electrons orbiting around the nucleus
C. charged particles emitted by the nucleus
D. neutral particles.

Q.30 _____________is a pressure wave; regions of high (compressions) and low pressure (rarefactions) are established as the result of the vibrations of the sound source.
A. Magnetic energy   **B.** Chemical Energy
C. Sound waves   **D.** Electrical energy

General Awareness

Q.31 The first woman Secretary general of SAARC is from which country?
A. Bhutan   **B.** India
C. Sri Lanka   **D.** Maldives

Q.32 ZnSO₄.7H₂O is the chemical formula of which substance?
A. White Vitriol   **B.** Bleaching powder
C. Blue Vitriol   **D.** Green Vitriol

Q.33 Guru Gobind Singh was the ___ Sikh Guru.
A. eighth   **B.** fifth   **C.** tenth   **D.** ninth

Q.34 In january 2019, Indian space research organisation launched a special programme for school children named ___ to inculcate and nurture space research fervour in young minds.
A. Young Scientist programme
B. Yound Thoughts programme
C. Young Mind programme
D. Young Blood programme

Q.35 Article _______ of the constitution of India provides special rights and priveleges to permanent residents of Jammu and Kashmir
A. 34A   **B.** 32A   **C.** 35A   **D.** 31A

Q.36 A petition has been filed by NGO ___ challenging the constitutional validity of both, Article 35A and Article 370.
A. We The Indians   **B.** We The Citizens
C. We The Challengers   **D.** We The Opposers

Q.37 The Imperial Bank Of India was renamed as ___ in 1955.
A. Punjab National Bank
B. The State Bank Of India
C. Central Bank Of India
D. Allahabad Bank

Q.38 Which of the following banks in NOT a public sector bank?

A.   Canara Bank
B.   State Bank Of India
C.   Jammu and Kashmir Bank Ltd.
D.   IndusInd Bank

Q.39 Which of the longest tributary of the river Indus?

A. Beas   **B.** Chenab   **C.** Jhelum   **D.** Sutlej

Q.40 Which of the following metals is found in free state in nature?

A. Copper   **B.** Potassium
C. Aluminium   **D.** Sodium

Basic English

Q.41 Select the word with the correct spelling.

A. circulate   **B.** cordonned
C. binomeal   **D.** fontannel

Q.42 Improve the bracketed part of the sentence.

The footballers (has been) arguing with the coach since morning.

A. was   **B.** had been
C. have been   **D.** no improvement

Q.43 In the following question, a sentence has been given in Active/Passive voice. Out of four alternatives suggested, select the one, which best expresses the same sentence in Passive/Active voice.

The storm destroyed several huts in the village.

A.   The storm in the village had destroyed several huts.
B.   Several huts in the village have been destroyed by the storm.
C.   The storm was destructive for the several huts in the village.
D.   Several huts in the village were destroyed by the storm.

Ques (44-48):Directions: In the following passage, some of the words have been left out. Read the passage carefully and select the correct answer for the given blank out of the four alternatives.

But what does this enthusiasm for voting actually ___(1)______? One popular theory ___(2)_____ that poor people ___(3)___ because they are intimidated into doing so. Intimidation occurs for sure but why then, voters in places where there is no intimidation do so? Another theory is that people vote in return for _____(4)_____. But recent research across India ___(5)___ that those who spend the most do not always win elections and voters do not feel any obligation to vote for those handing out freebies. In fact, they often accept the goodies from all parties but vote for only one.

Q.44 Choose the appropriate word for the blank (1)

A. answer   **B.** signify   **C.** ponder   **D.** suppose

Q.45 Choose the appropriate word for the blan

A. poses   **B.** supposes   **C.** disposes   **D.** proposes

Q.46 Choose the appropriate word for the blank(3)

A. vote   **B.** are voting

C. have voted   **D.** voted

Q.47 Choose the appropriate word for the blank(4)

A. valuables   **B.** favours
C. inducements   **D.** help

Q.48 Choose the appropriate word for the blank(5)

A. show   **B.** has shown
C. had shown   **D.** showed

Q.49 Rearrange the parts of the sentence in correct order.

The Finance Minister, under

P-whose supervision this

Q-has not made any definite statement

R-has taken place,

A. RPQ   **B.** QRP   **C.** PRQ   **D.** QPR

Q.50 Select the synonym of **"metropolitan"**

A. idyllic   **B.** arcadian   **C.** bucolic   **D.** urbane

// Smart Answer Sheet //

Correct   Indicates percentage of students who answered questions correctly.

Skipped   Indicates percentage of students who skipped questions.

Q.	Ans.	Correct / Skipped	Q.	Ans.	Correct / Skipped	Q.	Ans.	Correct / Skipped	Q.	Ans.	Correct / Skipped	Q.	Ans.	Correct / Skipped
1	D	85.42 % / 11.14 %	11	B	85.19 % / 10.56 %	21	A	79.8 % / 13.6 %	31	D	85.82 % / 13.79 %	41	A	78.53 % / 17.35 %
2	B	82.25 % / 12.98 %	12	D	87.41 % / 10.71 %	22	A	83.27 % / 14.58 %	32	A	80.36 % / 19.63 %	42	C	83.68 % / 10.44 %
3	B	76.72 % / 14.8 %	13	D	89.82 % / 10.09 %	23	D	87.8 % / 10.41 %	33	C	85.59 % / 11.47 %	43	D	82.97 % / 11.68 %
4	C	78.01 % / 10.72 %	14	A	88.63 % / 10.26 %	24	A	79.09 % / 13.39 %	34	A	76.97 % / 17.23 %	44	B	83.0 % / 10.62 %
5	C	88.93 % / 10.31 %	15	D	84.81 % / 11.93 %	25	B	78.72 % / 20.62 %	35	C	89.03 % / 10.4 %	45	D	83.08 % / 15.33 %
6	B	83.29 % / 15.0 %	16	B	89.07 % / 10.41 %	26	C	89.7 % / 10.16 %	36	B	86.45 % / 10.28 %	46	A	87.67 % / 10.37 %
7	A	87.78 % / 11.01 %	17	B	77.32 % / 18.49 %	27	B	78.97 % / 14.86 %	37	B	82.87 % / 14.31 %	47	C	79.46 % / 16.35 %
8	B	86.14 % / 13.36 %	18	B	86.47 % / 12.85 %	28	B	84.06 % / 10.21 %	38	D	83.6 % / 14.95 %	48	B	89.69 % / 10.11 %
9	A	87.94 % / 11.45 %	19	B	82.51 % / 13.58 %	29	C	88.02 % / 10.1 %	39	D	78.4 % / 18.11 %	49	C	83.58 % / 10.21 %
10	B	81.34 % / 18.03 %	20	C	84.85 % / 10.57 %	30	C	84.39 % / 10.09 %	40	A	81.76 % / 11.87 %	50	D	77.73 % / 15.11 %

Performance Analysis	
Avg. Score (%)	34.0%
Toppers Score (%)	68.0%
Your Score	

//Hints and Solutions//

1. Let the sales in 2008 be 100

Sales in 2009 will be 20

Sales in 2010 is 100

Increase from 2009 to 2010 = 80

% increase = (80 ÷20) × 100 = 400%

2. Let 1 day's work by A, B and C be x y and z respectively.

Then Efficiency of $(A \cdot B)$ together $-\dfrac{1}{36}$ Efficiency of

$(C \cdot B)$ together $-\dfrac{1}{24}$ Efficiency of $(A + C)$ together $=\dfrac{2}{18}$

Adding (i), (ii) and (iii), we get

$2 \times$ eff. of $[A + B + C] = \dfrac{9}{72}$

Or, eff. Of $|A + B + C| = \dfrac{9}{144} = \dfrac{1}{16}$

The three working together can finish the work in 16 days

3. If the height of the godown be h meter, then

$2(15 \times 12) = 2 \times h(15 + 12)$

$\Rightarrow 27h = 15 \times 12$

$\Rightarrow h = \dfrac{15 \times 12}{27} = \dfrac{20}{3}$ meter

Volume of the godown $= \dfrac{15 \times 12 \times 20}{3}$

$= 1200 cu$ meter

4. $\dfrac{p^2-q^2+r^2}{p^{-2}-q^{-2}+r^{-2}} = \dfrac{p^2-q^2+r^2}{\frac{1}{p^2}-\frac{1}{pr}+\frac{1}{r^2}}$

$= \dfrac{p^2-q^2+r^2}{r^2-pr+p^2} = \dfrac{(p^2 r^2)(p^2-q^2+r^2)}{p^2 r^2}$

$= \dfrac{(p^2 r^2)(p^2-pr+r^2)}{(r^2-pr+p^2)}$

$= p^2 r^2 = (pr)^2 = (q^2)^2 = q^4$

5. Average speed = total distance traveled/total time taken
Given, length and breadth of the rectangle are in the ratio 2: 1
Let the sides be 2 a and a respectively.
Given, a training plane flies along the four sides of a rectangle at
the speeds of 400,400,1200 and $800 km/h$ starting from the
longer side.

Total time $= \dfrac{2a}{400} + \dfrac{a}{400} + \dfrac{2a}{1200} + \dfrac{a}{800} = \dfrac{25a}{2400} = \dfrac{a}{96} hr$

Total distance travelled $= 2a + a + 2a + a = 6a$

Average speed $= 6a/(a/96)$

Average speed $= 96*6 = 576 km/hr$

6.

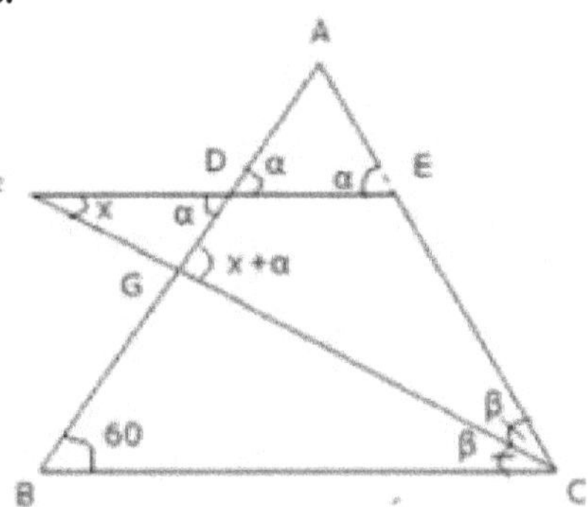

$In \Delta EFC$

$a - \beta + x - \cdots - (1)$

$In \Delta BGC$

$x + a - 60 + \beta - \cdots - \cdots$ (ii)

$\Rightarrow x + \beta + x = 60 + \beta$

$\Rightarrow 2x = 60$

$\Rightarrow x = 30$

$\angle EFC = 30°$

7. Let d be the number that needs to be added such that

$16a^2 - 12a + d$ is perfect square.

let it be the square of 4a-n.

$(4a-n)^2 = 16a^2 - 8n + n^2$

$8n = 12a$

$n = 3/2$

$d = n^2 = 9/4$

8. Let amount invested at the rate of 4% be $Rs.$ x and the
amount at the rate of 5% be $Rs.$ y Annual interest at $4\% = \dfrac{x \times 4 \times 1}{100} = \left[\dfrac{4x}{100}\right]$

Amount interest at $5\% = \dfrac{y \times 5 \times 1}{100} = \dfrac{5y}{100}$

So , $\dfrac{4x}{100} + \dfrac{5y}{100} = 153 \Rightarrow 4x + 5y = 15300$

and (by condition) we know that $x + y = 3500$ On solving,
we get $x = 2200$ \& $y = 1300$ Hence, amount invested at
5% is Rs. 1300

9. 1/3 × P = 1/4 × Q

$\Rightarrow$ P/Q = 3/4

And, 1/4 × Q = 1/5 × R

$\Rightarrow$ Q/R = 4/5

Hence, P : Q : R = 3 : 4 : 5

R will receive the highest money = 5/(3 + 4 + 5) × 3480 = Rs. 1450

10.

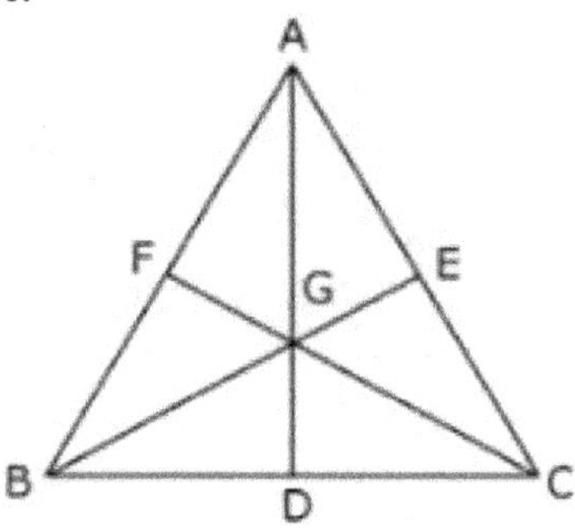

$$AG = \frac{2}{3} \times 9cm = 6cm$$

$$BG = \frac{2}{2} \times 12 = 8cm$$

$$GC = \frac{2}{3} \times 15 = 10cm$$

Area of $\triangle ABG = \frac{1}{2} \times 6 \times 8$

$$= 24cm^2$$

So, Area of $\triangle ABC = 3 \times 24 = 72cm^2$

Alternative method

If u, v, w are the medians of the triangle then Area $=$

$$4/3^* \sqrt{(s(s-u)(s-v)(s-w)}$$

Where

$s = (u+v+w)/2$ Area $= 4/3^* \sqrt{(18(9)(6)(3))} = 72$

11. $\alpha + \beta = \frac{-b}{a} = 3$

$$\alpha\beta = \frac{c}{a} = -1$$

$$\beta = \frac{-1}{a}$$

$$S0, \alpha - \frac{1}{\alpha} = 3$$

$$\alpha^3 - \frac{1}{\alpha^2} = 3^3 + 3 \times 3 = 36$$

$$and\, \alpha^2 + \frac{1}{\alpha^2} = 3^2 + 2 = 11$$

$$\alpha^4 + \frac{1}{\alpha^4} = 11^2 - 2 = 119$$

$$Now, \left(\alpha^2 - \frac{1}{\alpha^2}\right)\left(\alpha^4 + \frac{1}{\alpha^4}\right) = \alpha^7 - \alpha + \frac{1}{\alpha} - \frac{1}{\alpha^7}$$

$$\left(\alpha^3 - \frac{1}{\alpha^2}\right)\left(\alpha^4 + \frac{1}{\alpha^4}\right) = \alpha^7 - \frac{1}{\alpha^7} - \left(\alpha - \frac{1}{\alpha}\right)$$

Hence, $\alpha^7 - \frac{1}{a^7} = \left(a^3 - \frac{1}{a^3}\right)\left(a^4 + \frac{1}{a^4}\right) + \left(a - \frac{1}{a}\right)$

$$a^7 - \frac{1}{a^7} = 36 \times 119 + 3$$

$$a^7 - \frac{1}{a^7} = 4287$$

$$a^7 + \frac{-1}{a^7} = 4287$$

$$a^7 + \beta^7 = 4287$$

Required answer is 4287

12. B's capital - Rs. X A's capital = Rs. 2x. Ratio of equivalent capitals A and B for 1 month $2x \times 10 + \frac{3x}{2} \times 2 : 8x +$

$\frac{x}{2} \times 4$

$23x : 10x$

23 : 10

13.

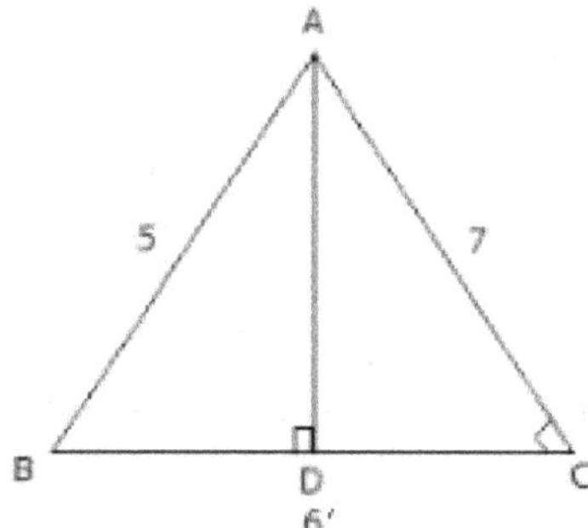

In $\triangle ABC$, applying cosine rule, $cosB = \frac{BD}{5} = \frac{5^2 + 6^2 - 7^2}{2 \times 5 \times 6}$

$$\Rightarrow BD = 1cm$$

14. Let price of 1 pen = x

Price of 1 pencil = y

Price of 1 notebook = z

According to question,

2x + 3y + 4z = 11 ------ (i)

3x + 5y + 2z = 17 ------ (ii)

We need to find the value of 3x + 4y + 10z =?

By equation (i) × 3 – equation (ii), we get

3x + 4y + 10z = 11×3 – 17 = Rs.16

∴ the answer is Rs.16

15. Let Cost Price (CP) of rice be Re.1 per gm. Now, for a transaction of 1000gms, he charges Rs. 800/- from a customer after giving him a discount of 20% but gives him wheat worth Rs. 900 only (as he uses 900gm weight instead of 1000gms). So, he loses Rs. 100/- .

His loss is worth Rs. 100 by giving rice of worth Rs. 900. So, his loss percent = 100/900*100 = 11.11%

16.

$$(C_6H_{10}O_5)n + nH_2O \xrightarrow{\ H^+\ } nC_6H_{12}O_6 \atop D-Glucose$$

17. Ans.(2) Helix is stabilised by hydrogen bonds.

18. Amide linkage is present in Nylon.

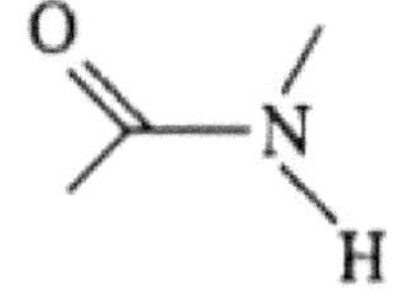

19.

$$\frac{N_0}{20} = N_0 e^{-0.18t} \text{ or } \log_{10} 20 = 0.18 \times t \times \log_{10} e$$

or $1.3 = 0.18 \times 0.4343 \times t$ or $t = \dfrac{1.3}{0.18 \times 0.4343}$

or $t = 16.5$ day.

29. Ans.

(c) Beta rays are emitted from nucleus. ${}_0 n^1 \to {}_1 H^1 + (-1\beta^0)$

A neutron disrupts into a proton and a beta particle. The beta par'ticle is ejected from the nucleus. The beta particles are fast moving electrons.

30. A sound wave is a pressure wave; regions of high (compressions) and low pressure (rarefactions) are established as the result of the vibrations of the sound source. These compressions and rarefactions result because sound. a. is more dense than air and thus has more inertia, causing the bunching up of sound.

31. Fathimath Dhiyana Saeed is a Maldivian diplomat and was the Secretary-General of the South Asian Association for Regional Cooperation (SAARC).

32. Zinc Sulfate is a white crystalline, water-soluble compound. The hydrated form, zinc sulfate heptahydrate, the mineral goslarite, was historically known as "white vitriol" and can be prepared by reacting zinc with aqueous sulfuric acid.

33. Guru Gobind Singh, the tenth Sikh Guru and founder of the Khalsa, was born on December 22, 1666, in Patna in present-day Bihar.

34. The Indian Space Research Organisation (ISRO) has launched a special programme for School Children called "Young Scientist Programme" "YUva VIgyani KAryakram" from this year.

35. Article 35A is a provision incorporated in the Constitution giving the Jammu and Kashmir Legislature a carte blanche to decide who all are 'permanent residents' of the State and confer on them special rights and privileges in public sector jobs, acquisition of property in the State, scholarships and other public aid and welfare.

36. A petition has been filed by NGO We The Citizens challenging the constitutional validity of both, Article 35A and Article 370.

37. On 1 July 1955, the Imperial Bank of India became the State Bank of India.

38. IndusInd Bank Limited is a Mumbai based Indian new generation bank, established in 1994.It is not a public sector bank.

39. Sutlej River

Sutlej River, Ancient Greek Zaradros, Sanskrit Shutudri or Shatadru, longest of the five tributaries of the Indus River that give the Punjab (meaning "Five Rivers") its name. It rises on the north slope of the Himalayas in Lake La'nga in southwestern Tibet, at an elevation above 15,000 feet (4,600 metres).

40. Only Gold,silver, copper and the platinum metals occur in nature in free state.

---

20. Ans.(3) DNA has two pyrimidine bases. Thymine and cytosine.

21. According to Modern periodic law, the physical and chemical properties of the elements are the periodic function of their atomic number.

22.

$$\int_{l=\infty}^{l=0} \vec{E} \cdot \vec{dl} = \text{Potential at the centre of the ring.}$$

$$= \frac{1}{4\pi\varepsilon_0} \frac{q}{r} = \frac{(9 \times 10^9) \times (1.11 \times 10^{-10})}{0.5} = 2 \text{ volt}$$

23. Resistor (R) and capacitor (C) are connected in parallel. They are connected across a 1.5 volt source of negligible resistance.Since the capacitor is directly connected to voltage source and there is no resistance in the path, The time required for the capacitor is zero.

24. Ans.(b) Electric potential at any point inside a hollow metal sphere is constant. The potential at the surface is 10 volt. The potential at the centre will also be 10

25. The two identical metal plates set up fields with intensities E_1 and E_2

$$E_1 = \frac{Q_1}{2\varepsilon_0 A}, \quad E_2 = \frac{Q_2}{2\varepsilon_0 A} + Q_1$$

$$\therefore E = E_1 - E_2$$

or $E = \dfrac{1}{2\varepsilon_0 A}(Q_1 - Q_2)$

$$\therefore V = Ed$$

$$V = \frac{(Q_1 - Q_2)d}{2\varepsilon_n A} = \frac{Q_1 - Q_2}{2C}$$

26. Ans.(c) Electric lines of force do not end at positive charge as shown in (a). The option is therefore incorrect. Electric lines of force never form a closed loop. Options (b) and (d) are incorrect.Option (c) represents correct answer. Mutual repulsion between similar charges is depicted in figure.

27. Ans.(2) Molish test for carbohydrates : when a drop or two drops of alcoholic solution of oc- naphthol is added to sugar solution and then cone. H_2SO_4 is added along the sides of test tube, formation of violet ring at the junction of two liquids conforms the sugar.

28. (b) $N = N_0 e^{-\lambda t}$ where $\lambda = \dfrac{0.693}{3.8} = 0.18$

41. Circulate means move continuously or freely through a closed system or area.

42. Because 'footballers" is a plural noun, so we use 'have been" instead of 'has been'.

43. Several huts in the village were destroyed by the storm.

44. But what does this enthusiasm for voting actually signify?

45. One popular theory proposes that poor people

46. poor people vote because they are intimidated into doing so.

47. Another theory is that people vote in return for inducements.

48. But recent research across India has shown that those who spend the most do not always win elections and voters do not feel any obligation to vote for those handing out freebies. In fact, they often accept the goodies from all parties but vote for only one.

49. The Finance Minister, under whose supervision this has taken place, has not made any definite statement.

50. Metropolitan means relating to or denoting the parent state of a colony. Hence urbane is the correct choice.

Mathematics

Q.1 Ram, Shyam and Aman jointly thought of engaging themselves in a business venture. It was agreed that Ram would invest Rs. 6500 for 6 months, Shyam Rs. 8400 for 6 months and Aman, Rs. 10,000 for 3 months. The profit earned was Rs. 11100. Calculate the share of Shyam in the profit

A. Rs. 3900 **B.** Rs. 3306 **C.** Rs. 5400 **D.** Rs. 3300

Q.2 Total number of four digit odd numbers that can be formed using 0,1,2,3,5,7 (using repetition allowed) are:-

A. 100 **B.** 720 **C.** 620 **D.** 120

Q.3 Five digit number divisible by 3 is formed using 0,1,2,3,4,6 and 7 without repetition. Total number of such numbers are

A. 60 **B.** 216 **C.** 120 **D.** 0

Q.4 Two friends A and B simultaneously start running around a circular track . They run in the same direction. A travels at 6 m/s and B runs at b m/s. If they cross each other at exactly two points on the circular track and b is a natural number less than 30, how many values can b take?

A. 1 **B.** 2 **C.** 3 **D.** 4

Q.5 Two friends A and B leave City P and City Q simultaneously and travel towards Q and P at constant speeds. They meet at a point in between the two cities and then proceed to their respective destinations in 54 minutes and 24 minutes respectively. How long did B take to cover the entire journey between City Q and City P?

A. 60 min **B.** 50 min **C.** 10 min **D.** 80 min

Q.6 Car A trails car B by 50 meters. Car B travels at 45km/hr. Car C travels from the opposite direction at 54km/hr. Car C is at a distance of 220 meters from Car B. If car A decides to overtake Car B before cars B and C cross each other, what is the minimum speed at which car A must travel?

A. 67.5 km/hr. **B.** 25 km/hr.
C. 15 km/hr. **D.** 57.5 km/hr.

Q.7 A is x% more than B and is x% of sum of A and B. What is the value of x?

A. 42% **B.** 62%
C. 52% **D.** None of these

Q.8 In a class, if 50% of the boys were girls, then there would be 50% more girls than boys. What percentage of the overall class is girls?

A. 15% **B.** 25% **C.** 10% **D.** 20%

Q.9 The area of a circle is increased by 88 cm^2 when its radius is increased by 2 cm. The original radius of the circle is:

A. 6 cm **B.** 5 cm **C.** 3.5 cm **D.** 4.5 cm

Q.10 Pipe A, B and C are kept open and together fill a tank in t minutes. Pipe A is kept open throughout, pipe B is kept open for the first 10 minutes and then closed. Two minutes after pipe B is closed, pipe C is opened and is kept open till the tank is full. Each pipe fills an equal share of the tank. Furthermore, it is known that if pipe A and B are kept open continuously, the tank would be filled completely in t minutes. How long will it take C alone to fill the tank ?

A. 34 minutes. **B.** 24 minutes.
C. 44 minutes. **D.** 36 minutes.

Q.11 4 men and 6 women complete a task in 24 days. If the women are at least half as efficient as the men, but not more efficient than the men, what is the range of the number of days for 6 women and 2 men to complete the same task?

A. 36 to 33.6 days **B.** 30 to 33.6 days
C. 20 to 33.6 days **D.** 40 to 33.6 days

Q.12 If $(343)^{20} \times (49)^x \times (7)^{12} = (7)^{80}$, then find the value of x?

A. 6 **B.** 4 **C.** 27 **D.** 11

Q.13 3sinx + 4cosx + r is always greater than or equal to 0. What is the smallest value 'r' can to take?

A. 0 **B.** 2 **C.** 5 **D.** 1

Q.14 A fruit vendor buys apples at the rate of 20 for ₹ 100. How many should he sell for ₹ 100, so that he makes a profit of 25% ?

A. 5 **B.** 16 **C.** 7 **D.** 8

Q.15 Cylindrical cans of cricket balls are to be packed in a box. Each can has a radius of 7 cm and height of 30 cm. Dimension of the box is l = 76 cm, b = 46 cm, h = 45 cm. What is the maximum number of cans that can fit in the box?

A. 15 **B.** 21 **C.** 19 **D.** 17

Science

Q.16 α -D $(+)$ − glucose and $\beta - D(+) - g$ lucose are

A. enantiomers **B.** conformers
C. anomers **D.** epimers

Q.17 The polymer containing strong intermolecular forces e.g. hydrogen bonding, is:-

A. Nylon 6,6 **B.** Teflon
C. Natural rubber **D.** None of these

Q.18 What is the boiling point for methanol?

A. 100°C **B.** 64.7 °C **C.** 62°C **D.** 46°C

Q.19 Synthesis of each molecule of glucose in photosynthesis involves:-

A. 18 molecules of ATP
B. 10 molecules of ATP
C. 20 molecules of ATP
D. 30 molecules of ATP

Q.20 Which one is classified as a condensation polymers ?

A. Acrylonitrile   **B.** Dacron
C. Neoprene   **D.** Teflon

Q.21 Which of the vitamins given below is water soluble ?
A. Vitamin B
B. Either Vitamin B or Vitamin C
C. Vitamin C
D. Vitamin K

Q.22 Curie temperature is the temperature at which _______.
A. Matter becomes radioactive
B. A metal loses magnetic properties
C. A metal loses conductivity
D. Transmutation of metal occurs

Q.23 _______ is one of the heaviest materials on earth.
A. Silver   **B.** Gold   **C.** Osmium   **D.** Lead

Q.24 Who discovered the neutrons?
A. James Chadwick   **B.** J.J. Thomson
C. Chadwick   **D.** Rutherford

Q.25 If the distance between the earth and the sun were half its present value, the number of days in a year would have been:-
A. 130   **B.** 129   **C.** 119   **D.** 110

Q.26 _____________ leaf has its leaflets radiating outwards from the end of the petiole, like fingers off the palm of a hand.
A. Pinnately compound leaf
B. Palmately compound leaf
C. Compound leaf
D. Simple leaf

Q.27 A simple pendulum has a time period T_1 when on the earth's surface, and T_2 when taken to a height R above the earth's surface, where R is the radius of the earth. The value of T_2/T_1
A. 2   **B.** 1   **C.** 1/2   **D.** 3

Q.28 .An energy of 24.6 eV is required to remove one of the electrons from a neutral helium atom. The energy (In eV) required to remove both the electrons form a neutral helium atom is:
A. 89 eV   **B.** 79 eV   **C.** 69 eV   **D.** 59 eV

Q.29 A radioactive material decays by simultaneous emission of two particles with respective half-lives 1620 and 810 year. The time, in year, after which one-fourth of the material remains is:
A. 180 year   **B.** 108 year
C. 1080 year   **D.** None of the above

Q.30 _________________ is a group of plant species of the family Crassulaceae that is usually included as a section within the genus Kalanchoe, but has also been considered to be a separate genus.
A. Hydra   **B.** Bryophyllum
C. Paramecium   **D.** Microcrondiea

General Awareness

Q.31 Who first discovered urea?
A. Marie Curie   **B.** J. J Thomson
C. Friedrich Wöhler   **D.** None of the above

Q.32 Poor vision in human can be due to the dificiency of __.
A. Vitamin A   **B.** Vitamin D
C. Iodine   **D.** Iron

Q.33 Name the annual fair of Rajasthan at which camel is a major event?
A. Sonepur Mela   **B.** Maru Mela
C. Suraj Kund Mela   **D.** Pushkar Mela

Q.34 Which of the institutions is to set up Space Technology Cell (STC) in collaboration with ISRO?
A. IIT-Hyderabad   **B.** IIT-Delhi
C. IIT-Bombay   **D.** IISc Bangalore

Q.35 Who among the following Indian Journalists have won the prestigious International Press Freedom Award?
A. Rajdeep Sardesai   **B.** Barkha Dutt
C. Arnab Goswami   **D.** Neha Dixit

Q.36 In January 2019, the Supreme Court gave its nod to the on-going projects under India Nepal Buddhist Tour Plan, which connects four holly places by all-weather roads.Which of the following is NOT one of them.
A. Badrinath   **B.** Kedarnath
C. Yamunotri   **D.** Sabrimala

Q.37 Which vitamin is prepared by our body in presence of sunlight?
A. Vitamin B   **B.** Vitamin A
C. Vitamin D   **D.** Vitamin C

Q.38 Which is largest freshwater lake in India?
A. Pangong tso   **B.** Wular Lake
C. Udai sagar   **D.** Chilka Lake

Q.39 Who was the first Indian to ski to the North pole?
A. Sanjay Thapar   **B.** Ajeet Bajaj
C. Arun Nayyar   **D.** Neal Paramjeet

Q.40 ____ temple In Karnataka is the most extravagant architectural showpiece of Hampi.
A. Vittala   **B.** Akshardham
C. meenakhsi   **D.** Lingaraj

Basic English

Q.41 Direction: In the following question, the sentence given with blank to be filled in with an appropriate word. Select the correct alternative out of the four and indicate it by selecting the appropriate option.

I _______ to return by the 3rd of the month.
A. strategize   **B.** program
C. plan   **D.** project

Q.42 Direction: Improve the bracketed part of the sentence.
Einstein was one (of the wisest men) that ever lived.

A. of the wisest man	**B.** wise man
C. wisest man	**D.** no improvement

A. made a sorry figure	**B.** made a sad figure
C. cut a sorry face	**D.** no improvement

Q.43 Direction: Select the word with the correct spelling.

A. oxidieser   **B.** thespian   **C.** appruval   **D.** secreetes

Q.44 Direction: In the following question, out of the four alternatives, select the alternative which is the best substitute of the phrase.

To sweep over something so as to surround it completely.

A. engulf   **B.** imbibe   **C.** drown   **D.** plunge

Q.45 Direction: Improve the bracketed part of the sentence.

Venezuelans (were being) deprived of food and medicines for the past year.

A. were	**B.** are
C. have been	**D.** no improvement

Q.46 Direction: In the following question, out of the four alternatives, select the alternative which best expresses the meaning of the idiom/phrase.

Turn a blind eye

A. Not able to see the obvious truth

B. Hide the ugly truth from someone

C. Pretend not to notice

D. Stay away from bad habits

Q.47 Direction: In the following question, a sentence has been given in Direct/Indirect speech. Out of the four alternatives suggested, select the one, which best expresses the same sentence in Indirect/Direct speech.

The girl in the red dress said to me, "Where is the film studio?"

A. The girl in the red dress inquired me where the film studio is.

B. The girl in the red dress asked me where is the film studio.

C. The girl in the red dress asked me where the film studio is.

D. The girl in the red dress asked me where the film studio was.

Q.48 Direction: Select the synonym of "Sheath"

A. weapon	**B.** hide
C. encourage	**D.** coat

Q.49 Direction: In the following question, a sentence has been given in Direct/Indirect speech. Out of the four alternatives suggested, select the one, which best express the same sentence in Indirect/Direct speech.

'Have you come from Japan?' said the shopkeeper to the tourist.

A. The shopkeeper asked the tourist whether she had come from Japan.

B. The shopkeeper asked the tourist that if she had come from Japan.

C. The shopkeeper asked the tourist that whether she had came from Japan.

D. The shopkeeper asked the tourist if she came from Japan.

Q.50 Direction: Improve the bracketed part of the sentence.

The hapless kid (cut a sorry figure) in his first performance on the stage.

// Smart Answer Sheet //

Correct Indicates percentage of students who answered questions correctly.

Skipped Indicates percentage of students who skipped questions.

Q.	Ans.	Correct / Skipped
1	B	83.58 % / 15.08 %
2	B	85.98 % / 13.9 %
3	B	84.48 % / 14.08 %
4	C	88.09 % / 10.96 %
5	A	83.68 % / 15.36 %
6	A	87.32 % / 10.88 %
7	B	88.59 % / 10.21 %
8	D	83.67 % / 15.87 %
9	A	81.76 % / 12.89 %
10	B	78.73 % / 20.94 %
11	B	81.97 % / 16.11 %
12	B	85.43 % / 11.19 %
13	C	83.42 % / 13.66 %
14	B	89.05 % / 10.83 %
15	B	89.97 % / 10.0 %
16	C	82.0 % / 12.08 %
17	A	85.03 % / 10.05 %
18	B	89.88 % / 10.11 %
19	D	78.76 % / 20.5 %
20	B	84.89 % / 14.33 %
21	B	83.01 % / 14.64 %
22	B	80.22 % / 15.45 %
23	C	83.04 % / 13.83 %
24	A	84.06 % / 13.66 %
25	B	89.58 % / 10.05 %
26	B	78.96 % / 11.25 %
27	A	77.44 % / 12.73 %
28	B	83.83 % / 12.13 %
29	C	86.51 % / 13.1 %
30	B	80.31 % / 12.24 %
31	C	80.59 % / 15.36 %
32	A	86.16 % / 10.44 %
33	D	79.6 % / 10.5 %
34	B	82.32 % / 10.99 %
35	D	76.64 % / 20.81 %
36	D	82.52 % / 14.71 %
37	C	83.25 % / 15.46 %
38	B	83.45 % / 16.33 %
39	B	89.77 % / 10.0 %
40	A	81.79 % / 15.89 %
41	C	89.04 % / 10.05 %
42	D	76.72 % / 18.69 %
43	B	77.35 % / 16.84 %
44	A	76.2 % / 14.31 %
45	C	79.2 % / 14.84 %
46	C	82.74 % / 11.3 %
47	D	77.26 % / 18.75 %
48	D	77.4 % / 20.59 %
49	A	79.88 % / 11.42 %
50	D	89.26 % / 10.67 %

Performance Analysis

Avg. Score (%)	55.33%
Toppers Score (%)	58.67%
Your Score	

//Hints and Solutions//

1. Given, Ram invested Rs. 6500 for 6 months, Shyam Rs. 8400 for 5 months and Aman, Rs. 10,000 for 3 months.

Ratio of investments = 6500 × 6 : 8400 × 5 : 10000 × 5

⇒ Ratio of investments = 39 : 42 : 50

Profit earned will be in the same ratio as their investment.

Total profit earned = Rs. 10200

Share of shyam = 42/141 x 11100 = Rs.3306

2.

$$\text{Required number of numbers} = 5 \times 6 \times 6 \times 4$$
$$= 36 \times 20 = 720$$

3. Required number are $5! + 5! - 4! = 216$

4. Let track length be equal to T.

Time taken to meet for the first time $= \dfrac{T}{relativespeed} = \dfrac{T}{6-b}$ or $\dfrac{T}{b-6}$

Time taken for a lap for $A = \dfrac{T}{\frac{6}{}}$

Time taken for a lap for $B = \dfrac{T}{b}$

So, time taken to meet for the first time at the starting point $=$

$$LCM\left(\frac{T}{6}, \frac{T}{b}\right) = \frac{T}{HCF(6,b)}$$

Number of meeting points on the track = Time taken to meet at starting point/Time taken for

first meeting = Relative speed / HCF (6, b).

So, in essence we have to find values for b such that

$$\frac{6-b}{HCF(6,b)} = 2 \text{ or } \frac{b-6}{HCF(6,b)} = 2$$

The question is " If two people cross each other at exactly two points on the circular track and

b is a natural number less than $30,$ how many values can b take?"

$b = 2, 10, 18$ satisfy this equation. So, there are three different values that b can take.

Hence, the answer is 3 .

5. Let us assume Car A travels at a speed of a and Car B travels at a speed of b.

Further, let us assume that they meet after t minutes.

Distance traveled by car A before meeting car $B = a^*t.$

Likewise distance traveled by ca

before meeting car $A = b * t$

Distance traveled by car A after meeting car $B = a * 54.$

Distance traveled by car B after

$carA = 24 * b$

Distance traveled by car A after crossing car $B = $ distance

traveled by car B before cross

$A(\text{ and vice versa })$

$$\Rightarrow at = 54b$$

and $bt = 24a$

Multiplying equations 1 and 2

we have $ab^*t^2 = 54^*24^*$ ab

$$\Rightarrow t^2 = 54 * 24$$

$$\Rightarrow> t = 36$$

The question is " How long did B take to cover the entire journey between City Q and C

So, both cars would have traveled 36 minutes prior to crossing each other. Or, B would r

taken $36 + 24 = 60$ minutes to travel the whole distance. Hence, the answer is 60 mins.

6. To begin with, let us ignore car A. Car B and car C travel in opposite directions.

Their relative speed = Sum of the two speeds $= 45 + 54kmph = 99kmph.$

$$= 99 * \frac{5}{18} m/s = \frac{55}{2} m/s = 27.5 m/s$$

The relative distance $= 220m.$ So, time they will take to cross each other $= \dfrac{220}{27.5} = 8seconds$

Now, car A has to overtake car B within 8 seconds. The relative distance = 50m

$$\Rightarrow \text{Relative speed should be at least } \frac{50}{8} m/s = 6.25 m/s$$

$$\Rightarrow 6.25 * \frac{18}{5} kmph = 22.5 kmph$$

The question is " If car A decides to overtake Car B before cars B and C cross each other, what

is the minimum speed at which car A must travel? "

Car B travels at 45kmph, so car A should travel at at least $45 + 22.5 = 67.5 kmph.$

Hence, the answer is $67.5 kmph.$

7. $a = b(1 + x) \Rightarrow \dfrac{a}{b} = 1 + x$

$a = x(a + b),$ dividing by a through out

$$1 = x\left(1 + \frac{b}{a}\right)$$

$$1 = x\left(1 + \frac{1}{1/x}\right)$$

$$1 = x\left(\frac{x+2}{x+1}\right)$$

$$x + 1 = x^2 + 2x$$

$$\Rightarrow x^2 + x - 1 = 0$$

Now, we need to solve this equation. Using the discriminant method, when we solve this, x turns

out to be $\dfrac{-1+\sqrt{5}}{2}$

x has to lie between 0 and 1 and there for cannot be $\dfrac{-1-\sqrt{5}}{2}$

So, the only solution is $\dfrac{-1+\sqrt{5}}{2}.$ This is roughly 0.62

Or, x has to be 62% approximately. The ration 1.618 is also called the golden ratio, and is the conjugate and reciprocal of 0.618.

The golden ratio finds many mentions, from the Fibonacci series to Da Vinci. So, it is a big favourite of mathematician.

x has to be 62% approximately.

Hence, the answer is 62%

8. In the final state, the number of girls should be 1.5 * the number of boys.

When 50% of the boys are taken as girls, let the number of boys = x

Number of girls = 1.5x

Total number of students = 2.5x

Original number of boys = 2x (50% of boys = x)

Original number of girls = 0.5x

Girls form 20% of the overall class.

Girls form 20% of the overall class.

Hence, the answer is 20%

9. $\pi(r + 2)^2 - \pi r^2 = 88$

$\pi(r^2+4r+4-r^2) = 88$

$4\pi r + 4\pi = 88$

22/7 (4r+4) = 88

4r + 4 = 4*7

4r = 28 - 4

r= 6 cm

10. A is kept open for all t minutes and fills one-third the tank. Or, A should be able to fill the entire
tank in '3t' minutes.

A and B together can fill the tank completely in t minutes. A alone can fill it in $3t$ minutes.

A and B together can fill $\dfrac{1}{t}$ of the tank in a minute. A alone can fill $\dfrac{1}{3t}$ of the tank in a minute.

So, in a minute, B can fill $\dfrac{1}{t} - \dfrac{1}{3t} = \dfrac{2}{3t}$. Or, B takes $\dfrac{3t}{2}$ minutes to fill an entire tank.

To fill one-third the tank, B will take $\dfrac{t}{2}$ minutes. B is kept open for 10 minutes.

$\dfrac{t}{2} = t - 10, t = 20$ minutes.

A takes 60 minutes to fill the entire tank, B takes 30 minutes to fill the entire tank. A is kept open
for all 20 minutes. B is kept open for 10 minutes.
C, which is kept open for 8 minutes also fills one-third the tank.
Or, C alone can fill the tank in 24 minutes.

11. In one day, $4m + 6w = \dfrac{1}{24}$ of task.

In these questions, just substitute extreme values to get the whole range

If a woman is half as efficient as man

$4m + 3m = \dfrac{1}{24}, 7m = \dfrac{1}{24}, m = \dfrac{1}{168}$

$6w + 2m = 3m + 2m = 5m, 5m$ will take $\dfrac{168}{5}$ days

$= 33.6$ days

If a woman is as efficient as a man

$4m + 6w$ finish in 24 days

$10m$ finish $\dfrac{1}{24}$ of task in a day

$6w + 2m = 8m, 8m$ will take $\dfrac{240}{8} = 30$ days to finish the task.

So, the range $= 30$ to 33.6 days. The new team will take 30 to 33.6 days to finish the task.

12. $7^3 = 343,$

$7^2 = 49,$

So on solving the above equation, $(7)^{72+2x} = (7)^{80}$

$72 + 2x = 80 \Rightarrow x = 4.$

13.

$$3\sin x + 4\cos x \geq -r$$
$$5\left(\dfrac{3}{5}\sin x + \dfrac{4}{5}\cos x\right) \geq -r$$
$$\dfrac{3}{5} = \cos A => \sin A = \dfrac{4}{5}$$
$$5(\sin x\cos A + \sin A\cos x) \geq -r$$
$$5(\sin(x + A)) \geq -r$$
$$5\sin(x + A) \geq -r$$
$$-1 \leq \sin(\text{ang }]e) \leq 1$$
$$5\sin(x + A) \geq -5$$
$$r = 5$$

14. C.P. of each apple = 100/20 = Rs. 5

S.P. of each apple = Rs.5 x125/100 = Rs. 6.25

Number of apple sold for Rs. 100 = 100/6.25 = 16

15. This question requires a good deal of visualization. since, both the box and cans are hard
solids, simply dividing the volume won't work because the shape can't be deformed.

Each cylindrical can has a diameter of $14cm$ and while they are kept erect in the box will
occupy height of $30cm$

Number of such cans that can be placed in a row $= \dfrac{l}{\text{Diameter}} = \dfrac{76}{14} = 5$ (Remaining space will be vacant)

Number of such rows that can be placed $= \dfrac{Width}{Diameter} = \dfrac{46}{14} = 3$

Thus $5 * 3 = 15$ cans can be placed in an erect position.

However, height of $box = 45cm$ and only $30cm$ has been utilized so far

Remaining height $= 15cm > 14cm$ (Diameter of the can)

So, some cans can be placed horizontally on the base.

Number of cans in horizontal row $= \dfrac{Length of box}{Height of can} = \dfrac{76}{30} = 2$

Number of such rows $= \dfrac{Width of box}{Diameter of can} = \dfrac{46}{14} = 3$

$\therefore 2 * 3 = 6$ cans can be placed horizontally

∴ Maximum number of cans = 15+6 = 21

16. Ans.

(3) $\alpha - D(+)$ – glucose and $\beta - D(+)$ – glucose are anomers.

17. Nylon 6,6 is a polymer of adipic acid and hexamethylene diamine.

18. 64.7 °C, Methanol, also known as methyl alcohol amongst other names, is a chemical with the formula CH_3OH. It is a light, volatile, colourless, flammable liquid with a distinctive alcoholic odour similar to that of ethanol.

19. Ans.1) Eighteen ATP units.

The chemical reaction that takes place during photosynthesis is given below:
$$6CO_2 + 6H_2O \rightarrow C_6H_{12}O_2 + 6O_2 + 18ATP + 12 NADPH$$
Thus, synthesis of each molecule of glucose involves 18 molecules of ATP

20. Ans.(2) Dacron is the condensation polymer Neoprene, teflon and acrylonitrile are addition polymers.

21. Ans.(1) Vitamin B and Vitamin C are water-soluble.

22. Curie point, also called Curie Temperature, temperature at which certain magnetic materials undergo a sharp change in their magnetic properties. In the case of rocks and minerals, remanent magnetism appears below the Curie point—about 570 °C (1,060 °F) for the common magnetic mineral magnetite.

23. Osmium is one of the heaviest materials on earth, weighing twice as much as lead per teaspoon. Osmium is a chemical element in the platinum group metals; it's often used as alloys in electrical contacts and fountain pen nibs

24. The essential nature of the atomic nucleus was established with the discovery of the neutron by James Chadwick in 1932 and the determination that it was a new elementary particle, distinct from the proton.

25. (b) According to Kepler's law, $T^2 \propto R^3$
$$\therefore \left(\frac{T_2}{T_1}\right)^2 = \left(\frac{R_2}{R_1}\right)^3 \quad \therefore T_1 = 365 \text{ day}$$
$$\text{or } \therefore \left(\frac{T_2}{T_1}\right)^2 = \left(\frac{R_1/2}{R_1}\right)^3 = \frac{1}{8} = 0.125$$
or $T_2 = 129$ days

26. A palmately compound leaf has its leaflets radiating outwards from the end of the petiole, like fingers off the palm of a hand. Examples of plants with palmately compound leaves include poison ivy, the buckeye tree, or the familiar house plant Schefflera sp. (commonly called "umbrella plant").

27. For a simple pendulum, $T = 2\pi\sqrt{\dfrac{1}{g}} \quad \therefore \dfrac{T_2}{T_1} = \sqrt{\dfrac{g_1}{g_2}}$

Now, $g_1 = \dfrac{GM}{R^2}, g_2 = \dfrac{GM}{(2R)^2} = \dfrac{GM}{4R^2}$

$$\therefore \frac{T_2}{T_1} = \sqrt{\frac{GM}{R^2} \times \frac{4R^2}{GM}} = \sqrt{\frac{4}{1}} = \frac{2}{1}$$

28. When one of the electrons is removed from a neutral helium atom, energy is given by E_n $E_n = \dfrac{13.6Z^2}{n^2} eV$ per atom

For helium ion, $Z = 2$, when doubly ionised. For first orbit,

$n = 1 \therefore E_1 = -\dfrac{13.6}{(1)^2} \times (2)^2 = -54.4 eV$

∴ Energy required to remove it $= 54.4 eV$

∴ Total energy required $= 54.4 + 24.6 = 79 eV$

29. $\because \dfrac{N}{N_0} = e^{-\lambda t}$

∴ There is a simultaneous emission of two particles. $\therefore \dfrac{N}{N_0} = e^{-(\lambda_1 + \lambda_2)t}$ or $\dfrac{N_0}{4N_0} = e^{-(\lambda_1 + \lambda_2)t}$

or $\log 4 = (\lambda_1 + \lambda_2)t \log e$

Now $\lambda_1 = \dfrac{0.693}{1620}$ and $\lambda_2 = \dfrac{0.693}{810}$

$$\therefore 2.303[2 \times 0.3] = 0.693\left[\frac{1}{1620} + \frac{1}{810}\right]$$

or $t = \dfrac{2.303 \times 0.6 \times 1620}{0.693 \times 3}$ or $t = 1080$ year

30. Bryophyllum is a group of plant species of the family Crassulaceae that is usually included as a section within the genus Kalanchoe, but has also been considered to be a separate genus. There are about forty species in the group, native to South Africa, Madagascar, and Asia

31. In 1828, the German chemist Friedrich Wöhler obtained urea artificially by treating silver cyanate with ammonium chloride. This was the first time an organic compound was artificially synthesized from inorganic starting materials, without the involvement of living organisms.

32. Night blindness caused by nearsightedness, cataracts, or vitamin A deficiency is treatable.

33. The Pushkar Fair, also called the Pushkar Camel Fair or locally as Kartik Mela or Pushkar ka Mela is an annual multi-day livestock fair and cultural fête held in the town of Pushkar Rajasthan.

34. IIT Delhi is to collaborate with the Indian Space Research Organization (ISRO) for establishing a Space Technology Cell (STC). IIT Delhi will become an academic partner of ISRO in research areas like Artificial Intelligence, nanotechnology, functional textiles, smart manufacturing. The Space Technology Cell will emphasize in carrying out research projects in the space technology.

35. Indian journalist Neha Dixit was one of several recipients of the 2019 International Press Freedom Awards, awarded by the Committee to Protect Journalists (CPJ), a non-profit organization whose aim is to enable journalists to work without fear of reprisal.

36. Sabrimala is not the part of India Nepal Buddhist Tour Plan, which connects four holly places by all-weather roads.

37. Vitamin D is known as the sunshine vitamin because our bodies can actually make and absorb vitamin D from sun exposure.

38. Wular Lake is the largest fresh water lakes in India. It is sited in Bandipora district in Jammu and Kashmir, India.

39. Ajeet Bajaj is the first Indian to ski to the North Pole and the South Pole within a year.

40. The Vittala Temple in Hampi is an ancient monument that is well-known for its exceptional architecture and unmatched craftsmanship. It is considered to be one of the largest and the most famous structure in Hampi.

41. an intention is always represented by "plan".

42. No improvement

43. thespian: relating to drama and the theatre.

44. engulf: a natural force sweep over something so as to surround or cover it completely.

45. As the "duration" has been given thus present perfect or present perfect continuous should be used. However "v3" has been given thus the voice used is passive. S

Venenzuela have deprived of food and medicine for the past year. (incorrect)

Venenzuela have been deprived of food and medicine for the past year. (correct).

46. turn a blind eye: pretend not to notice.

Management often turn a blind eye to bullying in the workplace.

47. The girl in the red dress asked me where the film studio was.

48. sheath: a close-fitting cover for the blade of a knife or sword.

49. Here 2 rules applies in the question.

Rule1-If the reported verb is in past then in reporting speech present perfect tense should be changed into past perfect tense,

Rule 2- if a question gives the reply in the form of "yes/no", we use the conjunction "if/whether" to join reported verb and reported speech.

50. No improvement

Mathematics

Q.1 In two mixtures respective ratio of milk and water is 3:5 and 7:5 respectively. In what ratio both mixtures should be mixed to make ratio of milk and water 1:1?

A. 3:2 **B.** 1:3 **C.** 2:3 **D.** 2:5

Q.2 ABC is a right angle triangle $\angle A$ = 90, $\angle B$ = 60. A perpendicular AD is drawn on BC. Find the ratio of areas of $\triangle ACD$ and $\triangle ABD$.

A. 4 : 1 **B.** 3 : 1 **C.** 2 : 1 **D.** 1 : 1

Q.3 If the roots of a quadratic equation are 20 and -8, then find the equation?

A. $x^2 + 12x - 160 = 0$ **B.** $x^2 - 12x + 160 = 0$
C. $x^2 - 12x - 160 = 0$ **D.** $x^2 + 12x + 160 = 0$

Q.4 A invests Rs. 64000 in a business: After few months B Joined him with Rs. 48000. At the end of year, the total profit was divided between them in the ratio 2 :1.After how many months did B join?

A. 8 **B.** 4 **C.** 6 **D.** 7

Q.5 Respective ratio of the present age of Reena and Beena is 2: 3. 4 years hence the resepective ratio of their ages will be 5: 7 then what is the difference between their ages?

A. 8 years **B.** 6 years **C.** 4 years **D.** 5 years

Ques (6-10):Direction: Study the following graph carefully and answer the questions given beside.

Following chart shows the percentage of infected people by epidemic 'SARS'

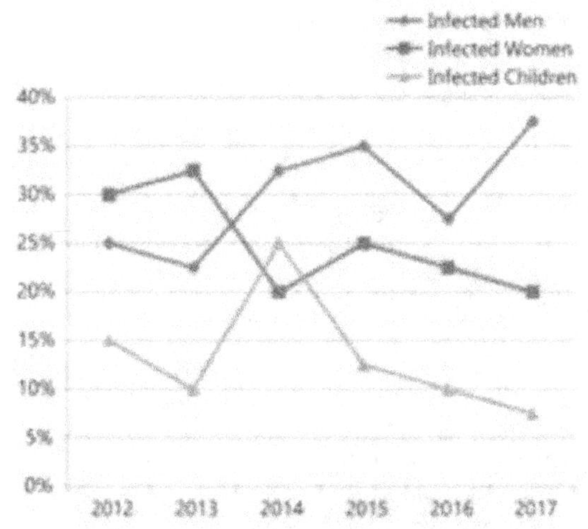

Total Number of Men, Women and Children in district over the years.

Years	Men	Women	Children
2012	44000	39000	12000
2013	75000	64000	21000
2014	63000	60000	12000
2015	70000	54000	16000
2016	70000	68000	20000
2017	78000	75000	45000

Q.6 What was the approximate average of infected men, infected women and infected children in 2014?

A. 12683 **B.** 12795 **C.** 11825 **D.** 12843

Q.7 The number of infected men in the year 2013 was what percent to the men not suffering from SARS in the same year?

A. 45% **B.** 29% **C.** 30.5% **D.** 25.5%

Q.8 What was the ratio of the infected women in 2014 to the infected men in the year 2016?

A. 6:7 **B.** 21:65 **C.** 15:73 **D.** 48:77

Q.9 What is the difference between the number of infected women and infected children together in the year 2017 and the number of infected men in the same year?

A. 10875 **B.** 15745 **C.** 14530 **D.** 31650

Q.10 What is the percent of non-infected women in 2012 to non-infected men in 2015?

A. 60% **B.** 55% **C.** 70% **D.** 85%

Q.11 Two trains of equal lengths take 10 seconds and 15 seconds respectively to cross a telegraph post. If the length of each train be 120 metres, in what time (in seconds) will they cross each other travelling in opposite direction?

A. 10 **B.** 12 **C.** 15 **D.** 20

Q.12 Each of the questions given below consists of a question followed by three statements. You have to study the question and the statements and decide which of the statement(s) is/are necessary to answer the question?

What is the speed of the train?

I. The train crosses a signal pole in 18 seconds.

II. The train crosses a platform of equal length in 36 seconds.

III. Length of the train is 330 metres.

A. I and II only
B. II and III only
C. I and III only
D. III and either I or II only

Q.13 A takes twice as much time as B or thrice as much time as C to finish a piece of work. Working together, they can finish the work in 2 days. B can do the work alone in

A. 4 days **B.** 6 days **C.** 8 days **D.** 12 days

Q.14 Ayesha's father was 38 years of age when she was born while her mother was 36 years old when her brother four years younger to her was born. What is the difference between the ages of her parents?

A. 6 years
B. 8 years
C. 2 years
D. None of these

Q.15 In covering a distance of 30 km, Abhay takes 2 hours more than sameer. If Abhay double his speed, then he would take 1 hour less than Sameer. Abhay's speed is
A. 5 kmph
B. 6 kmph
C. 6.5 kmph
D. 5.6 kmph

Science

Q.16 Performing of different functions but having the same basic structure such an organ is called _______.
A. Vestigial organs
B. Homologous organs
C. Analytic organs
D. Analogous organs

Q.17 Yeast is a __________.
A. Bacteria
B. Fungi
C. Algae
D. Bryophyte

Q.18 How many chambers are in a crocodile heart?
A. 13
B. 4
C. 2
D. 10

Q.19 Which enzyme is present in all members of the animal kingdom except Protozoa?
A. Insulin
B. Pepsin
C. Renin
D. Amylase

Q.20 Which of the following Vitamin is helpful in making clots of blood?
A. Vitamin E
B. Vitamin K
C. Vitamin C
D. Vitamin A

Q.21 Speed of the aircrafts can be recorded with-
A. Speedometer
B. Machmeter
C. Sphygmomanometer
D. Osmometer

Q.22 Which of the following Waves are required for long distance wireless communication?
A. Radio waves
B. Ultraviolet rays
C. Alpha rays
D. infrared rays

Q.23 While ascending a hill, the driver of the vehicle keeps the gear ratio -
A. equal to 1
B. less than 1
C. greater than 1
D. either equal to or greater than 1

Q.24 The loudness of sound coming from the busy traffic is__________.
A. 80 dB
B. 60 dB
C. 70 dB
D. 10 dB

Q.25 At what temperature is the density of water maximum?
A. 14 degrees celsius
B. 4 degrees Celsius
C. 10 degrees Celsius
D. 6 degrees Celsius

Q.26 Brown stains in vessels and clothes indicate the presence of high quantities of _______ in water.
A. Magnesium
B. Calcium

C. Manganese
D. Chromium

Q.27 The isotope used for the production of atomic energy is______?
A. U-235
B. U-238
C. U-234
D. U-236

Q.28 Which of the following is correct mixture of producer gas ?
A. $CO + H_2$
B. $CO + N_2$
C. $CO + SO_2$
D. $CO + Cl_2$

Q.29 "In the manufacture of Vanaspati ghee from vegetable oils, which among the following gas is used?"
A. Oxygen
B. Carbon dioxide
C. Hydrogen
D. Nitrogen

Q.30 Which one of the following is also called stranger gas?
A. Argon
B. Neon
C. Xenon
D. Nitrous Oxide

General Awareness

Q.31 Identify the largest muscle in the human body.
A. LattissimusDorsi
B. Iliopsoas
C. Gluteus Maximus
D. Sartorius

Q.32 The Presidential order was issued under ___ of the constitution of India which allows the president to make certain "exceptions and modification" to the constitution for the benefit of 'State subjects' of Jammu and Kashmir.
A. Article 340(1)(d)
B. Article 304(1)(d)
C. Article 370(1)(d)
D. Article 314(1)(d)

Q.33 The fifth sikh guru compiled AdiGranth, the first official edition of sikh scripture.
A. Guru ArjanDev
B. Gure Amar Das
C. Gure Ram Das
D. Guru Gobind Singh

Q.34 _________Tiger reserve in Karnataka is home to the largest number of Asian elephants in the world.
A. Ranthambore Tiger Project
B. Nagarhole Tiger Reserve
C. Bandhavgarh National Park
D. Kanha National Park

Q.35 Article 35A was incorporated into the Indian constitution based on the _______Delhi agreement entered between then Prime minister of Jammu and Kashmir Sheikh Abdullah.
A. 1955
B. 1952
C. 1960
D. 1956

Q.36 The global talent competitive index prepared by the _______ in partnership with Tata Communications and Adecco Group was released on the first day of the World Economic Forum Annual Meeting 2019.
A. SGT Business School
B. GURU GOBIND Business School
C. INSEAD Business School
D. JAMNALAL Business School

Q.37 In Carbon dating, a weak C-14 molecule deteriorates and transforms into ___.

A. C-16   **B.** N-14   **C.** C-11   **D.** N-12

Q.38 Which amongst the following is NOT the member of BASIC group?

A. Australlia   **B.** South Africa
C. India   **D.** Brazil

Q.39 Which of the following is known as the study of earthquakes?

A. Histology   **B.** Lithology
C. Seisomology   **D.** Semiology

Q.40 Identify the SI unit of electrical resistance.

A. Ampere   **B.** Watt
C. Coulomb   **D.** Ohm

Basic English

Q.41 Direction : In the following questions, some of the sentences have errors and some have none. Find out which part of the sentence has an error. The number of that part is your answer. If there is no error, the answer would be (D).

Great Sanskrit poet (A)/ and scholar of Ancient India, (B)/ Mahakavi Kalidasa is regarded as Shakespeare of India. (C)/ No error (D)

A. A   **B.** B   **C.** C   **D.** D

Q.42 Direction : In the following questions, sentences are given with blanks to be filled in with an appropriate word (s) Some alternatives are suggested for each question. Choose the correct alternative out of the given alternatives as your answer.

I am __ interested in the project, I intend to do it sincerely and earn good grades in my third semester.

A. Very   **B.** So
C. Scarcely   **D.** Much

Q.43 Direction : In the following questions out of the four/five alternatives, choose the one which is best express the meaning of the given word.

SCOURGE

A. Curse   **B.** Blessing
C. Regards   **D.** Bravery

Q.44 Direction : In the following questions, choose the word opposite in meaning to the given word.

AMORPHOUS

A. Obviate   **B.** Structured
C. Complete   **D.** Compassion

Q.45 Direction : In the following questions a group of four/five words is given. One word in each group is mis-spelt. Choose this mis-spelt word.

(A) Tedium
(B) Acremonious
(C) Magnanimous
(D) Archetype

A. A   **B.** C   **C.** D   **D.** B

Ques (46-50):Direction : In the following passage some of the words have been left out. First read the passage over and try to understand what it is about. Then fill in the blanks with the help of the alternatives given.

Modern society ignores the individual. It only takes account of human beings. The confusion of the concepts of individual and of human beings has led industrial civilization to a fundamental error i.e. the --------- (20) of men. Men are categorized, and placed in their respective brackets according to their social status, education and standard of living. ____(21) we were all identical, we could be reared and made to live and work in great herds like cattle. Categorization of human beings is just like putting symbols or marks on cattle to identify this _____ (22) that. But each one has his own personality. He cannot be treated like a symbol. Children should not be placed, at a very early age in schools where they are educated on a________(23) basis. As is well known, most great men ____ (24) brought up in comparative solitude, or have refused to enter the mould of the school.

Q.46 Choose the correct option for 20.

A. Standards   **B.** Inconsistent
C. Standardization   **D.** Inconsistency

Q.47 Choose the correct option for 21.

A. Even if   **B.** If
C. Even when   **D.** Therefore

Q.48 Choose the correct option for 22.

A. From   **B.** And
C. Between   **D.** None of the above

Q.49 Chose the correct option for 23.

A. Retail   **B.** Trade
C. Wholesale   **D.** All

Q.50 Chose the correct option for 24.

A. Had been   **B.** Has been
C. Have   **D.** Have been

// Smart Answer Sheet //

Correct Indicates percentage of students who answered questions correctly.

Skipped Indicates percentage of students who skipped questions.

Q.	Ans.	Correct / Skipped	Q.	Ans.	Correct / Skipped	Q.	Ans.	Correct / Skipped	Q.	Ans.	Correct / Skipped	Q.	Ans.	Correct / Skipped
1	C	86.02 % / 10.1 %	11	B	78.24 % / 12.85 %	21	B	79.4 % / 19.95 %	31	C	89.15 % / 10.4 %	41	C	79.87 % / 11.7 %
2	B	81.26 % / 13.2 %	12	D	82.32 % / 15.9 %	22	A	76.56 % / 15.94 %	32	C	89.97 % / 10.02 %	42	D	87.63 % / 11.53 %
3	C	76.38 % / 23.52 %	13	B	85.59 % / 10.42 %	23	D	78.98 % / 16.1 %	33	A	80.64 % / 11.3 %	43	A	83.24 % / 11.24 %
4	B	87.59 % / 12.22 %	14	A	84.28 % / 12.69 %	24	C	83.81 % / 12.91 %	34	B	81.56 % / 13.84 %	44	B	78.96 % / 10.3 %
5	A	79.23 % / 19.61 %	15	A	88.54 % / 11.45 %	25	B	83.51 % / 10.01 %	35	B	79.12 % / 16.76 %	45	D	83.75 % / 15.18 %
6	C	88.91 % / 10.66 %	16	B	84.85 % / 15.02 %	26	C	85.65 % / 12.67 %	36	C	82.52 % / 12.02 %	46	C	84.53 % / 15.18 %
7	B	87.92 % / 11.12 %	17	B	82.77 % / 12.57 %	27	A	79.3 % / 17.03 %	37	B	79.53 % / 18.23 %	47	B	89.82 % / 10.1 %
8	D	88.83 % / 10.68 %	18	B	84.5 % / 14.4 %	28	B	86.0 % / 13.35 %	38	A	84.09 % / 14.02 %	48	A	84.86 % / 13.92 %
9	A	78.86 % / 16.25 %	19	D	77.74 % / 14.77 %	29	C	83.8 % / 11.7 %	39	C	79.93 % / 19.59 %	49	C	80.66 % / 18.17 %
10	A	78.68 % / 13.51 %	20	B	89.16 % / 10.37 %	30	C	85.66 % / 12.36 %	40	D	76.22 % / 11.1 %	50	C	83.82 % / 13.6 %

Performance Analysis

Avg. Score (%)	38.0%
Toppers Score (%)	60.67%
Your Score	

//Hints and Solutions//

1. Using allegation method

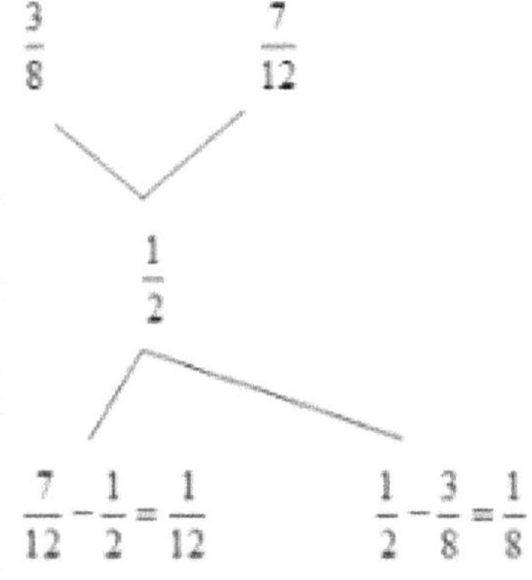

$$\frac{7}{12} - \frac{1}{2} = \frac{1}{12} \qquad \frac{1}{2} - \frac{3}{8} = \frac{1}{8}$$

Required ratio $= \frac{1}{12} : \frac{1}{8} = 2 : 3$

2.

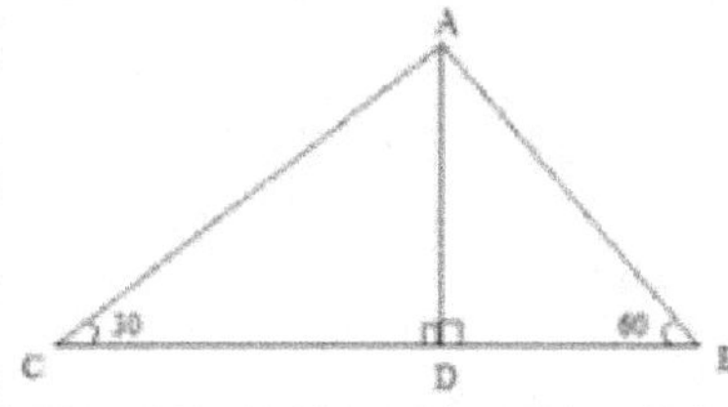

In $\triangle ABD$

$\tan 60 = \dfrac{AD}{DB}$

$AD = DB\sqrt{3}$

$In \triangle ACD$

$\tan 30 = \dfrac{AD}{CD}$

$\Rightarrow CD = \dfrac{AD}{\tan 30} = \dfrac{DB\sqrt{3}}{1/\sqrt{3}}$

$\Rightarrow CD = 3DB$

Area of $\triangle ACD$: Area of $\triangle ABD$ $\frac{1}{2} \times AD \times CD : \frac{1}{2} \times AD \times BD$

$D : BD$

$3BD : BD$

3 : 1 is the required answer.

3. Any quadratic equation is of the form

x^2 - (sum of the roots)x + (product of the roots) = 0 ---- (1)

where x is a real variable. As sum of the roots is 12 and product of the roots is -160, the quadratic equation with roots as 20 and -8 is: x^2 - 12x - 160 = 0.

4. B entered after x months.

Ratio of profits

$= 64000 \times 12 : 48000(12 - x)$

$= 16 : (12 - x)$

$\therefore \dfrac{16}{12 - x} = \dfrac{2}{1} \Rightarrow 24 - 2x = 16$

$\Rightarrow 2x = 8 \Rightarrow x = 4$ Months

5. Let present age of Reena and Beena be $2x$ and $3x$ years respectively

According to the question

$\dfrac{2x+4}{3x+4} = \dfrac{5}{7}$

$14x + 28 = 15x + 20 \quad \therefore x = 8$

Required difference $= 3 \times 8 - 2 \times 8 = 8$ years

6. Required average $= \dfrac{1}{3} \times \left(63000 \times \dfrac{325}{100} + 60000 \times \dfrac{20}{100} + 12000 \times \dfrac{25}{100} \right)$

$= \dfrac{1}{3} \times (20475 + 12000 + 3000)$

$= \dfrac{1}{3} \times 35475 = 11825$

7. Required percentage $= \dfrac{75000 \times \frac{22.5}{100}}{75000 \times \frac{100-22.5}{100}} \times 100$

$= \dfrac{22.5}{77.5} \times 100 = 29.03 \approx 29\%$

8. Required ratio

$= 60000 \times \dfrac{20}{100} : 70000 \times \dfrac{27.5}{100} = 6 \times 20 : 7 \times 27.5$

$= 48 : 77$

9. Reqd. difference

$= (78000 \times 37.5\%) - (75000 \times 20\% + 45000 \times 7.5\%)$

$= 29250 - (15000 + 3375) = 29250 - 18375 = 10875$

10. % of non-infected women $= 100 - 30 = 70\%$ % of non-infected men $= 100 - 35 = 65\%$ Required percentage $= \dfrac{39000 \times 70\%}{70000 \times 65\%} \times 100 = 60\%$

11. Speed of the first train $= \left(\dfrac{120}{10}\right) m/sec = 12 m/sec$

Speed of the second train $= \left(\dfrac{120}{15}\right) m/sec = 8 m/sec$

Relative speed $= (12 + 8) = 20 m/sec$

Required time $= \left(\dfrac{120+120}{20}\right) sec = 12 sec$

12. Let the speed of the train be x metres/sec.

Time taken to cross a signal pole $= \dfrac{\text{Length of the train}}{\text{Speed of the train}}$

Time taken to cross a platform $=$ $\dfrac{(\text{ Length of the train + Length of the Platform})}{\text{Speed of the train}}$

Length of train $= 330 m$

and III give, $18 = \dfrac{330}{x} \Rightarrow x = \dfrac{330}{18} m/sec = \dfrac{55}{3} m/sec$

II and III give, $36 = \dfrac{2 \times 330}{x} \Rightarrow x = \dfrac{660}{36} m/sec =$

$\frac{55}{3} m/sec$

Hence, D is correct.

13. Let A, B and C take $x, \frac{x}{2}$ and $\frac{x}{3}$ days respectively to finish the work. since, if they work together, the work will be finished in 2 days. Therefore. $\left(\frac{1}{x} + \frac{2}{x} + \frac{3}{x}\right) = \frac{1}{2}$

$\frac{6}{x} = \frac{1}{2}$

$x = 12$ days

Thus, B can finish the whole work in 6 days

14. Mother's age when Ayesha's brother was born = 36 years.

Father's age when Ayesha's brother was born = (38 + 4) years = 42 years.

∴ Required difference = (42 – 36) years = 6 years.

15. Let Let speed of Arun $=\times km/h$ speed of Anil $= y$ kmph

Distance covered $= 30km$ We have, I ime $= \frac{Distance}{Speed}$

Therefore, time taken by the Abhay to cover a distance of $30km$ by the speed of $\times km = \frac{30}{x}$ Time taken by the Sameer to cover a distance of $30km$ by the speed of $ykm = \frac{30}{y}$ According to 1 condition. $\frac{30}{x} - \frac{30}{y} = 2 \cdots (1)$

If Abhay double his speed, then he would take 1 hour less than Sameer. Therefore. $\frac{30}{y} - \frac{30}{2x} = 1 \cdots (2)$

Adding (1) and (2), we get $\frac{30}{x} - \frac{30}{2x} = 3$

$\frac{30}{2x} = 3$

$x = 5$

Hence Abhay's speed $= 5km/h$

16. Homologous organs are the organs that have the same origin in different organisms but they've been developed along different directions due to adaptations to different needs. For example -the forelimbs of man, cheetah, whale, and bat.

17. Yeast is a single-celled microorganism that is a member of the Fungi kingdom. Yeast is found in nature as well as within our bodies. It consumes sugar and produces by-products such as carbon dioxide, alcohol, and other chemical compounds. Yeast is an essential ingredient in baking, brewing, and wine making.

18. Crocodile has a four chambered heart and two ventricles because of the complex blood circulation system. As crocodiles have to spend lot of their time in water that is why their heart rate slows down to 1 or 2 beats/ minute. Thus the anatomy of their heart helps them to adapt water conditions and thus reduce blood flow so to save oxygen for them.

19. Amylase is present in all members of the animal kingdom except Protozoa. Amylase is an enzyme that catalyses the hydrolysis of starch into sugars. Amylase is present in the saliva of humans and some other mammals, where it begins the chemical process of digestion.

20. Vitamin K is helpful in making clots of blood. Normally clotting takes the time from 2 to 5 minutes.

21. Machmeter is an instrument that measures the speed of an aircraft relative to that of sound and displays it in Mach numbers.

22. Waves that are required for long distance wireless communication are radio waves. Radio waves are a type of electromagnetic radiation with wavelengths in the electromagnetic spectrum longer than infrared light. Radio waves have frequencies as high as 300 GHz to as low as 3 kHz, though some definitions describe waves above 1 or 3 GHz as microwaves, or include waves of any lower frequency.

23. While ascending a hill, the driver of the vehicle keeps the gear ratio either equal to or greater than 1.

24. Loudness of sound is proportional to the square of the amplitude of the vibration producing the sound It is expressed in decibel dB The loudness of the sound coming from busy traffic is 70 dB Above 80 dB the noise becomes physically painful.

25. When cooled from room temperature liquid water becomes increasingly dense, as with other substances, but at approximately 4 °C (39 °F), pure water reaches its maximum density. As it is cooled further, it expands to become less dense.

26. Iron and manganese can give water an objectionable color, taste or odor. Both can cause reddish brown stains on dishes, laundry, sinks and fixtures. Many cleaning products do not remove these stains, and some may even make them worse.

27. Uranium-235 (235U) is an isotope of uranium making up about 0.72% of natural uranium. Unlike the predominant isotope uranium-238, it is fissile, i.e., it can sustain a fission chain reaction.

28. Producer gas, a mixture of flammable gases (principally carbon monoxide or hydrogen) and nonflammable gases (mainly nitrogen or carbon dioxide) made by the partial combustion of carbonaceous substances, usually coal, in an atmosphere of air and steam. Producer gas has a lower heating value than other gaseous fuels, but it can be manufactured with relatively simple equipment; it is used mainly as a fuel in large industrial furnaces.

29. Vanaspati ghee is manufactured from vegetable oil by a process called 'hydrogenation'. By passing hydrogen gas.

30. Xenon was discovered in England by the Scottish chemist William Ramsay and English chemist Morris Travers. Ramsay suggested the name xenon for this gas from the Greek word [xenon], neuter singular form of [xenos], meaning 'foreigner', 'stranger', or 'guest'.

31. The gluteus maximus is the largest muscle in the human body. It is large and powerful because it has the job of keeping the trunk of the body in an erect posture.

32. Article 370 (1) (d) of the Constitution was issued under Presidential Order, the President can make certain 'exceptions and modifications' to the Constitution for the benefit of 'State subjects' of Jammu and Kashmir.

33. Guru Arjan(15 April 1563 – 30 May 1606) was the first of the two Gurus martyred in the Sikh faith and the fifth of the ten total Sikh Gurus. He compiled the first official edition of the Sikh scripture called the AdiGranth, which later expanded into the Guru Granth Sahib.

34. Nagarhole National Park, also known as Rajiv Gandhi National Park, is a wildlife reserve in the South Indian state of Karnataka. Part of the Nilgiri Biosphere Reserve, the park is backed by the Brahamagiri Mountains and filled with sandalwood and teak trees.

35. Article 35A of the Indian Constitution was an article that empowered the Jammu and Kashmir state's legislature to define "permanent residents" of the state and provide special rights and privileges to those permanent. It is based on the 1952 agreement between Jawaharlal Nehru and Sheikh Abdullah.

36. The Global Talent Competitiveness Index (GTCI) is an annual benchmarking report that measures the ability of countries to compete for talent. The report, which covers 125 economies and 114 cities, is based on research conducted by INSEAD.

37. Carbon-12 and Carbon-13 are stable, but Carbon-14 decays by very weak beta decay to nitrogen-14 with a half-life of approximately 5,730 years.

38. The BASIC countries are a bloc of four large newly industrialized countries – Brazil, South Africa, India and China – formed by an agreement on 28 November 2009.

39. Seismology is the study of earthquakes and seismic waves that move through and around the earth. A seismologist is a scientist who studies earthquakes and seismic waves.

40. The ohm (symbol: Ω) is the SI derived unit of electrical resistance, named after German physicist Georg Simon Ohm.

41. Correct Sentence - Great Sanskrit scholar and poet of Ancient India, Mahakavi Kalidasa is regarded as the Shakespeare of India.

'The' is an article of definiteness. It is used before Common Nouns which are names of things unique of their kind but not before any proper noun. Ex-The India or The Mohan is wrong. However in some cases when the proper noun is used in its general sense i.e. to refer to a class/group or some specific quality then usage of 'the' is essential. When the Article is placed before a Proper Noun it becomes a Common Noun.

The Shakespeare in the above-given sentence means a person possessing the qualities of Shakespeare hence 'the' is correct and it should come after as.

42. All these words are used as Adverbs i.e. they are defining the verb interested.

Very - used with the present participle

Much – is used with past participle

So- when there is a correlative

Never- this is not suitable as per the intended meaning of the sentence

Scarcely- Barely / hardly, this is not suitable as per the intended meaning of the sentence

43. Scourge- evil, misfortune, curse, torture, whip, thrash

Ex- Even the curable disease of polio continuous to be scourge in poor countries of Africa.

44. Amorphous – formless, shapeless, undefined or unorganized

Structured-construct or arrange according to a plan; give a pattern or organization to

Obviate – to prevent

Ex- Apart from the abstract paintings, the exhibition also featured some amorphous (shapeless) sculptures made of wood and metal.

45. Acrimonious – unfriendly, harsh, hostile, bitter

Tedium- Boredom, dullness

Magnanimous- generous, noble, upright

Archetype- Standard, classic, model

46. I.e. means 'in other words'. So, the before mentioned thing will be added upon in the subsequent part. Standardization means equality, homogeneity or in other words all things seen equally which is actually the confusion between the concepts of individual and of human beings. In context of the cloze passage human beings are treated as alike without having any individuality /uniqueness

47. The sentence is describing a consequence of an expected future situation so the word if is most appropriate.

48. This, that words are used to refer to identify two or more than two groups that are categorized. Here 'from' is suitable as the author considers it an error and wants to differentiate between two individuals.

Conjunction 'and' cannot be used here since this and that do not refers to same thing and between is also not suitable as this preposition is used to differentiate in comparison of two.

49. Wholesale means on a large scale/extensive/indiscriminate. It is suitable as it means that the children should not be educated without taking into consideration individual differences.

50. Have been is the correct answer because men (noun) is in plural form. Since this action started in the past and its effect continues at the time of speaking so have been + V 3 is appropriate.

Mathematics

Q.1 By selling 90 ball pens for ₹ 160 a person loses 20%. The number of ball pens, which should be sold for ₹ 96 so as to have a profit of 20% is

A. 36 **B.** 37 **C.** 46 **D.** 47

Q.2 4 smaller circles touch each other and larger circle as shown in the figure. Find the sum of perimeter of all the four small circles. Radius of smaller circles are r_1, r_2, r_3 r_4 and AB = 14 (dia. Of larger circle).

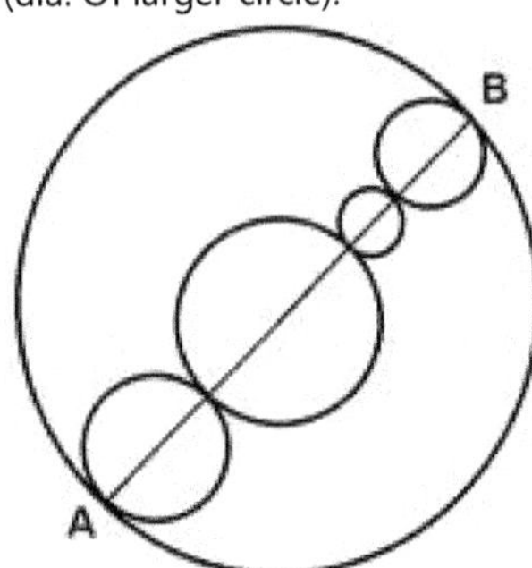

A. 28π
B. 7π
C. 14π
D. Cannot be determined

Q.3 The quotient when 10^{100} is divided by 5^{11} is :

A. 10^{25} **B.** 2^{75}
C. $2^{15} \times 10^{25}$ **D.** $2^{25} \times 10^{75}$

Q.4 Find the amount of Rs 4000 for two years compounded annually at the rate of 9% pa during first year and 10% during second year?

A. 4600 **B.** 4756 **C.** 4796 **D.** 4697

Q.5 In the following figure ABCDEF is a regular hexagon. M and N are two points on AB such that AM=MN=NB. Find the ratio of area of shaded region to unshaded region.

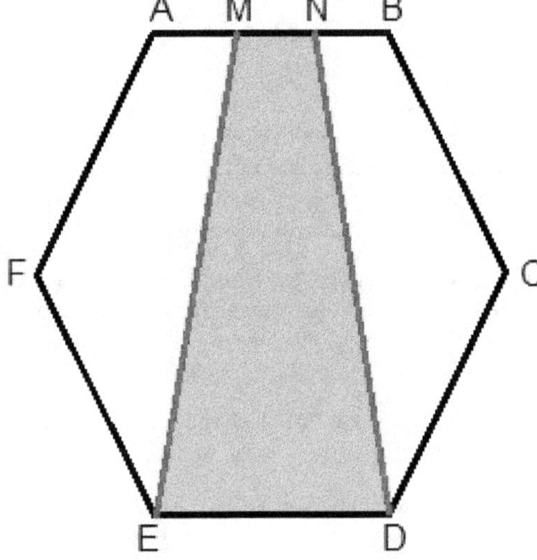

A. 4:5 **B.** 2:3 **C.** 5:4 **D.** 3:2

Q.6 In an exam there are 40 questions in each paper. Riya attempted 30 questions in geography paper and got 20% more marks than in history and 6.25% marks less than in English. The average marks in these three subjects is 130.5 .Then find that each question carries how much marks?

A. 4.5 **B.** 5 **C.** 2 **D.** 3.5

Q.7 A fruit seller buys some bananas at the rate of 25/dozen. He sells bananas such that the Selling price of first dozen is Rs.4, second dozen for Rs.8, third for Rs.12 and so on. if he wants to earn an overall profit of at least 20%. how many dozen of bananas he should sell?

A. 16 **B.** 24 **C.** 14 **D.** 12

Q.8 If $x = \dfrac{\sqrt{5}}{2}$ then, find the value of : $\dfrac{x-1}{x+1} + \dfrac{x+1}{x-1} + x$

A. $19 + \sqrt{5}/2$ **B.** $20 + \sqrt{5}/2$
C. $22 + \sqrt{5}/2$ **D.** $18 + \sqrt{5}/2$

Q.9 If x and y are both positive, then the minimum value of $(x + y)\left(\dfrac{1}{x} + \dfrac{1}{y}\right)$ is:

A. 0 **B.** 1 **C.** 2 **D.** 4

Q.10 The rate of simple interest per annum at which a sum of money double itself in 16⅔ yrs. is

A. 4% **B.** 5% **C.** 6% **D.** $6\frac{2}{3}\%$

Q.11 Samir is faster than Soumik and they individually travels 36 km. The summation of their speed is 21 km/hr. And the total time taken by both of them is 504 minutes. Find the speed of Samir.

A. 16 km/hr. **B.** 18 km/hr.
C. 15 km/hr. **D.** 13 km/hr.

Q.12 Let there be a regular octagon. Now ABCD and EFGH be two squares such that ABCD is the largest square that can fit inside that octagon and EFGH is the smallest square containing that octagon. What is the ratio of side of square ABCD to that of square EFGH.

A. 1:2   **B.** 1:3   **C.** 1:√2   **D.** 1:√3

Q.13 If $x^2 + y^2 + 2(y + 1) = 1$, then find the value of $x^{25} + y^{48}$

A. 0   **B.** 1   **C.** -1   **D.** 2

Q.14 The cost of diamond varies directly as the square of its weight, once this diamond broke into 4 pieces with weight in ratio 1:2:3:4, If the pieces were sold, the dealer would get Rs.70,000 less . Find the original price of the diamond

A. 2 lakh   **B.** 1.5 lakh   **C.** 1.3 lakh   **D.** 1 lakh

Q.15 Gary bought some balls for 2$ each and same number of balls for 3$ each and mixed all of them. After selling all the balls at 2.4$ per piece he suffered a loss of 10$. How many balls did he buy?

A. 20   **B.** 2   **C.** 50   **D.** 100

Science

Q.16 As per Bohr model, the minimum energy (in eV) required to remove an electron from the ground state of doubly ionized Li atom (Z = 3) is:

A. 122.4eV   **B.** -22.4eV   **C.** +122.4eV   **D.** -122.4eV

Q.17 The maximum kinetic energy of photoelectrons emitted from a surface when photons of energy 6 eV fall on it is 4 eV. The stopping potential in Volts is :

A. 8 volt.   **B.** 4 volt.   **C.** 3 volt.   **D.** 6 volt.

Q.18 Two radioactive materials X_1 and X_2 have decay constants 101 and 1 respectively. If initially they have the same number of nuclei, then the ratio of the number of nuclei of X_1 to that of X_2 will be 1/ e after a time of :

A. $1/10\ \lambda$ **B.** $9\ \lambda$ **C.** $10/9\ \lambda$ **D.** $1/9\ \lambda$

Q.19 What does rise of mercury in a barometer indicate?

A. fair weather   **B.** storm
C. rain   **D.** cold weather

Q.20 A solid cannot change its shape easily compared to liquid because of :-

A. stronger intermolecular force in solid
B. larger intermolecular separation in solid
C. bigger molecular size of solid
D. higher density of solid

Q.21 What is the freezing point of alcohol?

A. $-115°C$ **B.** $-95°C$ **C.** $-50°C$ **D.** $-145°C$

Q.22 Which acid is present in ant sting?

A. Lactic acid   **B.** Formic acid
C. Acetic acid   **D.** Tartaric acid

Q.23 In gas welding, which of the following gas is used to generate light?

A. Oxalic acid   **B.** Ethylene
C. Acetylene   **D.** Acetic acid

Q.24 What is the formula of benzopyrene?

A. $C_{20}H_{20}$ **B.** $C_{20}H_{12}$ **C.** $C_{20}H_{13}$ **D.** $C_{20}H_{14}$

Q.25 The gas which causes explosions in coal mines is:

A. Oxygen   **B.** Carbon dioxide
C. Carbon monoxide   **D.** Methane

Q.26 The temperature coefficient of resistance of a wire is 0.00125 per°C- At 300 K, its resistance is 1 ohm. This resistance of the wire will be 2 ohm at:

A. 1137 K   **B.** 2127 K   **C.** 1227 K   **D.** 1127 K

Q.27 A piece of copper and another of germanium are cooled from room temperature to 80 K. The resistance of :

A. each of them increases
B. each of them decreases
C. copper increases and germanium decreases
D. copper decreases and germanium increases.

Q.28 The electrical conductivity of a semiconductor increases when electromagnetic radiation of a wavelength shorter than 2480 nm is incident on it. The band gap (in eV) for the semiconductor is:

A. 0.9 eV   **B.** 0.1 eV   **C.** 0.7 eV   **D.** 0.5 eV

Q.29 The impurity atoms, with which pure silicon should be doped to make a p -type semiconductor, are those of :-

A. aluminum
B. boron
C. either boron or aluminum
D. none of the above

Q.30 .A triode has plate characteristics in the form of parallel lines in the region of our interest. At a grid voltage of -1 volt the anode current / (in milli ampere) is given in terms of plate voltage V(in volt) by the algebraic relation:

I = 0.125V-7.5 .

For grid voltage of -3 volt, the current at anode voltage of 300 volt is 5 milliampere. Determine the plate resistance (rp), transconductance (gm) and the amplification factor ( )for the triode.

A. 20   **B.** 200   **C.** 90   **D.** 100

General Awareness

Q.31 "Micro" and "Macro" words in economy was firstly used by –

A. Ragnar Frisch   **B.** I.Fischer
C. James Tobin   **D.** Garle

Q.32 Core Industries are-

A. Basic Industries
B. Consumer Goods Industries
C. Capital Goods Industries
D. Government Industries

Q.33 A person can be a member of the Council of Ministers without being a member of the Parliament for a maximum period of:-

A. one year
B. six months
C. three months
D. one month

Q.34 Which of the following is not a member of National Human Rights Commission?

A. Chairperson of National Commission for Scheduled Castes
B. Chairperson of National Commission for Scheduled Tribes
C. Chairperson of NITI Aayog
D. Chairperson of National Commission for women

Q.35 In which article of Indian Constitution the provision of Election Commission is mentioned?

A. Article 320
B. Article 322
C. Article 324
D. Article 326

Q.36 Which of the following is the most abundant metal on Earth's crust?

A. Magnesium
B. Iron
C. Copper
D. Aluminium

Q.37 Foehn is a local wind of

A. China
B. Japan
C. Korea
D. Switzerland

Q.38 The Kushans ruled in

A. 1st century AD
B. 2nd century BC
C. 3rd century AD
D. 5th century BC

Q.39 Consider the following events in the history of Indian freedom struggle

(1) Champaran Satyagraha

(2) Bardoli Satyagraha

(3) Ahmedabad Mill Workers Strike

(4) Chauri-Chaura Incident

Which one of the following is a correct chronological sequence of the above events starting from the earliest?

A. 1, 3, 2, 4   **B.** 1, 2, 4, 3   **C.** 1, 3, 4, 2   **D.** 3, 1, 2, 4

Q.40 Which of the following sectors are included in the priority sector lending?

A. Agriculture
B. Micro, Small and Medium Enterprises
C. Education
D. All the above

Basic English

Ques (41-45):Direction: Read the passage carefully and answer the questions that follow by choosing the best alternative:

What is the future which awaits our children? The underlying assumption of the question that Indian children have a common future is itself dubious. It can legitimately be asked whether a student who is well fed, attending a boarding school in the salubrious climate of the hills, and learning to use computers has any future in common with a malnourished child who goes to a school with no blackboards, if indeed he does go to school with no blackboards, if indeed he does go to school. The latter may have no worthwhile future at all. And it might be wroth while to analyze the significance of this marginalization of more than seventy five percent of the children of this country. The failure to provide an infrastructure for primary education in the villages of Indian more than 60 years after independence is in sharp contrast with the sophisticated institutions for technical institutes of higher education are funded by the government which essentially means that the money to support them comes from taxes. And since indirect taxation forms a substantial part of the taxes collected by the government, the financial burden is borne by all the people. L.K. Jha put it graphically when the observed that 25 paise of every rupee spent on educating an IIT student comes from the pockets of men and women whose children may never enter a proper classroom.

Q.41 The author is trying to highlight which of the following:

A. the greatness of L.K. Jha
B. need to have common future for Indian children
C. need of sophisticated education for rural poor
D. faulty system of direct taxes

Q.42 What seems to be likely answer of the author to the question posed by him in the first sentence of the passage?

(I) is no common future for the Indian children

(II) the future is worthwhile for majority of Indian children

(III)the majority may never enter a proper classroom

A. only I
B. only II
C. only III
D. both I and II

Q.43 Which of the following pairs have been termed as sharp contrast by the **author**?

(a) Infrastructure for technical education

(b) Lack of infrastructure for rural primary schools

(C) Twenty-five paisa of every rupee earned by the government is spent on education

(D) the financial burden of higher technical education is borne by all people

A. I and IV
B. II and III
C. III and IV
D. I and II

Q.44 According to the author, who among the following does not have a hopeful and a prosperous future

(A)All students from technical institutes

(B)All students financially supported by the government

A. only I
B. only II
C. both I and II
D. neither I nor II

Q.45 Which of the following statements is not true

(I)The author welcomes Govt's initiative on primary education

(II)75% of the children have a bright future

(III)25% cost of educating a technocrat comes from poor people

A. only I
B. only II
C. only III
D. only I and II

Q.46 Lytton Strachey's Eminent Victorians carries biographical sketches of writers and public figures. Identify the list below that correctly mentions those Eminent Victorians.

A. Cardinal Manning, Florence Nightingale, Thomas Arnold and General Gordon.

B. A.E.W. Mason, Sir Arthur Quiller Couch, Matthew Arnold, Robert Bridges.

C. E.F. Benson, Cardinal Manning, Lord Tennyson, Beatrice Webb.

D. George Harding, General Gordon, Robert Browning, Mrs. Humphrey Ward.

Q.47 One of the following statements about the eponymous saint of Dryden's "Song for St. Cecilia's Day" is incorrect. Identify that statement.

A. St. Cecilia was a Roman lady, an early Christian martyr.

B. St. Cecilia was an Armenian devotee of the Christian faith.

C. St. Cecilia's festival is celebrated on 22 November in England.

D. St. Cecilia was a patroness of music who was fabled to have invented the organ.

Q.48 Which of the statements on Michael Roberts's Faber Book of Modern Verse (1936) is not true?

A. His anthology canonized modern poetry and poets for quite some decades.

B. The collection begins with the poems of Robert Bridges.

C. Roberts omitted the Georgian poets in his anthology.

D. Yeats, Eliot and Pound find a place in the Faber Book of 1936.

Q.49 What does the phrase ut pictura poesis from Horace's Art of Poetry mean?

A. "as in painting, so in poetry".

B. "poetry beggars pictorial description".

C. "as in poetry, so in painting".

D. "picture above all poetry".

Q.50 Which of the following was not a dialect of Old English?

A. Irish

B. Northumbrian

C. Mercian

D. Mercian

// Smart Answer Sheet //

Correct Indicates percentage of students who answered questions correctly.

Skipped Indicates percentage of students who skipped questions.

Q.	Ans.	Correct / Skipped
1	A	78.61 % / 16.4 %
2	C	82.32 % / 12.8 %
3	C	83.01 % / 12.75 %
4	C	87.07 % / 10.69 %
5	A	81.58 % / 18.1 %
6	A	87.03 % / 10.38 %
7	C	80.44 % / 14.75 %
8	D	89.0 % / 10.02 %
9	D	86.98 % / 13.01 %
10	C	86.3 % / 10.01 %

Q.	Ans.	Correct / Skipped
11	C	87.62 % / 12.14 %
12	C	84.94 % / 10.41 %
13	B	81.25 % / 18.61 %
14	D	87.97 % / 11.01 %
15	D	87.56 % / 10.64 %
16	D	77.11 % / 17.62 %
17	B	78.4 % / 13.87 %
18	A	81.03 % / 17.95 %
19	A	76.75 % / 12.7 %
20	A	86.39 % / 11.02 %

Q.	Ans.	Correct / Skipped
21	A	80.1 % / 10.06 %
22	B	76.99 % / 21.6 %
23	C	83.46 % / 13.7 %
24	B	79.02 % / 12.17 %
25	D	81.73 % / 10.66 %
26	D	84.72 % / 11.65 %
27	D	82.03 % / 13.88 %
28	D	78.72 % / 18.78 %
29	C	81.68 % / 13.52 %
30	D	83.89 % / 12.82 %

Q.	Ans.	Correct / Skipped
31	A	88.56 % / 11.04 %
32	A	82.33 % / 12.67 %
33	B	77.75 % / 18.57 %
34	C	88.57 % / 10.4 %
35	C	76.36 % / 17.73 %
36	D	89.77 % / 10.08 %
37	D	84.2 % / 15.46 %
38	A	89.63 % / 10.34 %
39	C	79.25 % / 15.68 %
40	D	84.66 % / 12.23 %

Q.	Ans.	Correct / Skipped
41	B	84.44 % / 13.42 %
42	A	77.79 % / 21.0 %
43	D	88.81 % / 10.28 %
44	D	77.56 % / 10.99 %
45	B	84.6 % / 10.3 %
46	A	79.55 % / 10.82 %
47	B	78.71 % / 11.24 %
48	B	85.63 % / 10.68 %
49	A	76.45 % / 14.83 %
50	A	83.53 % / 16.12 %

Performance Analysis	
Avg. Score (%)	73.33%
Toppers Score (%)	74.67%
Your Score	

//Hints and Solutions//

1. Short Trick:

According to question SP of 90 pen = 160

Loss = 20%

Hence CP = (160/80)*100 = 200

To get a profit of 20%, new SP = 200*(120/100) = 240

So number of pen sold in rs 240 = 90

number of pen sold in rs 96 = (90/240)*96 = 36

2. Perimeter of all smaller circles $= 2\pi r_1 + 2\pi r_2 + 2\pi r_3 + 2\pi r_4$
$$= 2\pi(r_1 + r_2 + r_3 + r_4)$$
$$= 2\pi \cdot \frac{AB}{2}$$
$$= 2\pi \cdot \frac{14}{2}$$
$$= 14\pi$$

3. Required quotient $=$
$$\frac{10^{100}}{5^{11}} = \frac{(5\times2)^{250}}{5^{11}} = \frac{5^{100}\times2^{100}}{5^{11}}$$
$$= \frac{5^3\times5^{25}\times2^{100}}{5^7}$$
$$= 5^{25} \times 2^{100}$$
$$= 5^{25} \times 2^{25} \times 2^{15}$$
$$= 10^{25} \times 2^{15}$$

4. A= P(1+r1/100)(1+r2/100)

A= 4000(1+9/100)(1+10/100)

A= 4796

5.

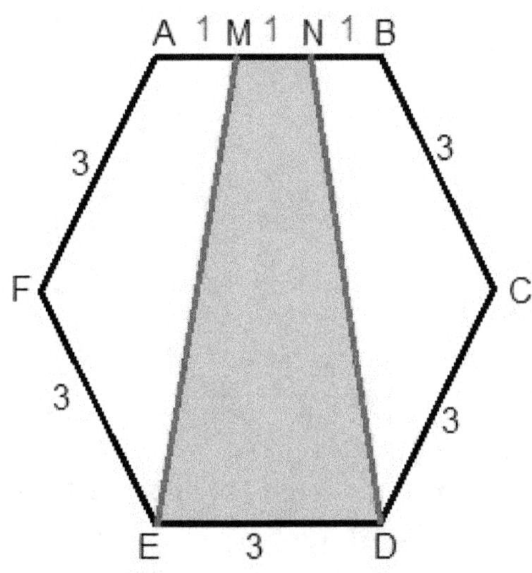

Let the side of regular hexagon = 3 units

Area of complete hexagon = (3√3/2)*32

= 27√3/2

Area of shaded region (trapezium) = h*(3+1)/2 = 2h

where h = height of the hexagon = √3*3 = 3√3

Area of shaded region (trapezium) = 2*3√3 = 6√3

Area of unshaded region = 27√3/2 - 6√3 = 15√3/2

Required Ratio = 6√3 : 15√3/2 = 12:15 = 4:5

6. Let one question be of 'm' marks.

Questions attempted in geography = 30

∴Marks in geography G = 30m

Let, Marks in History = H

Marks in English = E

Acc. To the ques.,

⇒ 30m = H*(1+20/100)

⇒ H = 25m

And,

⇒ 30m = E*(1 − 6.25/100)

⇒ E = 32m

Now, given that, average marks in three subjects = 130.5

⇒(G+H+E)/3 = 130.5

⇒(30m + 25m + 32m)/3 =130.5

⇒ m = 4.5

Therefore, one question carries 4.5 marks.

7. Let us assume he buys n dozen bananas.

∴C.P of bananas = 25n

A.T.Q

Total S.P should be equal to or more than 120% C.P.

∴ S.P of bananas =4+8+12+16........n terms

4+8+12+16........n terms ≥ 25n

$$\times \frac{120}{100}$$

4(1+2+3+4........n terms) ≥ 30n

The sum of first n terms = $\dfrac{n(n+1)}{2}$

$\therefore 4\times \dfrac{n(n+1)}{2}$

≥ 30n

∴ 2n² + 2n ≥ 30n

∴n² + n ≥ 15n

∴ n²-14n ≥ 0

$\therefore n(n-14) \geq 0$

$\therefore n \geq 14$

$\therefore$ He will sell 14 dozen bananas

8. $\dfrac{x-1}{x+1} + \dfrac{x+1}{x-1} = \dfrac{2x^2+2}{(x-1)(x+1)}$

$= \dfrac{2 \times \frac{5}{4} + 2}{\left(\frac{\sqrt{5}}{2} - 1\right)\left(\frac{\sqrt{5}}{2} + 1\right)}$

$= \dfrac{10+8}{(\sqrt{5}-2)(\sqrt{5}+2)}$

$= 18/(5-4) = 18$

Given expression:

$\dfrac{x-1}{x+1} + \dfrac{x+1}{x-1} + x = 18 + \sqrt{5}/2$

9. x>0 and y>0 (given that both are positive)

$\dfrac{(x+y)}{\frac{x}{y}}\left(\dfrac{1}{x} + \dfrac{1}{y}\right) = 2 + \dfrac{x}{y} + \dfrac{y}{x} = 2 + \left(k + \dfrac{1}{k}\right) where\ k =$

Since the minimum value of the expression (k+ $\dfrac{1}{k}$) is 2

Therefore minimum value of the given expression is 4

10. We know that, SI = prt/100

Here, SI = p

$\therefore$ r = 100/t

$\dfrac{100}{\frac{50}{3}}$

=6%

11. Samir and Soumik individually travels 36 km.

Let the speed of Samir be x km/hr.

The summation of their speed is 21 km/hr.

So, the speed of Soumik = (21 − x) km/hr.

And the total time taken by both of them is 504 minutes.

So, we can write now,

$\dfrac{36}{x} + \dfrac{36}{21-x} = \dfrac{504}{60}$

$\Rightarrow 36(21 - x) + 36x = x(21 - x) \times (42/5)$

$\Rightarrow 756 \times 5 = 42x(21 - x)$

$\Rightarrow 21x - x2 = 90$

$\Rightarrow x2 - 21x + 90 = 0$

$\Rightarrow x2 - 15x - 6x + 90 = 0$

$\Rightarrow x(x - 15) - 6(x - 15) = 0$

$\Rightarrow (x - 15)(x - 6) = 0$

Then, x = + 15 or x = + 6

As, the speed of Samir is greater than Soumik, so, we will take x = 15

$\therefore$ The speed of Samir = 15 km/hr.

12.

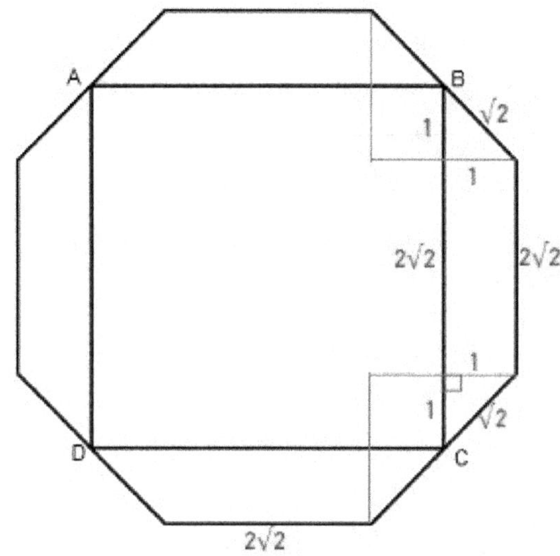

Let the side of regular octagon = 2√2 units

And every internal angle of regular octagon = 135 = 90+45

From figure each side of square ABCD = 1+ 2√2 + 1 = 2 (1+√2)

Now, consider square EFGH

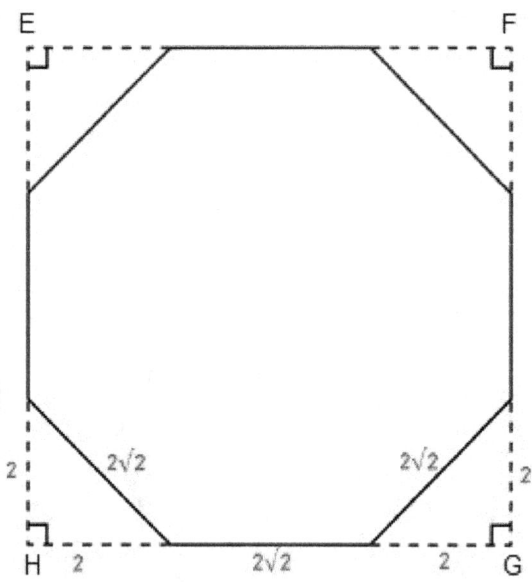

each side of square EFGH = 2 + 2√2 + 2 = 4+2√2 = 2√2(√2+1)

Required Ratio = 2 (1+√2) : 2√2(√2+1)

= 1:√2

13. $x^2 + y^2 + 2(y + 1) = 1$

$\Rightarrow x^2 + y^2 + 2y + 2 = 1$

$\Rightarrow x^2 + y^2 + 2y + 2 - 1 = 0$

$\Rightarrow x^2 + (y + 1)^2 = 0$

As, the sum of two square terms are equal to zero then the individual term will equal to zero.

So, x = 0

And, (y + 1) = 0

$\Rightarrow$ y = - 1

Hence,

$x^{25} + y^{48}$

$= (0)^{25} + (- 1)^{48}$

$= 0 + 1$

$= 1$

14. Given that,

Price $\propto$ Weight^2

$\Rightarrow$ p $\propto$ (w^2)

Let the weight of the diamond = 10x

$\Rightarrow$ p = k (10x)^2

$\Rightarrow$ p = k (100x^2) ------ (i)

Since the diamond has been broken into 4 pieces

10x will get divided into the ratio of 1:2:3:4

P1 = k(x^2), p2 = k (4x^2), P3 = k (9x^2), P4 = k (16x^2)

P1 + p2 + p3 + p4 = k (30x^2)

According to the question,

$\Rightarrow$ k (100x^2) - k (30x^2) = 70000

$\Rightarrow$ k70x^2 = 70000

$\Rightarrow$ kx^2 = 1000

From eq (i)

$\therefore$ Price = 1000 × 100 = Rs.1, 00,000

15. Let the total number of 2\$ balls be A then total number of 3\$ balls also equals A

Cost price of these 2A balls = 2A + 3A = 5A

Selling Price of these 2A balls = 2.4(2A)

CP = SP + loss

5A = 4.8A + 10

0.2A = 10

A = 50

Total number of balls = 2A = 100

16. Ans.

(d) For hydrogen atom and hydrogen like atoms $E_n =$

$-\dfrac{13.6z^2}{n^2} eV$

Therefore, ground state energy of doubly ionized lithium atom

$(Z = 3, n = 1)$ will be $\therefore E_1 = \dfrac{-13.6 \times (3)^2}{(1)^2} =$

-13.6×9 or $E_1 = -122.4 eV$

17. Ans.(b) Stopping potential is the negative potential which stops the emission of (K.E.)max electrons when applied.

Stopping potential = 4 volt.

18.

$$(d) \text{ Given}: \frac{N_1}{N_2} = \frac{1}{e} \because N = N_0 e^{-\lambda t}$$

$$\therefore \frac{N_0 e^{-10\lambda t}}{N_0 e^{-\lambda t}} = \frac{1}{e} \text{ or } \frac{1}{e^{9\lambda t}} = \frac{1}{e} \text{ or } 9\lambda t = 1 \text{ or } t = \frac{1}{9\lambda}$$

19. Rise of mercury indicates increase in atmospheric pressure. As air descends, it warms and contracts, which reduces or prevents the formation of clouds. Because of this effect, areas of high pressure often create clear, dry weather.

20. stronger intermolecular force in solid Explanation: In solids, the particles are arranged in a regular pattern, touching each other. They attract each other with a strong force (because they are so small and so close). This means that they cannot change places. So solids cannot change its shape.

21. Freezing point of alcohol is $-115°C$ while freezing point of mercury is $-39°C$ Hence, to measure below $-39°C$ alcohol thermometer is used.

22. In nature, formic acid is found in most ants and in stingless bees of the genus Oxytrigona. The wood ants from the genus Formica can spray formic acid on their prey or to defend the nest.

23. Acetylene is used to generate light, to weld metals. Oxygen and Acetylene are the gases used to produce the welding flame. The flame will only melt the metal. A flux is used during welting to prevent oxidations and to remove impurities. Metals 2mm to 50mm thick are welded by gas welding.

24. A benzopyrene is an organic compound with the formula C$_{20}$H$_{12}$. Structurally speaking, the colorless isomers of benzopyrene are pentacyclic hydrocarbons and are fusion products of pyrene and a phenylene group. Two isomeric species of benzopyrene are benzo[a]pyrene and the less common benzo[e]pyrene.

25. There are two main types of coalmine explosions: methane and coal dust. Methane explosions occur when a buildup of methane gas contacts a heat source and there is not enough air to dilute the gas level below its explosion point.

26. Ans.

(d) $R_0 =$ Resistance at 0^0C $1\Omega = R_0(1 + 27\alpha)$ and $2\Omega = R_0(1 + t\alpha)$

$\dfrac{2}{1} = \dfrac{1 + t\alpha}{1 + 27\alpha}$ or $t = 854^0C = 1127K$

27. Copper is a metal. Its resistance decreases when temperature falls. Germanium is a semiconductor. Its resistance increases when temperature falls.

28.

$$\text{Energy (in } eV) = \frac{12375}{\lambda (\text{in } A)}$$

$$\therefore \Delta E = \frac{12375}{24800} eV (\because 2480nm = 24800A)$$

$$\Delta E = 0.5eV \quad \therefore \text{ Band gap } = 0.5eV$$

29. p-type semiconductor is obtained when Si or Ge (tetravalent) is doped with group III trivalent impurities like aluminium, boron etc.

30. At $V_g = -1$ volt, $I_p = \left(0.125V_p - 7.5\right) \times 10^{-3}A$

$$\therefore \frac{dI_p}{dV_p} = 0.125 \times 10^{-3} \frac{A}{V}$$

or $r_p = \dfrac{dV_p}{dI_p} = \dfrac{1}{0.125 \times 10^{-3}} \dfrac{V}{A}$

or $r_p = 8 \times 10^3 \Omega \ldots\ldots\ldots\ldots. (i)$

Again, $I_p = \left(0.125V_p - 7.5\right)mA$

$I_p = \left(0.125 \times 300 - 7.5\right)$ at $V_p = 300V$

$V_g = -1$ volt

or $I_p = (37.5 - 7.5)mA$ or $I_p = 30mA$

In second case

$V_8 = -3$ volt , $V = 300$ volt , $I = 5mA$

$$\therefore g_m = \frac{\Delta I_p}{\Delta V_g} \text{ at } V_p \text{ constant}$$

$$g_m = \frac{(30-5)\times 10^{-3}}{[-1-(-3)]}$$

or $g_m = \dfrac{25 \times 10^{-3}}{2} = 12.5 \times 10^{-3}A/V$ ...(ii)

$\mu = r_p \times g_m = 8 \times 10^3 \times 12.5 \times 10^{-3} = 100$

31. Ragnar Frisch, Norwegian Economist, coined the terms 'micro' and 'macro' economics for the first time in 1933. He was the first Economics Nobel prize winner in 1969.

32. Core industries can be defined as main or key industries of the economy. In most countries, these particular industries are backbone of all other industries. In India, there are eight core sectors comprising of coal, crude oil, natural gas, petroleum refinery products, fertilizers, steel, cement and electricity

33. A Non-Member of a parliament can be a member of Council of Minister for a maximum period of 6 months.

34. Chairperson of NITI Aayog is not a member of National Human Right Commission.

35. Under Article 324 of the Constitution of India, the Election Commission of India, interalia, is vested with the power of superintendence, direction and control of conducting the elections.

36. Aluminum is the most abundant metal in the earth's crust, it is never found free in nature. All of the earth's aluminum has combined with other elements to form compounds.

37. Foehn is a local wind of Switzerland. A foehn is a type of dry, warm, down-slope wind that occurs in the lee (downwind side) of a mountain range. It is a rain shadow wind that results from the subsequent adiabatic warming of air that has dropped most of its moisture on windward slopes.

38. The Kushan Empire was a syncretic empire, formed by Yuezhi, in the Bactrian territories in the early 1st century AD. It spread to encompass much of Afghanistan, present-day Pakistan, and then the northern parts of India at least as far as Saketa and Sarnath near Varanasi, where inscriptions have been found dating to the era of the Kanishka the Great.

39. Champaran Satyagraha –1917, Ahmedabad Mill Workers Strike -1918, Chauri-Chaura Incident-1922, Bardoli Satyagraha – 1928.

40. Priority Sector includes the following categories:

(i) Agriculture

(ii) Micro, Small and Medium Enterprises

(iii) Export Credit

(iv) Education

(v) Housing

(vi) Social Infrastructure

41. The author is trying to highlight the need to have common future for the Indian children.

42. There is no common future for the Indian children.

43. There is a Sharp contrast between the failure to an infrastructure for primary education and Infrastructure for technical education.

44. Children who may never enter a classroom. They do not have a hopeful and prosperous future Therefore the option should be (4).

45. 75% children of this country have a bright future is the incorrect statement according to the passage.

46. Lytton Strachey's (1880-1932) 'Eminent Victorians' (first published in 1918) is a collection of biographies of four leading figures from the Victorian era. The figures include Cardinal Manning, Florence Nightingale, Thomas Arnold, and General Gordon. The work was critically acclaimed and was a financial success.

47. Option 2 is incorrect with reference to Dryden's song for St. Cecilia's Day.

"A Song for St. Cecilia's Day" (1687), is the first of two great odes written by poet laureate John Dryden. It was sung with music for the annual St. Cecilia's Day celebration, which was held every year from 1683 to 1703 on November 22. The celebration was sponsored by the London Musical Society.

St. Cecilia was a Roman and an early Christian martyr and patron saint of music. Cecilia is usually represented playing the organ, which serves as an allusion to her legend of having invented the instrument. According to the poem, "When to her organ, vocal breath was giv'n,/ An angel heard, and straight appear'd/ Mistaking earth for Heav'n".

48. Michael Roberts' (1902-48) Faber Book of Modern Verse was first published in 1936 and is considered as the most important and influential anthologies of the twentieth century. It canonized modern poetry and poets for quite some further decades. The book saw the publication of three more editions by Anne Ridler, Donald Hall and Peter Porter.

The collection included Roberts' awareness of the poetry scene, and his sense of the modern movement within it. He opted for poets who would "influence the future development of poetry and language". However, he excluded the Georgian poets like Edmund Blunden and Walter de la Mare because as they "seem to me to have written good poems without having been compelled to make any notable development of poetic technique".

The collection begins with the poems of Gerard Manley Hopkins. Some of the other poets who find a place in the 1936 edition are W. B. Yeats, T. E. Hulme, Ezra Pound, T. S. Eliot and Harold Monro.

49. The given phrase is in Latin and appears in Horace's 'Ars Poetica', an epistle presented as an informal letter to members of the Piso family. Quintus Horatius Flaccus or Horace (65 BC – 8 BC), was the leading Roman lyric poet during the time of Augustus (The age of Romans).

The given phrase means "as in painting, so in poetry" (poetry resembles painting). Horace explains, ""As is painting, so is poetry: some pieces will strike you more if you stand near, and some, if you are at a greater distance: one loves the dark; another, which is not afraid of the critic's subtle judgment, chooses to be seen in the light; the one has pleased once the other will give pleasure if ten times repeated . . . . "

50. There are four dialects of old English: Mercian, Northumbrian, Kentish, and West Saxon. Thus, "Irish" is the odd one out. Irish (Gaeilge) is a Goidelic (Gaelic) language that originated in Ireland and has been historically spoken by the Irish people.

Mathematics

Q.1 If A and B are complementary angles, then what is the value of $\sqrt{(\cos A \cosec B - \cos A \sin B)}$

A. tan A   **B.** cot A   **C.** cos A   **D.** sin A

Q.2 $2^x = 4^y = 8^z$ and $xyz = 288,$ then value of $\dfrac{1}{2x} + \dfrac{1}{4y} + \dfrac{1}{8z}$ is:

A. 11/12   **B.** 11/96   **C.** 29/96   **D.** 17/96

Q.3 $x^4 - ax^3 + bx^2 - cx + 8 = 0$ divided by $x - 1$ leaves a remainder of $4,$ divided by $x + 1$ leaves remainder $3,$ find b.

A. 2.1   **B.** 2.2   **C.** +5.5   **D.** -5.5

Q.4 A fruit-seller bought some mangoes at some price. He sold 3/5th of them in the morning at 25% profit. Due to festival on next day, he increased the prices in the evening and sold them at 40% profit. But, due to increased prices, his sales reduced and 25% of those remaining mangoes got wasted. Find his overall profit or loss percent.

A. 20% profit   **B.** 17% profit
C. No profit no loss   **D.** 24% loss

Q.5 Let ABCDEFGH be a cube of side a√2 unit. O be the centre of the face ABCD . Then find the distance of point O from any corner of opposite face EFGH.

A. √3a   **B.** 3a   **C.** 2√3a   **D.** √3a/2

Q.6 The system of equations 1.4x + 1.9y = 24.3 and 1.6x +2.4y – 31.6 = 0 has how many solutions?

A. Exactly two solutions
B. Infinite number of solutions
C. No solution
D. None of the above

Q.7 The population of a village is 25,000. One fifth are females and the rest are males. 5% of males and 40% of females are uneducated. What percentages on the whole are educated?

A. 75%   **B.** 88%   **C.** 55%   **D.** 85%

Q.8 In how many ways 11 identical toys be placed in 3 distinct boxes such that no box is empty?

A. 48   **B.** 45   **C.** 35   **D.** 55

Q.9 a, b, c are three distinct integers from 2 to 10 (both inclusive). Exactly one of ab, bc and ca is odd. abc is a multiple of 4. The arithmetic mean of a and b is an integer and so is the arithmetic mean of a, b and c. How many such triplets are possible (unordered triplets)?

A. 12   **B.** 5   **C.** 0   **D.** 4

Q.10 A batsman, in his 12th innings, makes a score of 63 runs and thereby increases his average score by 2. The average of his score after 12th innings will be how much?

A. 41   **B.** 42   **C.** 34   **D.** 35

Q.11 In how many years will Rs 1900 fetch interest of Rs 378 at 10%pa compounded annually?

A. 1.08   **B.** 2.08   **C.** 2   **D.** 5

Q.12 N is the foot of the perpendicular from a point P of a circle with radius 7 cm, on a diameter AB of the circle. If the length of the chord PB is 12 cm, the distance of the point N from the point B is

A. $6\frac{5}{7}cm$ **B.** $12\frac{2}{7}cm$ **C.** $3\frac{5}{7}cm$ **D.** $10\frac{2}{7}cm$

Q.13 If $x + \dfrac{1}{9x} = \dfrac{8}{3},$ then f ind $, 27x^3 + \dfrac{1}{27x^3}$

A. 222   **B.** 488   **C.** 484   **D.** 244

Q.14 Ram sold a book at the profit of 30%. If he sold it for 360 more then he would have made the profit of 60%. Find the selling price of the book.

A. 1460   **B.** 1680   **C.** 1500   **D.** 1560

Q.15 A seven-digit number comprises of only 2's and 3's. How many of these are multiples of 12?

A. 12   **B.** 10   **C.** 11   **D.** 9

Science

Q.16 Among the following, which metal has the highest resistivity?

A. Gold   **B.** Silver   **C.** Brass   **D.** Iron

Q.17 Two masses of 1 g and 4g are moving with equal kinetic energy. The ratio of the magnitudes of their momenta is :-

A. 2:1   **B.** 3:2   **C.** 1:2   **D.** 2:2

Q.18 Fleming's right hand rule is used to find the direction of the?

A. Alternating current   **B.** Direct current
C. Induced current   **D.** Actual current

Q.19 What is the speed of light in Glass?(in m/s)

A. 2.25 x 10⁸   **B.** 3 x 10⁸
C. 2 x 10⁸   **D.** 1.96 x 10⁸

Q.20 The speed of the block at point C, immediately before it leaves the second incline is:

A. $\sqrt{55}\,ms$ **B.** $\sqrt{120}\,ms$
C. $\sqrt{105}ms$ **D.** none of the above

Q.21 A ship of mass 3 x 10⁷ kg initially at rest is pulled by a force of 5 x 10⁴ N through a distance of 3m. Assuming that the resistance due to water is negligible, the speed of the ship is:-

A. 2 m/s   **B.** 0.2 m/s   **C.** 0.1 m/s   **D.** 1 m/s

Q.22 Which among the following gaseous non-metals present in air, reduces the rate of combustion making the air safe?

A. Oxygen
B. Carbon-di-oxide
C. Nitrogen
D. Argon

Q.23 Brass gets discoloured in air because of the presence of which of the following gases in air?

A. Oxygen
B. Nitrogen
C. Carbon dioxide
D. Hydrogen Sulphide

Q.24 Which gas is commonly known as laughing gas?

A. Nitric oxide
B. Nitrous oxide
C. Dry Carbon-di-oxide
D. Ammonic acid

Q.25 What is the chemical formula of potash alum?

A. $KAl(SO_4)_2 \cdot 12H_3O.$
B. $KAl(SO_4)_2 \cdot 12H_2O.$
C. $KAl(SO_5)_2 \cdot 12H_2O.$
D. None of these

Q.26 The biggest single-celled organism is -

A. Yeast
B. Acetabularia
C. Acetobacter
D. Caulerpa taxifolia

Q.27 Estrogen and Progesterone control and stimulate the growth in-

A. Pituary glands
B. Thyroid glands
C. Mammary glands
D. Super Renal glands

Q.28 Name the source from which Aspirin is produced?

A. Willow bark
B. Oak Tree
C. Acacia
D. Eucalyptus

Q.29 A banana plant fits into which of these groups?

A. trees
B. herbs
C. shrubs
D. flower

Q.30 Animal protein is called first class protein because it is-

A. delicious in taste
B. cheaper in the market
C. rich in essential amino acids
D. easily digestible

General Awareness

Q.31 S.I unit of lumnious intensity is

A. Lumen
B. lux
C. Candela
D. Watt

Q.32 Caliper is used to measure __________

A. Distance
B. Heat
C. Acceleration
D. Pressure

Q.33 Which of the following rays is used in oven ?

A. X-rays
B. UV rays
C. Microwave
D. Radiowave

Q.34 Which of the following plant hormone is mainly responsible for fruit ripening?

A. Cytokinin
B. Ethylene
C. Abscissic acid
D. None of these

Q.35 Which of the following organelles is called 'atom bombs'?

A. Microtubules
B. Nucleolus
C. Golgi bodies
D. Lysosome

Q.36 Which one of the following acids is used in battery?

A. Hydrochloric acid
B. Hydrofluoric acid
C. Sulphuric acid
D. Sulphurous acid

Q.37 Aspirin is common name of

A. salicylic acid
B. salicylate
C. methyl salicylate
D. acetyl salicylic acid

Q.38 Red color of tomato is due to the presence of

A. Lycopene
B. Chromoplast
C. Carotine
D. Betanine

Q.39 Minorites Right Day is observed in India on

A. 1st December
B. 23rd December
C. 18th December
D. 5th September

Q.40 How many number of the Biogeographic zones are present in India?

A. 4
B. 8
C. 10
D. 15

Basic English

Q.41 Fill in the blanks:-

I shall speak to him if he ____ here.

A. come
B. comes
C. will come
D. has come

Q.42 Complete the following sentences by filling articles:

Light travels faster than ____ sound.

A. the
B. a
C. an
D. none of the above

Q.43 What does the phrase ut pictura poesis from Horace's Art of Poetry mean?

A. "as in painting, so in poetry".
B. "poetry beggars pictorial description".
C. "as in poetry, so in painting".
D. "picture above all poetry".

Q.44 In how many parts did Cervantes publish his novel, Don Quixote?

A. three
B. five
C. two
D. twelve

Ques (45-49):Direction: Read the passage carefully and answer the questions that follow by choosing the best alternative:

What is the future which awaits our children? The underlying assumption of the question that Indian children have a common future is itself dubious. It can legitimately be asked whether a student who is well fed, attending a boarding school in the salubrious climate of the hills, and learning to use computers has any future in common with a malnourished child who goes to a school with no blackboards, if indeed he does go to a school with no blackboards, if indeed he does go to school. The latter may have no worthwhile future at all. And it might be wroth while to analyze the significance of this marginalization of more than seventy five percent of the

children of this country. The failure to provide an infrastructure for primary education in the villages of Indian more than 60 years after independence is in sharp contrast with the sophisticated institutions for technical institutes of higher education are funded by the government which essentially means that the money to support them comes from taxes. And since indirect taxation forms a substantial part of the taxes collected by the government, the financial burden is borne by all the people. L.K. Jha put it graphically when the observed that 25 paise of every rupee spent on educating an IIT student comes from the pockets of men and women whose children may never enter a proper classroom.

Q.45 The author is trying to highlight which of the following:
A. the greatness of L.K. Jha
B. need to have common future for Indian children
C. need of sophisticated education for rural poor
D. faulty system of direct taxes

Q.46 What seems to be likely answer of the author to the question posed by him in the first sentence of the passage?

(I) is no common future for the Indian children

(II) the future is worthwhile for majority of Indian children

(III) the majority may never enter a proper classroom

A. only I   B. only II
C. only III   D. both I and II

Q.47 Which of the following pairs have been termed as sharp contrast by the author?

(a) Infrastructure for technical education

(b) Lack of infrastructure for rural primary schools

(C) Twenty-five paisa of every rupee earned by the government is spent on education

(D) the financial burden of higher technical education is borne by all people

A. I and IV   B. II and III
C. III and IV   D. I and II

Q.48 According to the author, who among the following does not have a hopeful and a prosperous future

(A) All students from technical institutes

(B) All students financially supported by the government

A. only I   B. only II
C. both I and II   D. neither I nor II

Q.49 Which of the following statements is not true

(I) The author welcomes Govt's initiative on primary education

(II) 75% of the children have a bright future

(III) 25% cost of educating a technocrat comes from poor people

A. only I   B. only II
C. Only III   D. only I and II

Q.50 In the following questions , a sentence has been given in Direct/Indirect . Out of the four alternatives suggested, select the one which best expresses the same sentence in Indirect/ Direct .

The shopkeeper said, "Alas! There has been no sale today."

A. The shopkeeper exclaimed with sorrow that there had been no sale today.
B. The shopkeeper exclaimed that there was no sale that day.
C. The shopkeeper exclaimed with sorrow that there had been no sale that day.
D. The shopkeeper exclaimed that there had been no sale today.

// Smart Answer Sheet //

Correct   Indicates percentage of students who answered questions correctly.

Skipped   Indicates percentage of students who skipped questions.

Q.	Ans.	Correct / Skipped
1	D	89.86 % / 10.13 %
2	B	86.01 % / 13.03 %
3	D	85.77 % / 13.21 %
4	B	87.33 % / 11.86 %
5	A	76.99 % / 17.32 %
6	D	87.65 % / 11.24 %
7	B	82.63 % / 13.36 %
8	B	81.36 % / 13.18 %
9	D	84.17 % / 11.58 %
10	A	89.81 % / 10.03 %
11	A	77.15 % / 20.11 %
12	D	80.3 % / 11.1 %
13	B	81.74 % / 11.47 %
14	D	89.89 % / 10.06 %
15	C	88.87 % / 10.25 %
16	D	80.16 % / 19.25 %
17	C	80.6 % / 14.42 %
18	C	83.13 % / 13.93 %
19	C	76.72 % / 15.64 %
20	C	80.68 % / 16.24 %
21	C	84.11 % / 12.94 %
22	C	77.19 % / 19.05 %
23	D	76.78 % / 18.25 %
24	B	87.23 % / 12.04 %
25	B	89.12 % / 10.79 %
26	D	81.07 % / 14.76 %
27	C	78.52 % / 13.87 %
28	A	88.17 % / 10.83 %
29	B	82.8 % / 15.12 %
30	C	81.55 % / 17.28 %
31	C	83.49 % / 13.36 %
32	A	81.87 % / 13.31 %
33	C	86.28 % / 12.34 %
34	B	86.11 % / 11.33 %
35	D	85.95 % / 12.63 %
36	C	88.2 % / 11.47 %
37	D	81.58 % / 11.91 %
38	A	87.13 % / 11.47 %
39	C	83.08 % / 10.13 %
40	C	87.81 % / 11.54 %
41	B	86.77 % / 10.76 %
42	A	76.37 % / 22.17 %
43	A	79.92 % / 10.27 %
44	C	87.65 % / 11.51 %
45	B	80.45 % / 14.86 %
46	A	81.96 % / 12.4 %
47	D	83.01 % / 16.9 %
48	D	88.81 % / 10.94 %
49	B	89.3 % / 10.19 %
50	C	77.99 % / 11.63 %

Performance Analysis

Avg. Score (%)	46.67%
Toppers Score (%)	74.0%
Your Score	

//Hints and Solutions//

1. A and B are complementary angles which means
$(A + B) = 90$
Hence
$A = 90° - B$
Given expression:
$$\sqrt{(\cos A \operatorname{cosec} B - \cos A \sin B)} = \sqrt{\frac{\cos A}{\sin B} - \cos A \sin B}$$
$$= \sqrt{\frac{\cos A}{\cos(90° - B)} - \cos A \cos(90° - B)}$$
$$= \sqrt{\frac{\cos A}{\cos A} - \cos A \cos A}$$
$$= \sqrt{(1 - \cos^2 A)}$$
$$= \sqrt{(\sin^2 A)}$$
$$= \sin A$$

2. $2^x = 4^y = 8^z$
$2x = 2^{2y} = 2^{3z}$
$x = 2y = 3z = k(say)$
Then, $xyz = k^3/6 = 288$
$k^3 = 1728$
Therefore $k = 12$ so, $x = 12, y = 6, z = 4 = \frac{1}{2x} + \frac{1}{4y} + \frac{1}{8z} = \frac{11}{96}$

3. Let $f(x) = x^4 - ax^3 + bx^2 - cx + 8$
$f(1) = 4$
$1 - a + b - c + 8 = 4$
$-a + b - c = -5$ ..... Eqn (1)
$f(-1) = 3$
$1 + a + b + c + 8 = 3$
$a + b + c = -6$ ...... Eqn (2)
Adding Equation (1) and (2) we have
$2b = -11$
or $b = -5.5$

4. Let the seller buys "n" mangoes for Rs. 100 each CP of
$1 mango = Rs. 100$
$\Rightarrow CP$ of n mangoes $= 100n$
When $3/5^{th}$ of total was sold:
$\Rightarrow$ SP for 1 mango $= 100(1 + 25/100) = Rs. 125$
$\Rightarrow$ SP for $3n/5$ mangoes $= 125 * 3n/5 = 75n$
Now, Remaining mangoes $= 2n/5$ Out of these 25% wasted
So, Remaining $= \frac{2n}{5}\left(1 - \frac{25}{100}\right) = \frac{3n}{10}$
These are sold at 40% profit i.e. for Rs.140 each $\Rightarrow \therefore$ Total
$SP = 75n + 140 * 3n/10 = 117n$
We can see that, profit is made.
Profit $\% = \frac{117n - 100n}{100n} \times 100 = 17\%$

5.

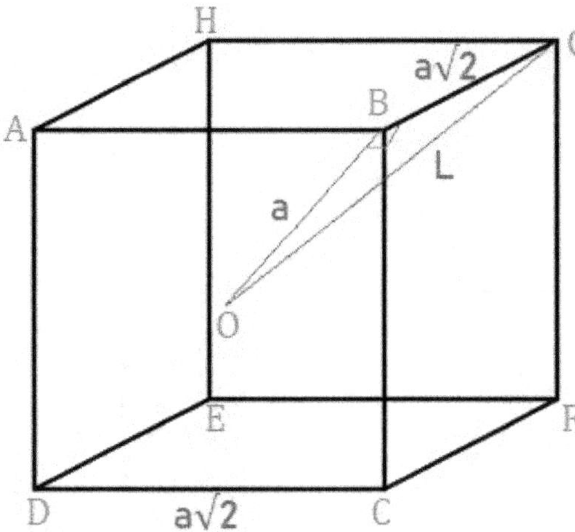

ABCDEFGH is a cube of side a√2.

diagonal BD = √2*(a√2) = 2a

OB = BD/2 = a

In triangle OBG,

OG² = OB² + BG²

L² = a² + (a√2)²

L² = 3a²

L = √3a

6. $\dfrac{A_1}{A_2} = \dfrac{1.4}{1.6} = \dfrac{7}{8}$

$\dfrac{B_1}{B_2} = \dfrac{1.9}{2.4} = \dfrac{19}{24}$

$\dfrac{A_1}{A_2} \neq \dfrac{B_1}{B_2}$

Therefore this system of lines has unique solution and represents a pair of intersecting lines.

7. The population of a village = 25000

One fifth are females = 1/5 (25000) = 5000

Rest are males = 25000 – 5000 = 20000

5% of males are uneducated, therefore number of uneducated males

= (5×20000)/100 = 1000

Therefore number of educated males = 20000 – 1000 = 19000

40% of females are uneducated, number of uneducated females

= (40×5000)/100 = 2000

Therefore number of educated females = 5000 – 2000 = 3000

Total number of educated people = 19000+3000 = 22000

% of educated people = 22000×100/25000 = 22×4 = 88%

8. This is nothing but the number of ways of having a, b, c such that a + b + c = 11, where a, b, c are natural numbers. By having them to be natural numbers, we ensure that no box can be empty. (no zeroes). $^{10}C_2$ = 45 ways

9. Exactly one of ab, bc and ca is odd => Two are odd and one is even.

abc is a multiple of 4 => the even number is a multiple of 4.

The arithmetic mean of a and b is an integer => a and b are odd.

and so is the arithmetic mean of a, b and c. => a + b + c is a multiple of 3.

c can be 4 or 8.

c = 4; a, b can be 3, 5 or 5, 9

c = 8; a, b can be 3, 7 or 7, 9

Four triplets are possible.

Hence the answer is "4"

10. Let the old average be A, then

(11A+63)/12 = (A+2)

11A+63 = 12A+24

A = 39

Hence, Average of the batsman up to 11 innings = 39

Required average = 39+2 =41

11. Amount=1900+378=2278

2278=1900(1+10/100)n

2278/1900=(11/10)n

1.19=(11/10)n

n=1.08

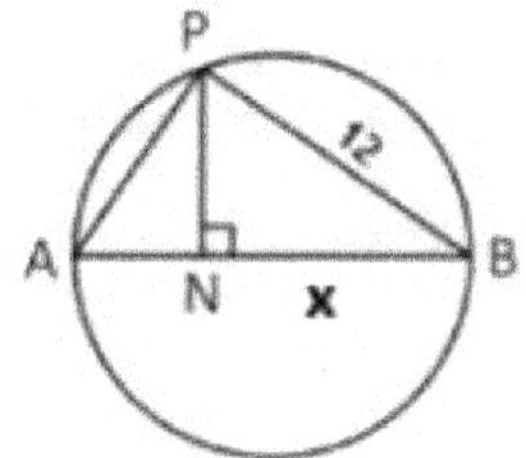

12.

Diameter, $AB = 2 \times 7 = 14cm$

$\angle APB = 90°$ ["angle in the semi-circle]

In $\triangle APB$, By Pythagoras theorem

$AP = \sqrt{AB^2 - PB^2} = \sqrt{14^2 - 12^2} = \sqrt{196 - 144}$
$= 2\sqrt{13}$

Let $BN = x$, then

$PN^2 = AP^2 - AN^2 = PB^2 - BN^2$

$\left(2\sqrt{13}\right)^2 - (14 - x)^2 = (12)^2 - x^2$

$52 - 196 + 28x - x^2 = 144 - x^2$

$28x = 144 + 196 - 52 = 288$

$x = \dfrac{288}{28} = \dfrac{72}{7} = 10\dfrac{2}{7}\, cm$

13. Given:

$x + \dfrac{1}{9x} = \dfrac{8}{3}$

Multiply by 3 on both sides, we get, $3x + \dfrac{1}{3x} = 8$

Take cube on both sides:

$27x^3 + \dfrac{1}{27x^3} + 3\left(3x + \dfrac{1}{3x}\right) = 512$

$27x^3 + \dfrac{1}{27x^3} = 512 - 3 \times 8 = 488$

14. Let the C.P be x.

Then the S.P = 130x/100 =1.3x

In second case,

Selling price = 1.3x + 360

S.P. = 160% of CP (according to second statement)

1.3x + 360 =1.6x

360 = 0.3x

x = 1200

S.P = 1.3x

1.3 * 1200 = 1560

So the selling price of the book will be Rs 1560.

15. Number should be a multiple of 3 and 4. So, the sum of the digits should be a multiple of 3. We can either have all seven digits as 3, or have three 2's and four 3's, or six 2's and a 3.

(The number of 2's should be a multiple of 3).

For the number to be a multiple of 4, the last 2 digits should be 32. Now, let us combine these two.

All seven 3's - No possibility.

Three 2's and four 3's - The first 5 digits should have two 2's and three 3's in some order.

No of possibilities $= \dfrac{5!}{3!2!} = 10$

Six 2 's and one 3 - The first 5 digits should all be 2 's. So, there is only one number 2222232 .

So, there are a total of $10 + 1 = 11$ solutions.

16. Resistivity is a measure of the resisting power of a specified material to the flow of an electric current. Iron has the highest electrical resistivity 9.9 x 10^{-8} Ohm.m

17. Ans.

(c) $p = \sqrt{2Em}$

where p denotes momentum, E denotes kinetic energy and m denotes mass. $\therefore \dfrac{p_1}{p_2} = \sqrt{\dfrac{m_1}{m_2}}$ or $\dfrac{p_1}{p_2} = \sqrt{\dfrac{1}{4}} = \dfrac{1}{2}$

18. Fleming's right hand rule (for generators) shows the direction of induced current when a conductor moves in a magnetic field.

19. The speed of light in a vacuum c = 3 x 10^8 m/s.

For crown glass Refractive index (n) = 1.5

v= c/n

$$\frac{3 \times 10^8}{1.5}$$

2 × 10^8 m/s

20. Mechanical energy conservation between point:

B and C gives $\quad v_C^2 = v_B^2 + 2gh$

or $v_C^2 = 45 + 2 \times 10 \times 3 \Rightarrow v_c = \sqrt{105} m/s$

21. Ans.

(c) $a = \dfrac{F}{m} = \dfrac{5 \times 10^4}{3 \times 10^7} = \dfrac{5}{3} \times 10^{-3} m/s^2$

velocity, $v = \sqrt{2 \, as}$

$$= \sqrt{2 \times \left(\frac{5}{3} \times 10^{-3}\right) \times 3} = 0.1 ms^{-1}$$

22. Nitrogen is a non-flammable, inert gas which does not support combustion, as oxygen does. So it reduces the chance of any explosion or fire during some electrical spark or vehicle accident.

23. Brass is a metallic alloy that is made of copper and zinc. H_2S gas is highly corrosive in nature which discolours it reacting with brass.

24. Nitrous oxide is commonly known as laughing gas or nitrous. It is a chemical compound and an oxide of nitrogen with the formula N_2O . At room temperature, it is a colourless non-flammable gas, with a slight metallic scent and taste.

25. Potassium alum, potash alum, or potassium aluminium sulfate is a chemical compound: the double sulfate of potassium and aluminium, with chemical formula $KAl(SO_4)_2$. It is commonly encountered as the dodecahydrate, $KAl(SO_4)_2 \cdot 12H_2O$.

26. Biologists used the world's largest single-celled organism, an aquatic alga called Caulerpa taxifolia, to study the nature of structure and form in plants. It is a single cell that can grow to a length of six to twelve inches.

27. Progesterone is a steroid hormone that is important for breast growth. It works alongside estrogen to maintain female reproductive health and female sex characteristics.

28. Aspirin, in the form of leaves from the willow tree, has been used for its health effects for at least 2,400 years.

29. Banana plants are not trees. They are, in fact, large herbs, as they do not have a persistent or woody stem. Although a banana plant has no wooden trunk, it can reach heights of as much as 40 feet, though, making it one of the tallest herbs grown on Earth.

30. First class proteins contain all the essential amino acids in sufficient amounts.Animal proteins are obtained from milk, egg, fish, meat etc. are first classproteins. These are also called adequate proteins.

31. Luminous intensity, the quantity of visible light that is emitted in unit time per unit solid angle. It's S.I unit is candela.

32. The Vernier Caliper is a precision instrument that can be used to measure internal and external distances extremely accurately.

33. Ovens are popular for reheating previously cooked foods and cooking a variety of foods.It uses Microwave rays for heating food.

34. Ethylene is an organic compound and gaseous substance, which is produced from amino acid.It is responsible for ripening of fruits.

35. Lysosome is called as "atom bombs".

 Lysosomes are also called suicide bags or atom bombs because if the single membrane surrounding the digestive enzymes breaks, the enzymes released may also destroy the cell itself.

36. Sulphuric acid is used in battery. It is highly corrosive strong mineral acid. It is used for a variety of other purposes in the chemical industry.

37. Aspirin, also known as acetylsalicylic acid (ASA), is a medication used to treat pain, fever, or inflammation.

38. Tomatoes use two colour pigment which are chlorophyll and lycopene. Chlorophyll is for green and lycopene is for red colour.

39. Minorities Rights Day was observed on 18 December across the Nation to create awareness on rights of minorities.

40. 10 Biogeographic zones are Trans Himalayan zone, Himalayan zone, Desert zone, Semiarid zone, Western ghat zone, Deccan plateau zone, Gangetic plain zone, North east zone, Coastal zone and Islands present near the shore line

41. I shall speak to him if he comes here.

42. Light travels faster than the sound.

43. The given phrase is in Latin and appears in Horace's 'Ars Poetica', an epistle presented as an informal letter to members of the Piso family. Quintus Horatius Flaccus or Horace (65 BC – 8 BC), was the leading Roman lyric poet during the time of Augustus (The age of Romans).

The given phrase means "as in painting, so in poetry" (poetry resembles painting). Horace explains, ""As is painting, so is poetry: some pieces will strike you more if you stand near, and some, if you are at a greater distance: one loves the dark; another, which is not afraid of the critic's subtle judgment, chooses to be seen in the light; the one has pleased once the other will give pleasure if ten times repeated . . . . "

44. 'Don Quixote' is a novel by Miguel de Cervantes (1547 – 1616). The book is considered to be the first modern novel and was published in two parts (1605 and 1615). It was first written in Spanish, and was soon afterwards translated to English by Thomas Shelton.

45. The author is trying to highlight the need to have common future for the Indian children.

46. There is no common future for the Indian children.

47. There is a Sharp contrast between the failure to an infrastructure for primary education and Infrastructure for technical education.

48. Children who may never enter a classroom. They do not have a hopeful and prosperous future Therefore the option should be (4).

49. 75% children of this country have a bright future is the incorrect statement according to the passage.

50. In reporting exclamations, the indirect speech is introduced by some verb expressing exclamation. 'Today' changes to 'that day'.

Structure of indirect speech in case of Exclamatory sentences are :

a. The reporting verb is changed into exclaim, cry, shout etc. according to the sense.

b. New words and phrases like. with joy/in joy, with sorrow/ in sorrow, in wonder etc. are used to express the meaning of exclamation. If the sense of exclamation is not clear, such phrases are not used.

c. That is used as a linking word.

d. The changed form becomes a statement form of the sentence.

Direct: The man said, "Alas! I am undone".

Indirect: The man cried out in sorrow that he was undone.

Direct: He said, "Hurrah! We have won the game".

Indirect: He exclaimed in joy that they had won the game.

Direct: He said to me, "What a funny boy you are!"

Indirect: He exclaimed in joy that I was a very funny boy.

Direct: He said, "What a fool I am!"

Indirect: He cried out with sorrow that he was a great fool.

Mathematics

Q.1 Profit of Rs 12,400 has to be divided between three partners A, B and C in the ratio 5:7:8. How much does B get (in Rs)?

A. 4340 **B.** 3440 **C.** 3340 **D.** 4430

Q.2 36 men together can build a wall 140 m long in 21 days, the number of men working at the same rate required to build the same wall in 14 days is:

A. 54 **B.** 48 **C.** 36 **D.** 18

Q.3 In the following figure, ABCDEF is a regular hexagon of side a. Line BE is extended to meet at Y-axis. Find the point of intersection of line BE and Y-axis.

A. $(0, 3\sqrt{3}a)$ **B.** $(0, 3\sqrt{3}a/2)$
C. $(0, 3\sqrt{2}a)$ **D.** $(0, 2\sqrt{3}a/3)$

Q.4 Two vessels A and B containing two types of liquid in the ratio 5:2 and 7:6 resp. Find the ratio in which these mixtures be mixed to obtained a new mixture in vessel C containing liquids in the ratio 8:5?

A. 4:3 **B.** 3:4 **C.** 5:6 **D.** 7:9

Q.5 The average of 17 results is 60. If the average of first 9 results is 57 and that of the last 9 results is 65, then what will be the value of 9th result?

A. 39 **B.** 78 **C.** 117 **D.** 156

Q.6 In the given figure 0 is the center of circle, $\angle AOB = 100°$ Find $\angle BCD$:

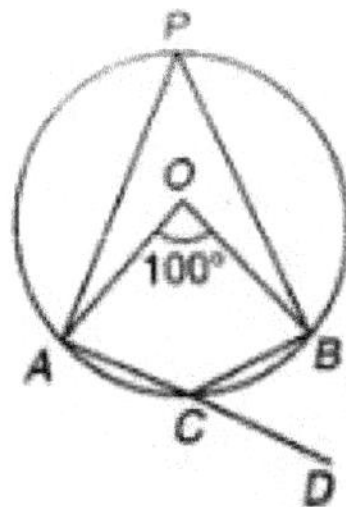

A. 80° **B.** 40° **C.** 60° **D.** 50°

Q.7 A clothing retailer gave a successive discount of 20% and 24% as a new marketing scheme. At what % higher than the cost price, should the clothes be marked to make a profit of 14%?

A. 100% **B.** 87.5% **C.** 95% **D.** 75%

Q.8 A can do a job in 10 days. B can do a job in 5 days. In how many days they can complete the job if they work together?

A. 3.33 days. **B.** 4 days
C. 5 days **D.** 2 days

Q.9 Two cars travel from city A to city B at a speed of 30 and 36 km/hr respectively. If one car takes 3 hours lesser time than the other car for the journey, then the distance between City A and City B is how much?

A. 648 km **B.** 810 km **C.** 432 km **D.** 540 km

Q.10 Find the area of shaded portion if the area of quadilateral BDEC is 380 cm²?

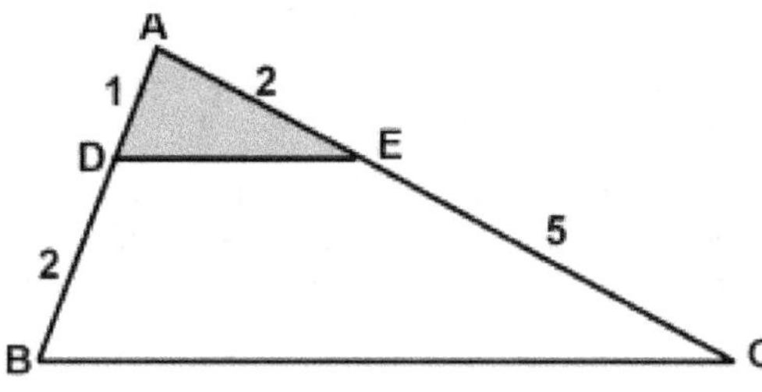

A. 10 **B.** 20 **C.** 30 **D.** 40

Q.11 A bag has Rs 43 in the form of 5 - rupee, 50 - paise and 10 - paise coins in the ratio of 1:5:11. What is the total number of 50 - paise coins?

A. 5 **B.** 25 **C.** 55 **D.** 50

Q.12 A boat covers 80% more distance in downsteem than upstreem. If speed of boat is 20 km/h in steel water then what is time required for boat to cover a distance of 50 km in upstreem?

A. 3.5 hrs **B.** 4.5 hrs **C.** 5 hrs **D.** 6 hrs

Q.13 A sphere of radius R is cut by a plane at a distance h from its centre, thereby breaking the sphere into two different pieces. The cumulative surface area of these two pieces is 25% more than that of the sphere. Find h.

A. R/√3 **B.** R/2 **C.** R/√2 **D.** R/3

Q.14 If (a+b) = 5 and (a-b) = 3, then the value of a^2+b^2 is _____.

A. 17 **B.** 15 **C.** 19 **D.** 20

Q.15 If {5/2, 3} is the solution set of a quadratic equation, find that quadratic equation.

A. $12x^2 - 11x -15 = 0$ **B.** $2x^2 + 11x +15 = 0$
C. $-2x^2 - 11x +15 = 0$ **D.** $2x^2 - 11x = -15$

Science

Q.16 The extension in a string, obeying Hooke's law, is x. The speed of sound in the stretched string is v. If the extension in the string is increase to $1.5x$, the speed of sound will be:

A. 0.012 V **B.** 0.09 V **C.** 1.22 V **D.** 1.33 V

Q.17 To make solar cells, which of the following elements is used?

A. Silicon **B.** Sodium
C. Calcium **D.** Aluminum

Q.18 What is the initial velocity of an object of mass 15kg that starts from the rest?

A. $\frac{15m}{8}$ **B.** 0   **C.** $\frac{5m}{8}$ **D.** $\frac{-2m}{8}$

Q.19 The phenomenon of change in direction of light when it passes from one medium to another is called-

A. Propagation   **B.** Reflection

C. Refraction   **D.** Dispersion

Q.20 When a beam of white light falls on a glass prism, the colour of light which will deviate least is:

A. Green   **B.** Violet   **C.** Red   **D.** Blue

Q.21 Consider the following statements.

1- D_2O is used to keep polio vaccine safe.

2- Boiling point of D_2O is less than ordinary water

Which of the statements given above is/are correct.?

A. 1 Only   **B.** 2 Only

C. 1 and 2   **D.** Neither 1 nor 2

Q.22 Nail polish remover contains?

A. Benzene   **B.** Acetic acid

C. Acetone   **D.** Petroleum ether

Q.23 Which type of glass is used for making lenses?

A. Soft Glass   **B.** Hard glass

C. Crook's Glass   **D.** Pyrex Glass

Q.24 Which of the following is a mixture of Paraffin wax and stearic acid?

A. Plastic   **B.** Rubber

C. Candle   **D.** None of these

Q.25 Which is the heaviest gas?

A. Xenon   **B.** Radon   **C.** Krpton   **D.** Florine

Q.26 Which of the following is the correct relation between enzyme or hormone & there function?

A. Ptyalin - Converts angiotensinogen in blood into angiotensin

B. Renin - Digests proteins

C. Oxytocin - Induces contraction of smooth muscles

D. None of these

Q.27 Light energy changes into the chemical energy by which of the following process-

A. By Respiration   **B.** By Transportation

C. By photosynthesis   **D.** By spewing

Q.28 Where is bile stored?

A. Liver   **B.** Kidney

C. Gall bladder   **D.** Spleen

Q.29 Penicillin which is used to treat bacterial infections is derived from :

A. Lichens   **B.** Fungi   **C.** Algae   **D.** Moss

Q.30 Hodophobia is the fear of which of the following?

A. Cattle   **B.** Water   **C.** Drugs   **D.** Travel

General Awareness

Q.31 Hygrometer is used to measure ?

A. Sound under water

B. Level of humidity

C. Boiling point of liquid

D. Pressure of gas

Q.32 Slug is unit of –

A. Current   **B.** Time   **C.** Distance   **D.** Mass

Q.33 The oil in the wick of an oil lamp rises up due to –

A. Capillary action   **B.** Low viscosity of oil

C. Gravitational force   **D.** Pressure difference

Q.34 " World Environment Day" is celebrated on:

A. 22 March   **B.** 22 April

C. 22 May   **D.** 5 June

Q.35 Which of the following salts in water causes "Blue Baby Syndrome"?

A. Cadmium   **B.** Sulphides

C. Carbonates   **D.** Nitrates

Q.36 Which of the following will be India's first solar mission ?

A. Aditya-LL mission   **B.** Aditya-L1 mission

C. Aditya-XL mission   **D.** Aditya-X1 mission

Q.37 Under whose chairmanship the 15th Finance Commission has been constituted by the Union Government?

A. Arvind Panagariya   **B.** Y.V Reddy

C. NK Singh   **D.** Shaktikanta Das

Q.38 Who is the author of the book 'The Ministry of Utmost Happiness' ?

A. Kiran Desai   **B.** Chetan Bhagat

C. Arundhati Roy   **D.** Jhumpa Lahiri

Q.39 Who is known as the father of the English language?

A. William Worth

B. Geoffrey Chaucer

C. William Shakespeare

D. None of the above

Q.40 'Boat race' is the part is which festival ?

A. Pongal   **B.** Onam   **C.** Bihu   **D.** Navratri

Basic English

Q.41 Who among the following writers was not the one identified with The Movement of the 1950's England?

A. Roy Fuller   **B.** Kingsley Amis

C. Philip Larkin   **D.** Donald Davie

Q.42 In the following series, which one has all the poets correctly matched with their poems?

A. Ezekiel, "Poet, Lover, Birdwatcher"; Ramanujan, "Small-scale Reflections on a Great House"; Dutt, "Sunset at Puri"; Mahapatra, "Our Casuarina Tree".

B. Ezekiel, "Sunset at Puri"; Ramanujan, "Small-scale Reflections on a Great House"; Dutt, "Our Casuarina Tree";

Mahapatra, "Poet, Lover, Birdwatcher".

Ezekiel, "Poet, Lover, Birdwatcher"; Ramanujan, "Sunset at
C. Puri"; Dutt, "Our Casuarina Tree"; Mahapatra, "Small-scale
Reflections on a Great House".

Ezekiel, "Poet, Lover, Birdwatcher"; Ramanujan, "Small-
D. scale Reflections on a Great House"; Dutt, "Our Casuarina
Tree"; Mahapatra, "Sunset at Puri".

Q.43 John Heywood wrote a farcical interlude called The Four
P's.

Who were the Four P's?

A. a Palmer, a Pedlar, a Pothecary, a Packer

B. a Printer, a Pedlar, a Pothecary, a Palmer

C. a Pedlar, a Parson, a Palmer, a Pothecary

D. a Palmer, a Pardoner, a Pothecary, a Pedlar

Q.44 Change into Imperative sentence:-

Bring your pen.

A. Let your pen be brought.

B. Your pen shall be brought.

C. Your pen should brought.

D. None of the above.

**Q.45 Direction: Each of the following twenty three items
consists of a word in capital letters followed by four words
or groups of words. Select the word or group of words that
is most similar in meaning to the word in capital letters.**

OBVIATE

A. Delaying the solution of a problem

B. To remove a difficulty

C. Make obstruction

D. Supercede

Q.46 Direction: In the following question, out of the four
alternatives, select the word similar in meaning to the given
word.

WRESTED

A. Took by force
B. Took away easily
C. Lost narrowly
D. Won easily

**Q.47 Direction: Each of the following twenty one items
consists of a word or a group of words in capital letters
followed by four words or groups of words. Select the
word or group of words that is farthest in meaning to the
word in capital letters.**

AT THE ELEVENTH HOUR

A. At night
B. At noon
C. Late
D. Early

**Q.48 Direction: In the following question, out of the four
alternatives, select the word similar in meaning to the
given word.**

CREDITABLE

A. Able to lend money
B. Bringing praise
C. Able to repay a loan
D. Fit to be believed

**Q.49 Direction: In the following question, out of the five
alternatives, select the word similar in meaning to the
given word.**

Hush up

A. Blow up
B. To keep quiet
C. To remove
D. Wind up

Q.50 Which of the following novels does not belong to
Nuruddin Farah's Blood In the Sun Trilogy?

A. Maps
B. Knots
C. Gifts
D. Secrets

// Smart Answer Sheet //

Correct — Indicates percentage of students who answered questions correctly.

Skipped — Indicates percentage of students who skipped questions.

Q.	Ans.	Correct / Skipped
1	A	80.64 % / 15.22 %
2	A	85.07 % / 14.53 %
3	B	80.09 % / 11.03 %
4	D	76.3 % / 17.56 %
5	B	85.38 % / 13.27 %
6	D	85.0 % / 14.18 %
7	B	82.43 % / 10.73 %
8	A	78.75 % / 13.18 %
9	D	86.64 % / 12.79 %
10	D	85.18 % / 12.41 %
11	B	87.42 % / 12.11 %
12	A	80.39 % / 12.4 %
13	C	88.03 % / 10.84 %
14	A	77.0 % / 22.72 %
15	D	80.57 % / 17.42 %
16	C	84.85 % / 12.88 %
17	A	86.63 % / 12.74 %
18	B	79.12 % / 10.68 %
19	C	85.75 % / 13.75 %
20	C	82.82 % / 12.96 %
21	A	77.11 % / 12.71 %
22	C	79.13 % / 13.3 %
23	C	83.94 % / 13.05 %
24	C	79.85 % / 11.49 %
25	B	81.59 % / 11.34 %
26	C	76.28 % / 17.23 %
27	C	79.21 % / 11.53 %
28	C	86.48 % / 10.35 %
29	B	86.64 % / 10.28 %
30	D	85.48 % / 11.47 %
31	B	89.15 % / 10.2 %
32	D	80.45 % / 16.51 %
33	A	89.0 % / 10.8 %
34	D	86.68 % / 12.42 %
35	D	86.79 % / 12.89 %
36	B	81.47 % / 11.4 %
37	C	79.71 % / 16.05 %
38	C	79.96 % / 17.66 %
39	B	77.72 % / 10.56 %
40	B	80.87 % / 18.2 %
41	A	84.76 % / 12.43 %
42	D	78.26 % / 11.05 %
43	D	79.65 % / 10.91 %
44	A	83.59 % / 12.54 %
45	B	82.87 % / 16.73 %
46	A	85.46 % / 11.81 %
47	D	88.02 % / 11.21 %
48	B	81.17 % / 16.83 %
49	B	83.99 % / 11.0 %
50	B	79.64 % / 17.48 %

Performance Analysis

Avg. Score (%)	43.33%
Toppers Score (%)	74.0%
Your Score	

//Hints and Solutions//

1. Amount to be divided = 12400

A:B:C = 5:7:8

So B share = $\dfrac{7}{5+7+8} x 12400 = \dfrac{7}{20} x\ 12400 = 4340$

2. Let the required number of men be 'x'.

As the length of the wall and the rate of working is same, but days are less then the number of men required will be more to build the 140 m long wall in 14 days.

This is the case of indirect proportion.

$\Rightarrow$ Men 36 : x

     : : 140 : 140

       21 : 14

$\Rightarrow$ (36*21*140) = (x*14*140)

$\Rightarrow$ 1960x = 105840

$\Rightarrow$ x = 105840/1960

$\Rightarrow$ x = 54 men

Hence, to build 140 m long wall in 14 days, 54 men will be required working at the same rate.

3.

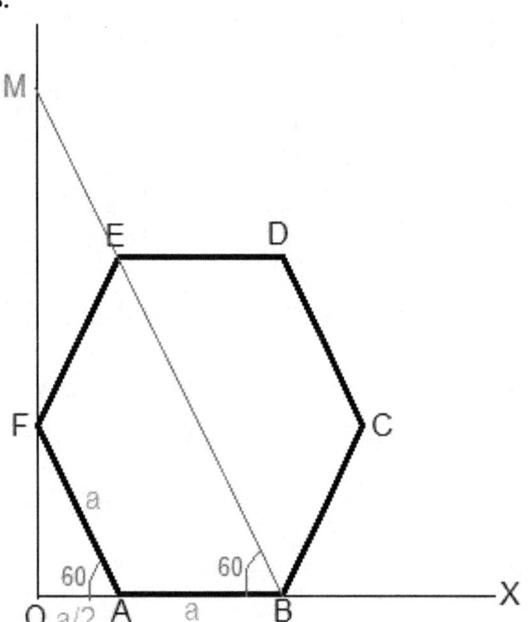

In triangle FAO,

OA = FA*cos60 = a/2

In triangle MBO,

tan60 = MO/OB

MO = OB*tan60

MO = (3a/2)*√3 = 3√3a/2

co-ordinates of point M = (0, 3√3a/2)

4. A   :   B

 5/7   7/13

    \   /

      (8/13)

    /   \

(1/13)   :   (9/91)

  7   9

Therefore required ratio = 1/13 : 9/91

= 7:9

5. Basic Method:

9th result = Sum of first 9 results + sum of last 9 results – sum of 17 results

= 9 × 57 + 9 × 65 - 17 × 60

= 513 + 585 – 1020

= 78

Short Trick:

60-3*9+5*9 =78 (in case of overlapping)

when overlapping is not there (take 8 in place of 9 in same question) then signs of '+' and '-' are interchanged.

6. $\angle APB = \dfrac{1}{2}\angle AOB = \dfrac{1}{2} \times 100° = 50°$

PACB is cyclic, therefore

$\angle ACB = 180° - \angle APB = 130°$

$\angle BCD = 180° - 130° = 50°$

7. Given, a clothing retailer gave a successive discount of 20% and 24% as a new marketing scheme.

Let the marked price be 'a'

Selling price after 1st discount% of 20% = a – 20% of a = 0.8a

Selling price after 2nd discount% of 24% = 0.8a – 24% of 0.8a = 0.76 × 0.8a

Now, he was able to make a profit of 14%.

Let the cost price be 'b'.

Selling price = b + 14% of b = 1.14b

Thus, 0.76 × 0.8a = 1.14b

$\Rightarrow$6b = 3.2a

$\Rightarrow$a = 15b/8

% higher than the cost price at which the clothes were

marked $= \dfrac{\frac{15b}{8}-b}{b} \times 100\% = 87.5\%$

8. Answer: Since A can do the job in 10 days, we can write the efficiency of A is equal to (100/10)% = 10%. Thus, A's efficiency =

10%. Similarly, we can say that B's efficiency is equal to 20%. Now we nee to find their combined efficiency as follows:

(A+ B) efficiency = (10 + 20)% = 30%. This means in one day A and B together can do 30% of the work. Therefore, Number of days A and B together take to do 100% of work = (100/3) days = 3.33 days.

9. Let the distance between city A and city B be $x km$, then
Time taken by first car - time taken by second car = 3 hours
or, $\dfrac{x}{30} - \dfrac{x}{36} = 3$
$\Rightarrow x = 540 km$

10. $\dfrac{\text{Area of } \Delta ADE}{\text{Area of } \Delta ABC} = \dfrac{\frac{1}{2} \times x \times 2y \times \sin\theta}{\frac{1}{2} \times 3x \times 7y \times \sin\theta}$

$\dfrac{\text{Area of } \Delta ADE}{\text{Area of } \Delta ABC} = \dfrac{2}{21}$

Area of $\Delta BDEC$ = Area of ΔABC − Area of ΔADE
$= 21 - 2 = 19$ unit
A. T.Q. 19 unit = 380 1 unit $= 20$ Required
Area of $\Delta ADE = 2$ unit $= 2 \times 20 = 40 cm^2$

11. Face value of 5 rupee 50 paise and 10 paise are in the ratio of
$5 : \dfrac{50}{100} : \dfrac{10}{100} = 5 : \dfrac{1}{2} : \dfrac{1}{10} = 5 : 0.5 : 0.1$
Number of coins are in the ratio of 1: 5: 11
Let the number of 5 rupee coins $= x$
50 paise $= 5x$
And 10 paise $= 11x$
Then $5x + 5x \times 0.5 + 11x \times 0.1 = 43$
$5x + 2.5x + 1.1x = 43$
$8.6x = 43$
$x = 5$
Number of 50 paise $coin = 5x = 5 \times 5 = 25$

12. Let speed of current be $x km/h$
According to the question
$20 + x = (20 - x)\dfrac{180}{100}$
$100 + 5x = 180 - 9x$
$14x = 80$
$x = \dfrac{40}{7} km/h$
Speed in upstream $= 20 \dfrac{40}{7} = \dfrac{100}{7} km/h$
Required time $= \dfrac{50 \times 7}{100} = 3.5 hrs$

13. 
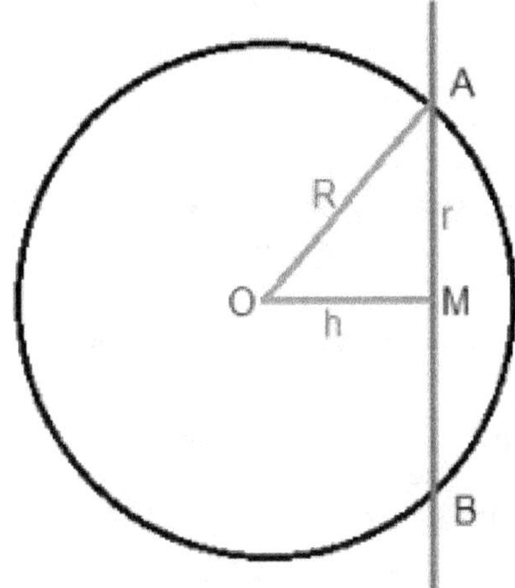

Area of the original sphere $= 4\pi R^2$ After the cut cumulative surface area $= 4\pi R^2 + \pi r^2 + \pi r^2 = 4\pi R^2 + 2\pi r^2$
According to question, $4\pi R^2 + 2\pi r^2 = 125\%$ of $4\pi R^2$
$2\pi r^2 = 25\%$ of $4\pi R^2$
$2\pi r^2 = \pi R^2$
$2r^2 = R^2$
Now in triangle OAM $h^2 = R^2 - r^2$
$h^2 = 2r^2 - r^2$
$h^2 = r^2 = R^2/2$
$h = R/\sqrt{2}$

14. Given equations:

a + b = 5

a − b = 3

Adding both equations:

2a = 8

a = 4

By putting a = 4 in above equation

b = 1

a^2 + b^2 = 16 + 1 = 17

15. α=5/2 & β= 3

α + β = 5/2 + 3 = 11/2

αβ = 15/2

Equation having the roots α and β is

X^2 − (α + β)x +αβ = 0

X^2 − (11/2)x + (15/2) =0

2x^2 -11x +15 = 0

16. Speed of sound $V = \sqrt{\dfrac{T}{\mu}}$ $V \propto \sqrt{T}$

Also

So

$$\frac{V_2}{V_1} = \sqrt{\frac{1.5x}{x}}$$

$$V_2 = \sqrt{1.5}V = 1.22V$$

17. Silicon is used for making solar cells. Solar cells are typically named after the semiconducting material they are made of. These materials must have certain characteristics in order to absorb sunlight.

18. The initial velocity of an object of mass 15kg is zero. As it is starting from the rest.

19. The bending of light as it passes from one medium to another is called refraction. The bending occurs because light travels more slowly in a denser medium.

20. A white light comprises of seven colours. The refractive index of a prism is different for different colours. The colour with greatest wavelength has least refractive index and vice versa. The red colour has greatest wavelength therefore, refractive index for this colour will be least and hence it will deviate least as it will pass through prism.

21. Boiling point of D_2O is more than ordinary water. Hence, option A is correct.

22. The most common remover is acetone. Repeated use can cause the skin around the nails to become dry or cracked. Acetone can also remove artificial nails made of acrylic or cured gel. An alternative nail polish remover is ethyl acetate, which often also contains isopropyl alcohol.

23. Crook's glass is used for making lenses and it also absorbs UV rays.

24. Candle is a mixture of Paraffin wax and stearic acid. Candle wax is a mixture of different alkanes that are solid at room temperature. Candles are usually made of paraffin wax that is a residue from the distillation of petroleum.

25. Radon is the heaviest noble gas with density 0.00973 g/cm³ and atomic number 86. he reason xenon might be considered by some people to be the heaviest noble gas is because it can, under certain conditions, form the Xe-Xe chemical bond of Xe_2

26. Ptyalin is an enzyme in the saliva that converts starch into dextrin and maltose. Pepsin is an enzyme that splits proteins into proteoses and peptones. Renin is a proteolytic enzyme secreted by the kidneys that convert angiotensin. Oxytocin is a polypeptide hormone, produced by the posterior lobe of the pituitary gland that stimulates contraction of the smooth muscle of the uterus.

27. In the process of photosynthesis, light energy changes into the chemical energy. Normally plants utilize sunlight but marine algae also use moonlight, photosynthesis even occurs in electric light.

28. Bile is produce in Liver and stored in Gall bladder.

Your gallbladder is a four-inch, pear-shaped organ. It's positioned under your liver in the upper-right section of your abdomen. The gallbladder stores bile, a combination of fluids, fat, and cholesterol. Bile helps break down fat from food in your intestine.

29. Penicillin is a group of antibiotics used to treat a large range of bacterial infections. They are derived from Penicillium fungi and can be taken orally or via injection.

30. Hodophobia is the irrational and intense fear of travel. It is a personalized phobia - some people may fear going a certain distance away from their house, others may fear certain types of transportation - planes, trains, boats, ships, road travel , etc.

31. Hygrometer is a instrument used in meteorological science to measure the humidity, or amount of water vapour in the air.

32. The slug is the unit of mass in the US common system of units.

33. The oil in the wick of an oil lamp rises up due to capillary action. Capillary action describes the ability of a liquid to flow against gravity in a narrow space such as a thin tube.

34. World Environment Day is held each year on June 5. It is one of the principal vehicles through which the United Nations (UN) stimulates worldwide awareness of the environment and enhances political attention and action.

35. Blue Baby Syndrome is caused by decreased ability of blood to carry oxygen, resulting in oxygen deficiency in different body parts.The disease can be caused by intake of water and vegetables high in nitrate, exposure to chemicals containing nitrate.

36. The Indian Space Research Organisation (ISRO) will launch the India's first mission to the Sun "Aditya-L1 mission".The aim of the solar mission is to improve the understanding of dynamical processes of the sun.

37. Under the chairmanship of NK Singh the 15th Finance Commission has been constituted by the Union Government. The commission will review the current status of the finance, deficit, debt levels, cash balances and fiscal discipline efforts of the Union and the states.

It will also recommend a fiscal consolidation road map for sound fiscal management.

38. The Ministry of Utmost Happiness is written by Arundhati Roy .The Ministry of Utmost Happiness is the second novel by Indian writer Arundhati Roy, published in 2017.

39. Geoffrey Chaucer was an English poet and author. Widely considered the greatest English poet of the Middle Ages, he is best known for The Canterbury Tales. He has been called the "father of English literature", or, alternatively, the "father of English poetry".

40. Onam is an annual Hindu festival of Kerala in India. 'Boat race' is part of Onam festival.

41. 'The Movement' was a term coined in 1954 to describe a group of writers including Philip Larkin, Kingsley Amis, Donald Davie, D. J. Enright, John Wain, Elizabeth Jennings, Thom Gunn and Robert Conquest. The term was coined by J. D. Scott. The Movement only included English poets. Those from the other parts of the United Kingdom of Great Britain and Northern Ireland were not involved.

The Movement poets were considered anti-romantic, but Larkin and Hughes showed romantic elements. The Movement took into account Britain's declining supremacy in world politics. The members of the Movement were opposed to modernism, which was reflected in the Englishness of their poetry. The noteworthy elements of the poems were the pastoral images that depicted nostalgia as Britain transited from the rural to the urban.

42. I. "Poet, Lover, Birdwatcher", by Nissim Ezekiel, was included in the volume 'The Exact Name' (1965). The poem resembles "The Lunatic, The Lover and The Poet, an Elizabethan Poem" taken from Shakespeare's A Midsummer's Night Dream. The poem deals with the patience which according to the poet is the only way for the Poet, the Lover and the Birdwatcher to succeed. In the poem, Ezekiel describes that the patience is the key to achieve the goal.

II. Published in 1971, "Small-Scale Reflections on a Great House" by A.K Ramanujan appears to be a poem about an ancestral house. However, it signifies the Great Indian Culture. The poet mentions that certain things that entered the house never left. They lost themselves amongst other things that had similarly a history of being lost. The house is said to possess the property of taking in whatever enters it, never allowing it to go back. This is similar to the Indian culture that has forever accommodated whatever had arrived at its threshold.

III. "Our Casuarina Tree" published in 1881 by Toru Dutt celebrates a huge tree that the speaker (a representation of Dutt herself) links with the happiness of her childhood in India.

IV. "Sunset in Puri" by Jayant Mahapatra is a symbolic and metaphorical poem where the poet talks about the shallowness of the rites and rituals common in Indian society.

43. John Heywood was an English writer known for his plays, poems, and collection of proverbs. He wrote a farcical interlude called 'The Four P's' which involves a debate among four men whose trades begin with the letter "P." Two are churchmen--a Pardoner and a Palmer; one is a medieval pharmacist (an aPothecary), and the last is a Pedlar. The first three argue which of them should "take the best place," or be considered the most important. The Pedlar suggests a competition where each one has to tell an elaborate lie; the best liar shall "most prevail."

44. Let your pen be brought. **OR**

Your pen should be brought.

45. Obviate means avoid, prevent or remove something.

1. The new treatment obviates many of the risks associated with surgery.

46. Wrested means forcibly pull something from person's grasp.

1. He tried to wrest control of the company from his uncle.

47. At the Eleventh Hour means late and its opposite will be early.

At the eleventh hour the lab technician saves the day, proving there is hope for closet cases in the 21st century.

48. Let's first find out the meaning of word 'creditable' :- deserving public acknowledgement and praise but not necessarily outstanding or successful; praiseworthy; laudable; admirable.

Now, find the meaning of following word :-

Able to lend money :- person or organization that has capacity to give any other person or org. money.

Able to repay a loan :- person or organization that has capacity to give back any other person or org. the money that is borrowed.

Clearly, we can observe that bringing praise is the most similar in meaning to given word 'defect'

49. Hush up = to be quiet.

Blow up = an outburst of anger.

Wind up = an attempt to tease or irritate someone.

50. Nuruddin Farah (1945-) is a Somalian novelist. He is considered as one of the greatest contemporary writers of the world. His trilogy "Blood in the Sun" (1986–99) is one of his major works. The novels included in 'Blood In the Sun Trilogy' are 'Maps', 'Gifts' and 'Secrets'. "Maps" takes place during the 1977 Ogadan border war with Ethiopia; "Secrets" takes place on the eve of civil war in the early '90s. "Gifts" reveals the motives behind the "gift" of aid to the Third World.

"Knots" (2006) is a separate novel by Farah, which accounts the story of a woman who returns to her roots and discovers much more than herself.

// Notes //

// Notes //